Sequence Comparison in Historical Linguistics
Johann-Mattis List

d|u|p

Hana Filip, Peter Indefrey, Laura Kallmeyer,
Sebastian Löbner, Gerhard Schurz & Robert D. Van Valin
(eds.)

Dissertations in Language and Cognition

1

Johann-Mattis List

2014

Sequence Comparison in Historical Linguistics

d|u|p

Bibliografische Information
der Deutschen Nationalbibliothek
Die Deutsche Nationalbibliothek verzeichnet diese
Publikation in der Deutschen Nationalbibliografie;
detaillierte bibliografische Daten sind im Internet
über http://dnb.dnb.de abrufbar.

D 61

© düsseldorf university press, Düsseldorf 2014
http://www.dupress.de
Einbandgestaltung: D. Gerland, C. Horn, J.-M. List, A. Ortmann
Satz: J.-M. List, LaTeX
Herstellung: docupoint GmbH, Barleben

Gesetzt aus der GNU FreeFont
ISBN 978-3-943460-72-8

Meinen Großeltern

Acknowledgements

This study is the result of three and a half years of doctoral studies at the Heinrich-Heine University in Düsseldorf, supported by the German Federal Ministry of Education and Research (BMBF) which generously funded the research project "Evolution and Classification in Biology, Linguistics, and the history of the Sciences" (EvoClass) from 2009 to 2012. During this time, I met many people from different places. We exchanged ideas, we shared coffee, and at evenings also beer and wine, and we agreed or disagreed in numerous discussions. Not always were the topics of our conversations directly related to the present study. Life is not only about computer algorithms and historical linguistics. But when looking back at this time, it is evident to me that all the moments I gladly recall contributed to this study in one or the other way, and it is hard, probably NP hard, to do justice to all who were involved. In the following, I will try to mention at least some of the people who accompanied me on my journey through the land of ivory towers, hoping that those who will not find mention here, will find their traces in the study itself.

The first one to mention is Hans Geisler, my supervisor. It is hard to find the right words to express how important he was for my studies. His incredible intuition about language change was an inexhaustible source of inspiration, and his calm and realistic attitude was a steady anchor of moderation. He always encouraged me to pursue my ideas, no matter how daring they were, while at the same time watching out that I would not give in to the temptation of sacrificing my work's linguistic foundation in favor of shiny results. I am very glad that I had the possibility to carry out my doctoral studies under his supervision, and I am extremely grateful for all his support.

When carrying out my research at the Heinrich Heine University, I was affiliated with the Institute of Romance Languages and Literature, where I was officially employed, and the Institute for Language and Information, where I was given the possibility to teach introductory courses. In both institutes I met many people who made my life a lot easier: Sebastian Löbner cordially welcomed me and invited me to take part in his seminar for doctoral candidates.

Although my work was only peripherily related to his research specialty, he always showed great interest and never hesitated to support me with helpful critics and encouraging advice. Wiebke Petersen, my second supervisor, carefully reviewed the formal and mathematical arguments of my thesis and gave me practical suggestions for typesetting and layout. I profited a lot from her scientific rigor and her keen mind. James Kilbury and Norbert Endres challenged me in fruitful discussions on various occasions and prevented me from being too easily satisfied with my work. Day after day, Christa Hohendahl and Tim Riebe helped me to navigate through the dark jungles of bureaucracy.

Given the interdisciplinary context of my research project, my studies were carried out in close cooperation with biologists from the Institute of Molecular Evolution at the Heinrich Heine University. After initial problems in finding a common language (which are probably typical for all kinds of interdisciplinary research), the collaboration turned out to be very fruitful, and it helped me to get inimitable insights into a different discipline and a fresh perspective on my own one. Working under the supervision of William Martin and Tal Dagan was a great and educational experience. They showed me how to focus, organize, and sell one's ideas without loosing enthusiasm for the ideas themselves. My fellow doctoral candidates Shijulal Nelson-Sathi and Ovidiu Popa never lost patience when being bothered by me with programming issues. Giddy Landan provided valuable insights into the evaluation of algorithms in biology. Apart from the technical support, I want to thank all people from the Institute of Molecular Evolution, especially Kathrin Hoffmann, David Bogumil and the aforementioned ones, for welcoming me so warmly as a visitor in their institute.

Many people supported my study by providing digital data or technical support. Jelena Prokić provided me with her multiple alignment benchmark of Bulgarian dialect data (Prokić et al. 2009). Michael Dunn shared parts of the *Indo-European Lexical Cognacy Database* (http://ielex.mpi.nl/). Simon Greenhill sent me parts of the *Austronesian Basic Vocabulary Database* (http://language.psy.auckland.ac.nz/austronesian/). Wang Feng provided me with a digital version of his Bai dialect data (Wang 2006a). Cecil Brown, Eric Holman, and Søren Wichmann shared their data on the most frequently recurring sound correspondences in the world's language families with me (Brown et al. 2013). Hans Geisler allowed me to use parts of his digitized version of the *Tableaux phonétiques des patois suisses romands* (TPPSR). Matthias Dickmanns, Sayako Maike Oetzel, and Karl Vogt digitized the Japanese dialect data of Shirō (1973) for me. Victor Persien helped to check the multiple alignment benchmark for formal errors. I am very grateful to all of the aforementioned people for their help. Johannes Wahle was so kind to point me to an erroneous formula in a draft version of this study.

Special thanks go to my fellow doctoral students at the Heinrich Heine University, Dorothea Brenner, Carina Füller, Daniel Schulzek, and Anselm Terhalle, with whom I spent countless lunch and coffee breaks discussing work, life, and frames. Without them, my time in Düsseldorf would not have been the same. I am very glad that I had the chance to meet them, and I am very grateful for all their support in personal and professional matters. Special thanks go also to all members of my family for not getting annoyed by my endless talks about linguistics and computers. It is a great gift to have a family, knowing that someone is and will always be there, no matter what happens.

Contents

1 Introduction   1

2 Historical Linguistics   9
- 2.1 Entities 10
  - 2.1.1 Languages 11
  - 2.1.2 Words 15
  - 2.1.3 Forms 18
  - 2.1.4 Meanings 21
  - 2.1.5 Representations 22
- 2.2 Change 24
  - 2.2.1 Sound Change 26
  - 2.2.2 Semantic Change 34
  - 2.2.3 Lexical Change 37
- 2.3 Relations 39
  - 2.3.1 Relations between Words 41
  - 2.3.2 Relations between Languages 44
- 2.4 Resemblances 47
  - 2.4.1 Resemblances in Form 48
  - 2.4.2 Resemblances in Meaning 50
- 2.5 Proof 51
  - 2.5.1 Laws 54
  - 2.5.2 Evidence 55
- 2.6 Methods 57

3 Sequence Comparison   61
- 3.1 Sequences 62
  - 3.1.1 Discrete and Continuous Entities ... 63
  - 3.1.2 Sequences and Sets 64
  - 3.1.3 A Formal Definition of Sequences ... 64

	3.2	Sequence Comparison	66
		3.2.1	Differences between Sequences	67
		3.2.2	Modelling Sequence Differences	69
		3.2.3	Alignment Analyses	72
	3.3	Pairwise Alignment Analyses	76
		3.3.1	The Basic Algorithm for Pairwise Alignment	77
		3.3.2	Structural Extensions of the Basic Algorithm	82
		3.3.3	Substantial Extensions of the Basic Algorithm	91
		3.3.4	Summary on Pairwise Alignment Analyses	99
	3.4	Multiple Alignment Analyses	99
		3.4.1	Progressive Alignment	100
		3.4.2	Enhancements for Progressive Alignment	108
		3.4.3	Summary on Multiple Alignment Analyses	115

4 Sequence Comparison in Historical Linguistics — 117

	4.1	Sequence Modelling	119
		4.1.1	Paradigmatic Aspects	121
		4.1.2	Syntagmatic Aspects	130
	4.2	Phonetic Alignment	134
		4.2.1	Previous Work	137
		4.2.2	SCA – Sound-Class Based Phonetic Alignment	139
		4.2.3	Specific Features	142
		4.2.4	Evaluation	147
		4.2.5	Examples	165
	4.3	Automatic Cognate Detection	169
		4.3.1	Previous Work	172
		4.3.2	LexStat – Multilingual Cognate Detection	173
		4.3.3	Specific Features	175
		4.3.4	Evaluation	185
		4.3.5	Examples	205

5 Conclusion — 209

Bibliography — 215

Sources — 229

Dictionaries and Databases — 231

Contents

Supplementary Material   **235**

List of Abbreviations   **237**

Indices   **239**
     Index of Topics 239
     Index of Persons 247
     Index of Languages 248
     Index of Word Forms 250
     Index of Reconstructed Forms 254

Appendix A   Language-Specific Resources   **255**
     A.1   Phonetic Transcriptions 255
     A.2   Etymological Sources 256

Appendix B   Sequence Modelling   **257**
     B.1   The DOLGO Scoring function 257
     B.2   The SCA Scoring function 258
     B.3   The ASJP Scoring function 259

Appendix C   Phonetic Alignment   **261**
     C.1   Covington's Testset 261
     C.2   Language-Specific Pairwise Alignments 262

Appendix D   Cognate Detection   **271**
     D.1   Comparison of Phonetic Distances 271
     D.2   Cognate Detection 274

List of Figures

1.1	Historical scenarios	4
2.1	Simplified representation of the variety space	13
2.2	The Saussurean model of the linguistic sign	16
2.3	A graph representation of the linguistic sign	17
2.4	Examples for graph representations of linguistic signs	17
2.5	The reference potential of the linguistic sing	21
2.6	Change in form and meaning	35
2.7	Comparing reference potentials of cognate words	36
2.8	Cognacy and ancestor-descendant relation	42
2.9	Ancestor relations vs. etymological relations	43
2.10	Ancestor-descendant relation between languages	45
2.11	Genetic relation between languages	46
2.12	Contact relation between languages	46
2.13	Common causes for formal resemblances	56
2.14	The iterative character of the comparative method	58
3.1	Sequences in our daily life: music, movies, recipes	62
3.2	Spectogram of Shanghainese *tàiyáng* 'sun'	64
3.3	Sequences as strings of colored beads	65
3.4	Comparing sequences of equal length	66
3.5	The basic types of segment correspondences	68
3.6	Transforming one sequence into the other	69
3.7	Crossed and complex matches	69
3.8	Traces, alignments, and listings	71
3.9	Comparing traces, alignments, and listings	72
3.10	Alignment analyses in different applications	73
3.11	The three states of each cell of the alignment matrix	79
3.12	The dynamic programming algorithm	81
3.13	Global vs. semi-global alignment	84

3.14	Semiglobal vs. local alignment	86
3.15	Primary vs. secondary alignment	91
3.16	Scoring matrix for a numerical keyboard	93
3.17	Alignment with extended scoring function	95
3.18	Linear vs. affine gap penalties	97
3.19	Traces vs. alignments of multiple sequences	100
3.20	Constructing the guide tree from pairwise distances	101
3.21	Ultrametric and additive distances	102
3.22	Demonstration of the UPGMA algorithm	103
3.23	Aligning sequences along the guide tree	106
3.24	Profile representation of an alignment	107
3.25	Calculation of the sum-of-pairs score	108
3.26	Matrix- vs. consistency-based MSA	109
3.27	Consistency with pairwise alignment libraries	111
3.28	Deriving scoring schemes from a primary library	112
3.29	Deriving scoring schemes from an extended library	113
3.30	Iterative refinement analyses	115
4.1	Discrete heritable units	120
4.2	Directonality of sound change patterns	126
4.3	Directionality of sound change in scoring functions	127
4.4	Multidimensional scaling of similarity models	129
4.5	Distances between the sounds of English	130
4.6	Deriving prosodic strings from sonority profiles	132
4.7	The basic working procedure of SCA analyses	139
4.8	SCA working procedure	141
4.9	Swaps in alignment analyses	145
4.10	Trace character in swap calculations	146
4.11	SCA method for the detection of swapped sites	147
4.12	Percentage idenity in the gold standard	150
4.13	Results of the PSA analysis	157
4.14	Results of the PSA analysis (tone language partition)	159
4.15	Results of the PSA analysis (different modes)	160
4.16	Results of the MSA analysis	162
4.17	Results on different gold standard partitions	163
4.18	Alignment of dialect variants of Dutch 'mountain'	165
4.19	Alignment of dialect variants of Chinese 'sun'	166

4.20	Alignment of reflexes of Proto-Germanic *xurnan	167
4.21	Alignment of Bai dialect words	168
4.22	Missed and detected swaps	170
4.23	LexStat working procedure	174
4.24	PID, NED, SCAD and LexStat distance	184
4.25	Flat clustering variant of UPGMA	186
4.26	Average scores for the subsets of the gold standard	196
4.27	B-Cubed F-Scores for the subsets	198
4.28	Comparing B-Cubed Scores	200
4.29	Sample size and ACD performance	201

List of Tables

1.1	Striking similarities between languages	3
2.1	"Northwind and Sun" in different speech varieties	12
2.2	Multilingual word list	23
2.3	Strange rhymes in the Book of Odes	25
2.4	Comparing Italian and Latin words	27
2.5	Split of Middle Chinese homophones in Shuāngfēng	30
2.6	Five basic types of sound change	33
2.7	Lexicostatistical word list	38
2.8	Basic relations between genes and words	39
2.9	Basic historical relations between words.	44
2.10	Basic historical relations between languages	47
2.11	Cognate words in Italian and French	49
2.12	Contact-induced systematic similarities	50
3.1	Correspondence vs. edit perspective	70
3.2	The scoring scheme of the edit distance	77
3.3	A simple scoring scheme for the NW algorithm	78
3.4	Comparison of the results of different alignment modes	87
3.5	Primary vs. secondary alignment	90
3.6	Extended scoring scheme	93
3.7	Scoring scheme with affine gap penalties	96
3.8	Rate-corrected distances	104
4.1	Parallels between species and languages	118
4.2	Dolgopolsky's original sound class model	123
4.3	The SCA sound class model	124
4.4	Default weights for tone and none-tone languages	133
4.5	The LingPy framework of sequence modelling	133
4.6	The importance of multiple phonetic alignment.	134
4.7	Different alignments of similar reflexes	135

4.8	Data sources of the gold standard	148
4.9	Four subsets of the MSA benchmark	149
4.10	Row and column score bias.	152
4.11	Bias in pair precision and pair recall.	154
4.12	Performance on the Covington benchmark	155
4.13	Results of the PSA Analysis	156
4.14	Results of the PSA analysis (tone language partition)	158
4.15	Results of the PSA analysis (different modes)	159
4.16	Results of the MSA analysis	161
4.17	Results on different gold standard partitions	163
4.18	Results of the swap-identification task	164
4.19	Proportion of cognates within word lists	171
4.20	Input and output format of LexStat	176
4.21	Aligned output of LexStat	177
4.22	n-Point Average Precision of string distances	179
4.23	Attested vs. expected frequencies of residue pairs	182
4.24	The *general partition* of the ACD gold standard	187
4.25	The *specific partition* of the ACD gold standard	189
4.26	The pair perspective in clustering evaluation	190
4.27	Pairwise decisions in reference and test set	191
4.28	Average scores for the subsets of the gold standard	195
4.29	F-Scores for the six subsets	197
4.30	Comparing the B-Cubed scores	199
4.31	Sample size and B-Cubed recall	202
4.32	Results on the KSL test set	204
4.33	Cognate judgments for the item 'dig'	206
4.34	Cognate judgments for the item 'mouth'	207

1
Introduction

> Die Sprache ist das Alleralltäglichste: es muss ein Philosoph sein, der sich mit ihr abgiebt.
>
> Nietzsche (1869 [1920]: Gedanken zur Einleitung, 21)

In *Murder on the Orient Express*, a famous piece of detective fiction written by Agatha Christie (1890 – 1976), Belgian's most famous detective, Hercule Poirot, is confronted with a very tricky murder case. Boarding the Orient Express to return from a trip in the Middle East, a passenger, Mr. Ratchett, gets killed during the second night on the train, having been stabbed twelve times. The circumstances are deeply mysterious. There are as many as twelve suspects who could have committed the murder, but all have an alibi. Furthermore, the stab wounds differ to a large extent, some appearing to have been inflicted by a right-handed person, and some by a left-handed one, some being very deep and lethal, and some being mere glancing blows. Based on the evidence, Hercule Poirot comes to the only possible conclusion, namely that *all twelve suspects* committed the murder *together*:

> I fancy, though I may be wrong, that each person in turn entered Ratchett's darkened compartment through that of Mrs. Hubbard – and struck! They themselves would never know which blow actually killed him. (Agatha Christie, *Murder on the Orient Express*, Chapter 9)

Several clues lead Hercule Poirot to come to this conclusion. In a first instance it is the behaviour of the suspects which can be best explained by assuming that they cooperate:

> I was particularly struck by the extraordinary difficulty of proving a case against any one person on the train, and by the rather curious coincidence that in each case the testimony giving an alibi came from what I might describe as an "unlikely" person. (ibid.)

The "twelve murderer hypothesis" can also best explain the "nature of the wounds – each inflicted by a different person" (ibid.). Putting these pieces of evidence together, it results in

> a perfect mosaic, each person playing his or her allotted part. It was so arranged that, if suspicion should fall on any one person, the evidence of one or more of the others would clear the accused person and confuse the issue. (ibid.)

Hercule Poirot bases his conclusion on a rule which one might call the "rule of the least unlikely explanation", or, as Sherlock Holmes would say, the

> maxim [...] that when you have excluded the impossible, whatever remains, however improbable, must be the truth. (Sir Arthur Conan Doyle, *The Adventure of the Beryl Coronet*)

Given that there are twelve different stab wounds and twelve different suspects, all having an aliby provided by somebody who is a suspect him- or herself, the least unlikely explanation covering all facts is to assume that all twelve suspects committed the murder. This rule plays an important role in many whodunit stories where the reader is led astray by a plot that offers many seemingly possible explanations while the only really possible explanation seems to be completely unlikely.

When during the end of the 18th century scholars stumbled over some striking similarities between Sanskrit, the classical language of India, and Latin and Old Greek, the classical languages of Europe (see Table 1.1), their conclusion was – given the spirit of the age – somewhat similar to the solution of a murder case by a least unlikely explanation. If these similarities between the three languages were not a pure coincidence, the only possible explanation was to assume that "all three [...] have sprung from some common source, which, perhaps, no longer exists" (Jones 1798: 423). Today, the hypothesis that Sanskrit, Old Greek, and Latin have developed from a common ancestor language has lost the sensational character it must have had during the end of the 18th century, when many scholars still stuck to the biblical paradigm in believing that the diversity of languages resulted from the *Confusion of Tongues* (*Genesis* 11:1-9). During the more than 200 years since the genealogical relatedness of the languages was first suspected, scholars have substantiated the hypothesis with a large body of evidence. More and more languages could be shown to be also related with the former three, and today the "Indo-European" language family covers more than 400 living languages (count based on Lewis and Fennig 2013).

Meaning	Sanskrit		Old Greek		Latin	
	Orth.	Pron.		Pron.	Orth.	Pron.
'field'	अज्र	aɟra	ἀγρός	agrɔs	*ager*	ager
'I carry'	भरमि	bʰarami	φέρω	pʰeroː	*fero*	feroː
'yoke'	युग	juga	ζυγόν	dzugon	*iugum*	jugum
'father'	पितृ	pitr̥	πατήρ	pateːr	*pater*	pater
'brother'	भ्रातृ	bʰraːtr̥	φράτηρ	pʰrateːr	*frater*	frater

Table 1.1: *Striking similarities between Sanskrit, Old Greek, and Latin. The examples are adapted from Anttila (1972: 246) in a slightly altered form. Greek and Latin nouns are given in the nominative, Sanskrit nouns are given in their root form.*

All languages constantly change. Words are lost when speakers cease to use them, new words are gained when new concepts evolve, and even the pronunciation of the words changes slightly over time. Slight modifications that can rarely be noticed during a person's live time sum up to great changes in the system of a language over centuries. When the speakers of a language depart, their speech keeps on changing independently in the two communities, and at a certain point of time the independent changes are so great that they can no longer communicate with each other: what was one language has become two.

Proving that two languages once were one is one of the major tasks of *historical linguistics*, a subdiscipline of linguistics that deals with the *history* of languages. The task exhibits some interesting parallels to crime investigations. Both disciplines make use of circumstantial evidence in order to draw a scenario of past events that explains a given situation in the present. While a detective employs evidence found at the crime scene to reconstruct the progression of events that led to the crime, a historical linguist employs evidence found in attested languages to reconstruct their unattested history. Since language change is rather gradual than abrupt, the traces of common origin can often still be detected through comparison. In historical linguistics, specific methods have been developed to identify these traces. Their analysis results in the construction of *historical scenarios* which shed light on how languages evolved from their common ancestor into their current shape.

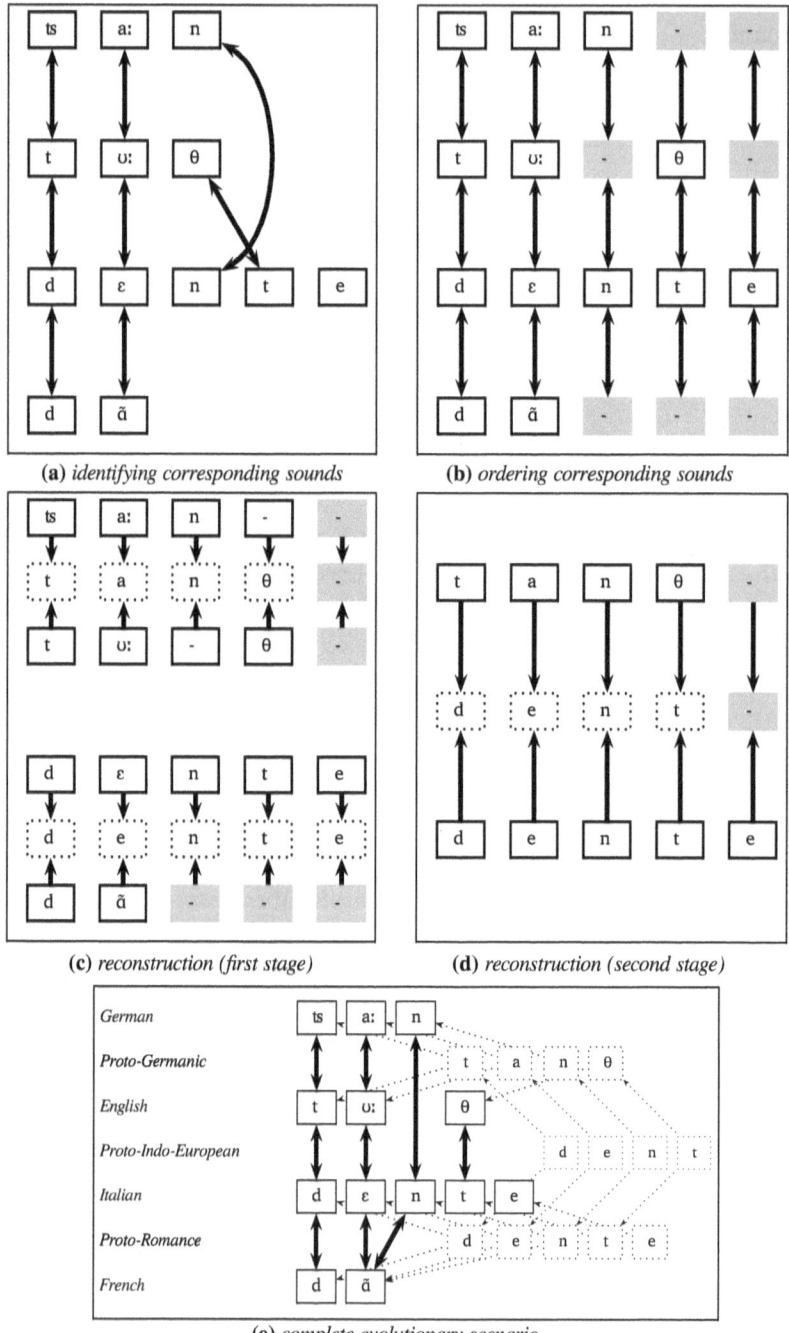

Figure 1.1: *Reconstructing historical scenarios from words* [1]

An example for the construction of such a historical scenario is given in Figure 1.1: The four words German *Zahn* [tsaːn] 'tooth', English *tooth* [tʊːθ], Italian *dente* [dɛnte] 'tooth', and French *dent* [dã] 'tooth' are successively traced back to their ancestor form Proto-Indo-European **dent*, via the intermediate stages Proto-Germanic **tanθ* and Proto-Romance **dente*.[1] The label "proto" that is added to the ancestor languages indicates that these languages are not attested in written sources. There is, however, strong evidence that these languages once existed. The development of such a scenario goes through two major stages. In a first stage, *cognate words*, i.e. words that are supposed to go back to a common ancestor word, have to be detected and *corresponding sounds* in the cognate words have to be identified (Figure 1.1a and b). In a second stage, *proto-values* for the corresponding sounds have to be reconstructed (Figure 1.1c and d). For the first stage, I will adopt the term *cognate detection*. The second stage is commonly called *linguistic reconstruction* (Fox 1995).

Cognate detection is based on the comparison of words in different languages. Words themselves can be described as *sequences of sounds* denoting a specific meaning. Cognate detection can therefore be seen as a specific kind of sequence comparison. In historical linguistics, sequence comparison is usually carried out manually. Linguists compare word lists from different languages, identify probably related words and set up lists of corresponding sound segments. This is a very tedious task, since the number of word pairs which could be compared grows exponentially with the number of languages being investigated. Ethnologue (Lewis and Fennig 2013), a large database collecting information for all languages in the world, lists as many as 7105 languages that are spoken at the moment. Comparing all these languages with each other yields a total of $\frac{7105^2 - 7105}{2} = 25\,236\,960$ pairs. So far, research in the field of historical linguistics has led to the postulation of 128 different language families, but – due to the tediousness of manual language comparison – only a small amount of these language families have been thoroughly investigated so far. Given the fact that the amount of digitally available data for the languages of the world is growing from day to day, while there are only a few historical linguists who are trained to carry out the comparison of these languages, the use of automatic methods to aid the task of sequence comparison seems inevitable in the future.

---

[1] Note that these reconstructions are simplified versions, based only on the evidence which can be derived from the four words themselves.

In this study, I will present automatic methods for sequence comparison and cognate detection in historical linguistics. The method is based on a larger framework of computational tools that I implemented as a Python library (LingPy, see Supplementary Material and http://lingpy.org). These tools are supposed to aid the work of historical linguists by automatizing several steps of the traditional methods for language and sequence comparison. The strategy I pursued when developing the new method was to follow the traditional methods as closely as possible, while at the same time trying to find solutions that had been developed for similar problems in other disciplines. If the task of cognate detection in historical linguistics is understood as a specific type of sequence comparison, one should be able to find solutions to similar problems in those disciplines which explicitly deal with this task, such as computer science, and evolutionary biology. The major work carried out for this study was therefore to get a very close insight into the basic approaches to sequence comparison in these disciplines in order to adapt them for the specific needs of historical linguistics.

This study consists of three main parts. In Chapter 2, I will give an introduction into some major aspects of historical linguistics. I will define its basic *entities*, languages and words (Section 2.1); I will describe the basic types of *change* to which these entities are subject (Section 2.2), and I will point to the basic *relations* between these entities that result from the basic types of change (Section 2.3). Language change leaves its traces in specific kinds of *resemblances* between languages and words (Section 2.4). These resemblances are crucial for the *proof* of language relations (Section 2.5). All these aspects play an important role for the comparative method, the core method for cognate detection and linguistic reconstruction in historical linguistics, which will be briefly outlined in Section 2.6.

Having pointed to some of the fundamental theoretical and practical aspects of historical linguistics, I turn to the formal aspects of sequence comparison in Chapter 3. After a brief introduction into some basic aspects of *sequences* (Section 3.1), and *sequence comparison* (Section 3.2), I turn to the more specific, especially algorithmic aspects of *alignments* and *alignment analyses*. Alignments are a specific way to model differences between sequences. Alignment analyses are an algorithmic framework to compute alignments. For reasons of computational complexity, alignment analyses are usually divided into *pairwise alignment analyses*, which are treated in Section 3.3, and *multiple alignment analyses*, which are treated in Section 3.4.

In Chapter 4, I present the new approaches to automatic sequence comparison in historical linguistics. The new methods presented combine the most recent research in the disciplines of computer science and biology with novel approaches to sequence modelling in historical linguistics. Since the sound sequences that are compared in historical linguistics show some crucial differences compared to sequences in biology and computer science, the approach is based on a new framework for *sequence modelling*, which is introduced in Section 4.1. This framework constitutes the core of a new method for *phonetic alignment*, i.e. the alignment of sound sequences, outlined in Section 4.2. Finally, the task of cognate detection is addressed in Section 4.3, where a new method for automatic cognate detection which builds on the new approaches to sequence modelling and sequence alignment is presented.

2
Historical Linguistics

> Was die menschliche Rede im Innersten bewegt, was sonst die Wissenschaft von den Sprachen der Völker zu einer der lebensvollsten macht, das tritt hier zurück [...]. [D]er Sprachhistoriker steht draussen vor seinem Gegenstande: hier der Anatom, da der Cadaver.
>
> Gabelentz (1891: 145)

When, during the end of the 18th century, more and more scholars became interested in the striking similarities between certain languages, such as Sanskrit and Old Greek, they had but a fuzzy idea about languages, language history, and language change. Often, they confused the *results* with the *processes*. Instead of making a strict distinction between the specific patterns of similarity between languages that *result* from language change with the *process* of change itself, they directly identified the patterns with the process.[1] As a result, the first historical linguists assumed that the relation between Sanskrit and other Indo-European languages, such as Old Greek and Latin, was like the relation between a mother and her children, the latter being the *offspring* of the former. It took scholars more than half a century to realize that a direct line of descent could not be drawn between Sanskrit and the European languages, and that it was more likely that they all were the children of a common, unknown ancestor language.[2] A similar confusion arose from the specific "organic" notion of languages which was propagated by some scholars. According to this notion,

---

[1] This notion is prevalent in most of the literature on language comparison in the first half of the 19th century. It is also reflected in the common terminology itself. Thus, the famous German term "Lautverschiebung" (*sound shift*), points to a process, although all the examples by which the process is usually described are merely its results (see, for example, Grimm 1822: 584).

[2] This is explicitly expressed in the work of August Schleicher (1821 – 1868) who justified the use of proto-forms by emphasizing "die Grundlosigkeit der noch immer nicht ganz verschollenen Annahme, daß auch die nicht indischen indogermanischen Sprachen vom altindischen

languages were comparable to organisms, i.e. they went through the stages of birth, youth, middle age, old age, and – finally – death.³

Today, after 200 years of research in the field of historical linguistics, we have a much clearer picture of language, language history, and language change. Many questions, however, still remain unsolved, many ideas about the entities, the processes, and the relations that are dealt with in historical linguistics have remained fuzzy. This fuzzyness is also reflected in the common methodology by which languages are compared and language history is inferred. Historical linguistics is a *historical* discipline that – in a first instance – deals with *individual events* rather than with general laws. It therefore bears certain resemblances with the work of historians who laboriously join tiny pieces of evidence into a larger mosaic of past events. While historians draw the evidence from direct or indirect sources, historical linguists seek the evidence in the systems of languages as they are given in the present. Due to the "individuality" of the processes that historians and historical linguistics commonly deal with, their methods tend to be impressionistic. The individual intuition of the researcher plays a major role, and the methods and theories that are commonly employed in both disciplines are not explicitly codified.

In the following, I will try to make the implicit theoretical and practical assumptions of historical linguistics more explicit by giving a short introduction into its main entities (Section 2.1), the basic change processes to which these entities are subject (Section 2.2), and the crucial relations (Section 2.3) and resemblances between the entities (Section 2.4) that result from these processes. I will then briefly address the question of how to prove that specific relations hold between the entities (Section 2.5), and, in the end, briefly describe how all these aspects cumulate in the common practice of the *comparative method*, the fundamental technique of historical linguistics (Section 2.6).

2.1 Entities

It is important for a scientific discipline to define its object of research. Only then it is possible to define the specific questions that the discipline is supposed to investigate, and only than it is possible to develop specific methods

---

(Sanskrit) abstammen" in the second edition of his *Compendium* (Schleicher 1861 [1866]: 8).

[3] Compare, for example, the discussion of the common stages of language history ("Sprachengeschichte") in Schleicher (1848: 16f).

2.1 Entities

and theories that are adequate for the given discipline. Unfortunately, not all scientific disciplines are in the comfortable situation that they can construct their research object independently of the real world (like mathematics) or that they can exclude the imponderableness of human behaviour (like physics and chemistry). Being on the borderline between science and humanities, it is especially difficult for the discipline of linguistics to define its research objects. Should linguistics only deal with the structure of concrete languages, or are languages less important than the general *language faculty*, i.e. the specific ability of humans to *speak*? Should linguistics only deal with the system of a language as it is given at a certain *point* of time, or should it deal with the *change* of language systems?

While it is impossible to settle these questions for the discipline as a whole, the subdisciplines, including historical linguistics, often answer them implicitly. While there are only a few explicit discussions regarding the definition of the research objects in the literature, there are certain implicit assumptions regarding the basic "entities" of historical linguistics and their basic characteristics which manifest themselves in the research practice and the common theories. Since the goal of this study is to develop automatic approaches to some of the major tasks of historical linguistics, it is important to give an explicit account on these basic entities.

2.1.1 Languages

It is not an easy task, to give an exact definition of the term "language" as it is applied in linguistics. The reason can be found in the daily use of the term in non-linguistic contexts: What one calls a language, i.e. which traditions of speech one classifies as belonging to one language, does not, usually, depend on purely linguistic but rather on social and cultural criteria (Barbour and Stevenson 1998: 8). Thus, one tends to say that the people from Shànghǎi, Běijīng, and Měixiàn all speak "Chinese", while, on the other hand, people from Scandinavia speek "Norwegian", "Swedish", or "Danish".

Table 2.1 gives phonetic transcriptions of translations of the sentence "*The North Wind and the Sun were disputing which was the stronger*"[4] in three Chinese "dialects" (Běijīng Chinese, Hakka Chinese[5], and Shànghǎi Chinese),

---

[4] This is the first sentence of Aesop's fable *The Northwind and the Sun*, which is traditionally used in phonetic studies to illustrate the phonetic system of a language.

[5] This is the traditional name given to the Chinese variety spoken in Měixiàn and some other regions of China.

Běijīng Chinese	1	iou²¹	i⁵⁵	xuei³⁵	pei²¹fəŋ⁵⁵	kən⁵⁵	tʰai⁵¹iaŋ¹¹	tʂəŋ⁵⁵ tsai⁵³ naɚ⁵¹			tʂəŋ⁵⁵luən⁵¹
Hakka Chinese	1	iu³³	it⁵⁵	pai³³a¹¹	pet³³fuŋ³³	tʰuŋ¹¹	ɲit¹¹tʰeu¹¹	hɔk³³		e⁵³	au⁵⁵
Shànghǎi Chinese	1	ɦi²²		tʰɑ⁵⁵ tsɿ²¹	poʔ³foŋ⁴⁴	taʔ⁵	tʰa³³ɦiã⁴⁴	tsəŋ³³ hɔ⁴⁴			ləʔ¹lə²³tsa⁵³
Běijīng Chinese	2	ʂei³⁵		də⁵⁵			pən³⁵ liŋ²¹ ta⁵¹				
Hakka Chinese	2	man³³	ɲin¹¹		kʷɔ⁵⁵	vɔi⁵³					
Shànghǎi Chinese	2	sa³³	ɲiŋ⁵⁵	ɦəʔ²¹		pəŋ³³ zɿ⁴⁴ du¹³						
Norwegian	1	nuːrɑʋinˀn̩	ɔ	suːln̩					krɑŋlət		ɔm
Swedish	1	nuːdanvɪndən	ɔ	suːlən	tvɪstadə	ən gɔŋ					ɔm
Danish	1	noʌʌnvenˀn̩	ʌ	soːlˀn̩	kʰʌm		eŋɡɑŋ		i sdʁiðˀ		ʌmˀ
Norwegian	2	ʋem	ɑ	dem	sm̩	ʋɑː	dn̩		stæɾkəstə		
Swedish	2	vɛm	av	dɔm	sɔm	va			staɪkast		
Danish	2	vɛmˀ	a	b̥m̩	d̥	va	d̥n̩		sd̥æʌɡ̊əsd̥ə		

Table 2.1: *Translations of the sentence "The Northwind and the Sun were disputing (1) which was the stronger (2)" in different varieties of Chinese and Scandinavian languages. The words are semantically aligned, i.e. all translational equivalents are placed in the same column. Words shaded in gray are further etymologically related. The data for Běijīng Chinese and Hakka Chinese follows Lee and Zee (2003 and 2009) with slight modifications for tone letters and some phonetic symbols. The data for Shànghǎi Chinese is taken from YINKU. The transcriptions for Norwegian (Oslo dialect) are taken from NORDAVINDEN, the transcriptions for Swedish and Danish follow Engstrand (1999) and Grønnum (1998).*

and three Scandinavian "languages" (Norwegian, Swedish, and Danish). In this table, all words which are semantically similar are aligned horizontally. The words which share a common etymological origin are further highlighted with a gray background.

As the phonetic transcriptions of the sentences show, the Chinese varieties seem to differ to a similar or even greater degree than the Scandinavian ones, in terms of both the amount of shared etymologically related words and the phonetic similarity between these words. Nevertheless, we address three speech traditions, which are largely mutually intelligible, as "Norwegian", "Swedish", and "Danish", while we classify the speech of the people in Shànghǎi, Běijīng, and Měixiàn (Hakka dialect), who can barely communicate with each other when relying on their native speech varieties, as being dialects of the same "Chinese" language.

2.1 Entities

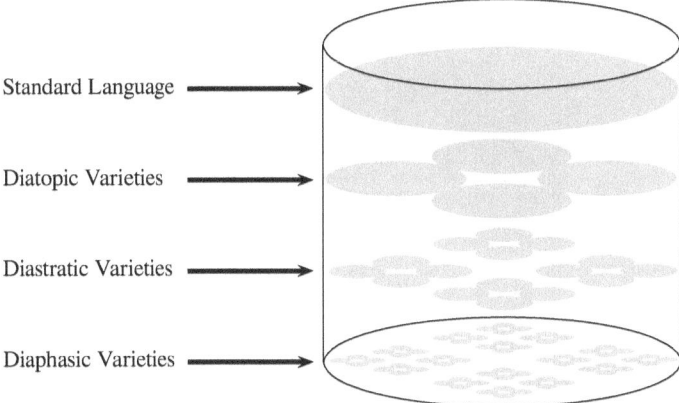

Figure 2.1: *Simplified representation of the variety space. On the top is the standard language which serves as a* Dachsprache *for the different varieties. These can be further subdivided into diatopic varieties (dialects), diastratic varieties (sociolects), and diaphasic varieties (speech varieties depending on the situation).*

In order to describe the complex heterogeneous structure of our modern languages being defined on a socio-cultural basis, the model of the *diasystem* is traditionally employed in sociolinguistics. This model goes back to the dialectologist Uriel Weinreich (1926 – 1967) who originally thought of a linguistic construct which would make it possible to describe different dialects in a uniform way (Weinreich 1954, see also Branner 2006: 209). According to the modern form of the model, a language is a complex aggregate of different linguistic systems, "die miteinander koexistieren und sich gegenseitig beeinflussen" (Coseriu 1973: 40). An important aspect for determining a linguistic diasystem is the presence of a *Dachsprache*, i.e. a linguistic variety serving as a standard for interdialectal communication (Goossens 1973: 11). The different linguistic varieties (dialects, sociolects) which are connected by such a standard constitute the *variety space* of a language (Oesterreicher 2001), as illustrated in Figure 2.1.

In historical linguistics, the term *language* is used in different ways, referring either to a certain language tradition spoken at a certain time, or to a speech tradition spoken during a certain period of time (Arapov and Xerc 1974: 7). The question, what a language actually *is*, is rarely stated, and complex models of language, such as the sociolinguistic model of the diasystem, are seldom applied. This lack of a theoretical model may be justified on the background of the specific goal of historical linguistics: historical linguistics seeks to *describe* how certain speech traditions *evolved*, i.e. "durch welche Veränderungen [...] die Sprache zu ihrem jeweiligen Zustande gelangt [ist]" (Gabelentz 1891: 149), and not to *explain* what languages actually *are*. Therefore, some scholars even claim that for most of the problems in historical linguistics, like classification or reconstruction,

> it is not important, what exactly we have in mind when using the term "language" as long as it is a discrete object x which we can distinguish from all other objects of this kind, and as long as one can give a certain period of time $t = [t_1, t_2]$ during which the object exists. (Arapov and Xerc 1974: 7)[6]

Although this might be true in certain contexts, the reluctance of many historical linguists to define their object of research has lead to many confusions and endless discussions which only arose because scholars were unaware of the fact that they were talking about different objects.[7] In order to avoid such a confusion in this study, it is important to define a language model, albeit a simple one, upon which most historical linguists would probably agree.

Following Ferdinand de Saussure's (1857 – 1913) traditional distinction between *langue* (language) and *parole* (speech, cf. Saussure 1916: 27-35), where *langue* is seen "as an abstract system of signs and rules", while *parole* corresponds to "the concrete realization of language as it is used" (Bussmann 1996: 657), the primary concern of historical linguistics is the abstract language system rather than its realization by the speakers. In a very broad notion, a *system* consists of a set of *elements* and a set of *relations* which hold between the elements (Marchal 1975: 462f). According to the traditional view in linguistics, the crucial *elements* of a language system are

(a) the *sounds* (phones / phonemes), and
(b) the *signs* (words / morphemes).

---

[6] My translation, original text: "[Когда мы классифицируем языки,] то не существенно, что именно мы имеем в виду под языком, лишь бы это был дискретный объект x, который мы можем отличить от всех объектов этого рода, и можно было бы говорить об определенном интервале времени $t = [t_1, t_2]$, в течение которого этот объект существует".

[7] An example for such a confusion is the so-called *realist-abstractionalist* debate dealing with the "nature" of proto-languages: This discussion arose solely because many scholars were confusing the ontological with the epistemological status of proto-languages (Kormišin 1988).

2.1 Entities

The crucial *relations* are

(a) the *phonotactic rules* by which the sounds are combined to form signs (phonotactics), and
(b) the *syntactical rules* by which the signs are combined to form sentences (syntax).

Given the fact that most of the traditional fields of historical linguistics (such as etymology and linguistic reconstruction) mainly focus on the *lexical* aspects of languages and language history, the grammatical rules can be ignored in the basic language model of historical linguistics. In the following, a language is thus defined as a system consisting of

(a) a set of sounds along with a set of phonotactic rules which constitute the *phonological system* of the language, and
(b) a set of words which constitutes the *lexicon* of the language.

In order to avoid to be dragged into the shallow waters of semiotics, I will use the term *sign* only when addressing the abstract characteristics of form-meaning pairs. When addressing concrete realizations of linguistic signs in a given speech variety, I will prefer the term *word* instead.

This model differs from the one favored by Katičić (1966) and Holzer (1996) who define a language as a set of linguistic signs, ignoring the set of phonemes and the set of phonotactic rules. While such a model may be sufficient in statistical applications dealing solely with lexical comparison on the sequence level, such as lexicostatistics (Swadesh 1950 1952, 1955, Lees 1953), its modern derivations (Atkinson and Gray 2006, Gray and Atkinson 2003, Starostin 1989), or certain alternative approaches (Holm 2000, Ross 1950), it is certainly not sufficient for approaches dealing with comparisons on the segment level, such as the one presented in this study.

2.1.2 Words

Roman Jakobson described the *bilateral sign model*, which was originally proposed by Ferdinand de Saussure, as follows:

> The sign has two sides: the sound, or the material side on the one hand, and meaning, or the intelligible side on the other. Every word, and more generally every verbal sign, is a combination of sound and meaning, or to put it another way, a combination of signifier and signified [...]. (Jakobson 1976 [1978]: 3)

In Saussure's original proposal the linguistic sign is characterized by its "image acoustique" and the mental "concept" which the speaker immediately asso-

Figure 2.2: *The Saussurean model of the linguistic sign*

ciates with the acoustic image (Saussure 1916: 98). Since the language model applied in this study is not based on a mental language conception, it is sufficient to distinguish the *form* (*signifier*) of a word from its *meaning* (*signified*), where the *form* corresponds to a "chain of sounds [which] acts as the support of meaning" (Jakobson 1976 [1978]: 32). Following this model, the form of the German word *Kopf* can be transcribed as [kɔp͡f] and the meaning can be glossed as 'head'. Accordingly, the form of English *cup* is [kʌp] and the meaning is 'cup' (see Figure 2.2).

Although this model is very simple, it is a significant improvement over older models in so far as the signified no longer directly denotes a real object but a certain concept which itself can be used to denote an object, as it is reflected in *triadic sign models* such as, e.g., the one proposed by Ogden and Richards (1923 [1989]: 10-12).

An important property of the linguistic sign is its *arbitrariness*. Being determined by convention, the form of the linguistic sign does not have to resemble its meaning, i.e. the connection between the form and the meaning of a sign does not have to be motivated. This does *not* mean that the connection between the form and the meaning of a linguistic sign *cannot* be motivated, it only means that there is no "necessary natural link [...], or a link due to some resemblance or similarity" between form and meaning (Merrell 2001: 31).

In addition to form and meaning as constitutive parts of the linguistic sign, every linguistic sign is characterized by the system to which it applies, i.e. by the *language* in which the sign is used. Without this information, the linguistic sign cannot be determined as such, and what we hear when hearing something which sounds like [kɔp͡f] without knowing that it belongs to the German language, it is just a sound sequence without any meaning (Ternes 1987: 22f). To

2.1 Entities

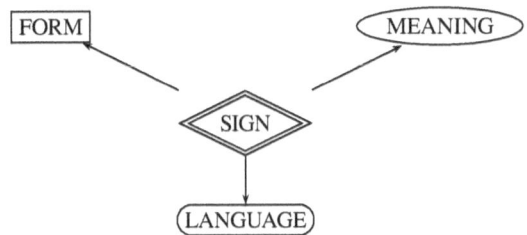

Figure 2.3: *A graph representation of the linguistic sign*

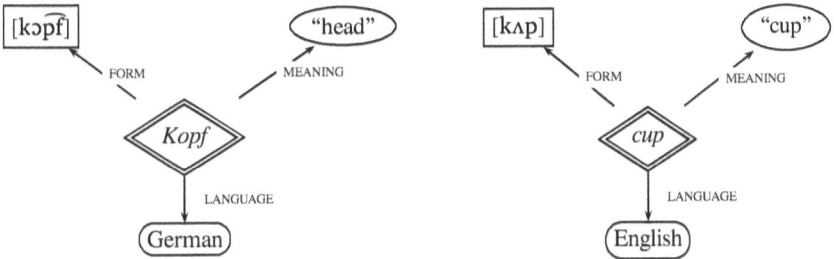

Figure 2.4: *Exemplary graph representation for two linguistic signs*

sum up, three parts are constitutive for the model of the linguistic sign which is applied in this study, namely

(a) the *form*, which will be given in phonetic transcription,
(b) the *meaning*, which will be rendered by a gloss, and
(c) the *language*, which will be addressed by the standard name of each given variety.

In order to display these three constitutive parts of the linguistic sign when dealing with words, a graph representation, as given in Figure 2.3, can be used. Figure 2.4 gives an example on how the words German *Kopf* [kɔpf͡] 'head' and English *cup* [kʌp] 'cup' can be represented.

This sign model is, of course, not exhaustive, and one might easily identify additional constitutive parts of the linguistic sign, such as, e.g., the way in which words can be combined with each other to form higher units of speech (Mel'čuk 2006: 384f). However, since such properties of linguistic signs belong to the range of the syntax, which is not included in the language model applied in this study, further parts of the linguistic sign can be ignored in most cases. Note that, although this is again a very simple model which contains many reductions, this is the way the matter is usually treated in historical linguistics.

2.1.3 Forms

Two aspects of the *form* of the linguistic sign are important in historical linguistics: its *substance* and its *structure*. Substance refers to the material properties of the form, i.e. to its sensually perceptible aspects. Structure, on the other hand, refers to the way the substance of the sign form is organized. The substance of the sign form can be addressed from two perspectives: the perspective of *production* which focuses on the articulatory movements characterizing speech, and the perspective of *perception* which characterizes its acoustic and auditive features (Hall 2000: 1f). The most striking aspect of the structure of the sign form is its *linearity*. The phonic substance is produced and perceived in dependence of time and can be measured "dans une seule dimension: c'est une ligne" (Saussure 1916: 103).

The substantial aspects of the sign form are usually addressed by dividing the continuum of speech into discrete units of "linguistically relevant" elements (*IPA Handbook* 1999: 4). These discrete units, the sound segments, do not find a direct reflection in reality, since speech production is not characterized by the succession but rather by the overlap of articulatory movements (Jakobson 1976 [1978]: 11, Geisler 1992: 10f). Nevertheless, the segmentation of speech into discrete sounds seems to be practically unavoidable, not only for historical linguistics but also for phonetic analysis in general.

It is common to distinguish two different levels of abstraction according to which sound segments can be described: the *phonetic* level and the *phonemic* level. The phonetic perspective deals with the substantial aspects of sound segments (*phones*), i.e. with the general acoustic and articulatory properties which characterize the sounds of different languages. The phonemic perspective, on the other hand, deals with the functional aspects of sounds (*phonemes*), that is, with the capacity of sounds or classes of sounds to distinguish the meaning of words in a given language (Hall 2000: 38). The main difference between the phonetic and the phonemic perspective lies in the level of abstraction applied in the transcription of sound segments. A phonemic (or broad) transcription assigns phonetically distinct sounds of a given language to the same category (expressed by the same phonetic symbol), if they are functionally equivalent, i.e. if they either do not change the meaning of a word when

2.1 Entities

occurring in the same context (*free variants*, ibid.: 46f), or if they are phonetically similar and occur in complementary distribution (*combinatory variants*, ibid.: 38-46). Different phones are thus grouped together into functional units which are reflected by contextual or facultative variants (*allophones*). A phonetic (or narrow) transcription, on the other hand, reflects the phonetic properties of the sound segments of a given language in greater detail, regardless of their contrastive function (*IPA Handbook* 1999: 28-30).

Based on the division of speech into discrete units, the structure of the sign form can be described as a *linear combination of segments*, i.e. as a *sequence of sounds*. Here, two different perspectives can be employed to describe the structure of the sign form in more detail: the *algebraic* and the *substantial perspective*. According to the algebraic perspective, segments are defined negatively and relatively, i.e. the comparison of segments in a given phonological system results in a binary decision, where two segments are either judged to be identical or different.[8] The substantial perspective, on the other hand, defines sound segments on the basis of additional properties, such as articulatory or acoustic features, and the comparison of segments results in different degrees of similarity, based on the features being employed to characterize the segments.

In historical linguistics, the algebraic perspective on sound sequences is especially important for the proof of genetic relationship and linguistic reconstruction. It finds a direct reflection in the strictly algebraic notion of *regular sound correspondences* which will be dealt with in greater detail in Section 2.4.1. When trying to prove that two words of different languages go back to a single ancestor form, the substance of the sounds plays a minor role, while the structural similarity of the sound sequences is of crucial importance: "Der *Abweichung* [= substantial differences in the form of cognate words, JML] sind keine Schranken gesetzt, solange sie als *regelmäßig* erwiesen werden kann" (Szemerényi 1970: 14).

In the substantial perspective, information regarding the acoustic or articulatory features of the sound segments is included in the structural description

---

[8] This perspective is mainly reflected in the work of early phonologists who emphasize the formal aspects of phonological systems while ignoring their substantial characteristics. Thus, according to Saussure (1916: 164), "[les] phonèmes sont avant tout des entités oppositives, relatives et négatives", and Sechehaye (1908: 151) claims that "on peut concevoir le système phonologique sous son aspect algébrique et remplacer les trente, cinquante ou cent éléments qui le composent dans une langue donnée, par autant de symboles généraux qui fixent leur individualité, mais non pas leur caractère matériel".

of sequences. This perspective is especially important for the explanation of sound change processes, and as a heuristic device in the early stages of language comparison. Thus, when investigating the High German Consonant Shift, during which, upon other terms, the Germanic voiceless plosives turned into fricatives in German,[9] the algebraic perspective can only state that a certain sound segment in English regularly corresponds to a certain other sound segment in German. Within the substantial perspective, on the other hand, one can compare this specific pattern with patterns attested in other languages and language families, and draw general conclusions regarding such processes of *lenition*. These conclusions can then be used to investigate languages whose genetic affiliation has not yet been resolved.

Apart from the role it plays in the description of sound change processes, the substantial perspective makes it also possible to describe certain characteristics of the structural organisation of sign forms as a result of their phonic substance, the most important being *phonotactic constraints*. Languages do not allow all possible combinations of their sound segments but only those who conform to specific *phonotactic rules* which may either be strictly *systematic*, i.e. specific to a given language or language family, or *natural*, i.e. determined by universal rules of "pronunciability" (Hall 2000: 59-61).

In historical linguistics, the form of the linguistic sign is traditionally not given in phonetic transcription but in the traditional orthography of the respective languages (compare, e.g., the popular handbooks of Lehmann 1962 [1992], Anttila 1972, and Trask 1996). This practice is surely due to the fact that the central languages in Indo-European studies (Sanskrit, Old Greek and Latin) are long extinct, forcing us to rely on their written sources whose pronunciation cannot be fully reconstructed. It might also result from the algebraic perspective on the sound substance which is prevalent in certain fields of historical linguistics, such as linguistic reconstruction. In order to underline the importance of the substantial perspective in historical linguistics, a phonetic representation of words, based on the International Phonetic Alphabet (IPA, cf. *IPA Handbook* 1999) will be maintained throughout this study. In order to maintain consistency, I have tried to base the transcriptions for each language on a single independent source. The sources for the languages used in this study are summarized in Appendix A.1.

---

[9] Compare, for example, the final consonant in English *ship* [ʃɪp] and German *Schiff* [ʃɪf] 'ship' which both go back to Proto-Germanic **skipa-* 'ship' (KROONEN: 446, OREL: 340).

2.1 Entities

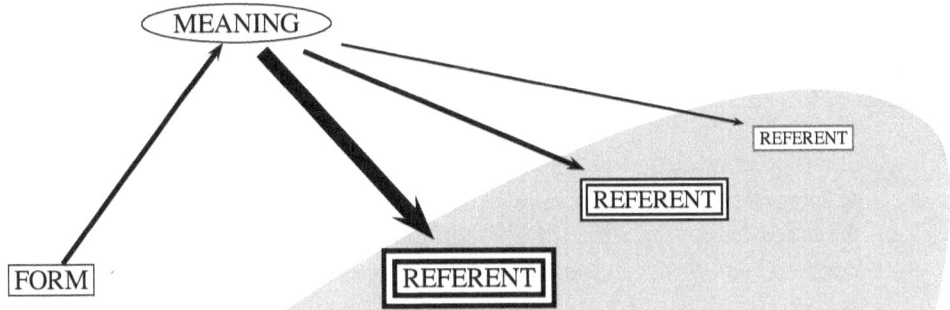

Figure 2.5: *The reference potential of the linguistic sign. The thickness of the arrows indicates the probability that the sign is used to refer to a given referent.*

2.1.4 Meanings

While – despite all problems mentioned in the previous section – the sign form can be pretty easily described as a sequence of sound segments, the "intelligible side" (Jakobson 1976 [1978]: 3) of the linguistic sign is less easily accessible. This is due to the fact that meaning lacks both substance and linearity. It lacks substance, since it is not sensually perceptible, and it lacks linearity, since it doesn't depend on time. The problem of accessibility comes along with the general problem that – as a result of the *arbitrariness* of the connection between sign form and sign meaning – "meaning is inherently fuzzy and non-systematic" (Hock and Joseph 1995 [2009]: 206), and up to today there is no semantic theory which finds basic support in the whole linguistic community.

Within the Saussurean model it is not specified how the linguistic sign is used to refer to the "real world". It is only emphasized that its meaning part should not be confused with the objects it denotes (Saussure 1916: 98). Triadic sign models (cf., e.g., Frege 1892, Ogden and Richards 1923 [1989]: 10-12) cope with this lack in detail by distinguishing the *meaning* of a word from its *reference*, the former determining a category and the latter determining a potential referent (Löbner 2003: 257).

Since the reference of a linguistic sign is only unique if the sign is used in a specific context, it is useful to make a further distinction between *reference* and *reference potential* (Schwarz 1996: 175). The reference potential of a sign is hereby understood as the set of all possible referents the sign can be used to denote (see the illustration in Figure 2.5).[10] The reference potential of a sign depends on its meaning: The more specific the meaning of a sign, the more restricted is its number of possible referents (Löbner 2003: 306). Thus, comparing the words German *Stein* [ʃtain] 'stone' and German *Ding* [dɪŋ] 'thing', the reference potential of *Stein* is more restricted compared to that of *Ding*, since the former usually denotes stones or stone-like objects, while the latter denotes all kinds of different objects. A further characteristic of the reference potential is its *heterogeneity*. Often, the possible referents of a sign do not comprise a uniform class, but may instead belong to different classes which can differ to a great extent. Thus German *Stein* may likewise refer to a certain material (*aus Stein gebaut*, 'built from stone'), or an object which consists of the material (*Steine werfen*, 'throw stones'). Such cases of polysemy resulting from different kinds of semantic shifts find a direct reflection in the structure of the reference potential.

In linguistics, the meaning of a sign, its reference, and its reference potential are not always distinguished in a strict manner. Often, the term *meaning* is used to refer to all three concepts, depending on the context. Since this study primarily deals with the formal part of the linguistic sign, I will generally follow this practice, and make use of the more exact terms only when the topic demands it.

2.1.5 Representations

The most common way to represent a language "practically" is to use a *word list*. A word list is henceforth understood as a collection of semantic glosses (henceforth called *items*), usually given in English, along with their "lexical representation" (Sankoff 1969: 2) in a given language or dialect (henceforth called *entries*). One can think of a word list as a simple table or spreadsheet where the first column contains the meaning of a word and the second column its form. In a practical realization, a word list is nothing else. In contrast to a *dictionary*, in which the form of a word in a given language serves as a key to the dictionary entry, which usually consists of an explanation of the word's meaning, a word list uses concepts (meanings) as keys for the word forms of a given language. Since the concepts are usually glossed by very simple English words, word lists make it easy to find semantically similar or identical words in different languages.

---

[10] For a similar view on the matter, see Allwood (2003) who uses the term *meaning potential*.

2.1 Entities

Items	Entries			
	German	**English**	**Dutch**	**Russian**
'hand'	hant	hænd	hɑnt	ruka
'tooth'	tsaːn	tuːθ	tant	zup
'head'	kɔpf	hɛd	hoːft	gəlɛva
...	...	...	...	...

Table 2.2: *Multilingual word list for German, English, Dutch, and Russian*

A word list does not necessarily have to be used to represent only one language (*monolingual word list*), but it can also be used to represent two languages (*bilingual word list*), or even multiple languages (*multilingual word list*). Whenever a word list represents more than one language, it is assumed that the words of the different languages are *semantically aligned*, i.e. that all words with an identical meaning are placed in the same row, and each language is given a separate column, as exemplified for a multilingual word list of German, English, Dutch, and Russian in Table 2.2.

In historical linguistics it is common to base the compilation of word lists on specific collections of semantic glosses. These collections are sometimes called *basic vocabulary lists*, but they are more often referred to as *Swadesh lists*, named after Morris Swadesh (1909 – 1967), who popularized the use of spreadsheet-like data in historical linguistics. Swadesh originally proposed a collection of 215 semantic glosses[11] which were intended to represent the *basic vocabulary* of all languages (Swadesh 1950). In theory, basic vocabulary refers to those concepts that are so general that they find simple expressions in all languages, independent of time and space (Sankoff 1969: 2). In practice, basic vocabulary is represented by a list of (English) glosses, such as, e.g. 'hand', 'foot', 'stone', etc.

Although the idea to design a list of cross-cultural basic meanings sounded well in theory, it turned out to be difficult to be realized in practice. Despite the fact that Swadesh himself (Swadesh 1952, Swadesh 1955) and other schol-

---

[11] In his first text from 1950, Swadesh mentions as many as 225 semantic glosses on page 161, but this is probably a typo: when counting all items listed on the page, there are exactly 215 items in the original list of English glosses.

ars (Alpher and Nash 1999, Bennet 1976, Dolgopolsky 1964, Geoffrey et al. 1969, Holman et al. 2008, Lees 1953) repeatedly revised the collection of basic glosses by reducing the number of items or modifying the glosses, no basic vocabulary list could be devised so far that would meet the requirement of cultural and temporal independence.

The term *Swadesh list* is often used ambiguously in historical linguistics, referring either to a concrete word list in which basic vocabulary items of a given Swadesh list are translated into a given language (Holman et al. 2011: 842), or a list of basic vocabulary items (Trask 2000: 331). In order to avoid this confusion, the term *basic vocabulary list* will be used to refer to lists of glosses that are supposed to reflect basic vocabulary items. The term *Swadesh list*, on the other hand, will exclusively be used to refer to word lists (in the sense defined above) which contain semantic glosses that correspond to a given basic vocabulary list. Thus, a *German Swadesh list* refers to a word list containing basic vocabulary items such as 'hand', 'foot', etc., and their translational equivalents in the German language, such as *Hand*, *Fuß*, etc. A Swadesh list for two or more languages is a simple bi- or multilingual word list whose items cover the range of a certain basic vocabulary list.

As I just mentioned, several authors have proposed different basic vocabulary lists, which differ in length and content. Among these, the most common lists are two lists proposed by Morris Swadesh himself, the first one containing 200 items (Swadesh 1952), the second one containing 100 items (Swadesh 1955). Since these lists are often used in the literature, I will call the first one the *Swadesh-200 basic vocabulary list*, and the second one the *Swadesh-100 basic vocabulary list*. When pointing to actual Swadesh lists that are based on these basic vocabulary lists, I will use the terms *Swadesh-200 word list*, and *Swadesh-100 word list*, respectively.

2.2 Change

The detection that languages change was not a necessary one to be made by scholars in the history of science. This is especially true for less obviously changing domains of language like the sound system. Table 2.3 gives an example for the effects of sound change: The Chinese poem, taken from the *Book of Odes* (ca. 1050–600 BC, *Shījīng*: 28.3), which is given in modern Pīnyīn transliteration along with a translation by Karlgren (1950), does not rhyme consistently throughout all rhyme words. Given the fact that we know

2.2 Change

燕	燕	於	飛,	下	上	其	音。	The swallows go flying, falling and rising are their voices;
yān	yān	yú	**fēi**	xià	shàng	qí	**yīn**	
之	子	於	歸,	遠	送	於	南。	This young lady goes to her new home, far I accompany her to the south.
zhī	zǐ	yú	**guī,**	yuǎn	sòng	yú	**nán**	
瞻	望	弗	及,	實	勞	我	心。	I gaze after her, can no longer see her, truly it grieves my heart.
zhān	wàng	fú	jí,	shí	láo	wǒ	**xīn**	

Table 2.3: *Strange rhymes in the* Book of Odes. *This is but one stanza of Ode 28, taken from the Book of Odes, an archaic collection of songs and poems created between 1050 and 600 BC. When the poem is read in the modern pronunciation (given here in Pīnyīn transliteration) the rhyme words (originally rhyming words shaded in the same color) do not necessarily rhyme, since the pronunciation of Old Chinese changed heavily compared to Modern Chinese.*

that the sound systems of languages change over time, this is not surprising when considering the great amount of time which elapsed between the creation of the poem (ca. 600 BC) and its modern reading.

Nevertheless, it took Chinese scholars almost one millenium of research to come to the conclusion that inconsistencies in the rhyme system of their sacred poems were indeed a result of language change rather than the result of lax rhyming conventions of their ancestors. Since the Chinese writing system denotes the form of the linguistic sign not on a phonemic, but on a morphemic basis (Chao 1968: 102), they simply had no clue – apart from the rhymes in their poems – that their language had changed greatly over the centuries. Starting from some early attempts in the middle of the first millennium to explain the strange rhymes as a result of "sound harmonization" practiced by their ancestors (*xiéyīn* 葉音, Baxter 1992: 153-157), it was the Chinese scholar Chén Dì 陳第 (1541 – 1606) who first explicitly stated that languages change over time:

> The writings of scholars must be made of adequate sounds. Even in the rural areas everybody orders the sounds harmonically. Can it be that the ancients solely did not have rhymes? One can say that in the same way in which ancient times differ from modern times, and places in the North differ from places in the South, characters change and sounds shift. This is a natural tendency. Therefore, it is

inevitable that reading the ancient writings with modern pronunciation will sound improper and wrong. (*Máoshī Gǔyīnkǎo*: 原序)[12]

In contrast to the Chinese scholars who were, roughly spoken, for a long time completely unaware of language change, Western scholars knew more or less that languages can change over time,[13] yet the way they investigated the issue was heavily influenced by the "Hebrew paradigm" which stated that all languages were descendants of Hebrew or the mysterious "Adamic language", and separated after the *Confusion of Tongues* (*Genesis* 11:1-9, Klein 1999, Klein 2004, Arens 1955: 72-80). This led to a *catastrophic view* on language change which stated that languages change within a sporadic and chaotic process lacking any observable systematics (Geisler and List 2013). Both views – the ignorant one of the Chinese and the catastrophic one of the Western scholars – held back one of the most important discoveries made by the first historical linguists at the beginning of the 19th century: the discovery that language change, or, more precisely, sound change, is a mostly regular and systematic process.

2.2.1 Sound Change

The very fact that the sounds of languages may change over time can be easily observed when comparing written sources of ancient languages with their descendant languages. Thus, when comparing a couple of Latin words with their Italian descendants, such as Latin *plūma* [pluːma] 'feather' vs. Italian *piuma* [pjuma] 'feather', Latin *clāvis* [klaːwis] 'key' vs. Italian *chiave* [kjave] 'key', and Latin *flōs* [floːs] 'flower' vs. Italian *fiore* [fjore] 'flower', one can easily observe that the similarity between the words is of a somewhat systematic nature, in so far as in all cases where a [j] occurs in an Italian word, the Latin ancestor word has an [l] (see Table 2.4). It is a straightforward conclusion to assume that the Latin [l] became a [j] in Italian. Adding more words to the comparison, such as Latin *lingua* [liŋgwa] 'tongue' vs. Italian *lingua*

---

[12] My translation, original text: 故士人篇章，必有音節，田野俚典，亦名諧聲，豈以古人之詩而獨無韻乎？蓋時有古今, 地有南北,字有更革,音有轉移,亦勢所必至。故以今之音讀古之作,不免乖剌而不入 。

[13] An awareness regarding language change is already reflected in the work of Plato (428/427 – 348/347 BC). Thus, in *Krátylos* (414c), Socrates says: "My friend, you do not bear in mind that the original words have before now been completely buried by those who wished to dress them up, for they have added and subtracted letters for the sake of euphony and have distorted the words in every way for ornamentation or merely in the lapse of time."

2.2 Change

[liŋgwa] 'tongue', Latin *lūna* [luːna] 'moon' vs. Italian *luna* [luna] 'moon', or Latin *lacrima* [lakrima] 'slow' vs. Italian *lacrima* [lakrima] 'tear', it becomes also obvious that the change of [l] to [j] did not affect all instances of [l], but only occurred in certain environments, namely when preceded by a plosive, such as [p] and [k], or a fricative, such as [f]. The list of examples for both cases, i.e. those where the [l] was preserved and those where it changed when preceded by a plosive or a fricative, can be easily extended when looking up the relevant entries in the literature (cf., e.g., REW).

When dealing with sound change, one can approach the phenomenon from different perspectives which emphasize its different aspects, namely, its *procedural aspects*, its *substantial aspects*, and its *systematic aspects*. The procedural perspective deals with general aspects of the process and its domain by distinguishing different *mechanisms* of sound change. The substantial perspective deals with the change in the substance of sounds by distinguishing different *types* of sound change. The systematic perspective deals with the impact of sound change on the phonological system by distinguishing different *patterns* of sound change.[14] The study of sound change patterns, especially the questions of *phoneme split*, *phoneme merger*, and *phoneme loss*, play a crucial role in linguistic reconstruction. However, since this study is not dealing

Meaning	Italian		Latin	
	Orth.	IPA	Orth.	IPA
'key'	*chiave*	kjave	*clāvis*	klaːwis
'feather'	*piuma*	pjuma	*plūma*	pluːma
'flower'	*fiore*	fjore	*flōs*	floːs
'tear'	*lacrima*	lakrima	*lacrima*	lakrima
'tongue'	*lingua*	liŋgwa	*lingua*	liŋgwa
'moon'	*luna*	luna	*lūna*	luːna

Table 2.4: *Italian words compared to their Latin ancestor words*

---

[14] This distinction follows the terminology used in Hoenigswald (1960), or at least, the terminology I infer from his work. Trask (2000) uses the terms *syntagmatic sound change* (ibid.: 246) and *paradigmatic sound change* (ibid.: 335) to distinguish between *types* and *patterns* of sound change.

with linguistics reconstruction, but only with its preliminary stages, only the mechanisms and the types of sound changes will be treated in the following.

Mechanisms of Sound Change

Approaching sound change from the procedural perspective, different mechanisms of sound change may be identified. If the example given in Table 2.4 was representative of the general mechanism of sound change, two major conclusions regarding the process could be drawn, namely that

(a) sound change is a *recurrent* process, i.e. it normally does not affect single words of a language sporadically but instead applies to many (if not to all) words of the lexicon, and
(b) sound change is *contextually restricted*, i.e. where a certain change occurs depends on its phonetic context.

These two observations are summarized in the traditional notion of the *regularity of sound change*: sound change is considered to be *regular*, since it follows certain rules by which certain sound segments to which the rules apply are changed in large parts of the lexicon of a language. That sound change may operate in this way was first detected by Rasmus Rask (1787 – 1832, cf. Rask 1818) and then popularized by Jacob Grimm (1785 – 1863, cf. Grimm 1822). The findings were met enthusiastically by the scholars of the 19th century and led to the even stronger notion of the *sound law* (*Lautgesetz*) which can already be found in the work of August Schleicher (1821 – 1868, cf. e.g. Schleicher 1861: 11). The hypothesis that sound change is a regular process which applies to the whole lexicon of a language is also called the *Neogrammarian Hypothesis*, since it found its strongest formulation in the so-called *Neogrammarian Manifesto* of Karl Brugmann (1849 – 1919) and Hermann Osthoff (1847 – 1909):

> Aller lautwandel, soweit er mechanisch vor sich geht, vollzieht sich nach *ausnahmslosen gesetzen*, d.h. die richtung der lautbewegung ist bei allen angehörigen einer sprachgenossenschaft, ausser dem Fall, dass dialektspaltung eintritt, stets dieselbe, und alle wörter, in denen der der lautbewegung unterworfene laut unter gleichen verhältnissen erscheint, werden ohne ausnahme von der änderung ergriffen. (Osthoff and Brugmann 1878: XIII)

This seemingly radical position which identified the phenomena with an exceptionless and law-like process did not find support among all scientists. Especially dialectologists who were working with empirical data of spoken lan-

2.2 Change

guages (as opposed to the written language data of scholars working in the Indo-European field) disagreed with the claim and proposed the opposite theory that *"every word has its own history"* (*"chaque mot a son histoire"*, a slogan that is often attributed to Jules Gilliéron, 1854 – 1926, cf. Campbell 1999: 189). While, strictly speaking, both theories were not incompatible, since the Neogrammarian Hypothesis did never claim that all words of a language necessarily change in a regular manner, but merely that idiosyncratic changes "could be accounted for [...] by certain less obvious mechanisms of borrowing and analogy" (Kiparsky 1988: 368), the linguistic community was for a long time split into two opposing camps, and the discussion went into a deadlock, since none of the views could find agreement among a majority of scholars. The situation changed in the sixties of the 20th century when new research – mainly conducted in the field of Chinese dialectology – led to the proposal of a different sound change mechanism which was somehow the opposite of the Neogrammarian Hypothesis. The Neogrammarians had claimed that sound change proceeds *lexically abrupt* and *phonetically gradual*:

> Regarding the lexicon [they assumed] that a change always affects the whole lexicon, and can therefore be seen as an abrupt change. Regarding the sounds [they assumed] that the change proceeded step by step, and can therefore be seen as a gradual change. (Wang 2006b: 109) [15]

The research of Chinese dialectologists, however, suggested that a certain mechanism of sound change, which was later labeled *lexical diffusion*, may operate in the opposite way, i.e. *lexically gradual* and *phonetically abrupt*:

> Phonological change may be implemented in a manner that is phonetically abrupt but lexically gradual. As the change diffuses across the lexicon, it may not reach all the morphemes to which it is applicable. If there is another change competing for part of the lexicon, residue may result. (Wang 1969: 9)

An example for the phenomenon of lexical diffusion is given in Table 2.5. The table gives three Chinese character pairs with identical readings in Middle Chinese (spoken around 600 AD) contrasted with their modern reflexes in the Shuāngfēng dialect which belongs to the Min group of Chinese dialects.[16] As can be seen from the table, the Middle Chinese homonyms split into two

---

[15] My translation, original text: "作為詞彙，要變就都變，因而是一種突變。作為語音，變化是逐漸的，因而是一種漸變".
[16] The data is taken from the electronic version of the *Hànyǔ Fāngyīn Zìhuì* (ZIHUI). Middle Chinese readings follow the system of Baxter (1992) with some slight changes.

different modern readings each, one where the Middle Chinese initial was preserved, and one, where it was devoiced and aspirated. Within the Neogrammarian Hypothesis, such splits of homonyms are difficult to explain, since, assuming regularity of change, all instances of a sound which occur in the same phonetic context should change in an identical way.

Such examples for the irregularity of change, however, do not necessarily contradict the Neogrammarian Hypothesis. As long as there are only a few of them, they can be explained by external factors, such as dialect borrowing or analogy. Chen (1972) presented a thorough statistical analysis of 616 character readings in Shuāngfēng which had a voiced initial in Middle Chinese. His findings show that there are many examples for the process of devoicing and aspiration of voiced initials, yet that there are also many cases where the voiced initials are preserved. This suggests that there is no strict *law* for devoicing and aspiration of Middle Chinese initials in Shuāngfēng, but rather a strong *tendency*. Such a tendency can best be explained by assuming that sound change does not necessarily affect the whole lexicon at once, but rather spreads from word to word at different paces:

> When a phonological innovation enters a language it begins as a minor rule, affecting a small number of words [...]. As the phonological innovation gradually spreads across the lexicon, however, there comes a point when the minor rule gathers momentum and begins to serve as a basis for extrapolation. At this critical cross-over point, the minor rule becomes a major rule, and we would expect

Character	Pīnyīn	Meaning	Middle Chinese	Shuāngfēng
步	bù	'to walk'	bo^3	bu^{33}
捕	bǔ	'to grasp'	bo^3	p^hu^{21}
刨	páo	'to dig'	$bæw^1$	$bə^{33}$
跑	páo	'to scrape'	$bæw^1$	$p^hə^{21}$
盜	dào	'to rob'	daw^3	$də^{33}$
導	dǎo	'to lead'	daw^3	$t^hə^{35}$

Table 2.5: *Split of Middle Chinese homophones in the Shuāngfēng dialect. Assuming that sound change affects all instances of a sound, regardless of the meaning of a word, the modern readings should be identical.*

2.2 Change

diffusion to be much more rapid. The change may, however, reach a second point of inflection and eventually taper off before it completes its course, leaving behind a handful of words unaltered. (ibid.: 474f)

When these phenomena were first presented, many researchers stated that lexical diffusion was the general mechanism of sound change and that the Neogrammarian Hypothesis was proven wrong. Yet, sociolinguistic research on ongoing sound change later gave strong support for the alternative explanation that there actually are two different mechanisms of sound change: Neogrammarian sound change, which was phonetically gradual and lexically abrupt, and lexical diffusion, which was phonetically abrupt and lexically gradual:

> There is no basis for contending that lexical diffusion is somehow more fundamental than regular, phonetically motivated sound change. On the contrary, if we were to decide the issue by counting cases there appear to be far more substantially documented cases of Neogrammarian sound change than of lexical diffusion. (Labov 1994: 471)

Including those cases where the sounds of the sign form change in a sporadic manner, due to such various reasons as language contact, analogy, or taboo, three different mechanisms of sound change can be distinguished:

(a) *Neogrammarian sound change* which is recurrent, phonetically conditioned, phonetically gradual, and affects the whole lexicon at once,
(b) *lexical diffusion* which is recurrent, not phonetically conditioned, phonetically abrupt, and spreads through the lexicon in different paces, and
(c) *sporadic sound change* which is not recurrent, neither phonetically conditioned, nor phonetically gradual, and does only sporadically affect the lexicon.

Types of Sound Change

The long tradition of research in historical linguistics has lead to the postulation of many different *types of sound change*. Unfortunately, the terminology which is used to address these types in the literature is rather "unsteady", ranging from very concrete terms covering very concrete sound changes to very general terms that refer to the change of abstract classes of sounds. Thus, what is labelled as *type of sound change* may cover the phenomenon of *rhotacism* (Trask 2000: 288), which, simply speaking, refers to the change of [s] to [r], as well as the process of *lenition*, which refers to any kind of change "in which a segment becomes less consonant-like than previously" (ibid.: 190). Many of the broad terms which cover a large range of distinct processes are "explanatory" rather than descriptive, since they also offer an explanation why the respective changes happened or happen. Thus, in common text book definitions of *assimilation*, this sound change type is not only described as "[a] change in which one sound becomes more similar to another", but it is also emphasized that this happens "through the influence of a neighboring, usually adjacent, sound" (Campbell and Mixco 2007: 16). Giving the explanation along with the description is problematic for a typology, since the latter builds on the former. As a result of this heterogeneous terminology which partially describes, partially explains, and partially classifies, it is difficult, if not impossible, to find a homogeneous and neutral classification of sound change types in the literature. Most authors confine themselves to giving examples which cover the most general and most frequently attested processes (cf., e.g., Anttila 1972: 57-83, Hock and Joseph 1995 [2009]: 113-149, Lehmann 1962 [1992]: 183-118).

A very broad classification of sound change types which is not in conflict with the linguistic literature, but would probably be regarded as rather trivial, can be derived when comparing the input and the output of sound change processes. Sound change can be thought of as a function which receives one or more sounds as input and yields one or more sounds as output. Since sound change may be contextually restricted, such a function may also require additional parameters, such as the sounds preceding or following, the syllabic environment, or suprasegmental aspects, such as stress or tone. When treating sound change in this way, one can assign concrete sound change events to one of five basic types, depending on the relation between the input and the output of the function, namely

(a) *continuation*,
(b) *substitution*,
(c) *insertion*,
(d) *deletion*, and
(e) *metathesis*.

Continuation does actually not refer to a sound change, but to its absence. As an example, compare Old High German *hant* [hant] 'hand' and its unchanged reflex German *Hand* [hant]. Substitution refers to all sound-change types in which a sound segment is replaced by another one. As an example, compare the initial consonant in Old High German *snēo* [sneːo] 'snow' with the initial consonant in its reflex German *Schnee* [ʃneː]. Insertion (Campbell and Mixco

2.2 Change

Type	Description	Representation
continuation	absence of change	$x > x$
substitution	replacement of a sound	$x > y$
insertion	gain of a sound	$\varnothing > y$
deletion	loss of a sound	$x > \varnothing$
metathesis	change in the order of sounds	$xy > yx$

Table 2.6: *Five basic types of sound change*

2007: 85) refers to all sound-change types in which a sound is inserted at a given position of a word, such as the [t] in German *jemand* [jeːmant] 'somebody' which was not present in Old High German *ioman* [joman]. In the literature, the term epenthesis is also used to refer to this type (Trask 2000: 107). Deletion (Campbell and Mixco 2007: 110f) refers to all sound-change types in which a sound is completely deleted, such as it happened with the [u] in Old High German *angust* [aŋust] 'fear' compared to German *Angst* [aŋst]. In the literature, the terms *loss* and *elision* are also used to refer to this type (Trask 2000: 202). In contrast to the previously discussed soundchange types, metathesis (Campbell and Mixco 2007: 122, Trask 2000: 211) does not involve a change in the substance of sounds, but merely the *order of segments*, although it is often also accompanied by additional types of sound change. Thus, comparing Proto-Slavic **žьltъ* 'yellow' with its reflexes Russian *жёлтый* [ʒoltɨj] and Czech *žlutý* [ʒluti:] (DERKSEN: 565), one can see that the Czech word swapped the [l] with the vowel originally preceding it. In Table 2.6 the five types are summarized.

From a formal perspective, this classification can be further modified. Not all distinctions are important. Thus, *continuation* and *substitution* can be assigned to one simple type which covers both processes. Metathesis can also be described in terms of deletion and insertion events, and often, this may even reflect the actual processes better. Thus, the metathesis by which Proto-Slavic **golvà* 'head' became Bulgarian *глава* [gləva] (DERKSEN: 176) may be more realistically understood as a process during which, in a first stage, a (weak) vowel was inserted after the liquid **golvà > *goləvà*. In a second stage, the preceding vowel was lost: **goləvà > [gləva]*. The intermediate state of this process is still reflected in Russian *голова* [gəlɐva] (Leskien 1871 [2002]: 35f). One further modification of this classification, which one might think of, is to add two further types of sound change, namely *split* and *fusion*, which refer to those cases in which one sound split into two or more sounds, or two or more sounds were fused into one sound. For the sake of simplicity, however, I prefer, to treat these changes as insertions and deletions which are eventually accompanied by additional substitutions.

2.2.2 Semantic Change

While in historical linguistics the change of the formal part of the linguistic sign is usually dealt with under the premise of "regularity", change in meaning, is traditionally considered to be notoriously irregular and unpredictable, and "there is [...] little in semantic change which bears any relationship to regularity in phonological change" (Fox 1995: 111). The reason for the problems one faces when dealing with semantic change can be found in the structural differences between sign form and sign meaning and the resulting processes by which both entities change. While the formal part of the linguistic sign is characterized by its sequential structure and sound change is characterized by the *alternation* of segments, the meaning part is better described as some kind of conceptual network, and semantic change is not based on an alternation but on the *accumulation* and *reduction* of potential referents, i.e. by a reorganization of the sign's reference potential (see Section 2.1.4).

This can be illustrated by taking the word German *Kopf* [kɔpf] 'head' as an example. Tracing the history of this word back in time, it probably goes back to Proto-Germanic **kuppa-* 'vessel' (KLUGE: 528, OREL: 224f, see Figure 2.6).[17] While the difference in meaning between the two words might seem implausible on the first sight (consider the English descendent *cup* [kʌp], whose meaning did not change greatly), the semantic change from 'vessel' to 'head' becomes less surprising when considering the fact that in many languages it is quite common to use a large bunch of words with different original meanings to denote 'head'. Thus, in German, one can use words like *Birne* [bɪrnə] 'peach', *Schädel* [ʃɛːdəl] 'skull', *Rübe* [ryːbə] 'weet', or *Dach* [dax] 'roof' in order to refer to the round upper part of the human body, and in English one can find similar types of denotation, such as, e.g., *melon* [mɛlən],

---

[17] This is a simplifying description of the etymology of the word. See page 43 for a more detailed account.

2.2 Change

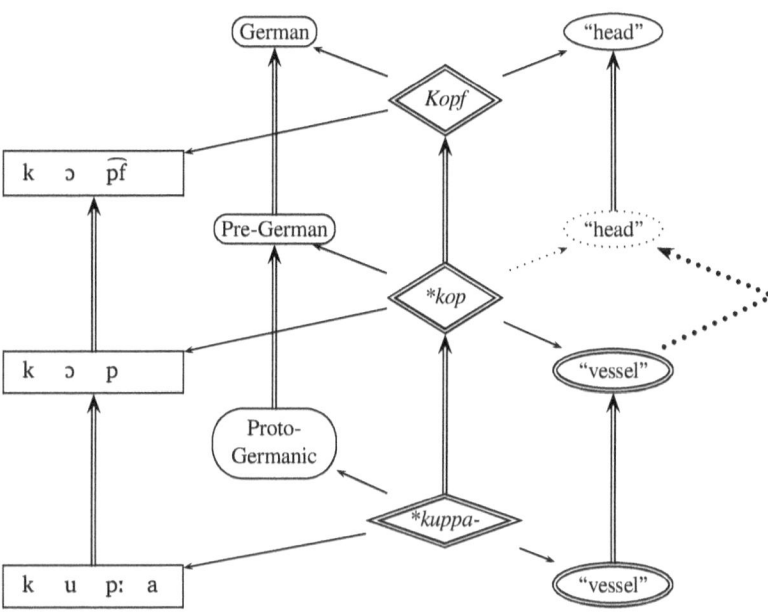

Figure 2.6: *Change in form and meaning: From Proto-Germanic* *kuppa- 'vessel' to German* Kopf *'head'.*

or *skull* [skʌl]. Keeping these examples in mind, the change from 'vessel' to 'head' can be easily explained as an initially sporadic use of the word [kɔpf] (commonly used to refer to 'cup') when referring to a 'head' in early German which later became its main use. Such a change basically goes through three phases: The initial phase where no change happened so far, the polysemic phase where the sign accumulates new meanings, and the final stage where the polysemy of the sign is reduced in favor of the meaning which was newly acquired in the polysemic phase (Wilkins 1996: 269). An intermediate stage of this change is attested in Dutch, where the word *kop* [kɔp] has both meanings 'head' and 'cup'.

Taking the aforementioned notion of the reference potential, and concentrating only on the most common referents of English *cup*, Dutch *kop*, and German *Kopf* (see Figure 2.7), one can find a certain continuum regarding the common referents of the words. This continuum does not only reflect the

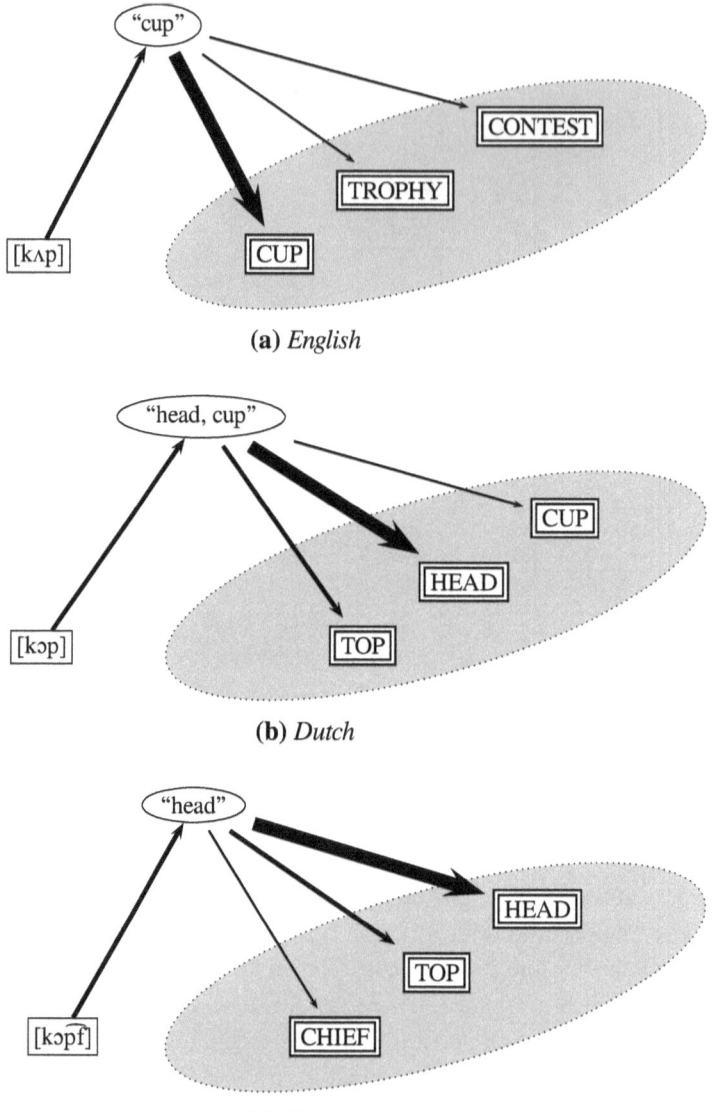

Figure 2.7: *Comparing the reference potentials of reflexes of Proto-Germanic* *kuppa- *'head' in English* (a), *Dutch* (b), *and German* (c), *as reflected by the most common meanings of the words. The thickness of the arrows indicates the most common referents of the words.*

2.2 Change

former processes of semantic change, but it may also point to future changes or general trends. For example, the shift from HEAD to CHIEF, probably via an intermediate stage TOP is also reflected in Chinese *shǒu* 首 [ʂou²¹⁴] 'chief, first' which originally meant 'head' (SCHUESSLER: 470). The original meaning is still reflected in the character of the word, which originally was a pictogram of an animal's head, as can be easily seen from the Oracle Bone version of the character: 𠙹. However, whether it is possible to generalize such trends remains an open question. Most linguists would probably subscribe to the claim that certain types of semantic change are more probable than other types. Many would probably also agree that there are universal processes of semantic change. However, so far, no universal processes could be identified, and it remains unproven whether they can be identified at all. The problem of semantic change remains unsolved as long as no data on actually attested semantic changes in a large number of different languages is available. In the meantime, historical linguists have to rely on their intuition when comparing languages and searching them for probably related words.

2.2.3 Lexical Change

If there was no semantic change, the lexicon of languages would remain stable during all times. Words might change their forms, but there would always be an unbroken tradition of identical patterns of denotation. Since this is not the case, the lexicon of all languages is constantly changing. Words are lost, when the speakers cease to use them, or new words enter the lexicon when new concepts arise, be it that they are borrowed from other languages, or created from native material via different morphological processes. Such processes of *word loss* and *word gain* are quite frequent and can sometimes even be observed directly by the speakers of a language when they compare their own speech with the speech of an elder or a younger generation.

An even more important process of lexical change, especially in quantitative historical linguistics, is the process of *lexical replacement*. Lexical replacement refers to the process by which a given word A which is commonly used to express a certain meaning x ceases to express this meaning, while at the same time another word B which was formerly used to express a meaning y is now used to express the meaning x. The notion of lexical replacement is thus nothing else than a shift in the perspective on semantic change. While semantic change is usually described from an *semasiological perspective*, i.e. from the

Items	Entries			
	German	English	Dutch	Russian
'hand'	hant 1	hænd 1	hɑnt 1	ruka 2
'tooth'	tsaːn 3	tuːθ 3	tɑnt 3	zup 4
'head'	kɔpf 5	hɛd 6	hoːft 6	gəlɐva 7
...	...	...	...	...

Table 2.7: *A lexicostatistical word list of German, English, Dutch, and Russian. The number to the right of each entry indicates assigns it to a specific cognate set. If two entries have the same number, they go back to a common ancestor word.*

perspective of the form, lexical replacement describes semantic change from an *onomasiological perspective*, i.e. the perspective of the meaning.

Lexical replacement plays a very important role in *lexicostatistics* (Lees 1953, Swadesh 1950, Swadesh 1952, Swadesh 1955) and its modern derivations (Gray and Atkinson 2003, Starostin 1989) where rates or concrete processes of lexical replacement are first inferred from multilingual word lists and then stochastically evaluated in order to reconstruct language phylogenies. Table 2.7 illustrates how processes of lexical replacement can be inferred from *lexicostatistical word lists*. A lexicostatistical word list is a word list which assigns words that go back to a common ancestor to *cognate sets*, i.e. sets of words that are *cognate* (see Section 2.3.1). Practically, this can be realized by giving each entry a specific cognate ID. If two entries have the same cognate ID, they are assumed to be cognate. From such a word list, lexical replacement can be inferred by comparing the entries of the different languages in a given meaning slot. If the languages that are represented by the word list share a common origin, one may assume that the distribution of cognate sets corresponding to a given item is the result of specific replacement events that took place in the past. For example, the distribution of cognate sets over the entries for 'head' points to a replacement event in the history of German, since German *Kopf* [kɔpf] 'head' is not cognate with Dutch *hoofd* [hoːft] and English *head* [hɛd]. The original word for 'head' in German was German *Haupt* [haupt] 'head, main'. It was replaced by *Kopf* during the 16th century (PFEIFER).

2.3 Relations

In order to describe how languages change, it is important to define certain relations which hold for such entities as words (in the sense of "form-meaning pairs") or languages (understood as "collections of words"). In contrast to evolutionary biology, where a rich terminological framework to describe the fundamental historical relations between genes and species has been established as a result of still ongoing discussions on theory and methodology (cf. the overview in Koonin 2005), linguists have rarely addressed these questions directly, but rather assumed that such relations as *cognacy*, or *genetic relationship* are more or less self-evident. The few examples where scholars explicitly tried to deal with these relations (cf., e.g., Arapov and Xerc 1974, Holzer 1996, Katičić 1966) have been largely ignored in the literature. As a result, the traditional terminology which is used to describe the fundamental relations between words and languages lacks precision and has led to a considerable amount of confusion in scholarly discussions.

In order to illustrate what I mean by this "lack of precision", consider the fundamental concept of *homology* in evolutionary biology. This term "designates a relationship of common descent between any entities, without further specification of the evolutionary scenario" (Koonin 2005: 311). In order to

Relations		Terminology	
		Biology	Linguistics
common descent	direct	orthology (homology)	? (cognacy)
	indirect	paralogy	oblique cognacy
	due to lateral transfer	xenology	?

Table 2.8: *Basic relations between genes (biology) and words (linguistics)*

address more specific relations, the terms *orthology*, *paralogy*, and *xenology* are further used in biology. Orthology refers to "genes related via speciation" (Koonin 2005: 311), i.e., genes related via *direct descent*. Paralogy refers to "genes related via duplication" (ibid.), i.e. genes related via *indirect descent*. Xenology, a notion which was introduced by Gray and Fitch (1983), refers to genes "whose history, since their common ancestor, involves an interspecies (horizontal) transfer of the genetic material for at least one of those characters" (Fitch 2000: 229), i.e. to genes related via *descent due to lateral transfer*. In historical linguistics, only one relation is explicitly defined, namely the *cognacy* relation (also called *cognation*), which usually refers to words related via "descent from a common ancestor" (Trask 2000: 63). Cognacy is strictly distinguished from descent due to lateral transfer (borrowing), but the term covers both direct and indirect descent. Indirect descent is sometimes labelled as *oblique cognacy* (ibid.: 234), but this term is rarely used, and in most cases, no further distinction between different kinds of cognate relations is being made.

In Table 2.8, the four basic relations between genes and words are contrasted with the terminology used in biology and linguistics. One might of course argue that the notion of xenology is not unknown to linguists, since the borrowing of words is a very common phenomenon in language history. However, the specific relation which is termed xenology in biology has no direct counterpart in historical linguistics, since the term *borrowing* refers to a distinct process, not to a relation. There is no common term in historical linguistics which addresses the specific relation between such words as German *kurz* [kʊrts] 'short' and English *short* [ʃɔːt]. These words are not cognate, since the German word has been borrowed from Latin *cŭrtus* [kurtus] 'mutilated' (KLUGE, PFEIFER), yet they share a common history, since Latin *curtus* and English *short* both (may) go back to Proto-Indo-European *(s)sker-* 'cut off' (LIV: 556f, VAAN: 158, PFEIFER).[18]

A specific advantage of the biological notion of *homology* as a basic relation covering any kind of historical relatedness compared to the linguistic notion of *cognacy* as a basic relation covering direct and indirect common descent is that the former is much more realistic regarding the epistemological limits of historical research. Up to a certain point, it can be fairly reliably proven that the basic entities in the respective disciplines (words and genes) share a common

---

[18] The cognacy of English *short* and Latin *cŭrtus* is rather presumed than considered to be definitely proven.

2.3 Relations

history. Proving that more detailed relations hold for the entities, however, is often much harder. The strict notion of cognacy has forced linguists to set goals for their discipline which might be far too ambitious to achieve. In the following, I will try to bring these goals into balance with the epistomological limits of our discipline by redefining the basic relations between words and languages.

2.3.1 Relations between Words

Given words from different languages one can define various kinds of relations between them. From a historical viewpoint, the most interesting question regarding relations between words is whether they are historically related, or, to put it in other words, whether they share a *common descent*. Common descent is the broadest way to describe historical relations between words, since no distinction is drawn to further characterize *how* the words are historically related. In order to address this form of relation, one may adopt the biological term *homology*, but I prefer to use the term *etymological relation* instead, since in historical linguistics this term is often used in a sense similar to the term *homology* in biology. From a formal viewpoint, the etymological relation is symmetric and transitive, i.e. if a word A is etymologically related to a word B, the word B is also etymologically related to the word A, and if a word A is etymologically related to a word B and word B is etymologicallly related to a word C, the same relation also holds for A and C.

One can define more specific relations between words. An important one is the relation between two words where one is the ancestor of the latter, i.e., one has evolved from the other via a *gradual* process of change. Such an *ancestor-descendant relation* is transitive and antisymmetric, i.e. if a word A is the ancestor of a word B, B cannot be the ancestor of word A, and if A is the ancestor of the word B which itself is the ancestor of the word C, A is also the ancestor of the word C. Such a relation holds, for example, for Old High German *swīn* [swiːn] 'pig' and German *Schwein* [ʃvain] 'pig', where the Old High German word is the ancestor of the German word, and, accordingly, the German word is the descendant of the Old High German word.

Given the ancestor-descendant relation, one can define another relation between words, namely the *cognate relation* (also termed *cognacy*, see above). If two words are *cognate*, they both are the descendants of a common ancestor, i.e., there is another word which is in an ancestor-descendant relation to both words. Following this notion, English *cup* [kʌp] and German *Kopf* [kɔ͡pf]

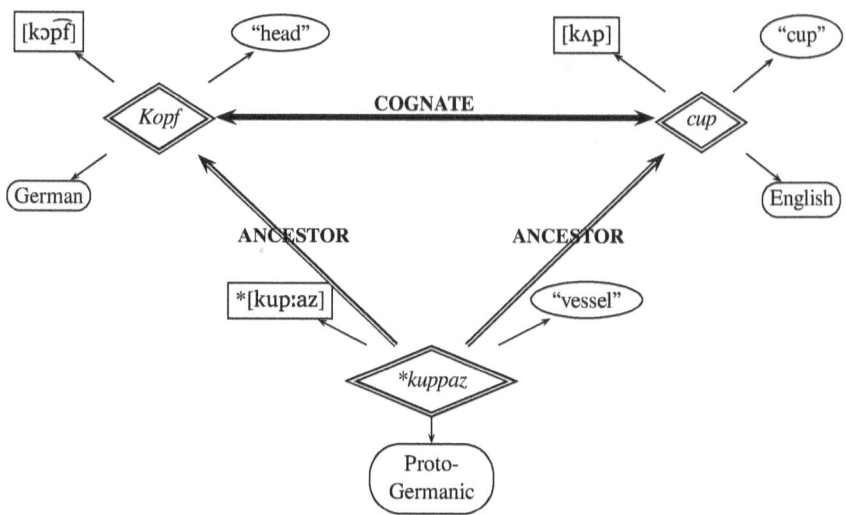

Figure 2.8: *Cognacy and ancestor-descendant relation*

'head' are cognate, since both are descendants of Proto-Germanic **kuppa-* 'vessel' (OREL: 224f), as illustrated in Figure 2.8. Similar to the etymological relation, cognacy is a also transitive, symmetric relation. It is useful to make a further distinction between a *direct cognate relation* and an *oblique cognate relation*. English *cup* and German *Kopf* are direct cognates, since the word forms have not been modified by morphological processes since the split of their ancestor language. As an example for an oblique cognate relation, compare Russian *птица* [ptitsa] 'bird' and Polish *ptak* [ptak] 'bird'. Both words are usually assumed to be cognate (VASMER: 3,398), but they are descendants of slightly different words in Proto-Slavic. While Polish word goes back to the masculine noun Proto-Slavic **pъtákъ* 'bird (male bird)', the Russian word goes back to the feminine noun **pъtìca* 'bird (female bird)' (DERKSEN: 424f). Both Proto-Slavic words are surely derived from a common root **pъt-* via morphological processes, but they the Russian and the Polish word are not directly, but only *obliquely* cognate.

The ancestor-descendant relation has to be distinguished from the *donor-recipient relation*, where one word is transferred from one language to another one. While the ancestor-descendant relation between two words is the re-

2.3 Relations

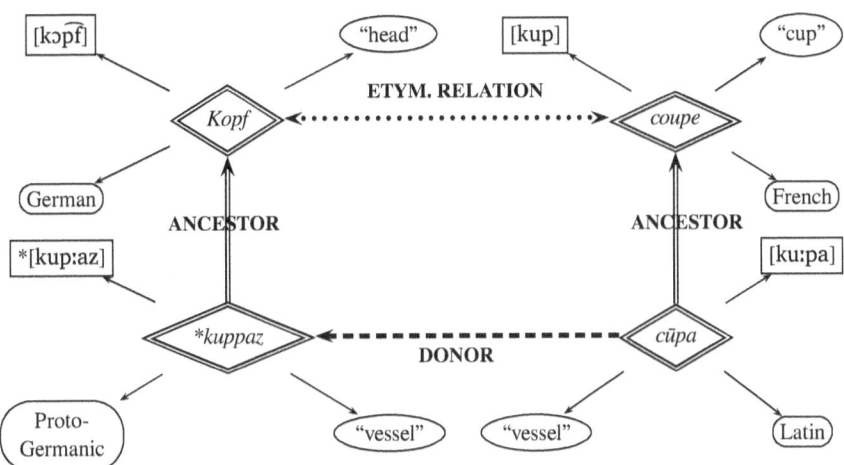

Figure 2.9: *Ancestor relations vs. etymological relations*

sult of a *gradual* process of change, whereby the ancestor word changes into the descendent word (i.e. both words are actually snapshots of the same word in different times), the donor-recipient relation is the result of a *discrete* process, where no continuous change is involved. Some linguists assume that Proto-Germanic *kuppa-* 'vessel' has been borrowed from Latin *cūpa* [kuːpa] 'vessel' (KLUGE: 528), which has a descendant in French *coupe* [kup] 'cup'.[19] Following the above stated, Latin *cūpa* is the donor of Proto-Germanic *kuppa-*, and French *coupe* and German *Kopf* are etymologically related, but not cognate, as illustrated in Figure 2.9. In order to address this specific symmetric and transitive relation, which is comparable to xenology in biology, I propose the term *oblique etymological relation*. The basic relations between words which were discussed in this section are summarized in Table 2.9.

---

[19] Not all scholars agree with this explanation, OREL classifies Proto-Germanic *kuppa-* as an inherited word, relating it to Latvian *gubt* 'to bend' (OREL: 224f).

Relations		Terminology
common descent — direct	etymological relation / cognate relation	direct cognate relation
common descent — indirect	etymological relation / cognate relation	oblique cognate relation
common descent — due to lateral transfer	etymological relation	oblique etymological relation

Table 2.9: *Basic historical relations between words*

2.3.2 Relations between Languages

Given the usual problems one always has with definitions in disciplines dealing on the borderline between social sciences and science such as linguistics, the description of relations between words can be carried out in a quite straightforward way. Describing relations between languages, however, is a bit more complicated, since, once we reduce languages to sets of words, relations between languages have to be derived from the relations between the words they contain. Words, however, may easily get lost during language history. In theory, this can lead to a situation in which a language once exhibited a certain relation with another language, but has lost all traces. This may be problematic – not only from an epistemological, but also from an ontological perspective. Nevertheless, since this study does not deal with the reconstruction of Proto-World, I will ignore these issues in the following.

Starting from two languages, spoken at different times, one can say that the former is the ancestor of the latter, if it is "an earlier language from which the later one is directly descended by the ordinary processes of language change" (Trask 2000: 21). As for words, we can also call this relation an *ancestor-descendant relation*. If the time span between ancestor and descendant language is not too large, one can assume that there is also a certain amount of words in the ancestor and the descendant language for which an ancestor-descendant relation holds. Figure 2.10 illustrates this relation: given the common processes as *word loss* and *word gain* (see Section 2.2.3), it is not neces-

2.3 Relations

sary that the ancestor-descendant relation holds for all words of the ancestor and the descendant language. There will always be a certain amount of words present in the ancestor language which are no longer present in the descendant language, and there are surely also words present in the descendant language which were not present in the ancestor language.

Given two languages which are spoken at the same time or at different times, they can exhibit two specific relations, namely a *genetic relation* and a *contact relation*. Simply speaking, two languages are *genetically related* if they "share a single common ancestor" (ibid.: 133).[20] The genetic relation between the two languages may be reflected by a certain amount of words in both languages which are in a cognate relation. The amount of cognate words in the languages may differ from the amount of words present in the common ancestor language. Both languages may have gained their own new words, and the words inherited from the ancestor language may also be different, as illustrated in Figure 2.11. Two languages are in a *contact relation* if a certain amount of the words of one language has been transferred to the other during a period of contact between the speakers of the languages. As a result, the

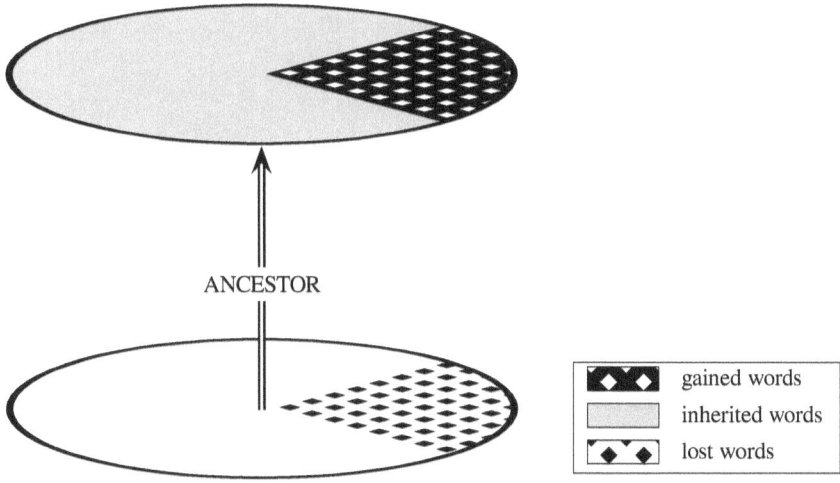

Figure 2.10: *Ancestor-descendant relation between languages*

---

[20] For a more precise definition see Ringe et al. (2002: 63).

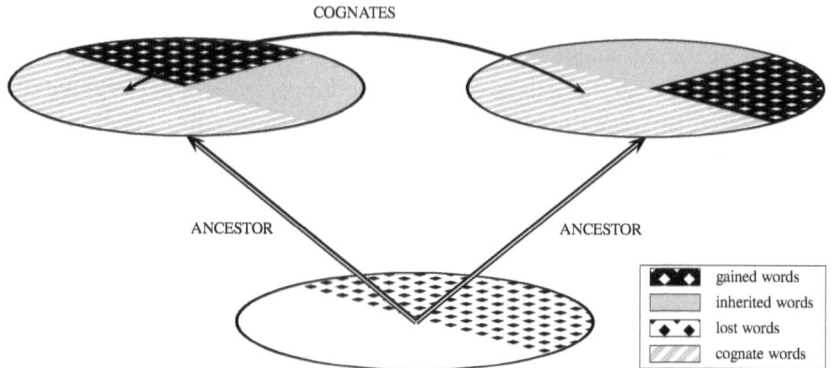

Figure 2.11: *Genetic relation between languages*

transferred words are in a donor-recipient relation. This relation is illustrated in Figure 2.12.

In contrast to the specific relations between words, the contact and the genetic relation between languages are not mutually exclusive. Two languages may well be genetically related *and* share a history of contact. For most genetically related languages, this is rather the rule than the exception. For example,

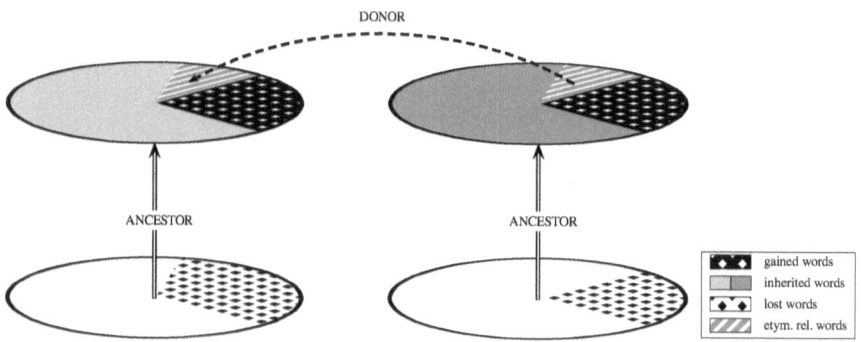

Figure 2.12: *Contact relation between languages*

2.4 Resemblances

Relations		
common history		
common descent		no comm. desc.
no contact	contact	

Terminology		
historical relation		
genetic relation		?
?	contact relation	

Table 2.10: *Basic historical relations between languages*

German and English are not only genetically related, but also share a still ongoing history of contact. Furthermore, since the genetic relation is stable, i.e., one usually assumes that a language does not loose its genetic status, contact relations can occur repeatedly during the history of languages. As a result, the lexicon of languages can be stratified into different layers of words reflecting different stages of contact with other languages. Similar to the terminology for word relations, there is no term to reflect that two languages share a common history without further specifying whether this involves common descent or contact. In the summary on basic relations between languages given in Table 2.10, I use the term *historical relation* to reflect this relation. There are likewise no specific terms to address that two languages are *not* genetically related, or that they have *never* come into contact. However, since these relations are not often addressed specifically, I leave them undefined.

2.4 Resemblances

So far, this study has dealt with the basic entities of historical linguistics (Section 2.1) and the basic processes by which these entities change (Section 2.2). As a consequenc of these basic change processes, basic relations between the entities could be established (Section 2.3). In the following, I want to deal with the *resemblances* between the entities which result from the basic processes of change. Investigating these resemblances by comparing languages represents the core of historical linguistic research, since both the inference of change patterns as well as the postulation of language relations directly depend on it.

2.4.1 Resemblances in Form

When discussing resemblances in the formal part of the linguistic sign, it is important to be clear of the kind of resemblance that shall be highlighted. The words German *schlafen* [ʃlaːfən] 'sleep' and German *Flaschen* [flaʃən] 'bottles', for example, are quite similar, both consisting of six different sound segments, which are almost identical, apart from the length of the vowel ([aː] vs. [a]). A similar kind of similarity holds for German *Post* [pɔst] 'post' and German *Obst* [oːpst] 'fruit'.

A different, less obvious, kind of similarity consists between German *Kerker* [kɛrkər] 'dungeon' and German *Tanten* [tantən] 'aunts'. Here, the similarity lies not in the *substance* of the sound sequences, but in their *structure*: both words consist of an identical chain of distinct characters, as can be easily seen when the words are *aligned*: | $\begin{smallmatrix} k & ɛ & r & k & ə & r \\ t & a & n & t & ə & n \end{smallmatrix}$ |. Every distinct segment of one of the two words corresponds directly to a distinct segment of the other word, and if one wants to convert one of the sound sequences into the other, all one has to do is to define a mapping between all unique segments, such as [k] ≈ [t], [r] ≈ [n]. Such a transformation is not possible for [flaʃən] compared to [ʃlaːfən], since these sound chains are not structurally equivalent. These two different kinds of similarities between words can be termed *substantial similarity* and *structural similarity*, respectively. The former emphasizes the similarities between the segments of the sequences while disregarding their order. The latter emphasizes the order of the sequences while disregarding the similarity of their segments.

The distinction between substantial and structural similarity might seem to be nothing more than an intellectual game. Similarity between two or more objects is always defined with respect to a given criterion, and one might easily think of other criteria, such as, e.g. the length of a word, whether it sounds pleasing to the ear, or whether it is easy to pronounce. When dealing with the similarities between etymologically related words, however, both the substantial and the structural similarity become crucially important. In Table 2.11, I have listed some cognate words between Italian and French. When comparing these words, their most striking resemblance is not due to their similarity in substance, but due to their similarity in structure. Although the substantial

2.4 Resemblances

Meaning	Italian		French	
	Orth.	IPA	Orth.	IPA
'key'	*chiave*	kjave	*klé*	kle
'feather'	*piuma*	pjuma	*plume*	plym
'flower'	*fiore*	fjore	*fleur*	flœʀ
'tear'	*lacrima*	lakrima	*larme*	laʀm
'tongue'	*lingua*	liŋwa	*langue*	lãg
'moon'	*luna*	luna	*lune*	lyn

Table 2.11: *Cognate words in Italian and French*

similarities might seem to be more evident, it is not difficult to observe that in all cases, where a [j] occurs in an Italian word, there is an [l] in the French word. It is further not difficult to observe that this is only the case when the [l] in French is preceded by a plosive, such as [p] or [k], or a fricative, such as [f], and the very fact that the sounds which are similar regarding their substance also occur in similar positions of the words reflects their structural similarity in a similar manner.

These structural similarities are a direct consequence of sound change. When the speakers of a language separate, the languages keep changing independently of each other. Since metathesis is rather rare, the order of the segments of the word forms is rarely affected by the processes of sound change. As a result, genetically related languages usually exhibit a striking amount of structural similarities between certain words. A specific characteristic of these similarities is their *systematic* nature, i.e. the structural similarity holds not only for a few words, but is reflected throughout the whole system of the languages. Lass (1997) calls this specific kind of similarity, which goes "beyond the stage of superficial comparison of individual words" (Hock and Joseph 1995 [2009]: 38), *genotypic* as opposed to *phenotypic similarity* (Lass 1997: 130). Genotypic similarity is reflected in *regular sound correspondences* (also called *systematic correspondences*, cf. Trask 2000: 336) which can be found between the sound segments of etymologically related words. Thus, for the examples in Table 2.11, one can find regular sound correspondences such as French [p] ≈ Italian [p], French [l] ≈ Italian [j] (befor labial plosive), and French [l] ≈

Meaning	English		German		Russian	
	Orth.	IPA	Orth.	IPA	Orth.	IPA
'fact'	*fact*	fækt	*Fakt*	fakt	*факт*	fakt
'function'	*function*	fʌŋkʃn̩	*Funktion*	fʊŋktsioːn	*функция*	funktsɨjə
'form'	*form*	foːm	*Form*	fɔrm	*форма*	formə

Table 2.12: *Systematic similarities resulting from contact relations*

Italian [1] (otherwise). The most crucial aspect of this correspondence-based, or genotypic similarity is that it is *language-specific* as opposed to *language-independent*. Phenotypic similarity is both substantial and structural, but it lacks the systematic aspect, since the resemblances are so spurious that they do not allow to derive regular correspondence patterns. As an example, consider Modern Greek θεός [θɛɔs] 'god' and Spanish *dios* [diɔs] 'god', which are only phonetically very similar, but not assumed to be cognate, since no further correspondence patterns can be found in the languages to support such a claim. Comparing the oldest ancestor forms of the words which are reflected in written sources, namely Old Latin *deivos*, and Mycenaean Greek *tʰehós* (Meier-Brügger 2002: 57f), it becomes further evident that the words originally were not that similar as they are now.

It is important to keep in mind that regular sound correspondences which can be established between languages do not necessarily result from their common descent but may also result from a period of contact. This can be can be seen from the examples of English, German, and Russian words given in Table 2.12, which all reflect striking recurrent structural similarities. These similarities, however, are not due to the common origin of the words, since in all languages the words have been directly or indirectly borrowed from Latin.

2.4.2 Resemblances in Meaning

The semantic aspects of linguistics are always notoriously problematic. The same holds for resemblances in meaning. In Section 2.2.2 I gave one example for the semantic shift from Proto-Germanic **kuppa-* 'vessel' to German *Kopf* 'head' which is reflected in its ancestral state in English *cup*, and as an intermediate state in Dutch *kop* 'head, cup'. To my knowledge, however, such cases are rather rare, and no empirical data which would make it possible to carry out statistical investigations on the frequency of certain patterns of semantic change is available at the moment. Therefore, no "deep" conclusions regarding the semantic resemblances between etymologically related words can be made at the moment. When searching for cognates in languages that have not yet been studied so far, the most reliable heuristic seems to start with semantic identity or near-identity. Other approaches have been discussed in the literature (List et al. 2013, Steiner et al. 2011), yet they have to be applied to more languages and tested on a larger amount of data in order to make it possible to draw valid conclusions.

2.5 Proof

In some branches of science, especially in the historical and social sciences, the object of investigation is not directly accessible to the researcher but can only be inferred by tests and theories. In historiography, for example, the events that took place at certain times (the *res gestae*) cannot be empirically testified. They have to be reconstructed by sifting the evidence as it is given in the sources (Schmitter 1982: 55f). In psychology, such attributes of people as "intelligence" cannot be directly observed but have to be inferred by measuring what they provoke or how they are "reflected in test performance" (Cronbach and Meehl 1955: 178). The same applies to historical linguistics. Once we assume that two languages are genetically related without having a complete written documentation of their common ancestor language, all we can say about the ancestor is what we can infer from the comparison of the descendant languages. When building and rejecting theories about the ancestor language, its sound system, its lexicon, or even its syntax, we never directly address the ancestor language as an *ontological fact* but only as an *epistemological reality* (Kormišin 1988: 92). We address the *construct*, i.e. the "fiction or story put forward by a theorist to make sense of a *phenomenon*" (Statt 1981 [1998]: 67), not the "real" object.[21]

Due to the fact that in historical linguistics we can investigate our research objects only via constructs, we are forced to rely on logical reasoning based on abduction (Anttila 1972: 196f). The term *abduction*, which was origi-

---

[21] This view was already emphasized by Johannes Schmidt (1843 – 1901) who characterized the reconstruction system of Proto-Indo-European as a "wissenschaftliche fiction" which cannot be treated as a "historisches individuum" (Schmidt 1872: 31).

nally coined by Charles Sanders Peirce (1839 – 1914), refers, as opposed to *induction* and *deduction*, to a "mode of reasoning [...] in which rather than progressing "logically" [...], one infers an antecedent condition by heuristic guessing from a present case" (Lass 1997: 334). Peirce himself explained the concept in the following way:

> Accepting the conclusion that an explanation is needed when facts contrary to what we should expect emerge, it follows that the explanation must be such a proposition as would lead to the prediction of the observed facts, either as necessary consequences or at least as very probable under the circumstances. A hypothesis then, has to be adopted, which is likely in itself, and renders the facts likely. This step of adopting a hypothesis as being suggested by the facts, is what I call *abduction*. I reckon it as a form of inference, however problematical the hypothesis may be held. (Peirce 1931/1958: 7.202)

Yet why should abduction be the only mode of reasoning available in historical linguistics? Contrasting the traditional kinds of logical reasoning (*induction* and *deduction*) may make this point clear: According to Peirce (ibid.: 2.623), all of them "involve the triad of 'rule', 'case' and 'result', but inference moves in different directions" (Lass 1997: 334). Given the rule "*All bunnies have long ears*", the case "**The thing that brings the Easter eggs is a bunny**", and the result "The thing that brings the Easter eggs has long ears", deduction infers the result from the rule and the case:

(2.1) "*All bunnies have long ears,* and **the thing that brings the Easter eggs is a bunny.** Therefore, the thing that brings the Easter eggs has long ears."

Induction infers the rule from the case and the result:

(2.2) "**The thing that brings the Easter eggs is a bunny,** and the thing that brings the Easter eggs has long ears. Therefore, *all bunnies have long ears.*"

But abduction will infer the case from the rule and the result:

(2.3) "*All bunnies have long ears,* and the thing that brings the Easter eggs has long ears. Therefore, **the thing that brings the Easter eggs is a bunny.**"

Given the fact that in historical linguistics we only *have* the rule and the result, abduction is the only kind of reasoning which *can* be applied:

(2.4) "*The sounds of languages change in a regular manner,* and the languages A and B show recurrent structural similarities in their lexical material. Therefore A **and** B **share a common history.**"

According to Schurz (2008), different *patterns* of abduction can be distinguished, depending on (1) "the kind of *hypothesis* which is abduced", (2) "the kind of *evidence* which the abduction intends to explain", and (3) "the *beliefs* or *cognitive mechanisms* which *drive* the abduction" (ibid.: 205). The kind of abduction which is commonly used in historical linguistics belongs to the family of *factual abduction*s, i.e. abductions in which "both the evidence to be explained and the abduced hypothesis are *singular facts*" (ibid.: 206). Since historical linguistics mainly deals with *unobservable facts* (constructs), we can further characterize it as historical-fact abduction (ibid.: 209).

In order to protect one's self from being stuck in the forest of wild speculations, historical-fact abduction has to be based on (1) *unique hypotheses*, i.e. "individual" cases in the terminology of Peirce, and (2) *cumulative evidence*, i.e. multiple results which can all be explained by the same hypothesis. The first point is already implied by the very nature of the problem: Seeking for an explanation for a specific result, the explanation has to be an "individual", i.e. a unique case which *solely* explains the results, as opposed to a type of case or a class of cases whose several instances all explain the result equally well. Otherwise, the explanation won't have any persuasive force. This view is reflected in Nichols (1996: 48) who claims that historical linguists tend to base their theories about genetic relationship on "individual-identifying evidence", i.e. "on evidence that identifies a unique individual protolanguage rather than on evidence that identifies a set of languages or a type of language". The second point results from the nature of the rules or general laws which are available in historical linguistics. In order to justify that there is only one singular hypothesis which explains a given result best, one needs either "strong" rules which – when applied to a specific case – will yield only one specific result, or multiple "pieces" of evidence which might "[fall] short of proof [when taking] each item separately" but become convincing when "all the items [are] combined" (Sturtevant 1920: 11).[22]

---

[22] Sturtevant emphasizes the importance of cumulative evidence in the context of the reconstruction of Old Greek and Latin pronunciation, yet this "multitude of decisions" ("множественность решений", cf. Makaev 1977: 88) is representative for almost all aspects of historical linguistics.

Being forced to rely on multiple pieces of evidence which – only when taken together – allow one to draw a rather convincing picture of the past, is not a unique problem of historical linguistics, but also of historiography – or crime investigations, as it has been already pointed out by Georg von der Gabelentz (1840 – 1893, cf. Gabelentz 1891: 154), and in later work on semiotics (cf. the papers in Eco and Sebeok 1983). The fact that in historical linguistics theories are built about cases (events, unique objects) as opposed to theories about general laws may also be the reason for the philological "style" prevalent in historical linguistic studies. Due to the complex nature of the inference process, a systematization of the comparative method (see Section 2.6) has never been carried out efficiently and intuition still plays a major role in the field, while statistical methods are rarely applied and often deemed with suspicion (Baxter and Manaster Ramer 2000: 169-172). This distrusting attitude of historical linguistics towards probability issues is surprising, since "probabilistic evaluation of causes and elimination of implausible causes plays a central role in factual abductions" (Schurz 2008: 207), since it reduces the search space when seeking an explanation for a given phenomenon (ibid.: 210f).

Given the fact that, as discussed above, historical linguistics has to make use of abduction as a primary inference pattern, it is important to distinguish the *evidence* (or the results in terms of Peirce) from the general *laws* (rules) when trying to prove that two words are cognate or that two languages are genetically related. In the following, I shall therefore discuss the evidence and the laws on which our hypotheses are normally based separately.

2.5.1 Laws

Strictly speaking, the laws or rules upon which historical linguists base their hypotheses are hypotheses themselves. The most important of these "laws" is the Neogrammarian Hypothesis regarding the *regularity of sound change* (see Section 2.2.1). Without this hypothesis, no (valid) conclusions regarding any historical relations between languages could be made. As I have pointed out in Section 2.2.1, the Neogrammarian Hypothesis has been directly questioned by the theory of lexical diffusion, yet later research in the field of sociolinguistics has provided evidence that both Neogrammarian sound change and sound change via lexical diffusion reflect basic mechanisms of sound change. It is important to note that the fact that lexical diffusion lacks the strict regularity of the Neogrammarian sound change mechanism does not invalidate it as a "law" for abductive reasoning. Although not being absolutely regular, lexical

2.5 Proof

diffusion usually manifests itself in strong tendencies. Since, as I have pointed out before, probabilistic evaluation is crucial in factual abductions, it does not make a huge difference whether one bases an abductive hypothesis on universal laws or strong tendencies. Hence, the regularity hypothesis does not loose its significance as the basic "law" of historical linguistics.

2.5.2 Evidence

When historical records are lacking for a given set of languages, the only way to shed light on their history is to infer historical events from a comparison of the synchronic systems of these languages. Based on the regularity hypothesis which serves as the background law in historical-fact abduction, historical language relations are inferred from resemblances which can be found in their "form material", i.e. in words and grammatical morphemes.

Many scholars make a distinction between two kinds of evidence, namely *grammatical* and *lexical evidence* (Dybo and Starostin 2008). In the notion of *systematic form resemblances*, which I prefer, this distinction is suspended. Strictly speaking, all kind of evidence is "lexical", in so far as "grammatical evidence" usually points to unique grammatical markers which are denoted by distinct morphemes, i.e. "forms", rather than abstract categories. Hence, "sound chains", be they grammatical morphemes or lexemes, provide the main evidence for the proof of historical language relations.

Resemblances in the form material of languages can be roughly divided into three classes, depending on their causes. They can be

(a) *coincidental*, i.e. they are simply due to chance,
(b) *natural*, i.e. they are due to general patterns of denotation observable in all human languages, and
(c) *non-natural*, or – in a stronger notion – *historical*, i.e. they are due to a shared history of the languages under observation.

The latter kind of resemblance can be further divided into *genetic* and *contact-induced* resemblances, i.e. resemblances due to common descent and resemblances due to a shared history of contact (cf. Figure 2.13, see also Section 2.3.2). Since the former two kinds of resemblances are not caused by historical events, they cannot serve as evidence and have to be discarded from the comparison. Fortunately, coincidental and natural similarities are not very frequent, and they can easily be detected. The latter two kinds of resemblances reflect language history and serve as the basic evidence. Unfortunately, both genetic and contact-induced resemblances can show up in form of regular sound correspondences between the languages under comparison (see Section 2.4.1). Thus, while regular sound correspondences which can be established between two or more languages provide direct evidence for their historical relatedness, they do not necessarily provide evidence for genetic relatedness.

In order to distinguish between sound correspondences resulting from donor-recipient and cognate relations, specific methods have to be applied. Thus, when dealing with multiple incompatible sound correspondences, one may stratify the correspondences and separate layers of inheritance and contact as Hübschmann (1877) did when proving that Armenian is an Indo-European language. For the process of stratification itself, it seems useful to turn to semantic criteria and to split the "basic lexicon" into separate parts which are more or less prone to borrowing (Chén 1996, Wang 2006a). Nevertheless, so

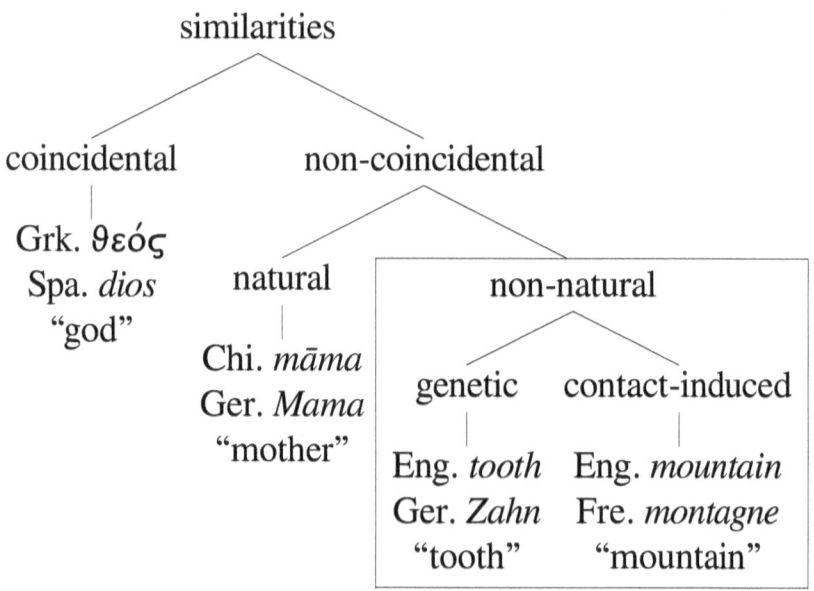

Figure 2.13: *Common causes for resemblances in the form material of languages: Both kinds of non-natural resemblances are "historical" and constitute one of the key objectives of historical linguistics.*

far, historical linguistics does not offer a straightforward method to distinguish between sound correspondences resulting from genetic and sound correspondences resulting from contact relations.

2.6 Methods

Almost all problems of historical linguistics, including those which were outlined so far, such as the proof of genetic relationship, or the identification of regular sound correspondences, and those which have only briefly been addressed, such as the genetic classification of languages, are addressed within the framework of the so-called *comparative method*. Although termed a *method*, the comparative method does not constitute a formal procedure which may be directly expressed in algorithmic terms, but rather covers a bunch of techniques that historical linguists commonly use to reconstruct the history of languages and language families. Following the descriptions in Durie (1996: 6f) and Trask (2000: 64-67), one may characterize the comparative method as a procedure roughly consisting of the following five stages: (1) proof of relationship, (2) identification of cognates, (3) identification of sound correspondences, (4) reconstruction of proto-forms, (5) internal classification. Note that all of these stages are intimately intertwined, and the order offers only a broad orientation. Thus, the ultimate proof of relationship should be based on the identification of cognates sets, but the identification of cognate sets itself should be based on the identification of regular sound correspondences which themselves can not only be found in cognate but also in obliquely etymologically related words. The reconstruction of proto-forms usually requires the internal classification of the language family to be known, but the internal classification of a language family traditionally requires that phonological or lexical innovations are known, which can only be identified after the reconstruction of proto-forms.

In order to circumvent this problem of circularity, historical linguists usually employ an iterative procedure in which all steps are constantly repeated and all conclusions are constantly revised (see Figure 2.14). In this context, the specific procedure for the identification of cognates constitutes the core of the method: First an initial list of putative cognate sets is created by comparing semantically and phonetically similar words from the languages to be investigated. In most of the literature dealing with the comparative method, the question of which words are most suitable for the initial compilation of cog-

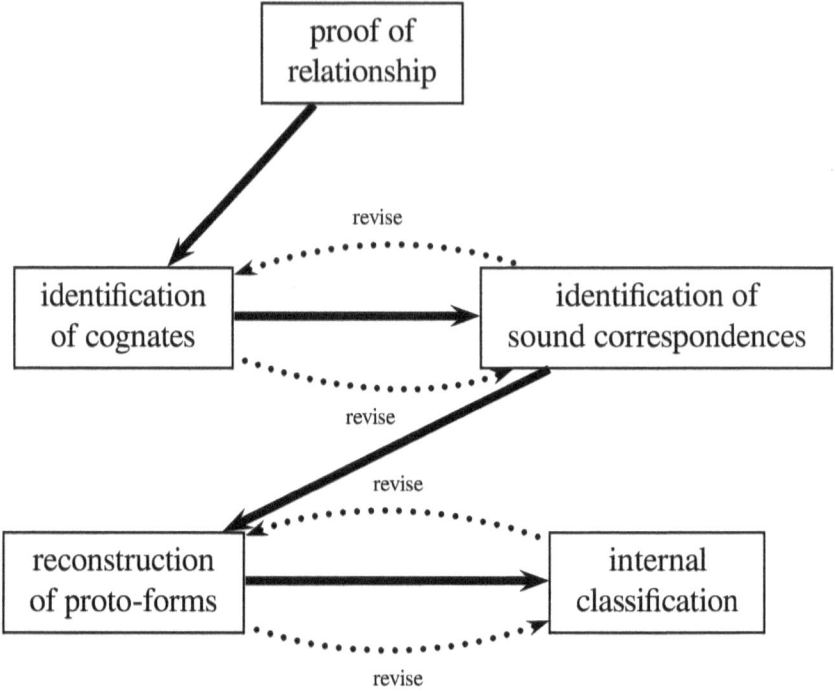

Figure 2.14: *The iterative character of the comparative method*

nate lists is not explicitly addressed, yet it seems obvious that the comparanda should belong to the basic vocabulary of the languages. Based on this *cognate list*, an initial list of putative sound correspondences (*correspondence list*) is created. Sound correspondences are determined by *aligning* the cognate words and searching for sound pairs which repeatedly occur in similar positions of the presumed cognate words.[23] After these initial steps have been carried out, the cognate list and the correspondence list are modified by

(a) adding and deleting cognate sets from the cognate list depending on whether or not they are consistent with the correspondence list, and

---

[23] The procedure of alignment will be dealt with in detail in Chapter 3.

2.6 Methods

(b) adding and deleting sound correspondences from the correspondence list, depending on whether or not they find support in the cognate list.

These steps are repeated until the results seem satisfying enough such that no further modifications, neither of the cognate list, nor of the correspondence list, seem to be necessary.[24]

The specific strength of the comparative method lies in the *similarity measure* which is applied for the identification of cognates: Sequence similarity is determined on the basis of *regular sound correspondences* as opposed to similarity based on surface resemblances of phonetic segments (see Section 2.4.1). Thus, comparing English *token* [təʊkən] and German *Zeichen* [tsaɪçən] 'sign', the words may not sound very similar, yet their cognacy is strongly suggested by the comparative method, since their phonetic segments can be shown to correspond regularly within other cognates of both languages.[25] The most crucial aspect of correspondence-based similarity is that it is *language-specific*: Genotypic similarity is never defined in general terms but always with respect to the language systems which are being compared (see Section 2.4). Correspondence relations can therefore only be established for individual languages, they can never be taken as general statements. This may seem to be a weakness, yet it turns out that the genotypic similarity notion is one of the most crucial strengths of the comparative method: It allow us to dive deeper in the history of languages in cases where phonetic change has corrupted the former identity of cognates to such an extent that no sufficient surface similarity is left.

---

[24] Note that in the comparative method it is tacitly assumed that a distinction between cognates and obliquely etymologically related words can be made, although, as has been mentioned earlier, no generally accepted method for this distinction has been proposed so far.

[25] Compare, for example, English *weak* [wiːk] vs. German *weich* [vaɪç] 'soft' for the correspondence of [k] with [ç], and English *tongue* [tʌŋ] vs. German *Zunge* [tsuŋə] 'tongue' for the correspondence of [t] with [ts].

3
Sequence Comparison

> The basic problem with sequence alignment is that it seems to be more an art than a science. For a science, the techniques are scarcely rigid enough, whereas for an art the results are usually rather prosaic. Perhaps, it is most justly treated as a sport, one for which no universal rules are presently formulated.
>
> Morrison (2010: 369)

In Chapter 2, I have outlined some of the most important theoretical and practical aspects of research in the field of historical linguistics. In the discussion of the form part of the linguistic sign (see Section 2.1.3), I have pointed to the *sequential* character of the sign form. Since language comparison in historical linguistics is mainly based on a comparison of sign forms (words, morphemes), language comparison can be seen as a very specific kind of *sequence comparison*.

Sequence comparison is an important topic in many different disciplines, especially in biology and computer science. Many solutions to common problems of sequence comparison have been developed in these scientific branches. When trying to develop automatic approaches to sequence comparison in historical linguistics, it seems therefore reasonable to start by reviewing those methods which have been already developed. In the following, I will therefore give an overview on general aspects of sequences and sequence comparison. I intentionally avoid to draw parallels to linguistics here, although many parallels are very striking. I think, however, that it is important to approach the topic from a maximally unbiased perspective in order to avoid to be led astray by the desire to find parallels in each and every detail, and – in the end – to construct them instead of finding them.

3.1 Sequences

Many structures we are dealing with – be it in daily life or in science – can be represented as *sequences*. The bird songs which awake us in the morning are sequences of sound waves, the movies we watch are sequences of pictures,

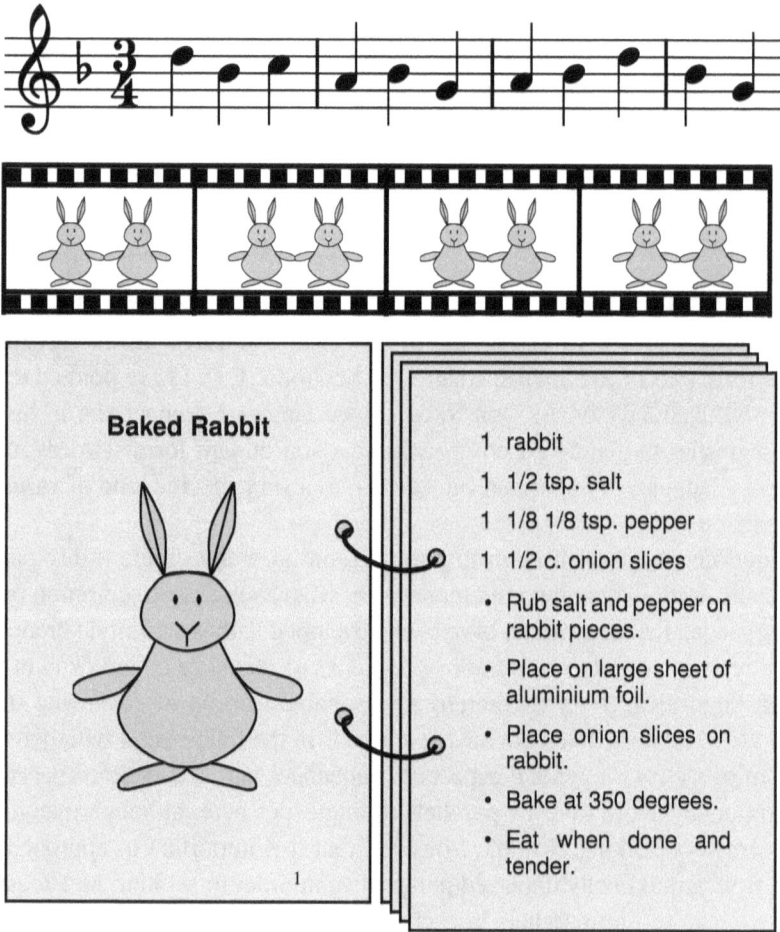

Figure 3.1: *Sequences in our daily life: music, movies, recipes*

3.1 Sequences 63

and the meals we cook are created by a sequence of instructions received from a recipe book.

What recipes, movies, and music have in common, or – to put it in other terms – what allows us to view them as sequences, is that they all can be seen as ordered chains of objects whose identity is a product of both their *order* and their *content*. In the following, I shall point to some general aspects which are important when investigating and comparing sequences. After discussing the problem of *discreteness* and *continuity*, I shall point to the differences between sequences and *sets*. In the end, a formal definition of sequences will be given.

3.1.1 Discrete and Continuous Entities

Many objects which we traditionally model as sequences are not discrete but rather appear as functions of a continuous variable (space, time, etc., cf. Kruskal and Liberman 1983 [1999]: 130). This holds for the music we listen as well as the words we speak. Treating these entities as sequences presupposes that they have been made discrete in a first instance.

In linguistics the act of making the continuous discrete has a long tradition. Since the way we look at language is traditionally influenced by "alphabetic thinking", it is often ignored that the continuum is the natural appearance of speech and that segmentation is the result of an explicit analysis applied to it: "Neither the movements of the speech organs nor the acoustic signal offers a clear division of speech into successive phonetic units" (*IPA Handbook* 1999: 5). This can be easily illustrated by having a look at the spectrogram of Shanghainese *tàiyáng*太陽 [$t^h a^{33} ɦiã^{44}$] 'sun' in Figure 3.2 [1]. There is no way to identify the five sound segments [t^h], [a], [ɦ], [i], and [ã] directly in the spectrogram. Furthermore, the phonetic representation of the word comes along with information regarding the tonal patterns of the two syllables, which are transcribed by superscript letters as if they were segments, but which are in fact suprasegmental in their nature, "involving the entire syllable rather than a single phone" (Sun 2006: 39).

Nevertheless, segmentation of speech into discrete units is one of the most common tasks in linguistics: "Phonetic analysis is based on the crucial premise that it is possible to describe speech in terms of a sequence of segments" (*IPA Handbook* 1999: 6). We should, however, always keep in mind that the seemingly discrete entities we are working with do not necessarily have to be dis-

---

[1] Sound data and phonetic data are taken from YINKU.

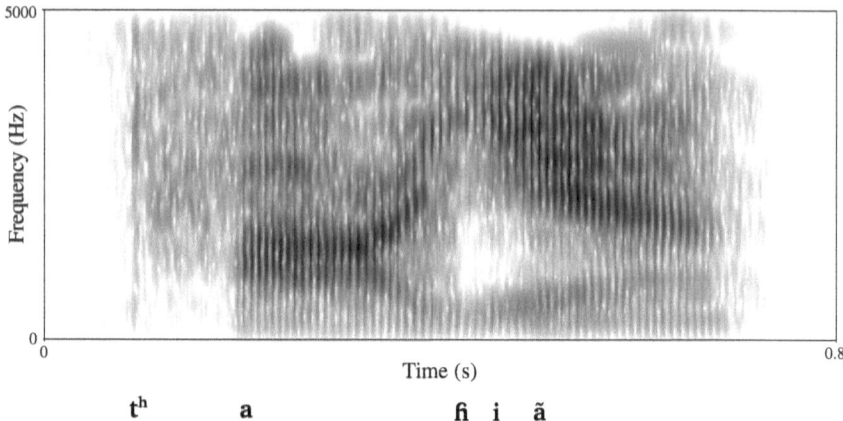

Figure 3.2: *Spectrogram of Shànghǎinese* tàiyáng *'sun'. Phonetic and sound data are taken from YINKU.*

crete by their nature, and that discrete approaches may therefore reach certain limits under certain circumstances.

3.1.2 Sequences and Sets

Sequences have to be distinguished from *sets*. While sets are *unordered* collections of *unique* objects, sequences are *ordered* lists of *non-unique* objects. This difference regarding uniqueness and orderedness is of crucial importance for the comparison of sets and sequences: While the objects of sets are easily distinguished because of their uniqueness, the objects of sequences receive a distinctive function only because of their order. Therefore, a comparison of different sets can be simply carried out by comparing the objects of the sets. A comparison of sequences, however, has to be based on a comparison of both the objects *and* the structure of the sequences.

3.1.3 A Formal Definition of Sequences

From a formal point of view, sequences can be roughly defined as follows:

Definition 3.1 Given an *alphabet* (a non-empty finite set, whose elements are called *characters*), a *sequence* is an ordered list of characters drawn from the al-

3.1 Sequences

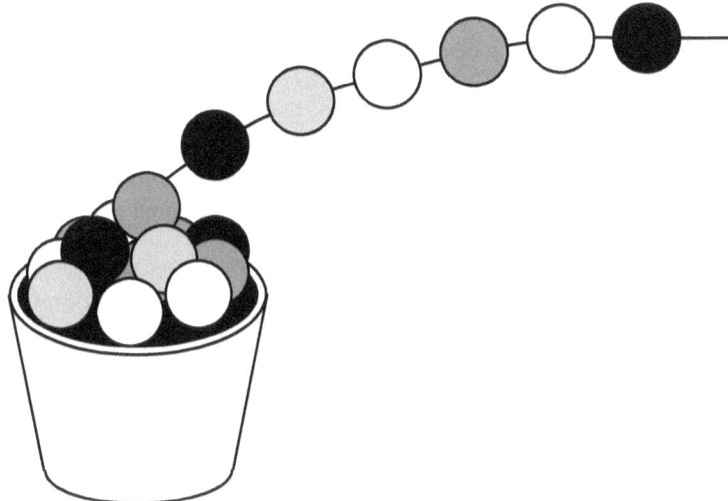

Figure 3.3: *Sequences as strings of colored beads. Only if the beads are lined up on the string, they are unique, in so far, as they can be defined by both their position in the sequence, and their color.*

phabet. The elements of sequences are called *segments*. The *length* of a sequence is the number of its segments, and the *cardinality* of a sequence is the number its unique segments. (cf. Böckenbauer and Bongartz 2003: 30f)

One can imagine a sequence as a string of colored beads. If we take the beads separately from the string, it is impossible to distinguish those beads which have the same color from each other. Yet having them lined up on a string, every bead is individual, since it has a position different from all the other beads on the string (see Figure 3.3).

Given Definition 3.1, it is useful to define some further common terms and notations which will be used again in this study.

Definition 3.2 Given two sequences s and t.

(a) t is a *subsequence* of s, if t can be derived from s by deleting some of the segments of s without changing the order of the remaining segments,

(b) *t* is a *substring* of *s*, if *t* is a subsequence of *s* and the derivation of *t* from *s* can be carried out by deleting only elements from the beginning and the end of *s*,

(c) *t* is a *prefix* of *s*, if *t* is a substring of *s* and the derivation of *t* from *s* can be carried out by deleting only elements from the end of *s*,

(d) *t* is a *suffix* of *s*, if *t* is a substring of *s* and the derivation of *t* from *s* can be carried out by deleting only elements from the beginning of *s*.

While the notion of *prefixes* and *suffixes* is intuitively clear, especially for a linguist, the distinction between *subsequences* and *substrings* is important not only for the formal definition of prefixes and suffixes, but also for the computational aspects of sequence comparison which will be dealt with in the remainder of this chapter.

3.2 Sequence Comparison

Comparing sequences may turn out to be a rather simple task. This is especially the case when it is known in advance, which segments of the sequences correspond to each other. Consider, e.g., two strings of colored beads which are of the same length: Comparing these sequences, we simply have to line them up and check whether the same colors appear in the same positions, as illustrated in Figure 3.4. It is also very easy to quantify the difference between the two strings by simply counting the number of positions in which both strings differ, which yields 2 for the two strings in the example, since the strings differ in positions three and four. The result of such a count is a

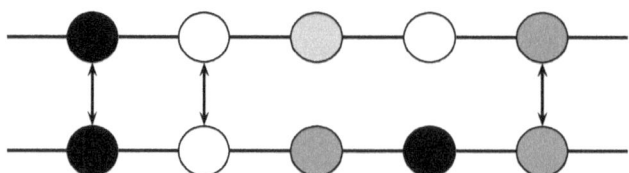

Figure 3.4: *Comparing sequences of equal length. If it is known in advance which segments of two sequences correspond to each other, the Hamming distance can be used to compare two sequences. It is defined as the number of positions in which two sequences differ.*

3.2 Sequence Comparison   67

distance in the strict mathematical sense, also known as *Hamming distance*, which was first introduced by R. W. Hamming (1915 – 1998) in a paper from 1950 (Hamming 1950).

While it is easy to compare sequences if the corresponding segments have already been identified, sequence comparison often has to deal "with the more difficult comparisons which arise when the correspondence is not known in advance" (Kruskal 1983: 201). In the following, I will introduce some main aspects regarding differences between sequences and general questions of sequence comparison. I will try to generalize the ways in which sequences may differ, I will discuss, how differences between sequences can be visualized, and I will introduce *alignments* as one of the most common ways to model differences between sequences.

3.2.1 Differences between Sequences

For the comparison of two sequences, of which we assume that they are in a certain relationship, it is important to determine how or if the segments of the sequences *correspond* to each other. When dealing with segment correspondences we should first distinguish whether the segments correspond at all. If one segment in a given sequence corresponds to a segment of another sequence, this is called a *proper match*. If one segment in a given sequence does not correspond to any segment of another sequence, I shall call this an *empty match*. Among the *proper matches*, we can further distinguish those cases where corresponding segments are identical (*uniform matches*) from those cases, where corresponding segments aren't identical (*divergent matches* or *mismatches*). [2] Figure 3.5 illustrates these different cases of correspondence and non-correspondence: Comparing both strings of colored beads, there are three uniform matches, one divergent match and one empty match.

Sequence comparison does not necessarily have to be based on the *correspondence perspective*. Another perspective which is very common in the literature on sequence comparison is the *edit perspective*. According to this perspective, differences between sequences are stated in terms of *edit operations*, i.e. the basic operations one needs in order to transform one sequence into the other. The most basic edit operations are *substitution* and *indels* (*insertions* and *deletions*). They were first introduced by the Russian scholar V. I. Lev-

---

[2] In the terminology commonly used in biology, the terms *match* vs. *mismatch* are often used instead of the terms *uniform* and *divergent match*.

enshtein. Compared to the above-mentioned correspondence types, substitutions correspond to divergent matches, since transforming one sequence into another presupposes that non-identical segments are transformed into identical ones, and indels correspond to empty matches, since missing or additional segments require either the insertion or the deletion of a segment. Figure 3.6 illustrates how the first string of Figure 3.5 can be transformed into the second string by means of the basic edit operations.

Some less basic but, nevertheless, common edit operations are *transpositions* (first introduced by F. J. Damerau, cf. Damerau 1964), and *compressions* and *expansions* (cf. Kruskal and Liberman 1983 [1999]). Transpositions allow to swap two adjacent segments when transforming the source sequence into the target sequence. From the correspondence perspective, these may be called *crossed matches* (see Figure 3.7a). Compressions and expansions allow to merge two or more adjacent segments into one or to split one segment into two or more adjacent segments, respectively. From the viewpoint of segment correspondence, these may be called *complex matches* (see Figure 3.7b).

The two perspectives regarding sequence similarities, namely the correspondence perspective and the edit perspective, are often treated as interchangeable in the literature. While it is true that both models are equivalent in many applications of sequence analyses, there is one great difference between them, in so far as the edit perspective emphasizes "putative *mutational events* that transform one [sequence] into another, whereas [the correspondence perspective] only displays a relationship between two [sequences]" (Gusfield 1997: 217). Furthermore, while the correspondence perspective treats all matchings of segments as being *equal*, the edit perspective allows to put all operations into a specific *order* and give them a certain *direction*. The

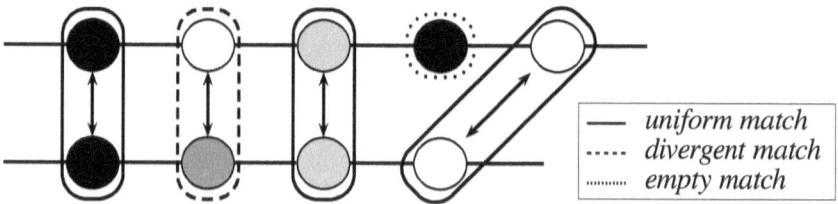

Figure 3.5: *The basic types of segment correspondences*

3.2 Sequence Comparison

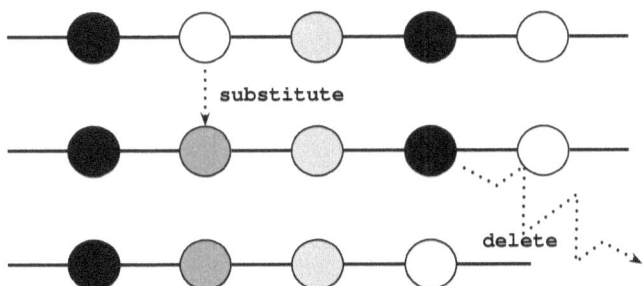

Figure 3.6: *Transforming one sequence into the other*

edit perspective is therefore more explicit than the correspondence perspective, since it allows to describe differences between sequences as a chain of events with a certain direction. This becomes obvious when summarizing the terms which were used so far in order to describe the different *matching types* (types of segment correspondences) and their corresponding edit operations as displayed in Table 3.1.

3.2.2 Modelling Sequence Differences

Regarding the visualization and modelling of sequence differences (be they in terms of the correspondence perspective or the edit perspective) three modes are distinguished in Kruskal (1983): *traces*, *alignments* and *listings*.

Trace: A *trace* is a relation which links all proper matches in two strings s and t, while empty matches are left unrelated (ibid.: 209-211).

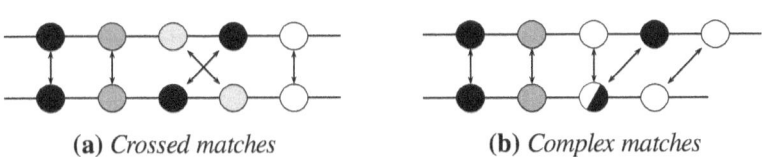

(a) *Crossed matches*   (b) *Complex matches*

Figure 3.7: *Crossed* (a) *and complex matches* (b) *between sequences*

	Perspective
Correspondence	**Edit**
uniform match	continuation
divergent match	substitution
empty match	insertion
	deletion
crossed match	transposition
complex match	compression
	expansion

Table 3.1: *Correspondence vs. edit perspective*

Alignment: An *alignment* is a matrix with two rows in which two sequences s and t are ordered in such a way that all proper matches appear in the same column. Empty matches are filled with gap symbols (Kruskal 1983: 211).

Listing: A *listing* is a sequence of *edit instructions* by which a source sequence s is successively transformed into a target sequence t. Every edit instruction consists of at least one edit operation, yet more than one edit operation is also possible (ibid.: 211-215).

Figure 3.8 illustrates the differences between the three presentation modes by taking the two sequences "GBWLG" and "GLWG" as examples. The three modes differ not only regarding the way they visualize sequence differences but also regarding the information displayed by them. Listings differ from traces and alignments in so far as they explicitly emphasize the edit perspective, while alignments and traces represent the information within the correspondence perspective. The difference between alignments and traces lies in the capability of alignments to distinguish the order of adjacent empty matches (ibid.: 211).

It becomes obvious that the information displayed by the three modes successively increases from traces via alignments to listings: The advantage of alignments over traces is their capability to display adjacent empty matches, which are simply ignored within the trace mode. Alignments, on the other hand, are indifferent regarding the order of edit operations (or the order of correspondences), in contrast to listings. Furthermore, listings "permit many

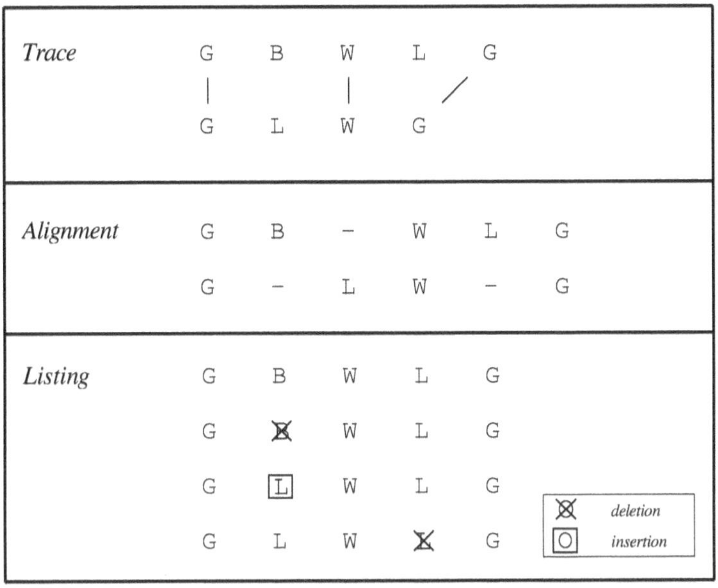

3.2 Sequence Comparison

Trace	G	B	W	L	G	
	|		|	/		
	G	L	W	G		

Alignment	G	B	–	W	L	G
	G	–	L	W	–	G

Listing	G	B	W	L	G
	G	⊠	W	L	G
	G	L̄	W	L	G
	G	L	W	⊠	G

⊠ deletion
☐ insertion

Figure 3.8: *Traces, alignments, and listings*

successive changes to be made in a single position and alignments permit only one" (ibid.: 214). Therefore, one alignment may have more than one corresponding listing, and one trace may have more than one corresponding alignment, as exemplified in Figure 3.9, where one trace corresponds to two alignments and to six different listings (not allowing successive changes for the construction of the listings).

Compared to traces and listings, alignments offer many advantages: They are more informative than traces, and they are indifferent regarding the perspective of sequence comparison one choses, be it the correspondence or the edit perspective. The last point is especially important when comparing alignment analyses to listings, since in most kinds of sequence analyses the information regarding the order of edit operations is either not needed, since the sequences which are compared are not in an ancestor-descendant relation, or simply impossible to retrieve (ibid.: 16-18). Furthermore, the computational realization for alignment analyses is much more straightforward than that for listings (ibid.: 12). One further advantage of alignments over both traces

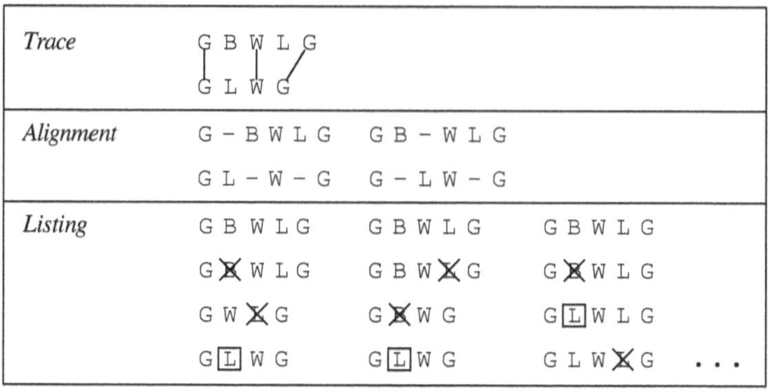

Trace	G B W L G G L W G	
Alignment	G - B W L G G L - W - G	G B - W L G G - L W - G
Listing	G B W L G G X W L G G W X G G L̄ W G	G B W L G G B W X G G X W G G L̄ W G	G B W L G G X W L G G L̄ W L G G L W X G ...

Figure 3.9: *Comparing traces, alignments, and listings. Taking the trace of the strings "GBWLG" and "GLWG" as a basic, there are two equivalent alignments, and six equivalent listings of which only three examples are shown in the figure.*

and listings lies in their capability to display resemblances between more than just two sequences: While traces of multiple sequences will result in complex networks, which are difficult to visualize, the directional structure of listings requires that ancestor-descendant relations among the sequences being compared are already reconstructed which is often not the case, because sequence comparison usually serves as the basis of the reconstruction of ancestor states.

3.2.3 Alignment Analyses

With the help of alignment analyses[3] all different kinds of sequences can be compared, regardless of where they occur or what the purpose of the comparison is. Thus, when trying to detect plagiarism in scientific work, alignment analyses can throw light on the differences between the original text and the plagiary (see Example (1) in Figure 3.10). In molecular biology, the alignment of protein and DNA sequences is a very common method and the basis of phylogenetic reconstruction (see Example (2) in Figure 3.10), and in type

---

[3] In the literature, the term *alignment* is often used interchangeably to refer either to the specific kind of analysis by which two or more sequences are aligned, or to the result of such an analysis. I try to maintain a strict distinction by using the term *alignment* only to refer to the result of the analysis, and the term *alignment analysis*, in order to address the specific process which yields an alignment.

3.2 Sequence Comparison

Type	Taxon	N.	Sequence
(1)	PLAGIARY	1	die Zurueckhaltung die im Umgang mit dem Foederalismusbegriff
	ORIGINAL	1	die Zurueckhaltung die im Umgang mit dem Foederalismusbegriff
	PLAGIARY	2	zu beobachten ist mag zu einem gewissen ..Teil. darauf zuruec
	ORIGINAL	2	zu beobachten ist mag ....n.ich.t zuletzt darauf zuruec
	PLAGIARY	3	kzufuehren sein dass sich ...waehre.nd. des 19 Jahrhunderts e
	ORIGINAL	3	kzufuehren sein dass sich im v.e.r.lauf des 19 Jahrhunderts e
(2)	HTL2	1	LDTAPCLFSDGS------PQKAAYVLWDQTIL---QQDITPLPSHETHSA QKGELLALIC
	MMLV	1	PDADHTWYTDGSSLLQEGQRKAGAAVTTETEVIWAKALDAG---T---SAQRAELIALTQA
	HTL2	2	GLRAAKPWPSLNIFLDSKYLIKYLHSLAIGAFLGTSAH---------QT-LQAALPPLLQG
	MMLV	2	LKMAEGKK-LNVYTDSRYAFATAHIHGEIYRRRGLLTSEGKEIKNKDE-ILALLKALFLPK
	HTL2	3	KTIYLHHVRSHT-NLPDPISTFNEYTDSLILAPL----------
	MMLV	3	RLSIIHCPGHQ-KGHSAEARGNRMADQAARKAAITETPDTSTLL
(3)	WRONG	1	two b- or not two b- that is the question
	CORRECT	1	t-o be or not t-o be that is the question
	WRONG	2	Leavins-t-ine distance is the addict distance betwean strings
	CORRECT	2	Le-venshtein- distance is the ed-i-t distance between strings
	WRONG	3	"ad-ress" "concensus" and "dependance" are of-en misspelled
	CORRECT	3	"address" "consensus" and "dependence" are often misspelled

Figure 3.10: *Alignment analyses in different applications: text comparison* (1), *protein analysis* (2), *and spelling correction* (3). *Source and plagiary in example* (1) *are taken with modifications from* Kommission "Selbstkontrolle" *(Appendix 3), example* (2) *is taken from* DIALIGN *(Manual).*

setting programs and search engines, sequence alignments can be used to detect spelling errors (see Example (3) in Figure 3.10).

Given the basic types of segment correspondences (uniform, divergent, and empty matches) as they were introduced in Section 3.2, an alignment of two or more sequences can be roughly defined as follows:

> **Definition 3.3** An *alignment* of n ($n > 1$) sequences is an n-row matrix in which all sequences are aranged in such a way that all matching segments occur in the same column, while empty cells, resulting from empty matches, are filled with gap symbols. The number of columns of an alignment is called its $length$ or its $width$, and the number of rows is called its $height$. (cf. Gusfield 1997: 216)

This definition is very general in so far as no difference is being made between the number of sequences that constitute an alignment. In many applications, however, it is useful to make a further distinction between *pairwise sequence alignments* (alignments of two sequences, PSA) and *multiple sequence alignments* (alignments of more than two sequences, MSA). This distinction between 'two' and 'many' is not arbitrary, since – for reasons of computational complexity – many algorithms and measures are only defined for pairwise alignments. As a consequence, the multiple perspective is often broken down to a pairwise perspective, when dealing with multiple alignments. In evolutionary biology, for example, a common measure to estimate the similarity between aligned sequence pairs is the so-called *percentage identity* (PID) which is defined as:

$$(3.1) \qquad PID = 100\frac{u}{u+d+i},$$

where u is the number of uniform matches in a given alignment, d is the number of divergent matches, and i is the number of internal empty matches.[4] For the pairwise alignment $\begin{vmatrix} G & B & W & L & G \\ G & L & W & - & G \end{vmatrix}$, for example the percentage identity is 60, since there are 3 uniform matches in the alignment, 1 divergent, and 1 empty match. While this score can be easily defined and computed for pairwise alignments, it is not possible to define it directly for multiple alignments. Therefore, the percentage identity of multiple alignments of height n is usually defined as the average of the pairwise percentage identities of all possible $\frac{n^2-n}{2}$ sequence pairs x_i and x_j:

$$(3.2) \qquad PID = \frac{2}{(n^2-n)} \cdot \sum_{j=1}^{n}\sum_{i=1}^{j} \text{pid}(x_i, x_j)$$

When dealing with alignment analyses it is of great importance to be aware of their potentials and limits. One limitation follows directly from Definition 3.3: since alignments are based on a linear representation of segment correspondences between sequences, they are not capable of displaying crossed and complex matches directly. Instead of a two-dimensional matrix, in which all columns are taken as independent from each other, a nested structure which allows to display relations between different columns has to be used. A further

---

[4] This definition of PID corresponds to PID1 in Raghava and Barton (2006). In biology there are a couple of different ways to measure percentage identity (see the overview in the Raghava and Barton 2006). They may – depending on the sequences being compared – yield quite different results . The PID measure applied in this study was chosen because of its simplicity compared to the other ones reported by Raghava and Barton.

3.2 Sequence Comparison

limitation follows from the fact that alignments mainly serve as an illustration of the correspondence perspective of sequence comparison (see Section 3.2.1). Alignments give an account on proper matches (uniform matches and mismatches) and empty matches (gaps). Therefore, alignment analyses, as mentioned above, are less rich regarding their information content than listings. We can take the information present in alignments in order to draw a scenario in which a source sequence is transformed into a target sequence, yet the decision which sequence is to be taken as the source and which as the target remains arbitrary as long as we lack further information.

Fortunately, in many applications (especially in historical linguistics and evolutionary biology), we do not need the edit perspective (see Section 3.2.1) to model sequence differences. The edit perspective may even be misleading, since in many cases neither of the sequences being compared is the source of the other one, but all sequences are the targets of an unknown source sequence such as the ancestor word in historical linguistics, or the ancestor gene in evolutionary biology. In these cases, any approach that models the differences between two or more sequences in an edit perspective is inappropriate. Approaches, such as alignment analyses, which model sequence differences within a correspondence perspective, however, can be used to *infer* the ancestor sequence.

Using alignments for inference and reconstruction, it is important to be aware of their ahistoric character: Given a divergent match between two segments, alignments do not tell us which of the segments has to be taken as the archaic one that was present in the common ancestor sequence. Given an empty match, alignments do not tell us whether the segment was present in the ancestor sequence and deleted, or whether it was missing and inserted. Therefore, I do not fully agree with the view that 'an alignment of two sequences poses a hypothesis on how the sequences evolved from their closest common ancestor' (Chao and Zhang 2009: 3). An evolutionary scenario which illustrates how sequences evolved from their common ancestor presupposes that we *reconstruct* the common ancestor sequence. The reconstruction, however, is not present in alignment analyses. It has to be inferred in a further step of investigation.[5]

Nevertheless, it would go too far to state that alignments are completely 'ahistorical', giving no clue for evolutionary events. Since alignments display

---

[5] This confusion between the results of a process and the process itself is, as I have pointed out in the beginning of Chapter 2, also present in historical linguistics.

corresponding segments of related sequences, certain conclusions regarding the descent of the sequences from a common ancestor can be drawn directly from the given matching type (Chao and Zhang 2009: 3):

> **Uniform Matches:** If two segments that are matched are identical, one can conclude that they were also present in the ancestor sequence.
> **Divergent Matches:** If two segments that are matched differ, one of them was supposedly present in the ancestor sequence, while the other one was substituted.[6]
> **Empty Matches:** If one segment does not match with any segment, it was either present in the ancestor sequence, or not.

An alignment may thus tell us which segments of related sequences were affected by certain types of change. Therefore, alignments can serve as a basis for reconstructive enterprises.

3.3 Pairwise Alignment Analyses

If one wants to align the two sequences "HEART" and "HERZ" (English *heart* and German *Herz*), a very simple automatic solution would be to start by building all possible alignments between them, such as $\left|\begin{smallmatrix} H & E & A & R & T & - & - & - & - \\ - & - & - & - & - & H & E & R & Z \end{smallmatrix}\right|$, $\left|\begin{smallmatrix} H & E & A & R & T & - \\ H & E & - & R & - & Z \end{smallmatrix}\right|$, $\left|\begin{smallmatrix} H & - & E & - & A & R & T \\ - & H & - & E & - & R & Z \end{smallmatrix}\right|$, etc. In a second step, all alignments could then be checked for their goodness by calculating their *alignment score*. This can easily be done by applying some *scoring scheme* which determines the similarity between the different types of correspondences (see Section 3.2.1) of the segment pairs. The score for all individual segment pairs of an alignment is then simply summed up to retrieve the general score. One such scoring scheme is the so-called Levenshtein distance (also called edit distance), named after V. I. Levenshtein's aforementioned proposal to model differences between sequences in terms of edit operations (Levenshtein 1965).

According to this scoring scheme, all divergent matches (mismatches) and empty matches (gaps) are penalized with 1 and uniform matches are penalized with 0 (see Table 3.2). As a result, differences between sequences are expressed by means of a distance: the more different two sequences are, the higher is the score. For the three alignments of the sequences "HEART" and "HERZ", which were given as examples above, the edit distance would re-

---

[6] Note that this assumption is unrealistic for applications in historical linguistics, since there is no reason to assume that an ancestral sound could not have changed in all descendant languages. This is also reflected in the standard reconstruction practice of most, if not all, etymological dictionaries.

3.3 Pairwise Alignment Analyses

Matching Type	Score	Example
uniform match	0	A / A
divergent match	1	A / B
empty match	1	A / -, - / A

Table 3.2: *The scoring scheme of the edit distance*

spectively be 9, 3, and 6. The *optimal alignment* (i.e. the alignment which minimizes the edit distance) of the two sequences is | H E A R T / H E - R Z |, and the edit distance of this alignment is 2, since we need two edit operations in order to convert one string into the other: the indel | A / - | and the substitution | T / Z |. Although such an approach would certainly yield the best alignment of two sequences in dependence of the scoring scheme being applied, the cost for the computation would be very high, given the large amount of possible ways in which two sequences can be aligned. The number N of possible alignments of two sequences with lengths m and n can be calculated with the formula of Torres et al. (2003):

$$(3.3) \qquad N = \sum_{k=0}^{\min(m,n)} 2^k \cdot \binom{m}{k} \cdot \binom{n}{k}.$$

For the alignment of the strings "HEART" and "HERZ", which are of length 5 and 4, there are therefore 681 possible alignments which might still easily be computed, but for two sequences of length 10 and 10, there are already 8 097 453 possible alignments, which makes it practically impossible to compute optimal alignments with this brute-force approach (cf. Rosenberg 2009b: 4). Fortunately, there is a rather simple algorithm for the computation of optimal alignments which circumvents the problem of computing and checking all alignments in a very elegant way.

3.3.1 The Basic Algorithm for Pairwise Alignment

The basic algorithm for the computation of an optimal alignment of two sequences was independently developed by different scholars from different scientific disciplines. In biological applications this algorithm is usually called

Needleman-Wunsch algorithm (NW), named after S. B. Needleman and C. D. Wunsch who published their algorithm as a solution for the sequence alignment problem in biology in 1970 (Needleman and Wunsch 1970). In general applications of computer science it is also common to refer to the algorithm as Wagner-Fischer algorithm, named after R. A. Wagner and M. J. Fischer's algorithm for the computation of the edit distance between two strings (Wagner and Fischer 1974). Both algorithms and their various extensions belong to the family of *dynamic programming algorithms* (DPA, cf. Eddy 2004, Gusfield 1997: 217f). The main idea of dynamic programming is to find an approach for the solution of complicated problems "that essentially works the problem backwards" (Rosenberg 2009b: 4). Thus, instead of checking all possible alignments between two sequences and looking for the best one in order to find an optimal alignment, an alignment is built up "using previous solutions for optimal alignments of smaller subsequences" (Durbin et al. 1998 [2002]: 19).

For the following description of the basic algorithm, I shall assume, that there are two sequences x and y of lengths m and n, where x_i denotes the i-th element of x, and y_j denotes the j-th element of y. In order to score the alignment, a scoring scheme which penalizes the basic matching types is needed. In this scoring scheme, the *matching* of segments is expressed by means of the *scoring function* score(A, B) which returns -1, if the segments A and B are different, and 1, if they are identical. Empty matches are expressed by means of the gap penalty g which is set to -1 (see Table 3.3). Note, that this scoring scheme is different from the aforementioned edit distance (see 3.2), since it expresses differences between sequences in terms of *similarity*: the more similar two sequences are, the higher the score.

Matching Type	Score	Example
uniform match	1	A / A
divergent match	-1	A / B
empty match	-1	A / -, - / A

Table 3.3: *A simple scoring scheme for the NW algorithm*

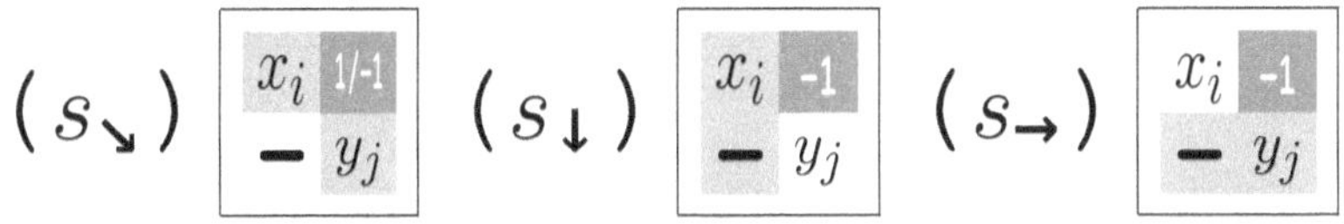

3.3 Pairwise Alignment Analyses

$$(s_\searrow) \quad \begin{array}{|c|} \hline x_i \; \text{1/-1} \\ -\; y_j \\ \hline \end{array} \quad (s_\downarrow) \quad \begin{array}{|c|} \hline x_i \; \text{-1} \\ -\; y_j \\ \hline \end{array} \quad (s_\rightarrow) \quad \begin{array}{|c|} \hline x_i \; \text{-1} \\ -\; y_j \\ \hline \end{array}$$

Figure 3.11: *The three states of each cell of the alignment matrix*

The algorithm which aligns x and y globally consists of four steps: (1) *matrix construction*, (2) *matrix initialization*, (3) *recursion*, and (4) *traceback*. In the first step, an $(m+1)\times(n+1)$ matrix is constructed. In this matrix, all segments of the two sequences are virtually confronted, either with each other, or with an additional gap symbol. Each cell of the matrix therefore covers three states (see also Figure 3.11):

($s_\searrow$) both segments are *matched* (x_i / y_j),
($s_\downarrow$) the first segment is *gapped* (x_i / –), and
($s_\rightarrow$) the second segment is *gapped* (– / y_j).

Since the first row and the first column of the matrix correspond to empty segments of x and y, and the matching of an empty segment with a non-empty segment is equivalent to an empty match between the segments, the three states in the cells in the first row and the first column of the matrix can be reduced to a single state ($s_\downarrow$ for the first row, and $s_\rightarrow$ for the first column).

In the second step the cell in the first row and the first column of the matrix is set to 0, since this cell corresponds to an alignment of two empty sequences. The first row and the first column of the matrix are "filled with increasing multiples of the gap cost" (Rosenberg 2009b: 8), reflecting the fact that an alignment of a sequence of length m with an empty sequence will always yield a score which is m times the gap cost.

In the third step the algorithm recursively calculates the total scores for the alignment of all substrings by filling the matrix from top to bottom and from left to right. In each step of filling the matrix, the current cell ($M[i][j]$) is set to one of the three possible states. Which state is chosen by the algorithm depends on both the individual score of the current cell and the alignment scores which have been already calculated for the closest smaller substrings.

Given the three states of each cell, there are three possible alignments, of which the best-scoring one has to be chosen:

(a) If the alignment ends with a proper match ($s_\searrow$), the total score will be the score of the alignment which ends in the cell to the *upper left* plus the score returned by the scoring function for the matching of the segments represented by the current cell: $M[i-1][j-1] + \text{score}(x_{i-1}, y_{j-1})$.[7]
(b) If the alignment ends with a gap in y ($s_\downarrow$), the total score will be the score of the alignment ending in the cell *directly above* plus the gap penalty: $M[i-1][j] + g$.
(c) If the alignment ends with a gap in x ($s_\rightarrow$), the total score will be the score of the alignment ending in the cell to the *left* plus the gap penalty: $M[i][j-1] + g$.

The score of the best alignment up to this point, which is the maximum value of the three possible scores, is then assigned to the current cell. Once the matrix is filled in this way, the total score of the global alignment of both sequences can be found in cell $M[m][n]$, i.e. the last row and the last column of the matrix.

While the matrix is being filled, it is important to keep track of the individual decisions which have been made. These decisions, which are usually stored in a separate traceback matrix, are then used in the last step of the algorithm. The traceback starts from the cell in the last row and the last column of the matrix and follows the "arrows" until the first cell of the matrix is reached.

Figure 3.12 illustrates the different steps of the algorithm for the sequences "HEART" and "HERZ": In ① the matrix has just been constructed, and the states of all cells are undefined, as the example for the state of the cell in the third row of the third column shows. In ② the matrix has been initialized and the first row and the first column are filled with multiples of the gap cost. ③ shows the recursion step at a certain point of the calculation along with the decision which is being made for the next cell. ④ gives the recursion step after all cells of the matrix have been filled, the last cell containing the alignment score, and ⑤ and ⑥ illustrate how the alignment is retrieved by backtracing from the last to the first cell of the matrix. For an alignment of the sequences "HEART" and "HERZ", the algorithm yields a similarity score of 1. Using the scoring scheme of the edit distance with distance scores instead of similarity scores, the resulting distance score is 2. The PID score (see Equation 3.1 on page 74) which is only defined for alignments and can therefore not be used for the computation of alignments themselves is $\frac{3}{3+1+1} = 0.6$.

---

[7] In these demonstrations, I follow the practice of most programming languages by starting the indices for arrays and strings from 0.

3.3 Pairwise Alignment Analyses

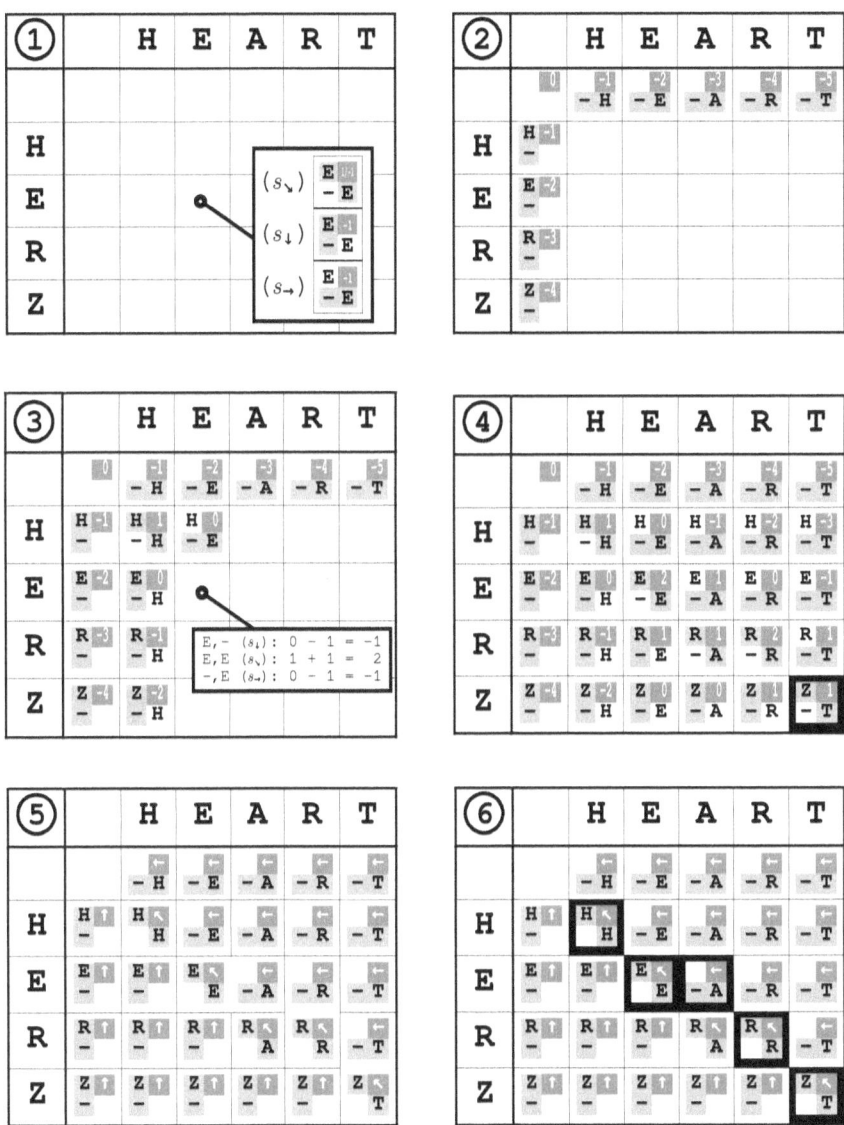

Figure 3.12: *The dynamic programming algorithm. ① shows the construction of the matrix with all cells corresponding to one of the three states. ② illustrates how the first cell and the first column of the matrix are filled. ③ gives an example on how the rest of the cells are successively filled from top to bottom and from left to right. ④ shows the filled matrix after the recursion. ⑤ and ⑥ illustrate the traceback procedure.*

Algorithm 3.1: Global(x, y, g, score)

/* matrix construction */

$M \leftarrow$ matrix(length(x) + 1, length(y) + 1)
$M[0][0] \leftarrow 0$

/* matrix initialization */

for $i \leftarrow 1$ to length(x)
  do $M[i][0] \leftarrow M[i][0] + g$
for $i \leftarrow 1$ to length(y)
  do $M[0][i] \leftarrow M[0][i] + g$

/* main loop */

for $i \leftarrow 1$ to length(x)
  do $\begin{cases} \text{for } j \leftarrow 1 \text{ to length}(y) \\ \quad \text{do } M[i][j] \leftarrow \max \begin{cases} M[i-1][j-1] + \text{score}(x_{i-1}, y_{j-1}) \\ M[i-1][j] + g \\ M[i][j-1] + g \end{cases} \end{cases}$

The essential part of the NW algorithm, i.e. the construction, the initialization, and the filling of the matrix, is given in pseudocode in Algorithm 3.1. The function requires four input parameters: the two sequences x and y, the gap cost gap and the scoring function score(A, B).

3.3.2 Structural Extensions of the Basic Algorithm

The basic algorithm which was presented in the previous section aligns two sequences in a *global* way, i.e. all segments of the sequences are treated equally in the calculation of the alignment, possible prefixes, infixes and postfixes contribute equally to the alignment score. A *global alignment* may, however, not be what one wants to achieve with an alignment analysis. Often, specific sites of two sequences are comparable, while others are not. Therefore, a couple of extensions have been proposed, which deal with the problem of comparability in different ways. I call these extensions of the basic algorithm *structural extensions* as opposed to *substantial extensions*, since they merely deal with the overall structure of the sequences, while the substantial part of the sequences, i.e. the segments, are not addressed by them.

Semi-global Alignment

If we align the sequences "CATFISH" and "FATCAT" globally, applying the scoring scheme given in Table 3.3, the algorithm for global pairwise alignment will yield | $\begin{smallmatrix} C & A & T & F & I & S & H \\ F & A & T & C & A & T & - \end{smallmatrix}$ | and the global score –3, which is equal to an edit distance of 5. This alignment is apparently not a good one, since what both strings have in common is the substring "CAT", yet the similarity between the substrings "CAT" and "FAT" forces the algorithm to accept a mismatch in the first position of the alignment. A good alignment would surely be | $\begin{smallmatrix} - & - & - & C & A & T & F & I & S & H \\ F & A & T & C & A & T & - & - & - & - \end{smallmatrix}$ |, but the similarity score of this alignment would be –4 (seven empty plus 3 uniform matches), and the edit distance 7, which is surely not the optimal score. The most convincing alignment would probably be an alignment which simply ignores the prefix "FAT" and the postfix "FISH", and only aligns the two identical substrings: $\begin{smallmatrix} --- \\ FAT \end{smallmatrix}$ | $\begin{smallmatrix} C & A & T \\ C & A & T \end{smallmatrix}$ | $\begin{smallmatrix} FISH \\ --- \end{smallmatrix}$. In order to find the right alignment in this case, one has to force the algorithm to exclude possible prefixes and postfixes from the alignment. This can be easily done by applying two slight modifications of Algorithm 3.1:

(a) Instead of initializing the matrix with increasing multiples of the gap cost, the gap cost is set to 0 in the first row and the first column of the matrix.
(b) When the main loop reaches the last row or the rightmost column of the matrix, the gap cost is likewise set to 0.[8]

This kind of alignment analysis is usually called *semi-global alignment*, or *alignment with overlap matches* (Durbin et al. 1998 [2002]: 26f), since the globality of the alignment is maintained inside the alignment, while the borders are set to a local mode. These modifications are displayed in Algorithm 3.2. Figure 3.13 contrasts the two resulting alignment matrices for global and semi-global alignment analyses applied to the strings "FATCAT" and "CATFISH".

Local Alignment

The semi-global alignment procedure maintains globality inside the sequences and ignores only their borders. This may yield some unwanted results. For example, the global alignment of the sequences "FATCAT" and "REDCAT",

---

[8] This procedure is not applied in the standard descriptions of the algorithm (cf. Durbin et al. 1998 [2002]: 26f, Böckenbauer and Bongartz 2003: 87-91), where, instead of setting the gap cost to 0, the traceback starts from the maximum value in the right and the bottom border of the matrix.

applying the scoring scheme from Table 3.3, will yield | $^{F\ A\ T\ C\ A\ T}_{R\ E\ D\ C\ A\ T}$ | as alignment with a score of 0 and an edit distance of 3. The semi-global alignment, however, will yield the alignment $^{----}_{REDC}$ | $^{F\ A\ T}_{-\ A\ T}$ | $^{CAT}_{---}$ with a score of 1 and an edit distance of 1 for the aligned sites. This seemingly strange behaviour results from the fact that the algorithm for semi-global alignment can only strip off prefixes and suffixes from the calculation, if the other sequence doesn't contain them, hence it cannot calculate an alignment like $^{FAT}_{RED}$ | $^{C\ A\ T}_{C\ A\ T}$ | which would surely be one of the best ways to align both strings. In order to get an alignment in which prefixes may be completely ignored, the algorithm has to be modified in such a way that only the most similar sites of two sequences are aligned, while the rest is simply ignored. This kind of alignment analysis is called *local alignment* (Durbin et al. 1998 [2002]: 22-24).

The algorithm which computes local alignments of two sequences is traditionally called the Smith-Waterman algorithm (SW), named after T. F. Smith and M. S. Waterman, who published the algorithm in a paper from 1981 (Smith and Waterman 1981). The algorithm for local alignment is essentially based on three modifications of the Needleman-Wunsch algorithm:

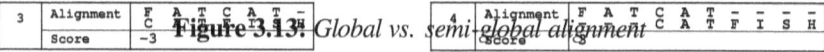

Figure 3.13: *Global vs. semi-global alignment*

3.3 Pairwise Alignment Analyses

Algorithm 3.2: SemiGlobal(x, y, g, score)

/* matrix construction (see Algorithm 3.1) */
...

/* matrix initialization */
for $i \leftarrow 1$ to length(x)
  do $M[i][0] \leftarrow 0$
for $i \leftarrow 1$ to length(y)
  do $M[0][i] \leftarrow 0$

/* main loop */
for $i \leftarrow 1$ to length(x)
  do $\begin{cases} \text{for } j \leftarrow 1 \text{ to length}(y) \\ \quad \text{do } M[i][j] \leftarrow \max \begin{cases} M[i-1][j-1] + \text{score}(x_{i-1}, y_{j-1}) \\ \text{if } j = \text{length}(y) \\ \quad \text{then } M[i-1][j] \\ \quad \text{else } M[i-1][j] + g \\ \text{if } i = \text{length}(x) \\ \quad \text{then } M[i][j-1] \\ \quad \text{else } M[i][j-1] + g \end{cases} \end{cases}$

(a) As in the algorithm for semi-global alignment, the first row and the first column of the matrix are initialized with 0, i.e. the gap cost is set to 0 for gaps introduced before the beginning of a sequence.
(b) In addition to the three scores, of which the maximum is chosen during the main loop, a zero-score is introduced.
(c) The traceback starts at the maximum value of the matrix and ends when it reaches a cell with the value 0.

Introducing a fourth possibility for the individual score of each cell prevents that the scores in the matrix can add up to negative values and "corresponds to starting a new alignment" (Durbin et al. 1998 [2002]: 23), whenever the algorithm reaches a site of low similarity. The modification of the traceback function results in an alignment in which only parts of the sequences are aligned, while the rest of them is left unaligned. Algorithm 3.3 shows, how the alignment matrix is computed according to the Smith-Waterman algorithm. Figure 3.14 contrasts the alignment matrices of semi-global and local alignments of the strings "FATCAT" and "REDCAT".

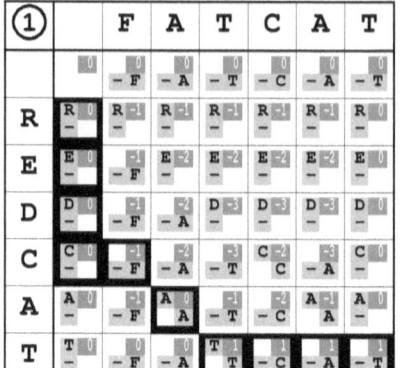

Figure 3.14: *Semiglobal vs. local alignment.*

Algorithm 3.3: Local(x, y, g, score)

/* matrix construction and initialization (see Algorithm 3.2) */

...

/* main loop */

for $i \leftarrow 1$ to length(x)

do { for $j \leftarrow 1$ to length(y)

do $M[i][j] \leftarrow \max \begin{cases} M[i-1][j-1] + \text{score}(x_{i-1}, y_{j-1}) \\ M[i-1][j] + g \\ M[i][j-1] + g \\ 0 \end{cases}$

Diagonal Alignment (DIALIGN)

A local alignment of two sequences x and y in terms of the Smith-Waterman algorithm is defined as "the best alignment between *subsequences* of x and y" (Durbin et al. 1998 [2002]: 22). Thus, given the two sequences "GREEN CATFISH HUNTER" and "A FAT CAT HUNTER", the Smith-Waterman algorithm, given the scoring scheme from Table 3.3, will only extract the best scoring subsequence, which is "HUNTER". Global alignment, on the other hand, aligns the substrings "GREEN" and "A FAT", and semi-global align-

3.3 Pairwise Alignment Analyses

ment matches the substrings "CAT" and "FAT". While none of these alignments is specifically "bad", it would be desirable to have a method which works globally, but nevertheless aligns only the most similar subsequences of two sequences, leaving the rest of the sequences unaligned.

Such a method is available with the DIALIGN algorithm (Morgenstern et al. 1996). While the scoring function of all previously discussed extensions of the Needleman-Wunsch algorithm is solely based on segment-to-segment comparison, DIALIGN employs an extended scoring function which searches for the best *diagonal* in each recursion step. A diagonal is an ungapped alignment of two subsequences, i.e. the alignment of two *substrings* of two sequences (see Definition 3.2). It describes a *diagonal* path through the alignment matrix.[9] Thus, instead of comparing only the segments in a given cell, the DIALIGN scoring function evaluates all possible diagonals up to that cell at each recursion step and selects the best one, i.e. the one which maximizes the overall score of the alignment.

In order to score diagonals, DIALIGN employs a specific scoring function (Morgenstern et al. 1998), yet, since diagonals are ungapped alignments, diagonal scores can likewise be calculated by summing up all scores for proper matches retrieved by the scoring scheme given in Table 3.3. Since only diagonals contribute to the overall alignment score, gap penalties are set to 0. Algorithm 3.4 shows how the basic algorithm has to be extended in order to conduct diagonal alignment analyses. Table 3.4 contrasts the output of

Mode	Alignment
global	G R E E N C A T F I S H H U N T E R A F A T C A T - - - - H U N T E R
semi-global	G R E E N - C A T F I S H H U N T E R - - - - - A F A T C A T H U N T E R
local	GREEN CATFISH ‖ H U N T E R A FAT CAT ‖ H U N T E R
diagonal	- - - - - G R E E N C A T F I S H H U N T E R A F A T - - - - - C A T - - - - H U N T E R

Table 3.4: *Comparison of the results of different alignment modes*

---

[9] Note that the terminology used here slightly differs from the terminology applied in Morgenstern et al. (1996): Morgenstern et al. use the term *segment* in order to refer to a *subsequence*. *Segments* in the sense used in this work are the smallest units of sequences, as described in Definition 3.1.

the different alignment modes for the alignment of the sequences "GREEN CATFISH HUNTER" and "A FAT CAT HUNTER".

Algorithm 3.4: Diagonal(x, y, score)

/* matrix construction and initialization (see Algorithm 3.2) */

...

/* main loop */

for $i \leftarrow 1$ **to** length(x)

$\quad$ **do** $\Bigg\{$ **for** $j \leftarrow 1$ **to** length(y)

$\qquad\qquad$ **do** $\Bigg\{$ /* loop over all diagonals */

$\qquad\qquad\qquad$ $s_{max} = 0$ /* maximum score */

$\qquad\qquad\qquad$ **for** $k \leftarrow 0$ **to** $\min(i, j)$

$\qquad\qquad\qquad\quad$ **do** $\begin{cases} s_{new} \leftarrow M[i-k-1][j-k-1] \text{ /* current score */} \\ \textbf{for } l \leftarrow k \textbf{ to } 0 \\ \quad \textbf{do } \{ s_{new} \leftarrow s_{new} + \text{score}(x_{i-l}, y_{j-l}) \\ \textbf{if } s_{new} > s_{max} \\ \quad \textbf{then } s_{max} \leftarrow s_{new} \end{cases}$

$\qquad\qquad\qquad$ /* determine the maximum for the current cell */

$\qquad\qquad\qquad$ $M[i][j] \leftarrow \max \begin{cases} s_{max} \\ M[i-1][j] \\ M[i][j-1] \end{cases}$

Secondary Alignment

So far, we have looked at sequences with regard to their primary structure only. The term *primary structure* refers to the *order of segments*. Segments are hereby understood in the sense of Definition 3.1, i.e. segments are the smallest units of a sequence which directly correspond to the characters of the alphabet from which the sequence is drawn. Apart from the primary structure, sequences can, however, also have a *secondary structure*, i.e. apart from segmentizing them into their primary units, they can further be segmentized into larger units of substrings consisting of one or more primary segments. In the following, these units shall be called *secondary segments* (as opposed to *segments* or *primary segments*). The criteria for the secondary segmentation of sequences may vary, depending on the objects one is dealing with, or the specific goal of the secondary segmentation. Thus, given the sequence "ABCEFGIJK", one may segmentize it into the three substrings "ABC", "EFG", and "IJK", since each of these substrings is also a substring of the se-

3.3 Pairwise Alignment Analyses

quence "ABCDEFGHIJK". The sequence "THECATFISHHUNTER" can be segmentized into three substrings ("THE", "CATFISH", and "HUNTER"), since each of them corresponds to a word of the English language. Given the sequence "KARAOKE", a possible meaningful secondary segmentation might be "KA", "RA", "O", "KE", since this reflects the different syllables of the word *karaoke*.

All alignment modes discussed so far compare sequences only with respect to their primary structure. Thus, given the sequences "THE CATFISH HUNTS" and "THE CAT FISHES", they will all yield an alignment in which the substring "CATFISH" of the first sequence is matched with the substring "CAT FISH" of the second sequence, yielding the partial alignment $| \begin{smallmatrix} C & A & T & - & F & I & S & H \\ C & A & T & & F & I & S & H \end{smallmatrix} |$ (see Table 3.5). While none of these alignments is particularly "bad", they all have the shortcoming that they only reflect the similarities of the primary sequence structure (the order of the letters) while disregarding the secondary sequence structure (the order of the words). Thus, the word "CATFISH" is aligned with the two words "CAT" and "FISHES". In contrast to these *primary alignments*, a *secondary alignment* displays the similarities of sequences with regard to both their primary and their secondary structure, aligning letters which belong to the same word in one sequence only with those letters in the other sequence which also belong to a single word (see the last row in Table 3.5). I shall call the problem of finding an alignment which reflects both the primary and the secondary structure of sequences the secondary alignment problem:

> **Secondary Alignment Problem:** Given two sequences s and t of lengths m and n, the primary structures $s_0, ..., s_m$ and $t_0, ..., t_n$, and the secondary structures $s_{0 \to i}, ..., s_{j \to m}$ and $t_{0 \to k}, ..., t_{l \to n}$, find an alignment of maximal global score in which segments belonging to the same secondary segment in s only correspond to segments belonging to the same secondary segment in t, and vice versa.

The primary alignment modes (global, semi-global, local, and diagonal alignment) can be made sensitive for secondary sequence structures by means of some slight modifications of the main loop of the basic algorithm. The main idea behind this secondary alignment algorithm that I want to propose in the following is to modify the scores for gaps and proper matches of the boundary segments of secondary segments in such a way that the algorithm is forced to go a path through the matrix in which primary segments can only be aligned within the boundaries of secondary segments.

Mode	Alignment																
global	T H E	C A T	-	F	I	S	H		H	U	N	T	S				
	T H E	C A T		F	I	S	H	-	E	-	-	-	S				
semiglobal	T H E	C A T	-	F	I	S	H	-	-	H	U	N	T	S			
	T H E	C A T		F	I	S	H	E	S								
local	T H E	C A T	-	F	I	S	H	HUNTS									
	T H E	C A T		F	I	S	H	ES									
diagonal	T H E	C A T	-	F	I	S	H	-	H	U	N	T	S				
	T H E	C A T		F	I	S	H	E	-	-	-	-	-	S			
secondary	T H E	C A T F I S H						H	U	N	T	-	S				
	T H E	C A T	-	-	-	-		F	I	S	H	E	S				

Table 3.5: *Primary vs. secondary alignment*

For the sake of simplicity, I shall assume in the following, that the secondary sequence structure of sequences is marked by some boundary marker r, which is introduced as a separator between all secondary segments. When dealing with sentences, this boundary marker will usually be a space character, yet it can be any character which does not occur as a segment of secondary segments in a given sequence. Given the sequences "AABCDE.E" and "A.BC.DE", where "." is the boundary character, a primary global alignment analysis based on the scoring scheme of Table 3.3 will yield the alignment $|\begin{smallmatrix} A & A & B & C & - & D & E & . & E \\ A & . & B & C & . & D & E & - & - \end{smallmatrix}|$. The corresponding secondary alignment would be $|\begin{smallmatrix} - & - & A & A & B & C & D & E & . & - & E \\ A & . & - & - & B & C & - & - & . & D & E \end{smallmatrix}|$. As becomes obvious from the comparison of the primary with the secondary alignment, two restrictions are needed in order to force the Needleman-Wunsch algorithm to carry out a secondary alignment analysis. These restrictions are:

(a) the matching of the boundary marker with all other segments, and
(b) the matching of the boundary marker with a gap which is introduced *inside* a secondary segment.

In the secondary alignment algorithm, these restrictions can be simply implemented by setting the relevant scores to $-\infty$. In order to check whether the first condition holds for a certain cell in the matrix, the scoring function can be modified in such a way, that it yields 0 for the matching of boundary markers with themselves, and $-\infty$ for the matching of the boundary marker with any other character. The check for the second condition can be implemented with

3.3 Pairwise Alignment Analyses

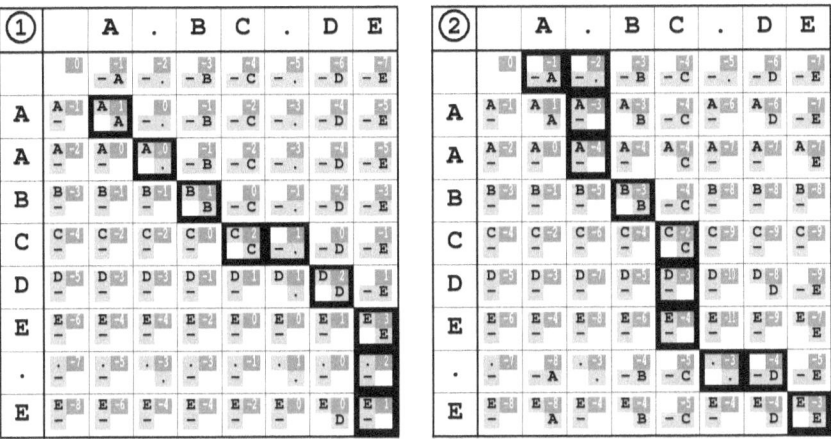

Figure 3.15: *Primary vs. secondary alignment*

help of an *if*-statement, as illustrated in Algorithm 3.5. Note that this algorithm yields results identical to the standard NW algorithm if the boundary marker *r* does not occur in the input sequences. Figure 3.15 shows the different alignment matrices of primary and secondary alignment analyses of the sequences "AABCDE.E" and "A.BC.DE".

3.3.3 Substantial Extensions of the Basic Algorithm

The extensions of the basic algorithm that were discussed in the previous section almost exclusively deal with the way sequences are compared with respect to their overall structure. These structural extensions may drastically change the results of automatic alignment analyses. Another way to modify the basic algorithm is to change the way the segments are being compared. In the basic algorithm segment-comparison is carried out with help of two functions which constitute the scoring scheme of pairwise alignment analyses: the *scoring function*, which returns scores for the proper matching of segments, and the *gap function*, which returns scores for the gapping of segments. Modifying these two functions may also have a great impact on the results of alignment analyses.

Algorithm 3.5: Secondary(x, y, g, r, score)

/* matrix construction and initialization (see Algorithm 3.1) */
...

/* main loop */
for $i \leftarrow 1$ to length(x)
do $\begin{cases} \text{for } j \leftarrow 1 \text{ to length}(y) \\ \text{do } \begin{cases} M[i][j] \leftarrow \max \begin{cases} M[i-1][j-1] + \text{score}(x_{i-1}, y_{j-1}) \\ \text{/* check for restriction 2 */} \\ \text{if } x_{i-1} = r \text{ and } y_{j-1} \neq r \text{ and } j \neq \text{length}(y) \\ \text{then } -\infty \\ \text{else } M[i-1][j] + g \\ \text{if } y_{j-1} = r \text{ and } x_{i-1} \neq r \text{ and } i \neq \text{length}(x) \\ \text{then } -\infty \\ \text{else } M[i][j-1] + g \end{cases} \end{cases} \end{cases}$

The Scoring Function

In the illustrations of pairwise alignment analyses presented so far, a very simple scoring scheme was used (see Table 3.3), which only distinguishes between uniform and divergent matches (mismatches). It is, however, easy to think of many situations in which it would be useful to have an extended scoring scheme which makes more fine-graded distinctions when matching segments. Consider, e.g., the alignment of the sequences "catwalk" and "CATWALK". According to the simple scoring scheme, these sequences are maximally unrelated with a score of −6, although they only differ regarding the case of their characters. Similarly, an alignment analysis of the sequences "catFAT" and "CATfat" will result in an unsatisfying alignment, such as $\left| \begin{smallmatrix} c & a & t & F & A & T & - & - & - \\ - & - & - & C & A & T & f & a & t \end{smallmatrix} \right|$. An extended scoring function may cope with the problem of case by assigning specific costs to divergent matches which only differ in case. Such a scoring function may be expressed in an extended scoring scheme like the one shown in Table 3.6, where uniform matches are scored with 1, uniform matches with case difference with 0.5, and divergent and empty matches with −1. Using this scoring scheme, both alignments of "catwalk"

3.3 Pairwise Alignment Analyses

Matching Type	Score	Example
uniform match	1	A / A
uniform match (case difference)	0.5	A / a
divergent match	−1	A / B
empty match	−1	A / -, - / A

Table 3.6: *An extended, case-sensitive scoring scheme for the NW algorithm.*

with "CATWALK" and "catfat" with "CATfat" will yield an alignment score of 3.

The extended scoring function in the scoring scheme in Table 3.6 is only one example for the various different ways in which the scoring of segments can be modified. In order to design an efficient spell-checker, for example, one might consider to design a scoring function which yields individual scores for the matching of all characters in the alphabet. Based on the assumption that a miss-spelled word often contains wrong characters that are topologically close to the right characters on the computer keyboard, one might use this

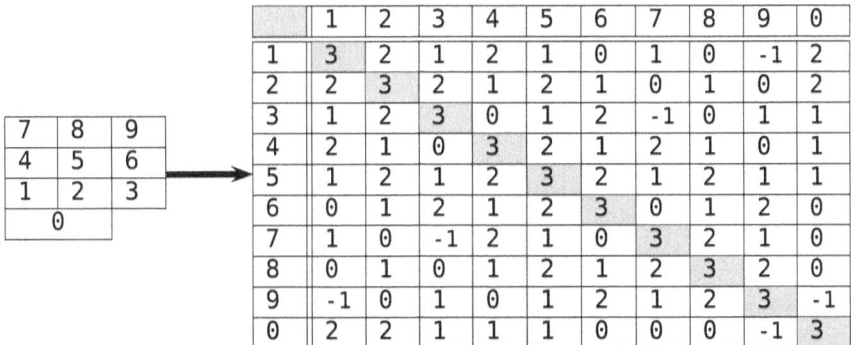

Figure 3.16: *Scoring matrix for a numerical keybord. The scores are derived in such a way that they reflect distances between the keys as similarity scores. The higher a score, the closer the two keys are located to each other.*

information in order to derive a weighted scheme in which, for example, the miss-spelled word "gand" is judged to be closer to the word "hand" than the alternative word "sand", since "h" can be found next to "g" on the keyboard, making it a more probable source character than "s".

In order to express such an extended scoring function which assigns individual matching scores for all characters in the alphabet, it is common to make use of a *scoring matrix* which contain scores for all possible character matchings. As an example, Figure 3.16 illustrates how a scoring matrix may be designed for a numerical keyboard. Defining the identity scores of all numerical keys, i.e. the matching of a character with itself, as 3, the scores for all $(N^2 - N)/2 = 45$ mismatches are derived from the identity scores by subtracting the distance between each pair of keys from the identity score. Distances between keys are defined as the length of the shortest path in a network where all keys are connected with the keys to the right and left, and to the top and bottom, but no diagonal edges are allowed. The distance between $\boxed{1}$ and $\boxed{2}$, for example, is 1, and the resulting similarity is $3 - 1 = 2$. Accordingly, the distance between $\boxed{1}$ and $\boxed{9}$ is 4 (since getting from $\boxed{1}$ to $\boxed{9}$ requires to follow a path which crosses three other keys, such as, e.g. $\boxed{2}$ - $\boxed{3}$ - $\boxed{6}$), and the similarity score is $3 - 4 = -1$. Using this scoring function, numeric strings can be compared for topological similarities on a numerical keyboard. Thus, a traditional alignment of the sequences "1234" and "6789" yields the alignment $|\begin{smallmatrix}1&2&3&4\\6&7&8&9\end{smallmatrix}|$ and the score -4. An analysis with the extended scoring function, however, yields the alignment $|\begin{smallmatrix}-&1&2&3&4\\6&7&8&9&-\end{smallmatrix}|$ with the score 1. This alignment correctly matches the most similar substrings of the sequences ("123" and "789"), both reflecting a continuous movement from the left to the right of the keyboard. Figure 3.17 shows the different alignment matrices resulting from a traditional alignment analysis and an alignment analysis with an extended scoring function.

While the example with the numerical keyboard will hardly be used in real-world applications, the use of scoring matrices is a very common strategy in pairwise alignment analyses in evolutionary biology, where they are commonly used to improve the analyses when searching for homologous sequences. Given the protein alphabet consisting of 20 amino acids, a popular way to derive scoring matrices for protein alignment is to calculate the log-odds scores from empirical data of known homologous sequences. A log-odds score is "the logarithm of the ratio of the likelihoods of [...] two hypotheses" (Eddy 2004: 1035). In the case of protein alignment the two hypotheses being

3.3 Pairwise Alignment Analyses

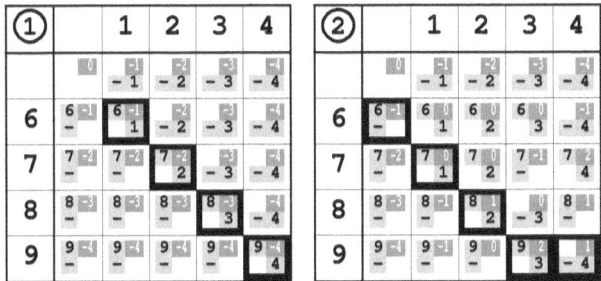

Figure 3.17: *Traditional alignment vs. alignment with extended scoring function.*

compared are "whether two sequences are homologous (evolutionary related) or not" (ibid.). Given a set of aligned, homologous protein sequences, the log-odds score $s(a,b)$ for each amino acid pair a and b can be calculated with the formula

$$(3.4) \qquad s(a,b) = \frac{1}{\lambda} \log \frac{p_{ab}}{q_a q_b},$$

where p_{ab} is the *attested frequency*, i.e. "the probability that we expect to observe residues a and b aligned in homologous sequence alignments" (ibid.), q_a and q_b are background frequencies, i.e. the "probabilities that we expect to observe amino acids a and b on average in any protein sequence" (ibid.), and λ serves as a scaling factor. Multiplying q_a and q_b yields the probability of the null hypothesis, i.e. the *expected frequency* of amino acid matches in evolutionary unrelated sequences. The resulting scores range from negative values for segment matchings that are very unlikely to occur, and positive scores for segment matchings that are very likely to occur in the alignments of homologous sequences. These matrices which are derived from aligned blocks of homologous sequences (Henikoff and Henikoff 1991) are called BLOSUM (blocks substitution matrix) matrices in evolutionary biology (Henikoff and Henikoff 1992). Based on specific clustering procedures by which the block databases are selected (ibid.), BLOSUM matrices are defined for different degrees of presumed evolutionary distances.

Extending scoring functions by designing specific scoring matrices may significantly improve alignment analyses. The drawback of scoring matrices lies in the loss in transparency when comparing them to simple, identity-based scoring schemes: Segment similarity can no longer be stated as a simple yes-no decision but is instead determined by a complex network of transition probabilities that quickly exceeds our intuitive capacities.

The Gap Function

In the previous illustrations of the Needleman-Wunsch algorithm the insertion of gaps was managed by defining a specific *gap penalty* for the insertion and the deletion of segments. Such a gap penalty is also called a *linear* gap penalty, since "the cost of introducing a new gap in a sequence is the same as the cost of extending an existing gap" (McGuffin 2009: 36). Instead of describing the gap penalty as a variable with a fixed value, as it was done in the previous sections, it can be useful to define it as a function. For the insertion of a gap of length l in an alignment, a linear gap function gap(l) returns the score

$$(3.5) \qquad \mathrm{gap}(l) = -l \cdot g,$$

where g is the general gap cost defined by the scoring scheme (Durbin et al. 1998 [2002]: 16f). Such a function treats all gaps equally, no matter where they were introduced. As a result, whether three gaps occur separately in different parts in a sequence, or whether one gap of length 3 is introduced at once, won't make a difference in a linear gap function.

In contrast to linear gap penalties, *affine gap penalties* "[differentiate] between the opening of a gap and extension of a gap" (McGuffin 2009: 36). Usually, the cost for the opening of a gap, the *gap opening penalty* (GOP), is given a higher cost than the extension of a gap, the *gap extension penalty*

Matching Type	Score	Example
uniform match	2	A / A
divergent match	−2	A / B
empty match (opening)	−2	A / -, - / A
empty match (extended)	−1	AB / --, -- / AB

Table 3.7: *Scoring scheme with affine gap penalties*

3.3 Pairwise Alignment Analyses

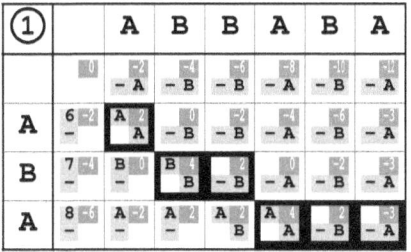
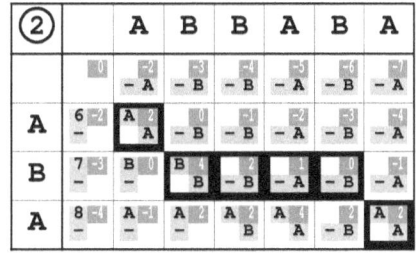

Figure 3.18: *Linear vs. affine gap penalties*

(GEP). This guarantees that "long insertions and deletions [are] penalised less than they would be by the linear gap cost" (Durbin et al. 1998 [2002]: 16). Given a gap of length l, an affine gap function $\text{gap}(l)$ returns the score

$$\text{gap}(l) = -g - (l-1) \cdot e, \tag{3.6}$$

where g is the gap opening penalty, and e is the gap extension penalty. As an example for the differences between alignment analyses with linear gap penalties and alignment analyses with affine gap penalties, compare the different outputs for the alignment of the sequences "ABBABA" and "ABA". A traditional analysis may yield the alignment $\left|\begin{smallmatrix}A&B&B&A&B&A\\A&B&-&A&-&-\end{smallmatrix}\right|$ as one optimal alignment among others. An analysis with a scoring scheme containing affine gap penalties (such as the one given in Table 3.7), however, yields only the alignments $\left|\begin{smallmatrix}A&B&B&A&B&A\\A&B&-&-&-&A\end{smallmatrix}\right|$ and $\left|\begin{smallmatrix}A&B&B&A&B&A\\A&-&-&-&B&A\end{smallmatrix}\right|$ since these are the only alignments, that not only optimize the alignment score, but also minimize the number of consecutively gapped regions.

Algorithm 3.6 shows how the traditional Needleman-Wunsch algorithm can be modified to be sensitive to affine gap penalties. In contrast to the modifications of the basic algorithm introduced earlier, the modification for affine gap penalties makes use of the traceback matrix T which stores the individual decisions made for each cell. The traceback is filled with the three integers 0, 1, and 2, serving as pointers. 0 points to the cell to the upper left, 1 points to the cell above, and 2 points to the cell to the left. During the main loop, the introduction of gaps is evaluated by checking the pointer in the traceback. If it indicates, that a gap has been already opened, the GEP is used instead of the

GOP, otherwise, the GOP is chosen.[10] Figure 3.18 shows the resulting alignment matrices for the alignment of the sequences "ABBABA" and "ABA" using linear and affine gap penalties.

Algorithm 3.6: AffineGaps(x, y, g, e, score)

/* matrix construction */

$M \leftarrow$ matrix(length(x) + 1, length(y) + 1)
$M[0][0] \leftarrow 0; M[1][0] \leftarrow g; M[0][1] \leftarrow g$

/* traceback construction */

$T \leftarrow$ traceback(length(x) + 1, length(y) + 1)
$T[0][0] \leftarrow 0; T[1][0] \leftarrow 2; T[0][1] \leftarrow 1$

/* matrix and traceback initialization */

for $i \leftarrow 2$ **to** length(x)
  do $\begin{cases} M[i][0] \leftarrow M[i-1][0] + e \\ T[i][0] \leftarrow 1 \end{cases}$
for $i \leftarrow 2$ **to** length(y)
  do $\begin{cases} M[0][i] \leftarrow M[0][i-1] + e \\ T[0][i] \leftarrow 2 \end{cases}$

/* main loop */

for $i \leftarrow 1$ **to** length(x)
  do $\begin{cases} \textbf{for } j \leftarrow 1 \textbf{ to length}(y) \\ \quad \textbf{do } M[i][j] \leftarrow \max \begin{cases} M[i-1][j-1] + \text{score}(x_{i-1}, y_{j-1}) \\ \textbf{if } T[i-1][j] = 1 \\ \quad \textbf{then } M[i-1][j] + e \\ \quad \textbf{else } M[i-1][j] + e \\ \textbf{if } T[i][j-1] = 2 \\ \quad \textbf{then } M[i][j-1] + e \\ \quad \textbf{else } M[i][j-1] + e \end{cases} \\ \text{/* fill the traceback */} \\ \textbf{if } M[i-1][j-1] + \text{score}(x_{i-1}, y_{j-1}) = M[i][j] \\ \quad \textbf{then } T[i][j] \leftarrow 0 \\ \textbf{else if } M[i-1][j] + g = M[i][j] \textbf{ or } M[i-1][j] + e = M[i][j] \\ \quad \textbf{then } T[i-1][j] \leftarrow 1 \\ \textbf{else } T[i][j-1] \leftarrow 2 \end{cases}$

Using affine gap penalties is not the only way to enhance the gap function of alignment analyses. Given the relevant information regarding the probability of gaps to occur in specific positions of a sequence, one may define a gap function gap(x_i) that returns individual gap penalties for each position i of an

---

[10] This solution differs from the one by Gotoh (1982) which is traditionally quoted. To my knowledge, the solution presented here works equally well compared with the one by Gotoh. At the same time, it has the advantage of being easier to implement, involving less matrices.

input sequence x. When defining these *position-specific* gap penalties as gap opening penalties, both approaches can be easily combined.

3.3.4 Summary on Pairwise Alignment Analyses

In this section, the basic algorithms for the computation of pairwise alignment analyses were introduced. Based on a detailed discussion of the basic algorithm for global alignment, two major ways to modify this algorithm were discussed: Structural extensions (semi-global, local, diagonal, and secondary alignment) modify the way the overall comparison of two sequences is handled by the algorithm. Substantial extensions (extended scoring and gap functions), on the other hand, modify the proper matching and gapping of segments in a first instance. Both extensions are often applied simultaneously in current alignment algorithms in evolutionary biology.

3.4 Multiple Alignment Analyses

In Section 3.2.2, it has been pointed out that one major advantage of alignments compared to traces and listings lies in their straightforwardness and simplicity. This is especially important when dealing with differences between more than two sequences. While the differences between the four strings "VOLDEMORT", "WALDEMAR", "VLADIMIR", and "VOLODYMYR" can be easily rendered in a multiple alignment matrix (Figure 3.19b), a trace would result in a network of 33 nodes and 46 edges which is hard to visualize, even when using three dimensions (Figure 3.19a). A listing, on the other hand, would require that the source sequence from which the sequences are derived is known, since listings explicitly model the edit perspective (see Section 3.2.1). If an explicit source-target scenario is – as in many cases – not given and not required, listings are simply too "rich" to deal with multiple sequence comparison.

The simplicity and straightforwardness of alignments compared to other models of sequence comparison has, however, an unwanted side effect: Being visually appealing, simple, and transparent, it is often not entirely clear how they should be interpreted. In the following description of some basic algorithmic aspects of multiple sequence alignment, this question will be ignored. I will deal with it in greater detail when discussing the application of automatic alignment analyses in historical linguistics.

3.4.1 Progressive Alignment

While an optimal solution for the pairwise alignment problem can relatively easy be achieved with the help of dynamic programming, the problem of finding an optimal multiple alignment, i.e. an alignment that maximizes the pairwise alignment scores between all sequences, is NP complete (Wang and Jiang 1994). Extending the traditional Needleman-Wunsch algorithm to three and more sequences will yield computation times that grow exponentially with the number of sequences being analyzed (Bilu et al. 2006). It is therefore common to employ certain heuristics which can only guarantee to find a near-optimal solution for multiple sequence alignments. The most popular algorithms applied in multiple sequence analyses are the so-called *progressive alignment techniques* (Feng and Doolittle 1987, Higgins and Sharp 1988, Hogeweg and Hesper 1984, Taylor 1987, Thompson et al. 1994). These approaches consist of two major stages: In the first stage, a *guide tree* is constructed to represent the relations between all sequences. In the second stage, this guide tree is used to align all sequences successively with each other, moving from its branches down to its root.

Guide Tree Construction

In order to construct the guide tree, most progressive strategies start by computing pairwise alignments of all possible sequence pairs. The pairwise distances that can be extracted from these alignments are stored in a distance matrix, and a traditional hierarchical cluster algorithm, such as UPGMA (Sokal

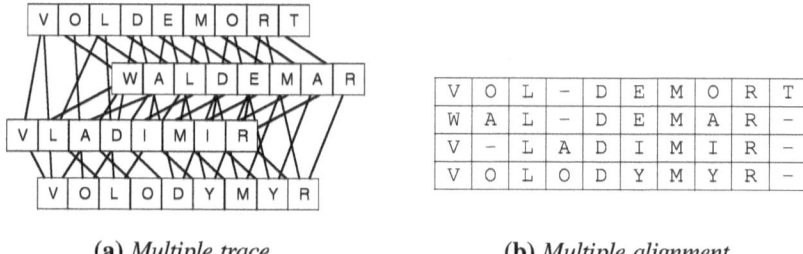

(a) *Multiple trace* (b) *Multiple alignment*

Figure 3.19: *Traces vs. alignments of multiple sequences*

3.4 Multiple Alignment Analyses

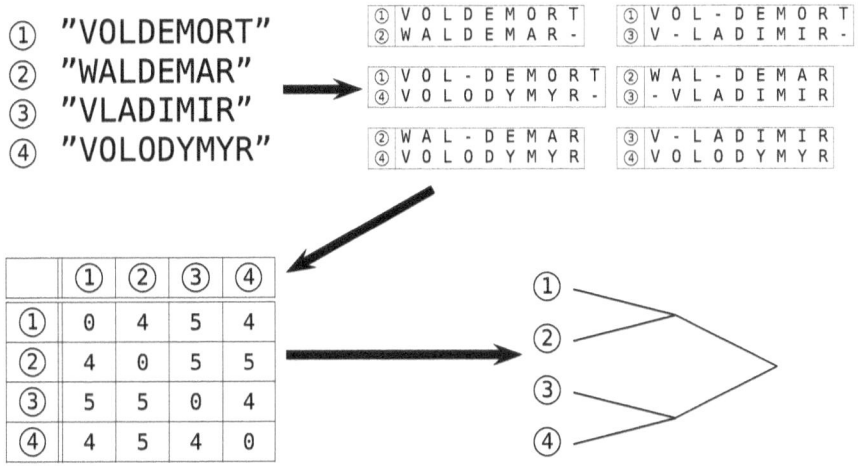

Figure 3.20: *Constructing the guide tree from pairwise distances*

and Michener 1958) or Neighbor-Joining (Saitou and Nei 1987), is used to calculate a tree from the distance matrix. As an example, consider the illustration in Figure 3.20: First, pairwise alignment analyses are carried out for all $(4^2 - 4)/2 = 6$ possible combinations of the sequences "VOLDEMORT", "WALDEMAR", "VLADIMIR", and "VOLODYMYR". Afterwards, the resulting edit distances are stored in a matrix, and the guide tree is constructed from the matrix with help of the UPGMA cluster algorithm.

Both the UPGMA algorithm and the Neighbor-Joining algorithm produce evolutionary trees from distance data and their original purpose is to explain observed distances between a set of taxonomic units (species, genomes) as an evolutionary process of split and divergence. The amount of divergence is displayed by the branch lengths of the evolutionary tree. Conceptually, both algorithms are quite different. UPGMA assumes that the distances are *ultrametric*. This means that evolutionary change should be *constant* along all branches of the tree. Divergence (as represented by the branch lengths) receives a direct *temporal* interpretation: UPGMA trees have a definite root, and all leaves (terminal nodes) have the same distance to it (Peer 2009: 144). If the observed distances between the taxonomic units can be interpreted in such a way, UPGMA will produce a tree which directly reflects the distance

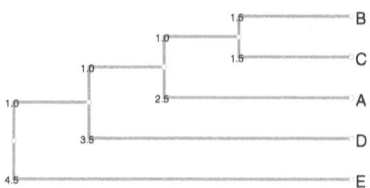

(a) *ultrametric distances and corresponding rooted tree*

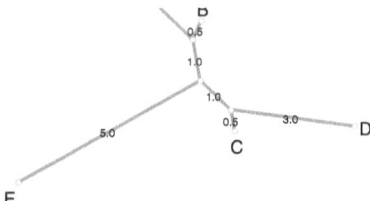

(b) *additive distances and corresponding unrooted tree*

Figure 3.21: *Ultrametric and additive distances. The distances in (a) are ultrametric and can be represented as a rooted tree in which the distance of all leaves to the root is the same. The distances in (b) are not ultrametric, but additive. They can be represented with help of an unrooted tree.*

matrix: The sum of the branch lengths connecting any two taxa will be the same as their pairwise distance in the distance matrix. Neighbor-Joining, on the other hand, allows for *varying divergence rates*. A direct temporal interpretation of the results is therefore not possible. Branch lengths only indicate the degree to which a node has diverged from its ancestral node. Neighbor-Joining assumes that the observed pairwise distances between the taxonomic units are *additive*. In simple terms, a distance matrix is additive, if there is an *unrooted tree* which directly reflects the pairwise distances between all taxonomic units (Peer 2009: 148). The differences between *ultrametricity* and *additivity* are illustrated in Figure 3.21 where an ultrametric and an additive distance matrix for five taxonomic units **A, B, C, D**, and **E** are given along with their corresponding rooted, ultrametric and unrooted, additive tree.

Computationally, the UGMA algorithm is much simpler than the Neighbor-Joining algorithm. An example for its basic working procedure is given in

3.4 Multiple Alignment

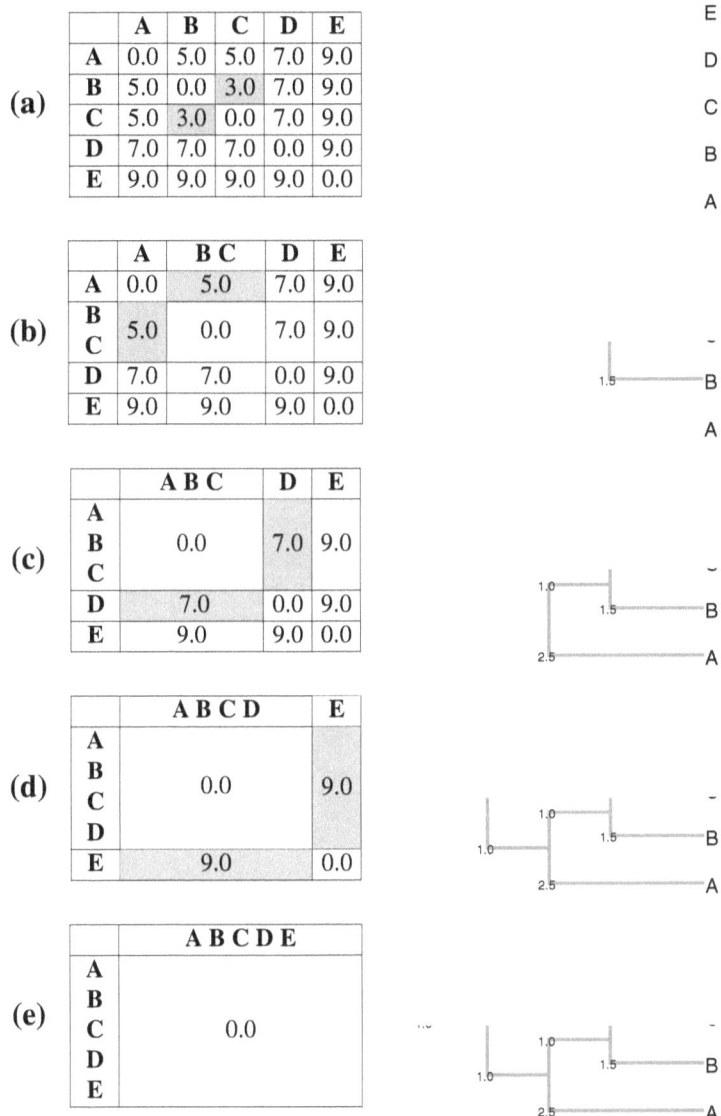

Figure 3.22: *Demonstration of the UPGMA algorithm for the five taxonomic units A, B, C, D, and E. In each iteration step, the closest units (gray-shaded cells in the distance matrices) are merged and the distance matrix is revised by calculating the average distances between the merged clusters and the remaining taxonomic units. If the ultrametric condition is met, the distances between all taxonomic units on the rooted tree directly reflect the observed distances in the initial distance matrix.*

Figure 3.22: Starting from the distance matrix, the taxonomic units with a minimal distance are successively merged into clusters and the distances of the new unit to the remaining units are recalculated by taking the average. This procedure is repeated until only one big cluster is left. Neighbor-Joining proceeds in a similar way, but instead of the initial distances, a *rate-corrected distance matrix* is calculated during each iteration step. This matrix takes the general distance of each taxonomic unit to all other taxonomic units into account (Peer 2009: 150-153). Given the initial distance d_{AB} between a pair of taxonomic units **A** and **B**, the rate-corrected distance R_{AB} is calculated with help of the formula

$$(3.7) \qquad R_{AB} = d_{AB} - \frac{r_A + r_B}{N - 2},$$

where r_A and r_B are the sum of the distances of **A** and **B** to all other taxonomic units, and N is the number of taxonomic units present in the respective iteration step. The benefit of this transformation is illustrated in Table 3.8, where the distance matrix from Figure 3.21b is given in its initial and in its rate-corrected form. In the initial form the taxonomic units **B** and **C** have the lowest distance from each other. In the rate-corrected form, the distance between **A** and **B** is minimal. Since UPGMA takes the matrix in Table 3.8a as input, the algorithm will erroneously join **B** and **C** into one cluster,

	A	B	C	D	E
A	0.0	3.5	5.5	8.0	9.0
B	3.5	0.0	3.0	5.5	6.5
C	5.5	3.0	0.0	3.5	6.5
D	8.0	5.5	3.5	0.0	9.0
E	9.0	6.5	6.5	9.0	0.0

(a) *general*

	A	B	C	D	E
A	0.0	-11.3	-9.3	-9.3	-10.0
B	-11.3	0.0	-9.3	-9.3	-10.0
C	-9.3	-9.3	0.0	-11.3	-10.0
D	-9.3	-9.3	-11.3	0.0	-10.0
E	-10.0	-10.0	-10.0	-10.0	0.0

(b) *rate-corrected*

Table 3.8: *General and rate-corrected distances in the Neighbor-Joining algorithm.*

3.4 Multiple Alignment Analyses

while Neighbor-Joining finds the correct evolutionary tree underlying the distances.[11]

From an evolutionary viewpoint, the basic assumptions underlying Neighbor-Joining are more realistic than those underlying UPGMA. For this reason, most multiple sequence alignment algorithms employ Neighbor-Joining rather than UPGMA for the task of guide tree reconstruction. Nevertheless, one should not overestimate the importance of the underlying evolutionary model. The guide tree is a tool that helps to reduce computation time when constructing multiple alignments. Its sole purpose is to sort the sequences in such a way that they can be successfully aligned. Whether it reflects "true" evolutionary history, or not, is of secondary importance, as long as it helps to find the best alignments. For this reason, the use of UPGMA instead of Neighbor-Joining may be equally justified in multiple alignment analyses, and it may even slightly improve the results (Edgar 2004: 1792).

Sequence Alignment

Once the guide tree is constructed, the sequences are aligned stepwise, following its branching structure (see Figure 3.23). While two sequences are naturally joined by traditional pairwise alignment algorithms, the joining of more than two sequences requires a different strategy. In one of the first proposals for guide-tree-based multiple sequence alignment, the Feng-Doolittle algorithm (Feng and Doolittle 1987), the adding of a sequence to a group or the joining of two already aligned groups of sequences is done by selecting the highest scoring pairwise alignment of all possible sequence pairs and aligning all sequences accordingly. Gaps that are introduced once in this phase remain fixed in order to guarantee that all alignments are consistent with previously joined ones (Durbin et al. 1998 [2002]: 146). As an example, consider the two alignments $\left|\begin{smallmatrix} V & O & L & D & E & M & O & R & T \\ W & A & L & D & E & M & A & R & - \end{smallmatrix}\right|$ and $\left|\begin{smallmatrix} V & - & L & A & D & I & M & I & R \\ V & O & L & O & D & Y & M & Y & R \end{smallmatrix}\right|$. In order to align these alignments, the Feng-Doolittle algorithm selects the most similar sequences of both alignments, such as, e.g., "VOLDEMORT" and "VOLODYMYR", and aligns them pairwise. In a second step, the gaps that were newly introduced in the alignment $\left|\begin{smallmatrix} V & O & L & - & D & E & M & O & R & T \\ V & O & L & O & D & Y & M & Y & R & - \end{smallmatrix}\right|$ are also introduced in the remaining sequences whereby the gaps that these sequences

---

[11] This is a very simplified description of the Neighbor-Joining algorithm. For a complete illustration of the algorithm, see Durbin et al. (1998 [2002]: 169-172) and Peer (2009: 150-153).

already contain remain fixed. As a result, the sequence "WALDEMAR-" becomes "WAL-DEMAR-" and "V-LADYMYR" becomes "V-LADYMYR-".

The apparent drawback of this procedure is that the information upon which an alignment is built only depends on pairwise sequence comparison throughout all stages of the algorithm. When a sequence is joined with a group of already aligned sequences, it would surely be "advantageous to use position-specific information from the group's multiple alignment to align a new sequence to it" (Durbin et al. 1998 [2002]: 146). A common strategy to cope with this problem is model an alignment as a sequence itself where the columns of the alignment matrix serve as segments. This sequence representation of alignments is called a *profile* (Gusfield 1997: 337, Durbin et al. 1998 [2002]: 146f). Profiles are often modeled as sequences of vectors in which each vector represents the relative frequency of the segments in all positions of the original alignment (see Figure 3.24), but since the vector representation is inherent in the alignment itself, it is sufficient to think of profiles as of *intermediate alignments* which are modeled as sequences during multiple alignment analyses. In profile-based approaches, once two sequences are aligned, they are further represented as profiles. When aligning already joined sequences, the traditional dynamic programming algorithm is used to align profiles with profiles, or profiles with sequences.

When conducting pairwise alignments of profiles, a score for the matching of the profile columns (the columns of the intermediate alignments) has to be determined. The most common approach taken in biology is to calculate the so-called *sum-of-pairs* score (SP). The SP score of an alignment of height n is defined as the sum of the pairwise alignment scores $\text{pw}(x_i, x_j)$ between all

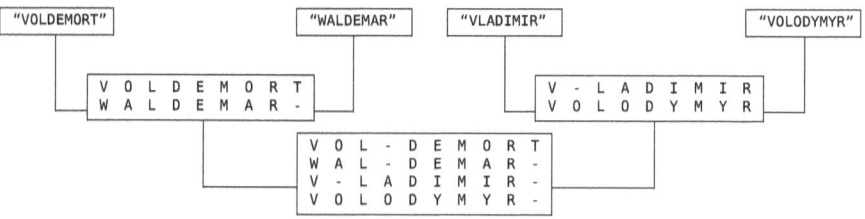

Figure 3.23: *Aligning sequences along the guide tree*

3.4 Multiple Alignment Analyses

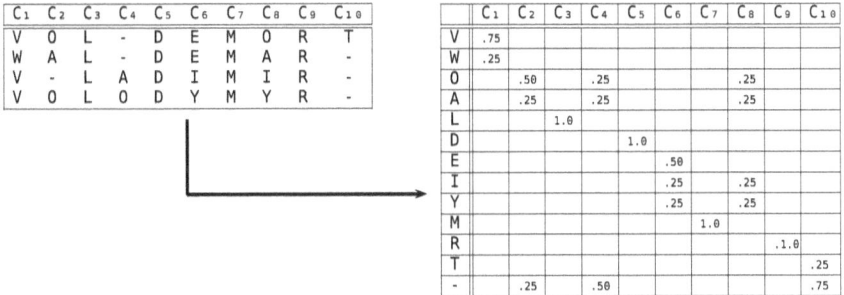

Figure 3.24: *Profile representation of an alignment*

$(n^2 - n)/2$ sequences x_i and x_j:

$$SP = \sum_{i<j}^{n} \text{pw}(x_i, x_j). \tag{3.8}$$

When dealing with only one column c of an MSA, this formula can be modified as:

$$SP = \sum_{i<j}^{n} \text{score}(c_i, c_j), \tag{3.9}$$

where c_i and c_j are the ith and the jth segments of column c, and score is the scoring function (ibid.: 140). In profile-profile alignment, only the crossed segment pairs of the SP score for one column have to be calculated (ibid.: 146f), and the formula for the calculation of the SP score in profile-profile alignment can thus be defined as:

$$SP = \frac{1}{m \cdot n} \cdot \sum_{i=1}^{m}\sum_{j=1}^{n} \text{score}(a_i, b_j), \tag{3.10}$$

where a is a column of the first alignment of height m, and b is a column of the second alignment of height n. Figure 3.25 illustrates how the SP score is calculated for columns C_7 and C_4 of the alignments $\left|\begin{smallmatrix} V & O & L & D & E & M & O & R & T \\ W & A & L & D & E & M & A & R & - \end{smallmatrix}\right|$ and $\left|\begin{smallmatrix} V & - & L & A & D & I & M & I & R \\ V & O & L & O & D & Y & M & Y & R \end{smallmatrix}\right|$. When comparing these two columns, there are

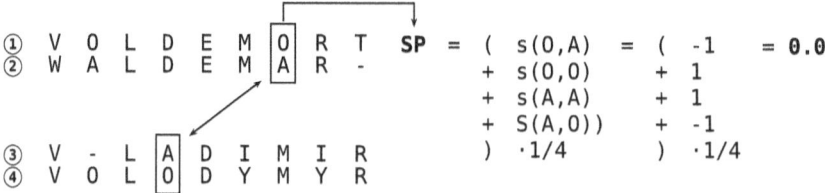

Figure 3.25: *Calculation of the sum-of-pairs score*

$2 \times 2 = 4$ possible matches between the segments of both alignments. Based on the scoring function in Table 3.3, the sum of all scores is 0, since there are two uniform and two divergent matches, and the average score of the columns is therefore also 0.

3.4.2 Enhancements for Progressive Alignment

The main drawback of progressive Alignment is the greediness of the algorithm: "[A]ny mistakes that are made in early steps of the procedure cannot be corrected by later steps" (Rosenberg 2009b: 19). In order to cope with this shortcoming, a couple of different modifications for the algorithm have been proposed. Among these modifications one can roughly distinguish two different kinds of methods: preprocessing methods and *postprocessing methods*. Preprocessing methods apply *before* the progressive alignment analysis has been carried out. Postprocessing methods apply *after* a first (preliminary) progressive alignment has been constructed.

Preprocessing Methods

Among the most popular preprocessing methods are those that make use of so-called *consistency-based* (as opposed to *matrix-based*) scoring schemes (Do et al. 2005, Notredame et al. 2000). The basic principle of these approaches is to "compile a collection of pairwise global and local alignments [...] and to use this collection as a position-specific substitution matrix during a regular progressive alignment" (Notredame 2007: 1405). The underlying idea is that a "good" multiple alignment of a set of sequences should be consistent with optimal alignments of its subsets (Notredame et al. 1998). The collection

3.4 Multiple Alignment Analyses

of pairwise alignments is called a *library* (ibid.: 409), and an optimal multiple alignment is defined as an alignment that is maximally consistent with all alignments in the library.

Traditional, matrix-based approaches rely on a fixed, general scoring scheme throughout all alignment stages (including sequence and profile alignment). As a result, they maximize the global alignment score within the limits of progressive heuristics. Maximally scoring alignments, however, are not necessarily maximally consistent with the alignments of subsets of the data. As an example, consider the two alignments of the sequences "REDCAT", "FATCAT", "CATFISH", and "CATFISHFAT", given in Figure 3.26: Alignment (a) is the output of a traditional progressive alignment analysis; alignment (b) is the output of a consistency-based alignment analysis with the substitution scores derived from a primary library of global and local pairwise alignment analyses.[12] While alignment (a) doubtlessly displays important similarities between all sequences, most people would probably agree that alignment (b) displays the similarities between all sequences in a much more consistent way. This is because the matrix-based analysis displays the similarities between the sequences in a global way, trying "to align the full lengths of the sequences with each other" (Notredame et al. 2000: 206), whereas the consistency-based analysis emphasizes global similarities *and* local similarities, i.e. similari-

①	R	E	D	–	–	–	–	C	A	T
②	F	A	T	–	–	–	–	C	A	T
③	C	A	T	F	I	S	H	–	–	–
④	C	A	T	F	I	S	H	F	A	T

(a) *Matrix-based*

①	R	E	D	C	A	T	–	–	–	–	–
②	F	A	T	C	A	T	–	–	–	–	–
③	–	–	–	C	A	T	F	I	S	H	–	–	–
④	–	–	–	C	A	T	F	I	S	H	F	A	T

(b) *Consistency-based*

Figure 3.26: *Matrix- vs. consistency-based MSA*

---

[12] Both analyses are based on the scoring scheme described in Table 3.3.

ties which hold only for certain parts of the sequences. The differences regarding global and local consistency between matrix-based and consistency-based approaches are further illustrated in Figure 3.27, where the consistency of matrix-based and consistency-based multiple alignments with the optimal global and local alignments of all sequence pairs is compared. Whenever a segment pair that matches in a given pairwise alignment also matches in the corresponding multiple alignment, the respective cell is colored gray. As can be seen from the figure, the consistency-based alignment reflects the pairwise local similarities much better than the matrix-based one.

Apart from being superior with respect to local consistency, alignment (b) is also superior regarding the general similarity of the sequences. Using the average percentage identity of all sequence pairs as a measure of alignment quality (cf. Equation 3.1 on page 74), the matrix-based alignment yields a score of 53, whereas the consistency-based one yields a score of 92. The reason for the better performance of consistency-based alignment analyses lies in the specific scoring schemes employed by the approaches. In contrast to the predefined, *general* scoring schemes of traditional progressive alignment analyses, consistency-based scoring schemes are directly derived from global and local alignment analyses of all sequence pairs. As a result, the scoring schemes are *position-specific*, i.e. identical "residues [segments, JML] will have potentially different scores if the indices of the residues are different" (Notredame et al. 1998: 410). As an example, consider the segment "A" which occurs twice in the sequence "FATCAT" and once in the sequence "REDCAT". In a general scoring scheme, the matching of either of the two instances of "A" in "FATCAT" will yield identical scores when being matched with the "A" in "REDCAT". In a position-specific scoring scheme, however, the second "A" may receive a higher score, since it aligns with the "A" in "REDCAT" in both the global analysis $\left|\begin{smallmatrix} R & E & D & C & A & T \\ F & A & T & C & A & T \end{smallmatrix}\right|$ and the local analysis $\begin{smallmatrix} RED \\ FAT \end{smallmatrix} \left|\begin{smallmatrix} C & A & T \\ C & A & T \end{smallmatrix}\right|$.

There are many different ways to convert the information present in a given library of pairwise alignments into a position-specific scoring scheme. In order to define a score for the matching of two segments x_i and y_j occurring at positions i and j in the sequences x and y, one might, for example, simply count the number of times both segments match in the library. If the library only contains global and local alignments, this would result in a maximal score of 2, if x_i and y_j are matched in both the global and the local alignment analysis, and a minimal score of 0. The disadvantage of this approach is, however, that all alignments in the library contribute equally to the creation of the scoring

3.4 Multiple Alignment Analyses

No.	global	local
① ②	R E D C A T F A T C A T	RED ‖C A T‖ FAT ‖C A T‖
① ③	R E D C A T - - - - - - - C A T F I S H	RED ‖C A T‖ ‖C A T‖ FISH
① ④	- - - - R E D C A T C A T F I S H F A T	RED ‖C A T‖ ‖C A T‖ FISHFAT
② ③	F A T - C A T C A T F I S H	FAT ‖C A T‖ ‖C A T‖ FISH
② ④	F A T - - - - C A T C A T F I S H F A T	‖F A T‖ CAT CATFISH ‖F A T‖
③ ④	C A T F I S H - - - C A T F I S H F A T	‖C A T F I S H‖ ‖C A T F I S H‖ FAT

(a) *Matrix-based*

No.	global	local
① ②	R E D C A T F A T C A T	RED ‖C A T‖ FAT ‖C A T‖
① ③	R E D C A T - - - - - - - C A T F I S H	RED ‖C A T‖ ‖C A T‖ FISH
① ④	- - - - R E D C A T C A T F I S H F A T	RED ‖C A T‖ ‖C A T‖ FISHFAT
② ③	F A T - C A T C A T F I S H	FAT ‖C A T‖ ‖C A T‖ FISH
② ④	F A T - - - - C A T C A T F I S H F A T	‖F A T‖ CAT CATFISH ‖F A T‖
③ ④	C A T F I S H - - - C A T F I S H F A T	‖C A T F I S H‖ ‖C A T F I S H‖ FAT

(b) *Consistency-based*

Figure 3.27: *Consistency with global and local libraries of pairwise alignments. Comparing the consistency of the pairwise alignments in* (a) *and* (b) *with the multiple alignments in Figure 3.26.*

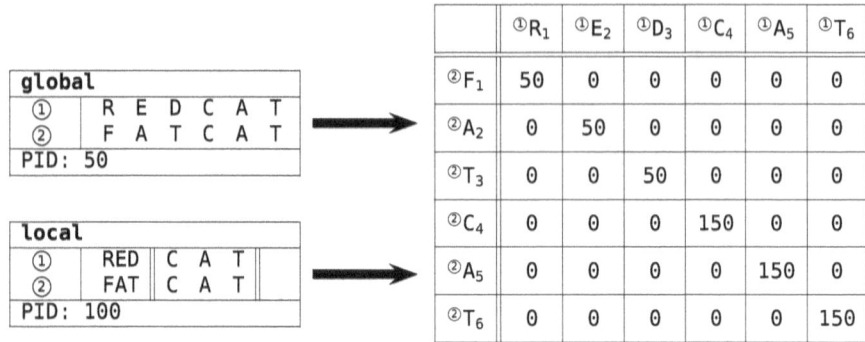

Figure 3.28: *Deriving scoring schemes from a primary library*

scheme, although not all of them are equally good. A method for scoring-scheme creation should also take the quality of the alignments in the library into account.

A rather simple, but nonetheless effective, procedure for the creation of the scoring scheme is employed by the T-Coffee algorithm (Notredame et al. 2000), one of the first approaches to consistency-based alignment analyses. It starts from a (position-specific) scoring matrix in which all cells are set to zero. In the first stage, a *primary library* is constructed by computing global and local alignments of all sequence pairs and determining specific *weights* for each sequence pair by calculating its percentage identity (cf. Equation 3.1). The scoring matrix is then filled by adding the sequence weights to each cell corresponding to a match in the primary library. In the second stage, an *extended library* is created. This library consists of pairwise alignments between all sequences x and y in the dataset which are extracted from the pairwise alignments of x and y with a remaining sequence z. The weights for these alignments are derived by taking the minimum of the primary weights for the alignment of x with z and y with z. The first stage is illustrated in Figure 3.28, where the global and local alignments of the strings "REDCAT" and "FATCAT" contribute initial values to the scoring scheme. Note the high values of 150 for the segment pairs $^{①}C_4/^{②}C_4$, $^{①}A_5/^{②}A_5$, and $^{①}T_6/^{②}T_6$. These are due to the fact that the respective segments match in both the global and the pairwise alignment. Figure 3.29 illustrates the second stage of library

3.4 Multiple Alignment Analyses

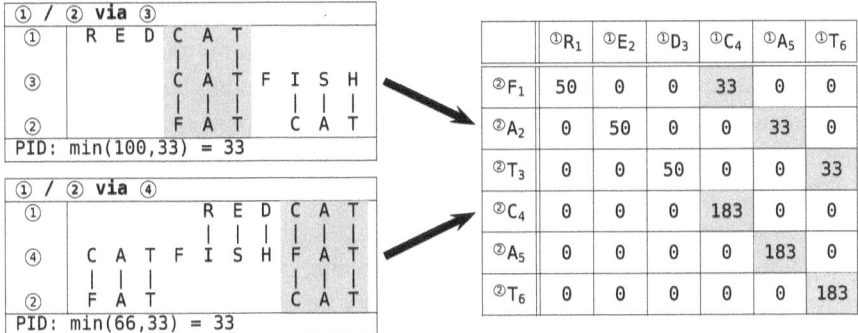

Figure 3.29: *Deriving scoring schemes from an extended library*

extension, where "REDCAT" and "FATCAT" are aligned through their alignment with the remaining sequences "CATFISH" and "CATFISHFAT".

Using consistency-based scoring schemes as a preprocessing method has many advantages. The scoring schemes derived from libraries are sensitive to both global and local similarities. The computational complexity of the approaches is relatively low, and the procedure is transparent and easy to implement. One further advantage is that the library of pairwise alignments does not necessarily have to consist of global and local alignment analyses only (Notredame et al. 1998: 409). Virtually all kinds of information extracted from all kinds of different analyses can be used to construct the library. As a result, consistency-based alignment approaches are very flexible and can easily be adapted for specific purposes.

Postprocessing Methods

Among the common methods for postprocessing, *iterative refinement* methods (Durbin et al. 1998 [2002]: 148f) are probably the most popular ones (Notredame 2009: 58). While iterative approaches have been proposed as an independent heuristic strategy for multiple alignment analyses (Barton and Sternberg 1987), they are more often used to refine a given multiple alignment (Gotoh 1996), or to cope for typical errors resulting from the greediness of the progressive alignment strategy (Do et al. 2005, Edgar 2004). The basic principle of all iterative refinement approaches is to partition an initially given MSA and to realign the parts. If the score of the new alignment (usually a variant of the sum-of-pairs score, cf. Equation 3.10) is better than the previous one, the new alignment is given the preference over the previous alignment, otherwise the previous alignment is retained. This procedure is repeated several times, until the alignment score reaches convergence (Rosenberg 2009a: 58).

Since the realignment itself follows the traditional paradigm of profile alignment as described in Section 3.4.1, the most crucial aspect of iterative refinement approaches lies in the heuristic strategy that is used to partition a given multiple alignment. Many different strategies for alignment partitioning can be found in the literature (see the descriptions in Hirosawa et al. 1995 and Wallace et al. 2005). They can be roughly divided into two subsets, namely into *single-type* and *multi-type* partitioning strategies. Single-type partitioning strategies split an alignment of height N into one subalignment of $N - 1$ sequences and one subalignment consisting only of one sequence (Hirosawa et al. 1995: 14f), i.e. during each iteration step, only one sequence is removed from the alignment and then realigned. Multi-type partitioning strategies split the alignment into subalignments of arbitrary length, depending on the specific criterion which is used to partition the alignment. The specific criteria which are used to partition the alignment vary widely. In single-type iterative refinements, for example, the simplest way is to remove and realign single sequences in a *round-robin* manner (ibid.: 14), i.e. the first sequence of a given MSA is removed and realigned, followed by the second sequence, and the third, until all sequences have been removed and realigned once (this procedure is used in Barton and Sternberg 1987). In multi-type iterative refinements *random* and *tree-dependent* partitioning strategies are the most popular ones. Random partitioning strategies split a given MSA into two randomly chosen subalignments (Do et al. 2005). In tree-dependent partitioning, the splitting of an alignment is "restricted to the ways indicated by branches of a guided tree" (Hirosawa et al. 1995: 15).

The basic stages of iterative refinements are illustrated in Figure 3.30, where the alignment in Figure 3.26a is enhanced using multi-type partitioning and realignment: The basic alignment is first partitioned into the two subalignments $\left|\begin{smallmatrix} R & E & D & C & A & T \\ F & A & T & C & A & T \end{smallmatrix}\right|$ and $\left|\begin{smallmatrix} C & A & T & F & I & S & H & - & - & - \\ C & A & T & F & I & S & H & F & A & T \end{smallmatrix}\right|$, the subalignments are then realigned, and the new alignment is retained, since it has both better SP and PID scores. Note that in the new partitions all columns which consist of gaps only are deleted, resulting in the partition $\left|\begin{smallmatrix} R & E & D & C & A & T \\ F & A & T & C & A & T \end{smallmatrix}\right|$ as opposed to $\left|\begin{smallmatrix} R & E & D & - & - & - & - & C & A & T \\ F & A & T & - & - & - & - & C & A & T \end{smallmatrix}\right|$. Oth-

3.4 Multiple Alignment Analyses

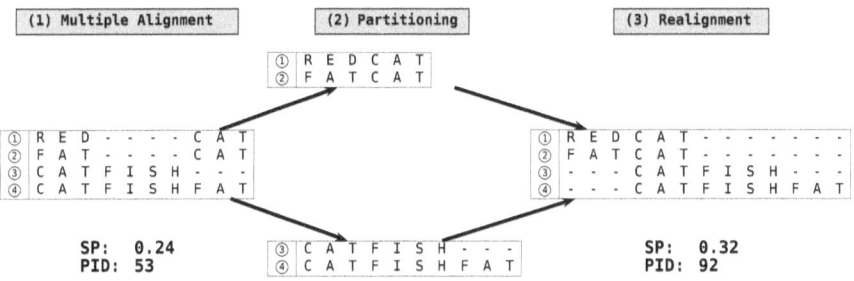

Figure 3.30: *Partitioning and realignment during iterative refinement*

erwise, new results could barely be achieved with this procedure. The resulting alignment is identical with the alignment in Figure 3.26b, i.e. the alignment achieved by consistency-based preprocessing. Both, the consistency-based scoring functions as a preprocessing method, and iterative refinements as a postprocessing method, can significantly improve traditional progressive alignment analyses. Taken together, even better results can be achieved.

3.4.3 Summary on Multiple Alignment Analyses

In this section, the basic algorithms for the computation of multiple alignment analyses were introduced. In contrast to pairwise alignment methods, most multiple alignment methods do not seek an optimal solution but instead rely on heuristics. Among the most common heuristics are the progressive techniques in which multiple sequences are successively aligned along a previously constructed guide tree. These methods can be further enhanced by various techniques for pre- and postprocessing. Among the preprocessing techniques, the most common representatives are consistency-based scoring schemes. Among the postprocessing techniques, the most common representatives are iterative refinement analyses.

4
Sequence Comparison in Historical Linguistics

Die Beobachtung ist in Beziehung auf Entstehung neuer Formen aus früheren auf sprachlichem Gebiete leichter und in grösserem Maassstabe anzustellen, als auf dem der pflanzlichen und thierischen Organismen. Ausnahmsweise sind wir Sprachforscher hier einmal im Vortheile gegen die übrigen Naturforscher.

Die Darwinsche Theorie und die Sprachwissenschaft, 17
Schleicher (1863)

That there are many seemingly striking parallels between biological evolution and language change has long since been noted by linguists as well as biologists. Starting from the rise of language studies as a scientific discipline in the early 19th century up to today scholars from both disciplines have repeatedly pointed to similarities between the respective research objects and models in biology and linguistics. It is therefore not surprising that these parallels have also lead to the transfer of methods between both disciplines. Thus, starting from the 1980s, biologists began to employ *transformational grammars* (Chomsky 1959), originally designed to model the syntax of natural languages, to address certain sequence analysis problems in biology (Searls 2002, Durbin et al. 1998 [2002]: 233). Some 20 years later, scholars began to employ biological methods for phylogenetic reconstruction to solve questions of genetic language classification (Gray and Atkinson 2003, Ringe et al. 2002), eventually triggering a 'quantitative turn' which lead to the establishment of a whole new branch of 'quantitative historical linguistics'. The key assumption of these new approaches is that the characteristic processes of language change and biological evolution are so similar that the methods designed for one discipline may also be used in the other one, despite the fact that the domains differ (Croft 2008: 225).

Aspects	Species	Languages
unit of heredity	gene	word
replication	(asexual and sexual) reproduction	learning
origination	cladogenesis	language splitting
forces of change	natural selection and genetic drift	social selection and trends
differentiation	treelike	treelike (?)

Table 4.1: *Some apparent parallels between species and languages*

The majority of the new methods in quantitative historical linguistics assumes a direct mapping of linguistic and biological entities. Table 4.1 lists some of the most common parallels between linguistics and biology which are often proposed in the literature. Thus, regarding the *unit of heredity*, the biological *gene* is usually set in analogy with the linguistic *word*, both being 'discrete heritable units' (Pagel 2009: 406). *Replication* of the heritable units is achieved via concrete mechanisms of *reproduction* in biological evolution and via *learning* in language history. From the perspective of *origination*, *cladogenesis* in biology is identified with *language splitting* in linguistics (ibid.). From the perspective of *change*, the driving forces of biological evolution, such as *natural selection* and *genetic drift* are compared with *social selection* and *trends*, eventually leading to language change (ibid.). Last not least, *differentiation* is usually assumed to be *treelike*, and the impact of 'horizontal forces' on evolution is considered to be rather low in both cases.

Assuming that these parallels hold, it seems perfectly plausible to use the methods developed for the application in one discipline in the other. However, it is important to be aware not only of the parallels but also of the differences between the research objects of both disciplines. The most striking difference between languages and genomes is that biological evolution manifests itself *substantially* while language history does not. In terms of Popper (1978), genome evolution and language evolution take place in different worlds: While biological organisms are part of world 1, the 'world that consists of physical bodies' (ibid.: 143), languages belong to world 3, the 'world of the products of the human mind, such as languages; tales and stories and religious myths' (ibid.: 144).[1]

The new automatic methods are usually thought to have a greater degree of objectivity and reliability compared to the traditional framework of the comparative method (McMahon and McMahon 2005: 26-29), which is a rather intuitive enterprise (Schwink 1994: 29), suffering from a lack of probabilistic thinking (Baxter and Manaster Ramer 2000: 169-172). However, it is interesting to note that the most crucial part of the analysis, namely the identification of sound correspondences and cognates (steps 2 and 3 of the working procedure outlined in Section 2.6), is still almost exclusively carried out manually. That this may be problematic was recently shown in a comparison of two large lexicostatistical word lists produced by different scholarly teams where differences in item translation and cognate judgments led to topological differences of more than 30% in the automatically calculated phylogenetic trees (Geisler and List forthcoming). Thus, new automatic approaches do not necessarily lead to an overall increase in objectivity and reliability, as long as they are applied to datasets produced by the intuitive, qualitative methods they are supposed to overcome.

The goal of this study is to cope with this gap by developing a new framework for automatic sequence comparison in historical linguistics. Based on novel approaches to sequence modelling (Section 4.1) and phonetic alignment (Section 4.2) a new method for automatic cognate detection has been developed (Section 4.3), which automatically performs the relevant steps 2 and 3 of the traditional comparative method (see Section 2.6).

4.1 Sequence Modelling

When dealing with automatic sequence comparison in historical linguistics, it is important to be clear about the underlying *sequence model*. Phonetic sequences differ crucially from biological sequences in several respects. The segmentation of sequences into phonetic segments (see Section 3.1.1), for example, poses a problem of itself which is addressed in the fields of phonology and phonetics. The processes dominating in biological evolution and language history may also differ quite significantly. Thus, the unit of heredity in biology, the gene, is built from a set of universal characters which can be found

---
[1] For a more detailed account on language as part of Popper's world 3, see Keller (1990: 164-174).

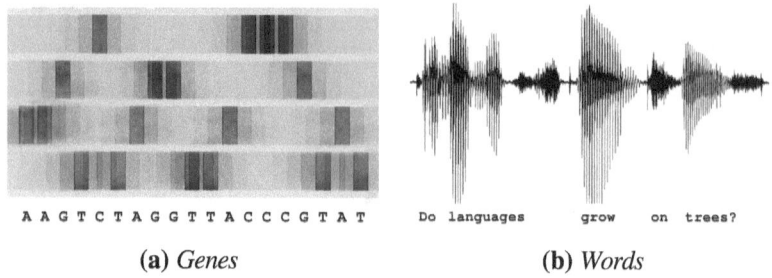

(a) *Genes* (b) *Words*

Figure 4.1: *Discrete heritable units: genes and words. While the biological alphabet manifest itself substantially and can be retrieved by means of gel electrophoresis* (a), *the sounds of languages are physically only present as acoustic waves* (b).

in all organisms. The unit of heredity in linguistics, the word, however, is built from a set of sounds which are distinct only with respect to the language they belong to (see Section 2.1.3). Unlike genes, words are not drawn from a universal alphabet, but from alphabets which themselves are subject to change (see Section 2.2.1). As a result, the problem of sequence alignment in historical linguistics differs fundamentally from the problem of sequence alignment in biology: While the latter requires only to find the best arrangement of two sequences in dependence of a scoring scheme that – once inferred – holds for all biological taxa,[2] the former requires to find both the best arrangement of two words *and* the best scoring scheme which matches the sounds of the two languages from which the words are taken.[3]

In order to address these specific characteristics of linguistic sequences, new models for the representation of sequences were developed for this study. These new models cover both paradigmatic and syntagmatic aspects of sound sequences and play a crucial role in the algorithms for phonetic alignment and automatic cognate detection that are presented in this study. Paradigmatic aspects of sequence modelling focus on the comparison of sequences on the segment level. Syntagmatic aspects of sequence modelling, on the other hand,

---

[2] In biology, different scoring schemes are used for different evolutionary distances, yet it is generally assumed that these scoring schemes apply globally to all biological taxa.

[3] In the literature this problem is sometimes stated as a cryptanalytic problem where neither the mapping between source and target texts nor the mapping between source and target alphabets is known (Hoenigswald 1959).

4.1 Sequence Modelling

focus on the comparison of sequences with respect to their structure. All models are part of a specific framework for sequence modelling which is implemented as part of the LingPy Python library which was written for this study (see Supplementary Material).

4.1.1 Paradigmatic Aspects

Sound Classes

A strict notion of genotypic similarity (see Section 2.4.1) is prevalent in historical linguistics. Genotypic similarity is defined in absolute terms. Only if two segments are judged to correspond systematically, they are judged to be similar. As an example, consider the two words English *mouth* [mauð] and German *Mund* [mʊnt] 'mouth'. From a genotypic perspective, these two words are maximally similar, since all correspondences, which are reflected in the alignment | $\begin{smallmatrix} m & au & - & ð \\ m & ʊ & n & t \end{smallmatrix}$ |, occur regularly, even the null-correspondence German [n] ≈ English [-] (Starostin 2010: 95).[4] Once the language-specific genotypic similarities are identified for a pair of languages, it is not difficult to design an alignment algorithm that optimally aligns all genotypically similar words of these two languages, thereby rejecting all phonetically more similar candidates, such as, e.g., English *mount* [maunt], or German *Maus* [maus] 'mouse'. All one has to do is to design a specific scoring function which reflects the regular sound correspondences in a given language pair.

However, in the first stages of language comparison, neither the cognate words nor the sound correspondences are known. In order to find cognates and correspondences, we need a heuristic which helps us to find *probably* corresponding segments rather than *absolutely* corresponding ones. Many authors (Holzer 1996: 174f, Szemerényi 1970: 14f) emphasize that phenotypic similarity can be neglected when establishing correspondence patterns, since, "[...] given a long enough time span, almost any sound can change into any other sound" (Arlotto 1972: 77). While it is true that there are good examples for sound change which are difficult to explain on pure phonetic terms, most scholars, however, would probably also agree that sound change often *does* follow certain patters, that "[...] even the most divergent languages show examples of phonetic change which are remarkably similar" (ibid.), and that "[not] all changes are [...] equiprobable" (Lass 1997: 136). The difference

---

[4] Compare, for example English *other* [ʌðər] ≈ German *anders* [andərs] 'different' and the alignment of the words: | $\begin{smallmatrix} ʌ & - & ð & ə & r & - \\ a & n & d & ə & r & s \end{smallmatrix}$ |.

regarding the probability of certain sound changes to occur will also show up in the patterns of *sound correspondences* which can be observed in genetically related languages, with certain patterns occurring more often and other ones being quite rare. Stating segment similarity in terms of *correspondence probability* will differ from a pure phenotypic notion of similarity, yet it will, nevertheless, come closer to it than the strict notion of genotypic similarity, which is ignorant of phonetic realization.

The first attempt to derive an empirical model for the probability of sound correspondences that is known to me is an approach by A. B. Dolgopolsky (Dolgopolsky 1964). Based on partially empirical observations of sound-correspondence frequencies in the languages of the world, which are – unfortunately – not further specified by the author, he divided speech sounds into ten types (see Table 4.2), and "[...] thereby distinguished [them] in such a way that phonetic correspondences inside a 'type' are more regular than those between different 'types'" (ibid.: 35). In a recent study, Dolgopolsky's sound-class model has been used as a heuristic device for automatic cognate detection (Turchin et al. 2010). According to this method, semantically identical basic words are judged to be cognate if their first two consonant sound classes match, otherwise, no cognacy is assumed. The advantage of this approach is that the number of false positives is usually considerably low (see the evaluation of the method in Section 4.3), the apparent disadvantage lies in the fact that many true positives are missed, since no true alignment analysis is carried out. Thus the cognate words German *Tochter* [tɔxtər] 'daughter' and English *daughter* [dɔːtər] do not match in their first two consonant classes ("TKTR" vs. "TTR"). An alignment analysis of the sound class strings, however, can easily show that three of four consonant classes match perfectly: $\left| \begin{smallmatrix} T & K & T & R \\ T & - & T & R \end{smallmatrix} \right|$.

The advantage of sound class representations of phonetic segments compared to pure phonetic representations lies in the specific probabilistic notion of segment similarity inherent in the sound class approach. Offering a stochastically based intermediate solution between the two extreme positions of genotypic and phenotypic similarity, sound classes seem especially suitable for automatic sequence comparison. Choosing strings of sound classes as internal representation format has many advantages: While, as has been mentioned before, sequence comparison in disciplines such as evolutionary biology always deals with the same *fixed set of characters*, such as the protein or DNA alphabets, the sound systems of the world's languages differ to a great degree (compare the overview given in Maddieson 2011), and the number of

4.1 Sequence Modelling

characters (including diacritics) of phonetic transcription systems such as the IPA will force the algorithms to handle a large bunch of phonetic values which will be meaningless in most applications. This is due to the fact that, on the one hand, there is a lot of variation regarding the way linguists transcribe languages: Apart from the difference between narrow and broad phonetic transcriptions, there are many cases in which linguists simply slightly differ in their judgments, especially in poorly studied languages. On the other hand, there are many correspondence patterns which occur so frequently, that it seems justified to give the respective sounds an identical value from the beginning. Thus, while probably no one would doubt that the velar unvoiced plosive [k] should be kept distinct from the labial unvoiced plosive [p], the distinction between the velar nasal [ŋ] and the uvular nasal [N] is far less obvious and it does not seem likely that the performance of any algorithm will suffer if both sounds will be merged into one.

In List (2012c), I proposed a revised version of Dolgopolsky's original sound-class model that was developed within a trial-and-error process when testing the suitability of different sound-class models for phonetic alignment. The **S**ound **C**lass-Based Phonetic **A**lignment (SCA) model consists of 28 sound classes. In contrast to the model by Dolgopolsky (henceforth called DOLGO model), the SCA model is more fine-graded, distinguishing 16 consonant, six vowel, and six tone qualities (see Table 4.3). Among the consonant classes in

No.	Cl.	Description	Examples
1	"P"	labial obstruents	p, b, f
2	"T"	dental obstruents	d, t, θ, ð
3	"S"	sibilants	s, z, ʃ, ʒ
4	"K"	velar obstruents, dental and alveolar affricates	k, g, ts, tʃ
5	"M"	labial nasal	m
6	"N"	remaining nasals	n, ɲ, ŋ
7	"R"	liquids	r, l
8	"W"	voiced labial fricative and initial rounded vowels	v, u
9	"J"	palatal approximant	j
10	"Ø"	laryngeals and initial velar nasal	h, ɦ, ŋ

Table 4.2: *Dolgopolsky's original sound class model*

No.	Cl.	Description	Examples
1	"A"	unrounded back vowels	a, ɑ
2	"B"	labial fricatives	f, β
3	"C"	dental / alveolar affricates	ts, dz, tʃ, dʒ
4	"D"	dental fricatives	θ, ð
5	"E"	unrounded mid vowels	e, ɛ
6	"G"	velar and uvual fricatives	ɣ, x
7	"H"	laryngeals	h, ʔ
8	"I"	unrounded close vowels	i, ɪ
9	"J"	palatal approxoimant	j
10	"K"	velar and uvular plosives	k, g
11	"L"	lateral approximants	l
12	"M"	labial nasal	m
13	"N"	nasals	n, ŋ
14	"O"	rounded back vowels	Œ, ɒ
15	"P"	labial plosives	p, b
16	"R"	trills, taps, flaps	r
17	"S"	sibilant fricatives	s, z, ʃ, ʒ
18	"T"	dental / alveolar plosives	t, d
19	"U"	rounded mid vowels	ɔ, o
20	"W"	labial approx. / fricative	v, w
21	"Y"	rounded front vowels	u, ʊ, y
22	"0"	low even tones	$11, 22$
23	"1"	rising tones	$13, 35$
24	"2"	falling tones	$51, 53$
25	"3"	mid even tones	33
26	"4"	high even tones	$44, 55$
27	"5"	short tones	$1, 2$
28	"6"	complex tones	214

Table 4.3: *The SCA sound class model*

the SCA model, the basic difference to the DOLGO model is the strict separation of the general sonority classes. Thus, affricates, plosives, and fricatives are now generally separated. The voicing distinction is still ignored, since voice

4.1 Sequence Modelling

is generally quite prone to assimilation and weakening, and many languages lack this distinction completely.

While sound classes in the original sense of Dolgopolsky are seldom applied in historical linguistics, the use of specific alphabets which reduce the large number of phonetic values attested in the languages of the world to smaller samples is quite common. The Automatic Similarity Judgment Program (ASJP), for example, uses a specific alphabet of 41 symbols (34 consonants, 7 vowels), called ASJP code (Brown et al. 2008), for its large collection of small word lists from more than 6000 languages of the world (Wichmann et al. 2010). In contrast to the DOLGO model, which was specifically designed for the purpose of historical comparison, the primary goal of the ASJP code was to ease the pain-staking labor of transcription, while at the same time reflecting the majority of most of the commonly occurring sounds of the languages of the world (Brown et al. 2008: 289). Nevertheless, since the ASJP code is also based on the idea to reduce the variation inherent in phonetic transcription in order to guarantee comparability, it fulfills the criterion of a sound-class model in the sense in which the term is used in this study. All three sound-class models (DOLGO, SCA, ASJP) that were discussed so far are implemented as basic models of sequence representation in the LingPy library. In order to guarantee the full applicability of the model, 6 tonal classes, originally not present, were added to the ASJP model, and the DOLGO model was extended by one class covering all vowels and one class covering all tones.

Scoring Functions

Dolgopolsky's original sound-class approach defined sound classes as absolute entities. Transitions between sound classes were not allowed, although they are surely desirable, since transitions between classes are well-known to every historical linguist. Transition probabilities between sound classes can be easily modeled in the scoring functions of alignment algorithms. Scoring functions can be based on *empirical* or *theoretical* approaches. Within empirical approaches, scoring functions are derived from studies on sound correspondence frequencies in the languages of the world. This approach has been applied in List (2012b) where a specific substitution matrix for the ASJP sound-class model was derived from a study on sound correspondence frequencies in the languages of the world as they are reflected in the ASJP database (Brown et al. 2013).

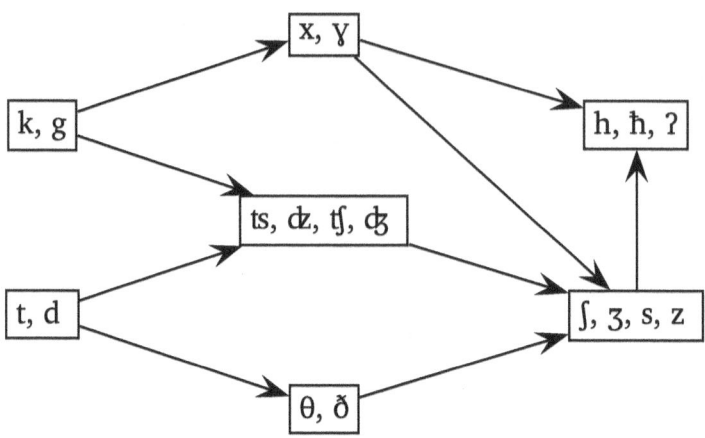

Figure 4.2: *Directionality of sound change patterns*

When deriving scoring functions from a theoretical basis, it is important to find a way to model the nature of sound change and sound correspondences. One crucial characteristic of certain well-known sound change types is their directionality, i.e. if certain sounds change, this change will go into a certain direction and the reverse change can rarely be attested. Other types of sound change are bidirectional and it cannot be decided which direction occurs more frequently. Thus, regarding velar plosives ([k, g]), we know that they can be easily *palatalized*, and that palatalization consists of certain steps, where the velars first become affricates and then turn into sibilants (e.g. [k, g] > [tʃ, ts, ʤ, ʣ] > [ʃ, ʒ, z, s]). The same process of palatalization may happen with dental plosives (e.g. [t, d] > [tʃ, ts, ʤ, ʣ] > [ʃ, ʒ, z, s]). The opposite direction of these changes, however, is rarely attested. Another directional type of sound change which also occurs quite frequently is *lenition* whereby velar plosives become velar fricatives ([k, g] > [x, ɣ]), and dental plosives become dental fricatives ([t, d] > [θ, ð]).

A direct consequence of the directionality of certain sound change types is that certain sound classes are very unlikely to occur in regular correspondence relations. This can be easily illustrated when displaying the possible transitions between sound classes resulting from common sound change types in a directed graph as it is done in Figure 4.2. As a rule, correspondence relations

4.1 Sequence Modelling

can only be assumed for those sound classes which either share a common ancestor, or are connected via a possible path through the graph. Hence, the correspondence [x, ɣ] ≈ [ts, dz, tʃ, dʒ] is possible, as is the correspondence [ts, dz, tʃ, dʒ] ≈ [θ, ð]. The correspondence [θ, ð] ≈ [x, ɣ], however is not possible (if the assumption of directionality holds), since there is no path which connects both sound classes. A scoring function which models the probability of sound classes to occur in correspondence relations should assign similarity scores which reflect the directionality of sound change types.

In order to define such a scoring function from a theoretical model, the following approach is applied: The scoring function is derived from a directed weighted graph. All sound classes which are known to be in very close connection to each other are connected by directed edges which reflect the direction of the respective sound changes. The assumed probability of the sound changes is defined by the edge weights. The higher the assumed probability of sound change, the smaller the weight. If sound change processes are not directional, both directions are reflected in the graph. This may, for example, be important for the scoring of vowels for which directional patterns of change are difficult to establish. The similarity score for two segments in the directed graph is calculated by subtracting the similarity score of one segment to itself from the length of the shortest path connecting two segments. In this context, the length of an edge in the directed graph is directly identified with the weight assigned to the edge. Figure 4.3 gives an example on how the similarity scores can be calculated for the above-mentioned cases of palatalization of dentals and ve-

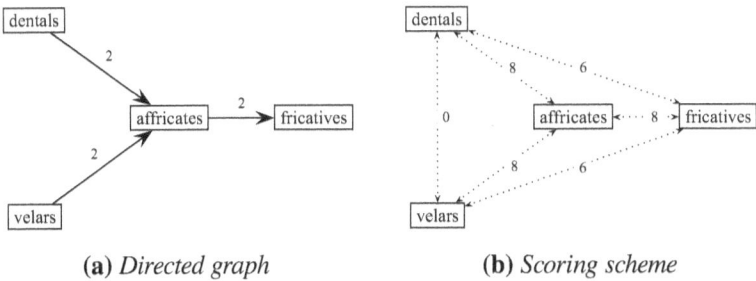

(a) *Directed graph*   (b) *Scoring scheme*

Figure 4.3: *Modelling the directionality of sound change in scoring functions. See the text for a detailed description.*

lars: The resulting similarity score for dentals and fricatives is calculated by subtracting the length of the shortest path (4) from the similarity score for a segment to itself (10). If no shortest path can be found, the similarity score is automatically set to 0.

Based on the above stated, LingPy defines three different scoring functions for each of the basic sound-class models (DOLGO, SCA, and ASJP). The scoring function of the DOLGO model is the simplest one. It prohibits the matching of the vowel class with the consonant classes, and otherwise assigns high scores for identical sound classes. The SCA scoring function is based on the weighted-graph method. The underlying transition graph incorporates palatalization and lenition as exemplified above. Furthermore, some classes, such as the nasals and the glides, were given high similarity scores among each other, since transitions among these classes are quite likely as a result of assimilation. The ASJP scoring function is based on the empirical scoring function derived from the above-mentioned study on sound correspondence frequencies (Brown et al. 2013).[5]

The differences between the three sound-class models and their respective scoring functions can be illustrated by comparing the consonants in the sound system of English as it was defined by Chomsky and Halle (1968: 177). Figure 4.4 shows the results of a multidimensional scaling analysis for the different models. In this analysis, all sounds belonging to the same sound class in a given model were automatically clustered into one set. Furthermore, the distances between all sound sequences were calculated by converting the scoring functions (which reflect similarities) into distance scores. The distances in the model of Chomsky and Halle are derived by calculating the Hamming distances (see Section 3.1) of their feature vectors (ibid.). As can be seen from the figure, the Chomsky-Halle model of feature-based distances is not a good candidate for historical comparison. The DOLGO model receives its "historical strength" from the rough lumping of sound classes, but no further patterns are recognizable, since no explicit further transition probabilities between the sound classes are defined. Comparing the empirically derived ASJP model with the theoretically derived SCA model, one can find a lot of similarities, but even more striking differences. Thus, the voicing distinction, which was discarded in the SCA model, is only partially reflected in the ASJP model, and the closeness of nasals to their non-nasal counterparts in the ASJP model is completely absent in the SCA model.

---

[5] Matrix representations of all three scoring functions are given in Appendix B.

4.1 Sequence Modelling

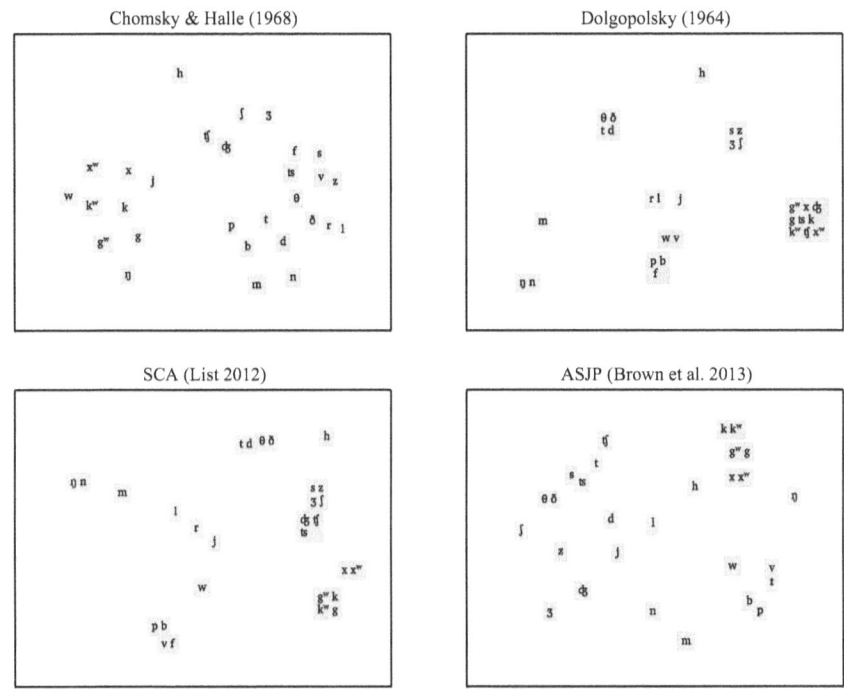

Figure 4.4: *Multidimensional scaling analysis illustrating the distances between the sounds of English in different similarity models.*

The differences between the different models are further visualized with the help of heat maps in Figure 4.5. Here, the fuzzy character of the Hamming distances derived from the features by Chomsky and Halle becomes especially evident. Of the larger clusters, only the velar group in the lower left of the matrices ([x^w, k^w, g^w, x, g, w]) finds a reflection in the other models. That the SCA model was derived from the DOLGO model can be easily spotted from a comparison of the respective matrices. Comparing the SCA with the ASJP model, the difference between empirical and theoretical models become quite obvious: While the ASJP matrix exhibits a broad range of partially very weak similarities between many different sound segments, the SCA model is much more restrictive.

4.1.2 Syntagmatic Aspects

Prosodic Context

In biological sequence analyses it is common to treat specific positions of certain sequences differently by modifying the scores for the introduction of gaps (Thompson et al. 1994). In the approach presented here, the idea of position-specific scoring is adopted to incorporate syntagmatic information in the sound-class representation of phonetic sequences. The main idea behind this modification is to account for the well-known fact that certain types of sound change are more likely to occur in specific prosodic contexts. For example, vowels are more likely to get modified or lost than consonants, and

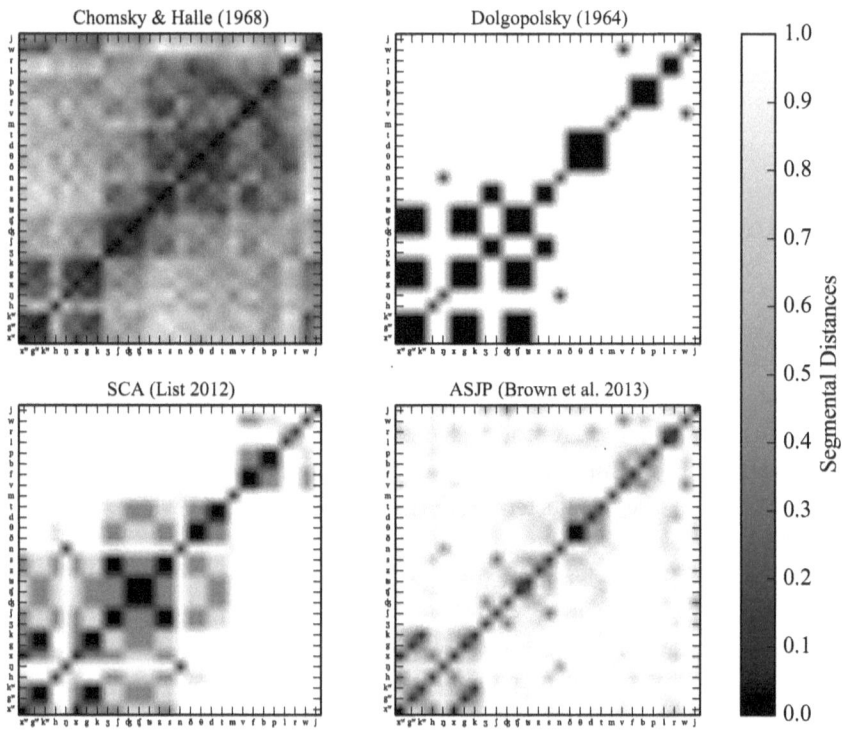

Figure 4.5: *Distances between the sounds of English in different similarity models.*

4.1 Sequence Modelling

consonants are more likely to get modified or lost in syllable-final than in syllable-initial position. It therefore seems fruitful to include this position-specific information in the general representation of phonetic sequences. The information itself can then be used in different parts of sequence analyses. In alignment analyses, for example, it can be used to derive position-specific gap penalties (see Section 4.2). When searching for regular sound correspondences, the position-specific information offers an alternative to traditional *n*-gram representations of sequences (see Section 4.3).

The LingPy framework of sequence representation employs a very simple method to model prosodic context: A phonetic sequence is not only represented by its sound-class sequence, but also by a *prosodic string*, which itself is derived from the sequence's *sonority profile*. The sonority profile is represented as a vector of integer weights representing the relative sonority of all segments in a sonority hierarchy, going from lower weights for less sonorous segments to higher weights for more sonorous segments. LingPy currently employs the sonority hierarchy given in Example 4.1, which follows Geisler (1992: 30) with an additional sonority class for affricates:

(4.1) | *plosives* | *affricates* | *fricatives* | *nasals* | *liquids* | *glides* | *vowels* |
       | 1 | 2 | 3 | 4 | 5 | 6 | 7 |

Once the sonority profile of a sequence is calculated, all segments can be assigned to different *prosodic contexts* according to their position in the profile. Given the fact that syllabification is often language-specific (Hall 2000: 226f), and that a given syllabification can become meaningless when multiple sequences are being compared, the framework for sequence modelling in LingPy employs a simplified strategy for the determination of prosodic context which is not based on syllabification. Given a sonority profile of a linguistic sequence, it is easy to determine peaks of *maximum* sonority, which will usually be represented by vowels. It is further possible to determine whether a given segment (which does not appear in a maximum peak position) is in a position of *descending* or *ascending* sonority. The derivation of these different prosodic contexts from a sonority profile is illustrated in Figure 4.6 for the sequence Bulgarian ябълка [jabəlka] 'apple'. Apart from the positions of ascending, descending, and maximum sonority, the word-initial and the word-final positions are treated as separate prosodic context, whereby a further distinction between vowels and consonants is being made. As a result, seven different prosodic contexts can be defined for phonetic segments, namely (1) "#" –

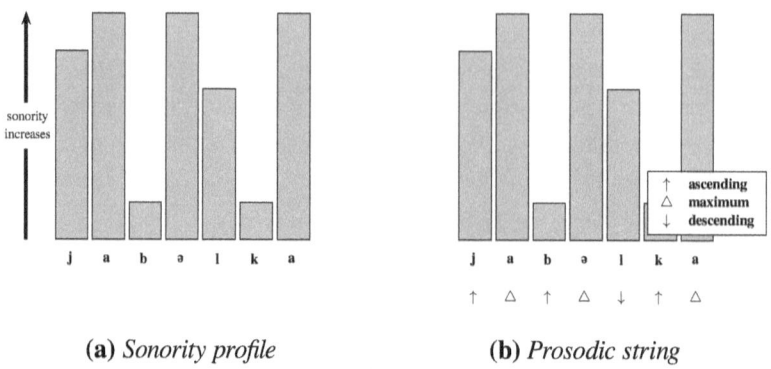

(a) *Sonority profile*   **(b)** *Prosodic string*

Figure 4.6: *Deriving prosodic strings from sonority profiles. See the text for a detailed description.*

word-initial[6] consonants, (2) "V" – word-initial[7] vowel, (3) "C" – ascending sonority, (4) "V" – sonority peak, (5) "C" – descending sonority, (6) "$" – word-final consonant, and (7) ">" – word-final vowel.

In order to derive position-specific weights, LingPy builds on an idea of Geisler (1992: 31-34) in assigning these contexts specific *weights*. These weights are defined in such a way that it is easier to introduce gaps in weak positions than in strong ones. The weights are represented as floating point numbers by which the GOP is multiplied. For example, a weight of 2.0 assigned to a specific environment will double the GOP for all segments occurring in this environment. The current default weights (see Table 4.4) have been determined by testing the performance of the SCA method for phonetic alignment (see Section 4.2) on a small representative sample of pairwise alignments. Two default sets are used: one for the alignment of South-East Asian tone languages, and one for all other languages. Using specific weights for tone languages is justified by the specific syllable structure of these languages that makes it necessary to assign high weights for vowels, and lower

---

[6] This refers to all syllable-initial consonants in the first syllable of a word.
[7] This refers to the first vowel in a word, regardless of whether it is preceded by a consonant or not.

4.1 Sequence Modelling

Set of Weights	Prosodic Context						
	#	V	C	c	v	$	>
Tone L.	1.6	3.0	1.2	1.1	3.0	0.5	0.7
Non-Tone L.	2.0	1.5	1.5	1.1	1.3	0.8	0.7

Table 4.4: *The sets of default weights for tone and non-tone languages*

weights for the position of descending sonority, since this position is seldom occupied.

The information regarding prosodic context is further used to modify the substitution scores slightly. They are increased if two segments belong to the same prosodic context. The amount by which the score is increased is also defined by a scaling factor, the default being 0.3. Thus, if two segments match regarding their scaling factor, the resulting score is increased by 30%. Table 4.5 summarizes the different representations of phonetic sequences applied by LingPy for Bulgarian *ябълка* [jabəlka] 'apple'.

Secondary Sequence Structures

The idea of *secondary sequence structures* has been proposed in Section 3.3.3, and it is straightforward to apply this idea in an extended model for the rep-

Phonetic Sequence	j	a	b	ə	l	k	a
SCA Model	J	A	P	E	L	K	A
ASJP Model	y	a	b	I	l	k	a
DOLGO Model	J	V	P	V	R	K	V
Sonority Profile	6	7	1	7	5	1	7
Prosodic String	#	V	C	v	c	C	>
Relative Weight	2.0	1.5	1.5	1.3	1.1	1.5	0.7

Table 4.5: *The LingPy framework of sequence modelling: Bulgarian ябълка 'apple' given in different representations.*

resentation of phonetic sequences. However, so far, the LingPy framework of sequence modelling is not capable to detect secondary sequence structures automatically. Therefore, only secondary structures which are explicitly marked as such by the user can be employed in the analyses. Thus, if a morpheme segmentation is included in the data, the alignment algorithm described in the next section, can carry out alignment analyses which are sensitive to secondary sequence structures. This is generally the case when dealing with South-East Asian tone languages, since the tone characters (which are represented by specific sound classes and are also assigned to a specific prosodic environment), automatically mark the syllable boundaries. Secondary alignment is especially useful in these cases, since the syllable in South-East Asian languages normally also reflects the morphemes. When aligning data containing sentences or phrases, the secondary structures (in form of white space characters) are usually also directly given along with the data. In all other cases, the data has to be manually or automatically preprocessed.

4.2 Phonetic Alignment

Although alignment analyses are the most general way to compare sequences manually and automatically, their application is still in its infancy in historical linguistics. Generally speaking, historical linguists have always aligned words. Without alignments, i.e. without the explicit matching of sounds, neither can regular sound correspondences be detected nor can cognacy between words or genetic relationship between languages be proven. However, although language comparison was always based on an implicit alignment of words, it was

Language	Alignment			
Choctaw	f	a	n	i
Cree	-	i	l̥	u

(a) *Pairwise alignment.*

Language	Alignment				
Choctaw	-	f	a	n	i
Koasati	i	p	-	l̥	u
Cree	i	-	-	l̥	u

(b) *Multiple alignment.*

Table 4.6: *The importance of multiple phonetic alignment (b) in comparison to pairwise phonetic alignment (a) illustrated for words meaning 'squirrel' in Muskogean (Fox 1995: 68, Haas 1969: 41).*

4.2 Phonetic Alignment

(a) *Global alignment.*

Language	Alignment						
Russian	s	-	ɔ	n	ts	ə	-
Polish	s	w	ɔ	nʲ	ts	ɛ	-
French	s	-	ɔ	l	-	ɛ	j
Italian	s	-	o	l	-	e	-
German	s	-	ɔ	n	-	ə	-
Swedish	s	-	uː	l	-	-	-

(b) *Local alignment.*

Language	Alignment							
Russian	s	ɔ	-	-	n	ts	ə	
Polish	s	-	w	ɔ	nʲ	ts	ɛ	
French	s	ɔ	l	-	-	-	-	ɛj
Italian	s	o	l	-	-	-	-	e
German	s	ɔ	-	-	-	-	-	nə
Swedish	s	uː	l	-	-	-	-	

Table 4.7: *Two different alignments of reflexes of Proto-Indo-European* *séh₂uel- *'sun'. In* (a) *all segments are globally aligned, resulting in an unrealistic scenario not reflecting known intermediate stages. In* (b) *all segments are locally aligned, whereby some elements are left unaligned, and the core block is shaded in gray. Segments connected via metathesis are displayed using a white font.*

rarely explicitly visualized or termed as such, and in the rare cases where scholars explicitly used alignments to visualize correspondence patterns in words, it merely served illustrational purposes (Anttila 1972: 229-263, Lass 1997: 128).

That alignment analyses, and especially multiple alignment analyses, are important, is nicely illustrated by Fox (1995: 67f) in an example taken from Haas (1969: 41), where a pairwise comparison of Choctaw [fani] 'squirrel' and Cree [iḷ] 'squirrel' leads to an incorrect matching of sound segments (see Table 4.6a), unless Koasati [ipḷu] 'squirrel' is added to the comparison (see Table 4.6b). It is, however, indicative that Fox does not use the term "alignment" but instead speaks of the problem of matching the correct "position in the string of phonemes" (Fox 1995: 67). This illustrates that linguists up to recently were unaware of the fact that the specific kind of sequence comparison they were carrying out had a close counterpart in other branches of science.

Another reason for this reluctance of linguists to make a broader use of alignment analyses may be that the representation of sequence differences with the help of alignments is not always apt to display the differences between phonetic sequences properly. Alignment analyses suggest a "holistic" picture of sequence differences where sequences are put into the matrix as a whole. As a result, it is difficult to display local similarities between sequences, especially when conducting multiple alignment analyses. As an example, consider Proto-Indo-European *séh₂u̯el- 'sun' and its reflexes Russian *солнце* [sɔntsə], Polish *słońce* [swɔnʲtsɛ], French *soleil* [sɔlɛj], Italian *sole* [sole], German *Sonne* [sɔnə], Swedish *sol* [suːl] (NIL: 606f). A seemingly obvious global alignment of these words is given in Table 4.7a. This alignment, however, does only partially reflect the real correspondences between the words as they are proposed by the comparative method. The problem is that not all words are fully cognate, but have been derived indirectly via different morphological processes. Thus, French *soleil* goes back to Vulgar Latin *sōlĭculus* 'small sun' (REW: § 8067), but Italian *sole* goes back to Latin *sōlis* 'sun' (REW: §8059). Similarly, German *Sonne* and Swedish *sol* are usually assumed to be cognate, but their Proto-Germanic ancestor had a complex, stem-alternating paradigm. The Swedish word is a reflex of the nominative stem Proto-Germanic *sōel- 'sun', and the German word goes back to the oblique stem Proto-Germanic *sunnōn- (KROONEN: 463f). Russian *солнце* and Polish *słońce* both go back to Proto-Slavic *sьlnьce 'sun' (DERKSEN: 479f), but the Proto-Slavic form cannot directly be traced back to Proto-Indo-European *séh₂u̯el-, but rather goes back to an early derivation *suh₂l-n- (NIL: 606). What further complicates an alignment of the words is the fact that the Polish word form results from a metathesis (Polish [w] < Proto-Slavic *l) which cannot directly be displayed in an alignment analysis. The primary purpose of alignment analyses in historical linguistics, but also in evolutionary biology, is to show which segments of different sequences are homologous. If we take this purpose seriously, the whole arrangement has to be rearranged drastically. In Table 4.7b, I have attempted to draw a more realistic scenario for the six words, leaving certain parts of the sequences unaligned, while at the same time using additional markup to display more specific relations.

Given the complexities and the problems to align remotely distant words realistically, it is surely not surprising that linguists so far have been reluctant

4.2 Phonetic Alignment

to conduct such analyses. Nevertheless, even if it might not be possible at the moment to design algorithms which are accurate enough to yield an alignment as the one displayed in Table 4.7b, a careful adaptation of the methods that have been recently developed in evolutionary biology may yield alignments which come closer to the ideal than any linguist would probably have imagined 20 years ago.

4.2.1 Previous Work

When discussing previous work, one should distinguish *implicit alignment algorithms*, i.e. those approaches where alignment analyses have been used to calculate distances between phonetic sequences, and *explicit alignment algorithms*, i.e. those approaches where alignment analyses have been used as an explicit tool for the visualization of segment correspondences. The former studies, which started with an application by Kessler (1995) and since then have been followed up in many different applications, mostly in dialectology (see the overview in Nerbonne and Heeringa 2010), but also in large-scale genetic language comparison (Holman et al. 2011), are of less interest here, since the alignment method that I propose in the following is explicitly intended to serve the latter purpose.

When discussing explicit alignment algorithms, it is further important to distinguish between applications for *pairwise phonetic alignment* (PPA) and applications for *multiple phonetic alignment*. The first one to propose an explicit pairwise phonetic alignment algorithm was Covington (1996). The basic characteristics of this algorithm are a rough weighting scheme which especially prohibits the matching of vowels and consonants, and the use of affine gap costs. In contrast to later approaches proposed by other scholars, the algorithm is not based on dynamic programming, but on an extensive, partially guided, tree search of the whole space of possible alignments. In 1999, Somers reported an algorithm which was developed in the end of the 1970s and was originally intended to align narrow phonetic transcriptions of children's speech with a corresponding adult model in order to test the articulation of children. In contrast to the exhaustive tree search conducted by the algorithm of Covington, Somers's algorithm employed a greedy strategy which is not guaranteed to find the optimal pairwise alignment. The first PPA algorithm that employed dynamic programming was proposed by Oakes (2000). This algorithm was part of a larger framework (JAKARTA) that was intended to identify regular sound correspondences between language pairs. The alignment algorithm in JAKARTA defines a considerably complex scoring scheme which reflects many different types of sound changes that are modeled by characterizing each sound segment with the help of three phonetic features (place, manner, voicing). Although JAKARTA defines a great number of different sound change types, the resulting distance function is rather rough, since the edit costs for divergent matches resulting from thesound change types are all set to 1. Among the most sophisticated algorithms for PPA analyses is the ALINE algorithm (Kondrak 2000). Similar to JAKARTA, ALINE is also based on dynamic programming. Apart from the basic matching types, the algorithm has been extended to account for complex matches (compressions and expansions, see Section 3.2). Among the different alignment modes, global, local and semi-global alignment are supported. The most remarkable feature of ALINE, however, is the scoring function which is based on a multi-valued feature representation of phonetic segments and specific salience values for the features. The advantage of this approach is that the impact of features on similarity scores can be weighted according to their relevance for PPA analyses. Kondrak's ALINE algorithm was a milestone in phonetic alignment. Largely outperforming previously proposed algorithms (see the comparison of ALINE with other algorithms in Kondrak 2002: 64, also given in Table 4.12), it introduced many new concepts in phonetic alignment analyses, such as local and semi-global alignment. The only drawback of the algorithm is its restriction to pairwise alignment analyses.

Covington was also the first one to propose an explicit algorithm for multiple phonetic alignment (Covington 1998). Similar to his PPA algorithm, the MPA algorithm is based on a tree search instead of using dynamic programming. While this strategy may still work for PPA analyses, it is surely unsuitable for MPA analyses, as can be also seen from the fact that the author only gives examples for a maximum of three aligned sequences. More than 10 years later, Prokić et al. (2009) employed the ALPHAMALIG algorithm (Alonso et al. 2004) to carry out MPA analyses of a dataset containing the translational equivalents of 152 glosses in 192 Bulgarian dialects (Buldialect). Although the algorithm was not specifically designed for the task of phonetic alignment, Prokić et al. (2009) report a high accuracy of the performance of the algorithm in comparison with their manually edited gold standard.

4.2 Phonetic Alignment

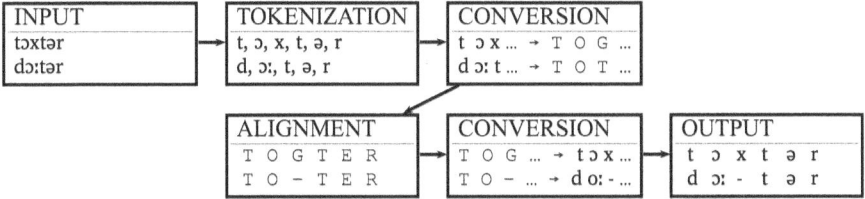

Figure 4.7: *The basic working procedure of SCA analyses*

4.2.2 SCA – Sound-Class Based Phonetic Alignment

The Sound-Class-Based Phonetic Alignment (SCA) method for pairwise and multiple phonetic alignment analyses was first introduced in List (2010), and successively revised in (List 2012b) and List (2012c). In the following, the most recent version of the method shall be introduced in detail. The SCA method combines both the current state of the art in general sequence alignment as it was outlined in Chapter 3 and the new approaches to sequence modelling that were presented in Section 4.1. The method is also implemented as part of the LingPy library (see Supplementary Material).

The main idea of the current version of SCA and all its predecessors is to distinguish between an *external* and an *internal* representation of phonetic sequences. The transition between the two representations is managed within a specific module which manages the conversion from external to internal format and vice versa. While the difference between external and internal format was merely a result of the conversion of IPA characters into capital letters reflecting sound-class models in the first version of SCA (List 2010), the current internal representation is a bit more complex, involving not only sound classes (see Section 4.1.1), but also prosodic strings (see Section 4.1.2). Distinguishing the external and internal representation of phonetic sequences has several advantages. Not only are the computational aspects easier to handle when working with a unified internal representation, the program is also much more flexible regarding the models that can be chosen for a given analysis. Since – from a technical viewpoint – sound classes merely constitute a substitution framework that accounts for the conversion of sequences drawn from one alphabet into sequences drawn from another one, there is no limitation regarding detail or roughness. One can conduct analyses where sounds are lumped into just a few general classes as proposed by Dolgopolsky (1964), as well as analyses which are virtually identical with narrow phonetic transcriptions.

Given that the IPA is chosen as the basic external representation format for phonetic sequences, a module in which IPA sequences are tokenized into meaningful phonetic segments precedes the first conversion stage. Hence, the basic working procedure of SCA consists of four stages: (1) tokenization, (2) class conversion, (3) alignment analysis, and (4) IPA conversion. In stage (1) the input sequences are tokenized into phonetic segments. In stage (2) the segments are converted into their internal representation format, whereas each sequence is further represented by its corresponding sound class sequence and its prosodic profile. The pairwise or multiple alignment analysis is carried out in stage (3). After the alignment analysis has been carried out, the aligned sequences are converted back to their original format in stage (4). This procedure is illustrated in Figure 4.7 for the words German *Tochter* [tɔxtər] 'daughter' and English *daughter* [dɔːtər].

Pairwise Alignment

The SCA method supports all structural extensions to the basic algorithm for pairwise sequence alignment mentioned in Section 3.3.2, including the extension for secondary alignment. When carrying out secondary alignment analyses, the boundary marker has to be defined by the user. By default, there are two different boundary markers: (1) tone letters as they are used in the system of phonetic transcriptions of Sinitic languages proposed by Chao (1930 [2006]), and (2) a marker for word boundaries, such as, e.g. the character "#". Substitution scores are based on the respective sound-class model which is being used. All three models mentioned in Section 4.1.1 are available (DOLGO, SCA, ASJP), but more models can be easily defined by the user. The respective substitution matrices are derived as described in the same section. All analyses also support the use of position-specific gap and substitution scores derived from prosodic strings as described in Section 4.1.2. The relative weights for the different prosodic contexts can be defined by the user.

Multiple Alignment

The SCA algorithm for multiple phonetic alignment is based on the progressive alignment paradigm. In order to cope for the known problems of progres-

4.2 Phonetic Alignment

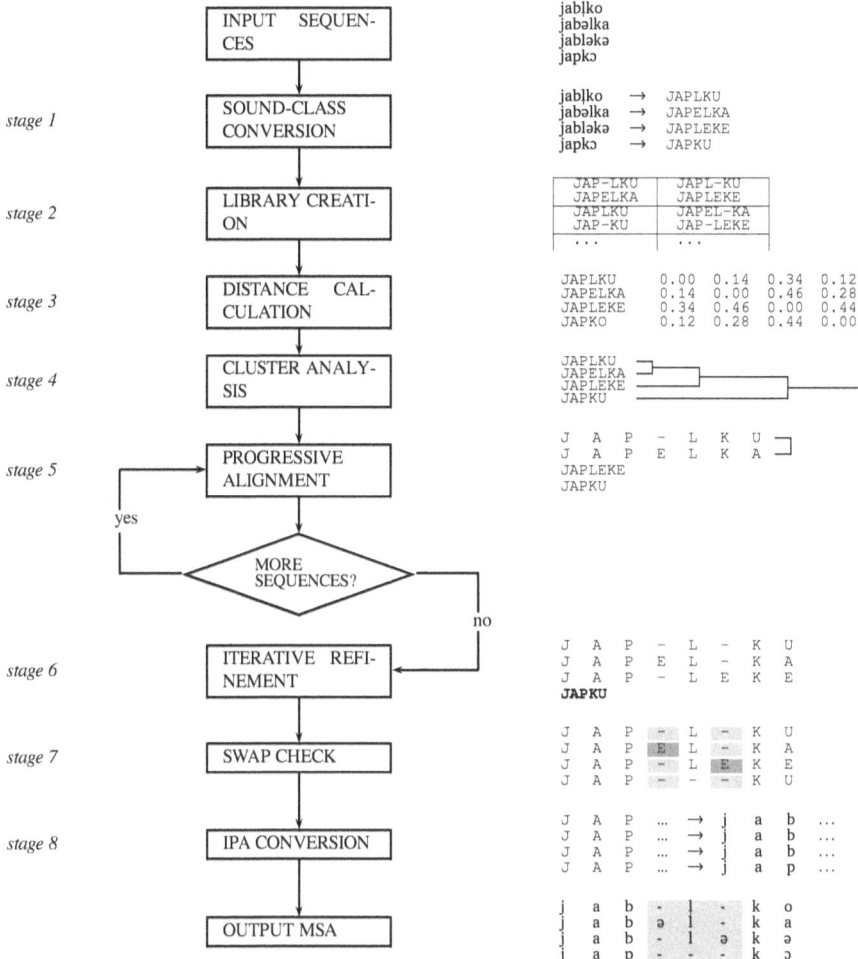

Figure 4.8: *Working procedure of the SCA method. See the text for a further description of each of the eight stages.*

sive algorithms, SCA makes use of pre- and postprocessing methods. For the preprocessing, SCA employs consistency-based scoring schemes. The postprocessing is based on iterative refinement (see Section 3.4.2). The working procedure of SCA consists of 8 stages as illustrated in Figure 4.8. In the figure, every stage is accompanied by an example which shows the current progress of the alignment of the four words Czech *jablko* [jabļko], Bulgarian *ябълка* [jabəlka], Russian *яблоко* [jabləkə] and Polish *jabłko* [japko] 'apple'.

In stage 1, the input sequences which are converted to sound classes, e.g. the word Czech *jablko* is converted to "JAPLKU" according to the SCA model. In stage 2, the library of pairwise alignments is created. As a default, global, local, and diagonal alignment analyses (see Section 3.3.2) are carried out of all possible word pairs. In stage 3, the distance matrix is computed from the pairwise similarity scores of all sound class sequences. The conversion of similarity into distance scores is carried out with the formula of Downey et al. (2008):

$$(4.2) \qquad D = 1 - \frac{2 \cdot S_{AB}}{S_A + S_B},$$

where S_A and S_B are the similarity scores of the sequences aligned with themselves, and S_{AB} is the similarity score of the alignment of both sequences. In stage 4, the sound-class strings are clustered with help of the Neighbor-Joining algorithm (Saitou and Nei 1987). The clustering procedure yields the guide tree that is used for the progressive alignment in stage 5, where all sequences are stepwise aligned with each other, following the branching order of the guide tree. In stage 6, iterative refinement methods are applied to the already aligned sequences in order to account for possible errors resulting from misaligned sequences. In stage 7, a method for swap detection (described in detail in Section 4.2.3) is applied. As can be seen from the example, the algorithm correctly identifies a swap for the alignment of the four input sequences. In stage 8, all sequences are converted from their internal representation back to their original IPA format.

4.2.3 Specific Features

Iterative Refinement

The basic principle of iterative refinement methods was described in Section 3.4.2. Since alignments in linguistics are much shorter than in biology, the heuristics for the partitioning of alignments in biology are not particularly apt for phonetic alignment. Therefore, three new strategies for alignment partitioning were developed for the SCA method, one single-type partitioning strategy, and two multi-type partitioning strategies. They may be called the

4.2 Phonetic Alignment

orphan partitioning, *flat-cluster partitioning*, and *similar-gap-sites partitioning* strategy, respectively.

The (single-type) orphan partitioning strategy,[8] splits and realigns the most divergent sequences from the MSA, whereas divergence is measured by taking the average distance of each sequence to all other sequences in the distance matrix. The flat-cluster partitioning strategy is based on a flat-cluster analysis of the data, using a flat-cluster variant of the UPGMA algorithm (Sokal and Michener 1958). In contrast to a traditional cluster analysis, the flat-cluster analysis stops to separate sequences when a certain threshold is reached. As a result, the set of input sequences in an alignment may be divided into a couple of subsets. The flat-cluster partitioning strategy for iterative refinement continuously splits off all sequences belonging to one of the flat clusters and realigns them, until all clusters have been split off and realigned once. The similar-gap-sites partitioning strategy also clusters the data into subsets, but not on the basis of sequence similarity, but on the basis of the current alignment. In an alignment, all rows can be assigned to a certain *gap profile*, depending on the positions at which they contain gaps. The similar-gap-sites partitioning strategy simply assigns all sequences to the same cluster, depending on whether they share an identical gap profile or not. Once the clusters are determined, the clusters are treated in the same way as in the flat-cluster partitioning strategy, i.e. each cluster is split off and realigned, until all clusters have been split off and realigned once.

Consistency-Based Scoring

Apart from traditional, matrix-based progressive alignment analyses, the SCA method also allows to carry out consistency-based alignment analyses as described in section 3.4.2. As mentioned before, the basic idea of consistency-based alignment is to use the information given in pairwise alignment analyses of the data to derive an alignment-specific scoring matrix. In the initial stage, the substitution scores for all residue pairs in the scoring matrix are set to 0. After the pairwise alignments have been carried out, the scoring matrix is extended by increasing the score for each residue pair which occurs in the primary library by a certain weight. While in consistency-based methods in biology, such as, e.g. the T-Coffee algorithm (Notredame et al. 2000), the

---

[8] In evolutionary biology, the term *orphan* is used to refer to "distant members of a [protein] family" (Thompson et al. 1999: 2684).

weights for the substitution matrix are derived from percentage identity (see Equation 3.1 on page 74), the SCA method employs a different strategy, since, in contrast to biology, sequence identity is not a reliable measure in linguistics. Given the sequences A and B, the weight W_{xy} for the residues x and y being matched in an alignment of A and B is derived by the formula:

$$(4.3) \qquad W_{xy} = \frac{1}{2} \cdot \left(\frac{S_{AB}}{L_{AB}} + M_{xy} \right),$$

where S_{AB} is the similarity score of the alignment of A and B, L_{AB} is the length of the alignment, and M_{xy} is the original substitution score for the residues. This equation combines both the general similarity of the aligned sequences and the individual similarity of the residue pair as defined by the scoring function. Apart from this modified weight formula, the consistency-based alignment of the SCA method does not differ from the description given in Section 3.4.2.

Detection of Swapped Sites

Swaps (crossed matches, see Section 3.2.1) are ignored in most approaches to phonetic alignment that have been proposed so far (Heeringa et al. 2006, Kessler 1995, Kondrak 2002, Prokić et al. 2009). Authors usually justify this ignorance for crossed matches by emphasizing the rareness of sound changes involving metathesis (Kondrak 2002: 50). A further problem is that it is quite difficult to extend the Needleman-Wunsch algorithm to account for transpositions, especially when dealing with specific scoring matrices instead of simple edit operations (Nerbonne and Heeringa 2010: 557). It may, however, nevertheless be useful to have a procedure that deals with swaps, since metathesis is not so rare as it is often claimed and it even regularly occurs in some languages (Hock 1991: 110).

The SCA strategy to deal with swaps differs from previous, formal solutions to the problem (Lowrance and Wagner 1975, Oommen and Loke 1997, Wagner 1975), in so far as it is not part of the basic alignment algorithm but a posterior procedure that is applied to already conducted multiple and pairwise alignment analyses. The basic idea of the method is to make use of the fact that the alignment of swaps in phonetic sequences often follows a similar pattern.

Given two hypothetical sequences "FORMA" and "FROMA", we may align and score them in different ways. When allowing for swaps, the Damerau-

4.2 Phonetic Alignment

 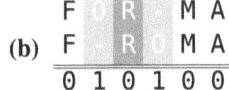 

Figure 4.9: *Different representations of swaps in alignment analyses*

Levenshtein distance (named after the work of F. J. Damerau and V. I. Levenshtein, cf. Damerau 1964 and Levenshtein 1965) can be used. It builds on the edit distance (cf. Table 3.2), but it provides an additional penalty of 1 for crossed matches. A gap-free alignment of "FORMA" with "FROMA" will therefore yield a total score of 1, since the sequences only differ by one transposition (see Figure 4.9a). Once we exclude transpositions in the scoring scheme, we arrive at a score of 2. With a different scoring scheme where gaps are scored as 1, but mismatches are scored as 2, we can force the algorithm to avoid mismatches by spreading the swapped region over three columns instead of two (see Figure 4.9b and c).

This is exactly the situation we find in most phonetic alignments, where swapped regions in sequences are aligned over three columns instead of being crushed into one. The usual alignment of Russian *яблоко* [jabləkə] and Bulgarian *ябълка* [jabəlka] 'apple' is | $\begin{smallmatrix}j\\j\end{smallmatrix}$ $\begin{smallmatrix}a\\a\end{smallmatrix}$ $\begin{smallmatrix}b\\b\end{smallmatrix}$ $\begin{smallmatrix}-\\ə\end{smallmatrix}$ $\begin{smallmatrix}l\\l\end{smallmatrix}$ $\begin{smallmatrix}ə\\-\end{smallmatrix}$ $\begin{smallmatrix}k\\k\end{smallmatrix}$ $\begin{smallmatrix}ə\\a\end{smallmatrix}$ |, rather than | $\begin{smallmatrix}j\\j\end{smallmatrix}$ $\begin{smallmatrix}a\\a\end{smallmatrix}$ $\begin{smallmatrix}b\\b\end{smallmatrix}$ $\begin{smallmatrix}ə\\ə\end{smallmatrix}$ $\begin{smallmatrix}l\\l\end{smallmatrix}$ $\begin{smallmatrix}k\\k\end{smallmatrix}$ $\begin{smallmatrix}ə\\a\end{smallmatrix}$ |. This is due to the fact that most phonetic alignment approaches, including the one presented in this study, disfavor the matching of consonants and vowels. Since most cases of metathesis involve the transposition of vowels and consonants, the natural representation of swaps in phonetic alignment analyses is the one that spreads them over three columns.

Detecting complementary columns in a given alignment is not difficult, and the computational effort is also rather low, since phonetic alignments are usually very short. Regions containing complementary columns, however, do not necessarily contain swaps. The easiest way to test whether complementary regions really point to swaps in an alignment is to calculate a *swap score* (an alignment score that allows for swaps), and to compare it with the original score: if the swap-score is better (higher in case of similarities, lower in case of distances), the swap is confirmed, if not, it is rejected.

There are surely many different ways to calculate an alignment score which allows for swaps. Within the SCA approach, the calculation of swap-scores

Figure 4.10: *Calculating the swap-score with help of a trace character*

is done by introducing a *trace character* ("+") into the sound class alphabet. This character scores only when it is matched with a gap, the score being the swap penalty. When matched with itself the trace character scores 0, and it scores ∞ (or $-\infty$ when dealing with similarities) when being matched with any other character. The character is introduced into the gapped columns of a complementary site instead of all non-gap characters. The characters themselves are moved to the position where they would appear, if there was no swap in the alignment. The trace character "+" thus moves the original character by inducing a swap penalty at the same time. When transforming a given alignment in this way, the resulting score is identical with the Damerau-Levenshtein distance (if the swap penalty is set to 1), yielding 1 for two similar sequences which only differ by one transposition (see Figure 4.10).

One specific advantage of this procedure compared to the formal approaches to swap detection is that it works for pairwise as well as multiple alignments. Being a posterior method, it has the further advantage that it does not influence the computational complexity of the basic algorithm. It is left to the user to decide whether a search for swapped regions should be carried out in addition to the basic alignment analysis, or not.

The method for swap detection is illustrated in Figure 4.11 for the alignment of the four cognate words Czech *žlutý* [ʒlutiː], Russian жёлтый [ʒoltɨj], Polish *żółty* [ʒoltɨj], and Bulgarian жълт [ʒɤlt] 'yellow' (DERKSEN: 565). In stage ①, the alignment is searched for complementary sites and the sum-of-pairs score is calculated. In stage ②, two copies of the alignment are created, one which is identical with the original one, and one in which the three columns of the probably swapped region are shifted in such a way that the outer columns appear as the inner column and the inner column is split into two outer ones. In stage ③, the trace character is inserted in the rightmost column and the rightmost non-gap characters are inserted in the first column. In stage ④, the sum-of-pairs scores for both new alignments are calculated. The comparison

4.2 Phonetic Alignment

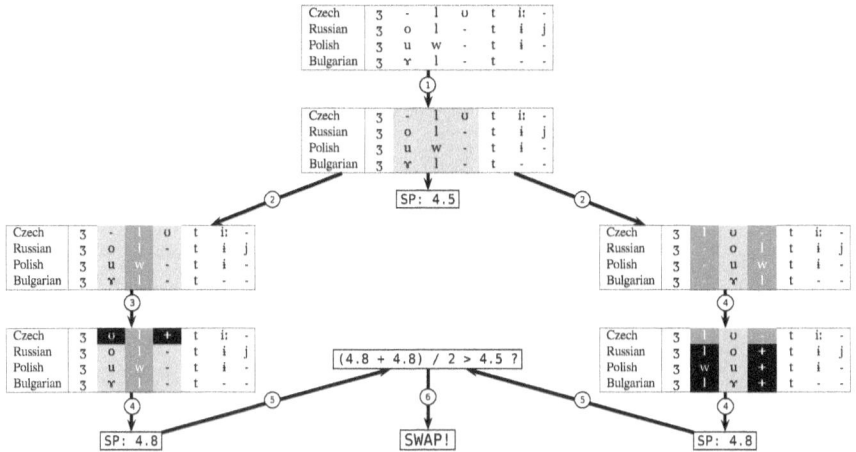

Figure 4.11: *SCA method for the detection of swapped sites*

of the average of the new scores with the original score in stage ⑤ yields the final decision in stage ⑥.

4.2.4 Evaluation

Gold Standard

Since automatic sequence comparison in historical linguistics is still in its infancy, the number of benchmark databases which are available is very limited. Covington (1996) tested his algorithm for pairwise phonetic alignment on a small dataset consisting of 82 sequence pairs (henceforth called the Covington Benchmark). Unfortunately, he only presented the results, without providing a gold standard. The test set has nevertheless been used as a benchmark for pairwise phonetic alignment algorithms in a couple of studies (Kondrak 2000, Somers 1999), and the results for the comparison of the algorithms by Covington (1996), Oakes (2000), and Somers (1999), and Kondrak (2000) are given in Kondrak (2002), which makes it very convenient to compare theim with the current proposal.

For multiple phonetic alignments, Prokić et al. (2009) compiled a benchmark database (henceforth called the BulDial Benchmark) consisting of 152

Dataset	Languages	PSA	MSA	Words	Taxa	PID	Source
Andean	Andean dialects (Aymara, Quechua)	619	76	883	20	55	SAL
Bai	Bai dialects	889	90	1416	17	32	BDS, Wang 2006a
Bulgarian	Bulgarian dialects	1515	152	32418	197	48	Prokić et al. 2009
Dutch	Dutch dialects	500	50	3024	62	44	MAND
French	French dialects	712	76	3810	62	41	TPPSR
Germanic	Germanic languages and dialects	1110	111	4775	45	32	LOE
Japanese	Japanese dialects	219	26	224	10	40	Shirō 1973
Norwegian	Norwegian dialects	501	51	2183	51	46	NORDAVINDEN
Ob-Ugrian	Uralic languages	444	48	689	21	45	GLD
Romance	Romance languages	297	30	240	8	37	LOE
Sinitic	Chinese dialects	200	20	20	40	35	YINKU
Slavic	Slavic languages	120	20	81	5	38	DERKSEN

Table 4.8: *Data sources of the gold standard for phonetic alignment*

manually edited MSAs covering 197 taxa and more than 30 000 words taken from Bulgarian dialect data (Buldialect). Prokić et al. (2009) also reported the results of the ALPHAMALIG algorithm for multiple sequence alignment (Alonso et al. 2004) on the BulDial Benchmark. These results were directly compared with those obtained by an early version of SCA (List 2012b). In List (2012c) a new manually edited benchmark dataset was presented. Including the BulDial Benchmark, kindly provided by the authors of Prokić et al. (2009), it consists of 600 MSAs covering six different language families, 435 different taxa, and a total of 45 947 words. The extended benchmark database also included a pairwise partition which was directly extracted from the MSAs by taking the 5 506 most divergent, unique word pairs.

For this study, an extended version of the previously used benchmark databases was compiled. The new phonetic alignment benchmark consists of manually edited pairwise and multiple alignment analyses.[9] The MSA partition of the phonetic alignment benchmark consists of 750 manually edited MSAs, covering eight language families, 528 different taxa (language varieties), and 50 089 words (14 217 of them unique). The database consists of 12 partitions which either correspond to a language family, or to the dialects of a single language variety. The dataset is further divided into four subsets, covering different regions of diversity, whereas diversity is measured as the average percentage identity of an alignment (see Equation 3.2 on page 74).

---

[9] The full data is available as part of the supporting online material accompanying this study (see Supplementary Material I).

4.2 Phonetic Alignment

The subsets and their range are listed in Table 4.9. The PSA benchmark, consisting of 7 126 sequence pairs, was extracted automatically by selecting the most divergent sequence pairs from each partition of the benchmark for multiple phonetic alignments, using percentage identity as a measure of divergence. The alignments were edited manually by different contributors. Table 4.8 gives an overview over the different partitions of the data, along with the number of files, words and taxa, the average percentage identity (PID) of the respective partition, and the data sources. In Figure 4.12 the similarity of alignments in the pairwise and the multiple partition of the benchmark is plotted in histograms.

Thompson (2009: 154f) lists four requirements for benchmark databases for computational tasks in biology: (1) relevance, (2) solvability, (3) accessibility, and (4) evolution. *Relevance* refers to the tests in the benchmark which should be "representative of the problems that the system is reasonably expected to handle in a natural [...] setting" (ibid.: 154). *Solvability* refers to the tasks presented by the benchmark. They should not be "too difficult for all or most tools" (ibid.: 154f), in order to allow for comparisons between different algorithms and methods. *Accessibility* refers to both the easiness to obtain and to use the data. *Evolution* refers to the requirement that benchmarks change constantly in order to avoid that programs are being optimized with respect to the benchmark instead of the general task the benchmark was designed to represent. The current version of the phonetic alignment benchmark was designed to fulfil these requirements as good as possible: The number of datasets from different languages was drastically increased, both in comparison to the Covington Benchmark and the BulDial Benchmark. In order to guarantee solvability, only cognate sets with little morphological variation are included.

Subset	Range	MSAs	PID Ø
PID_100	100 – 70	15	76
PID_70	70 – 50	207	57
PID_50	50 – 30	438	38
PID_30	30 – 0	90	19

Table 4.9: *Four subsets of the benchmark for multiple phonetic alignment*

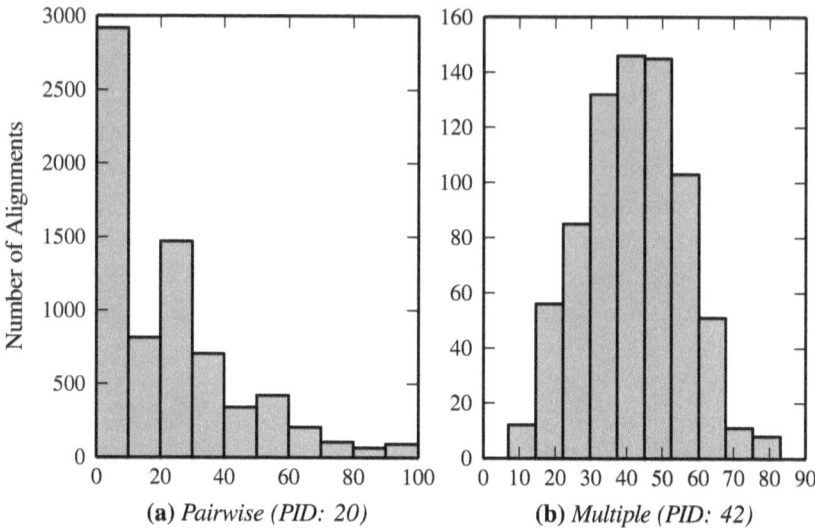

Figure 4.12: *Percentage Identity (PID) of the alignments in the gold standard for pairwise* (a) *and multiple alignments* (b).

In order to guarantee consistency and applicability, all words are encoded in IPA. Only the last of the four requirements cannot be addressed at the moment. Since – in contrast to biology – phonetic alignment at the moment still plays a minor role in historical linguistics, it is not clear whether it will be possible to find the resources to change the current benchmark regularly.

Evaluation Measures

Given a reference set (a gold standard) and a test set (the output of an algorithm), the simplest way to test how well an alignment algorithm performs is to calculate the *perfect alignments score* (PAS), i.e. the proportion of alignments which are identical in test set and gold standard. Since this score only reveals very strong tendencies, a couple of different methods have been proposed to test how well alignment algorithms perform in comparison with benchmark datasets (Prokić et al. 2009, Thompson et al. 1999). The comparison of alignments produced by automatic methods with alignment benchmarks, however, is a complicated task, and all these methods bear certain shortcomings.

4.2 Phonetic Alignment

When comparing two alignments, there are two basic perspectives that can be taken, namely (1) the *row perspective*, and (2) the *column perspective*. The former focuses on the rows in both the reference and the test alignment, and the latter focuses on the columns. A simple way to compare a reference with a test alignment is to base the comparison solely on one of the two perspectives. For the row perspective, such a comparison is very straightforward, since both the reference and the test alignment have always the same number of sequences (rows). One may therefore simply calculate a *row score* (RS) by applying the formula:

$$(4.4) \qquad RS = 100 \cdot \frac{|R_t \cap R_r|}{|R_t|},$$

where R_t is the set of rows in the test alignment and R_r is the set of rows in the reference alignment. The RS is not used in biological applications. This may be due to the fact that the score may yield some intuitively strange results, especially when only two sequences are aligned. Thus, in case of pairwise alignments, one may encounter the strange situation that one of the rows is identical in test and reference set, while the other row is not. The resulting score of 0.5 seems to be meaningless in such a case, since nothing is said about the degree of difference between test and reference alignment.

For the column perspective, the comparison becomes a little bit more complicated, since the number of columns in test and reference alignment may differ. In applications of information retrieval it is common to evaluate algorithms by calculating their *precision* and *recall*. Precision refers to the proportion of items in the test set that also occur in the reference set. Recall refers to the proportion of items in the reference set that also occur in the test set (Witten and Frank 2005: 171). Transferring this to the column perspective, one can define the *column precision* (CP) as:

$$(4.5) \qquad CP = 100 \cdot \frac{|C_t \cap C_r|}{|C_t|},$$

where C_t is the set of columns in the test alignment and C_r is the set of columns in the reference alignment. Accordingly, the *column recall* (CR) may be defined by modifying Equation 4.5 into:

$$(4.6) \qquad CR = 100 \cdot \frac{|C_t \cap C_r|}{|C_r|}.$$

No.	Reference				Test (columns)					Test (rows)				
(a)	A	B	C	D	A	B	C	-	D	A	B	C	-	D
	A	B	-	D	A	B	-	D	-	A	B	-	D	-
	A	-	C	-	A	-	C	-	-	A	-	C	-	-
(b)	A	B	C	D	A	B	C	D		A	B	C	D	
	A	B	-	D	A	B	-	D		A	B	-	D	
	A	-	C	-	-	A	-	C		-	A	-	C	

Table 4.10: *Row and column score bias resulting from small errors in single sequences. Shaded regions indicate rows and columns which differ from the reference alignment.*

Since both CP and CR measure different aspects of alignment similarities (Rosenberg and Ogden 2009: 198), it is useful to define a more general score that combines both of them. Following the suggestion of Lassmann and Sonnhammer (2002) and Rosenberg and Ogden (2009: 186), a general *column score* (CS) can be defined by taking the average of $|C_t|$ and $|C_r|$ (which is equivalent with calculating the harmonic mean of both scores):

$$(4.7) \quad CS = 100 \cdot \frac{|C_t \cap C_r|}{\frac{1}{2} \cdot (|C_r| + |C_t|)} = 100 \cdot 2 \cdot \frac{|C_t \cap C_r|}{|C_r| + |C_t|}.$$

In contrast to the RS, the CS is often used in biology (Lassmann and Sonnhammer 2002, Thompson et al. 1999). The definition for the CS, however, varies in the literature. In most approaches, it corresponds to the column precision as it was defined in Equation 4.5, but in practice it seldom differs from the average of column precision and recall. For reasons of consistency and simplicity, I will therefore only use the general CS as defined in Equation 4.7 in this study.

Both measures, the row score and the column score, have specific drawbacks. Since neither of them distinguishes degrees of similarity between columns and rows, errors resulting from small differences in test and reference alignment may yield large differences in the scores. Table 4.10 illustrates this bias, by giving examples where (a) one misaligned sequence results in the difference of all rows, and (b) one misaligned sequence results in the difference of all columns. As a result, the RS of (a) and the CS of (b) is 0, suggesting that there is no similarity at all between reference and test alignment. Nevertheless,

4.2 Phonetic Alignment

both scores are useful to give a rough estimation of alignment accuracy. Being very conservative, they are especially capable to point to large differences and strong tendencies when comparing the performance of several algorithms.

More fine-graded measures for the evaluation of alignment accuracy in biology are based on the comparison of reference and test alignment on a pairwise basis. This can easily be done by comparing the aligned residue pairs (segment pairs) in reference and test alignment. Similar to the calculation of columns scores, the *pair precision* (PP) can be defined as:

$$(4.8) \qquad PP = 100 \cdot \frac{|P_t \cap P_r|}{|P_t|},$$

where P_t is the set of all aligned residue pairs in the test alignment and P_r is the set of all aligned residue pairs in the reference alignment. Accordingly, the *pair recall* (PR) can be defined as:

$$(4.9) \qquad PR = 100 \cdot \frac{|P_t \cap P_r|}{|P_r|},$$

and a general *pair score* (PS) can be defined by taking the harmonic mean of pair precision and pair recall:

$$(4.10) \qquad PS = 100 \cdot 2 \cdot \frac{|P_t \cap P_r|}{|P_r| + |P_t|}.$$

PR is the most widely used pair score in biology, where it is usually termed *sum-of-pairs score* (SPS, cf. Thompson et al. 1999). Using only the PR, and not the more general PS, however, has certain drawbacks. Since gaps are ignored, in all pair scores, a situation may arise where pair precision or pair recall yield a score of 1, indicating full identity of reference and test alignment, although they are in fact different. Thus, the PR (or SPS) for reference and test alignment in Table 4.11a is 1 since all pairs which occur in the reference alignment *also* occur in the test alignment. That the test alignment itself has two more pairs which do *not* occur in the reference alignment, is ignored by this measure. The same holds for the PP when comparing reference and test alignment in Table 4.11b. Using the more general PS instead, these problems can be easily avoided. Instead of 1, the PS for 4.11a is $100 \cdot 2 \cdot \frac{7}{16} = 87.5$ and for 4.11b it is $100 \cdot 2 \cdot \frac{4}{11} = 72.0$.

Prokić et al. (2009) propose two additional scores as a measure of alignment accuracy: the *column dependent evaluation* (CDE) and the *modified rand index* (MRI). The CDE is similar to the CS, but it takes the similarity instead of

No.	Reference	Test	Pairs (Reference)	Pairs (Test)
(a)	A - C D A B - D A - C -	A C D A B D A C -	AA, -B, CC, DD, AA, --, C-, DD, AA, -B, -C, DD	AA, CC, DD, AA, CB, DD, AA, BC, DD
(b)	A - C D A B - D A - C -	A - C D - A B - - D A - C - -	AA, B-, C-, DD, AA, --, CC, DD, AA, -B, -C, DD	AA, B-, C-, D-, -D AA, --, CC, --, -- AA, -B, -C, -D, D-

Table 4.11: *Bias in pair precision (a) and pair recall (b). Pairs shaded in light gray indicate gaps and are ignored when calculating the scores. Pairs shaded in dark gray are ignored in the calculation.*

the identity of the columns into account. The MRI is similar to the pair scores, since it ignores the placement of gaps, and compares reference and test alignment from a pairwise perspective. Both the CDE and the MRI generally yield similar tendencies as either the column score or the pair score. For this reason and because of the broad use of column and pair scores in biology, only RS, CS, and PS will be taken as evaluation measures in the following.

Results

All results which are reported in the following were achieved by using the most recent version the SCA method along with identical parameters for the different parts of the analysis. All parameters correspond to the default settings of the SCA method as they are implemented in LingPy. In all alignment analyses, the GOP was set to -2. The relative weights for the modification of gap penalties follow the default parameters of LingPy (see Table 4.4). Instead of a fixed gap extension penalty, SCA employs a gap extension *scale*, by which an extended gap is modified. This value was set to 0.5. Thus, in extended gaps the gap scores were halved by the algorithm. These settings were used in both PPA and MPA analyses. In all MPA analyses, the guide tree was calculated using the Neighbor-Joining algorithm (Saitou and Nei 1987). In consistency-based MPA analyses, the GOP for global alignments was set to -2, and for local alignments it was set to -1. All results of the analyses which are discussed in the following are available as part of the supporting online material accompanying this study (see Supplementary Material II).

4.2 Phonetic Alignment

Subset	PSA	Score						
		Covington	Somers	Oakes	Kondrak	SCA		
						DOLGO	SCA	ASJP
Spanish-French	20	19.0	17.0	15.0	20.0	18.0	20.0	20.0
English-German	20	18.0	18.0	16.0	18.5	20.0	20.0	19.0
English-Latin	25	18.1	19.5	9.0	24.0	24.0	24.0	24.0
Fox-Menomini	10	9.0	9.0	9.0	9.5	9.0	9.0	10.0
Other	7	4.7	3.0	4.0	6.0	5.0	7.0	7.0
Total	82	68.8	66.5	53.0	78.0	76.0	80.0	80.0

Table 4.12: *Performance of different alignment algorithms on the Covington benchmark.*

Pairwise Phonetic Alignment Kondrak (2002) uses the Covington Benchmark in order to compare the performance of the algorithms of Covington (1996) and Somers (1999), and Oakes (2000) with his ALINE algorithm (Kondrak 2000). The evaluation measure is roughly identical with the above-mentioned PAS score, i.e. the number of identically aligned sequence pairs in reference and test set is counted. If an algorithm yields more than one output for a given pair, the results are averaged. In order to get a first impression regarding the general quality of SCA alignments in comparison with other methods for pairwise sequence comparison, the Covington Benchmark was analyzed using the three standard models of LingPy (DOLGO, SCA, ASJP) with their respective default parameters and the semi-global extension to the Needleman-Wunsch algorithm. The results for the three models along with the scores achieved by the other algorithms (taken from Kondrak 2002: 64) are listed in Table 4.12. As can be seen from the table, both the SCA and the ASJP model perform slightly better than Kondrak's ALINE, whereas the DOLGO model performs slightly worse, although it still outperforms all the other algorithms.[10]

Although often used for the assessment of alignment quality, the Covington Benchmark is clearly no good benchmark for pairwise sequence alignments. Apart from being too small, both regarding the number of sequence pairs and the number of languages being covered, many of the alignments simply fail to be a real challenge for an alignment algorithm (ibid.: 61). This is also

---

[10] The items where the three models differ from the gold standard are given in Appendix C.1.

reflected in the average PID of 37, which is rather high for a pairwise alignment benchmark. The pairwise gold standard of the phonetic alignment benchmark consists of 7 126 aligned word pairs with an average PID of 20. It should therefore be much more challenging than the Covington Benchmark.

The PSA gold standard was analyzed using the three different sound-class models provided by LingPy and the traditional Needleman-Wunsch algorithm for global pairwise alignment. In order to test to what degree the new approaches to sequence modelling discussed in Section 4.1 would influence the results of pairwise alignment analyses, four different analyses for each of the three different modes were carried out: (1) a simple global alignment analysis (Basic), (2) a global alignment analysis in which gap costs and substitution scores were scaled in dependence of prosodic environments (Scale), (3) a simple global alignment analysis which was sensitive to secondary sequence structures as extracted from tone markers in South-East Asian languages and word boundaries in the Dutch partition of the pairwise phonetic alignment benchmark (Secondary), and (4) a global alignment analysis which was sensitive to both prosodic environments and secondary sequence structures (Sec-Scale).

Model	Measure	Mode			
		Basic	Scale	Secondary	Sec-Scale
DOLGO	PAS	80.52	83.23	81.74	84.87
	RS	84.47	85.86	85.39	87.01
	CS	88.31	90.55	89.26	91.31
	PS	92.70	94.21	93.33	94.70
ASJP	PAS	83.64	84.62	85.00	86.09
	RS	86.48	86.82	87.49	87.89
	CS	91.00	91.63	91.88	92.47
	PS	94.53	94.97	95.09	95.50
SCA	PAS	84.98	86.57	86.29	88.18
	RS	87.59	88.33	88.61	89.54
	CS	91.69	92.83	92.68	93.74
	PS	94.90	95.67	95.54	96.24

Table 4.13: *Results of the PSA Analysis*

4.2 Phonetic Alignment

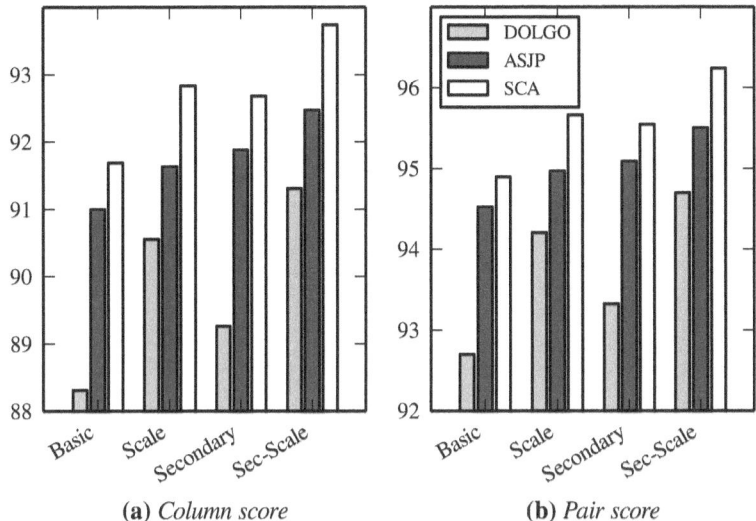

(a) *Column score*   (b) *Pair score*

Figure 4.13: *Results of the PSA analysis*

As can be seen from the results shown in Table 4.13 and Figure 4.13, all three complex modes (Scale, Secondary and Sec-Scale) improve the accuracy of the pairwise alignment analyses compared to the Basic mode independent of the evaluation measure. The improvement is significant in all cases with $p < 0.01$, using the Wilcoxon signed rank test as suggested by Notredame et al. (2000). The combination of both the Scale and the Secondary mode shows the greatest improvement, yielding the highest scores regardless of measure or model. In all analyses, the SCA model performs best, followed by the ASJP model and the DOLGO model, the differences being significant between all models ($p < 0.01$, using the Wilcoxon test). Apparently, both prosodic context and secondary alignment are very useful extensions for automatic alignment analyses.

Secondary alignment is, of course, only useful, if secondary sequence structures are relevant for an alignment analysis, as it is the case for tone languages. However, of the 7 126 alignments in the pairwise benchmark, only 1 089, i.e. 15%, come from South-East-Asian languages like Chinese or Bai. Given the fact that only 15% of the data apparently account for a significant improve-

Model	Measure	Mode			
		Basic	Scale	Secondary	Sec-Scale
DOLGO	PAS	75.30	75.76	83.65	84.94
	RS	81.31	82.05	87.60	88.80
	CS	81.43	84.58	87.51	88.85
	PS	87.80	89.85	91.90	92.62
ASJP	PAS	79.06	79.89	87.60	88.98
	RS	83.79	84.62	90.08	91.14
	CS	87.11	88.60	92.32	93.36
	PS	91.83	92.73	95.27	95.85
SCA	PAS	79.43	79.71	87.88	89.44
	RS	83.43	83.98	89.94	91.23
	CS	85.19	87.76	91.33	92.81
	PS	90.52	92.22	94.64	95.50

Table 4.14: *Results of the PSA analysis (tone language partition)*

ment in alignment accuracy, a further analysis was carried out. This time, only the 1 089 alignments belonging to tone languages were analyzed. As can be seen from the results given in Table 4.14 and Figure 4.14, the improvement resulting from the new sequence models becomes even more apparent. Comparing only the PAS, reflecting the number of perfectly aligned word pairs, the Sec-Scale analyses are all between 9 and 10% better than the Basic analyses in all models. The improvement of the complex modes compared to the Basic mode is again significant in all cases ($p < 0.01$) As in the previous analyses, the DOLGO model performs worse than ASJP and SCA. This time, however, the ASJP model performs better than SCA in all modes.

So far, all tests were based on global alignment analyses only. Hence, as a final part of the evaluation of pairwise sound-class-based phonetic alignments, the performance of the four different alignment modes (global, semi-global, local, and diagonal, see Section 3.3.2) on pairwise benchmark was tested. Since the output of pairwise local alignment analyses differs from the output of the other modes, the evaluation of the local alignments was only based on the core part of the alignments, i.e. the part which remains when all consecutive gaps in the beginning and the end of an alignment are stripped of.

4.2 Phonetic Alignment

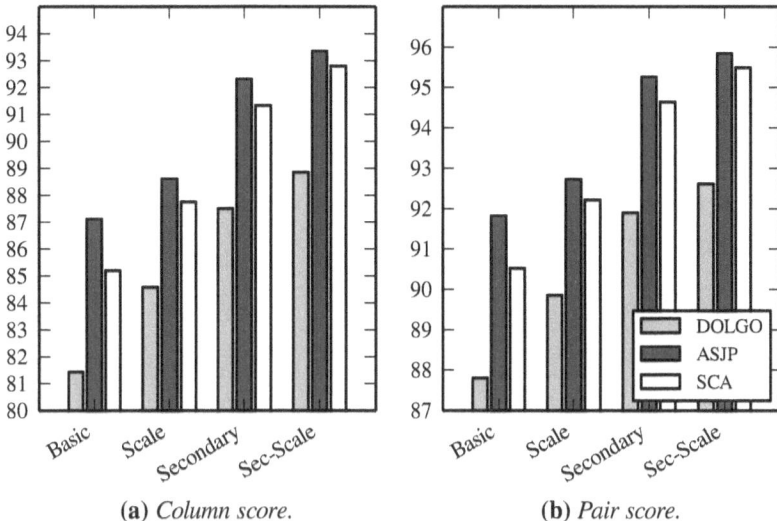

(a) *Column score.* (b) *Pair score.*

Figure 4.14: *Results of the PSA analysis (tone language partition)*

For this analysis, only the Sec-Scale mode was used, since it showed the best performance in the previous analyses.

Model	Measure	Mode			
		Global	**Semi-Global**	**Local**	**Diagonal**
DOLGO	PAS	84.87	85.22	85.56	84.23
	RS	87.01	87.17	85.76	86.32
	CS	91.31	91.35	92.72	91.30
	PS	94.70	94.68	95.03	94.84
ASJP	PAS	86.09	85.87	85.52	83.53
	RS	87.89	87.83	86.05	84.75
	CS	92.47	92.23	92.89	91.93
	PS	95.50	95.35	95.15	95.17
SCA	PAS	88.18	88.25	84.51	76.76
	RS	89.54	89.42	84.87	76.70
	CS	93.74	93.61	93.78	90.18
	PS	96.24	96.12	95.79	94.39

Table 4.15: *Results of the PSA analysis for different alignment modes*

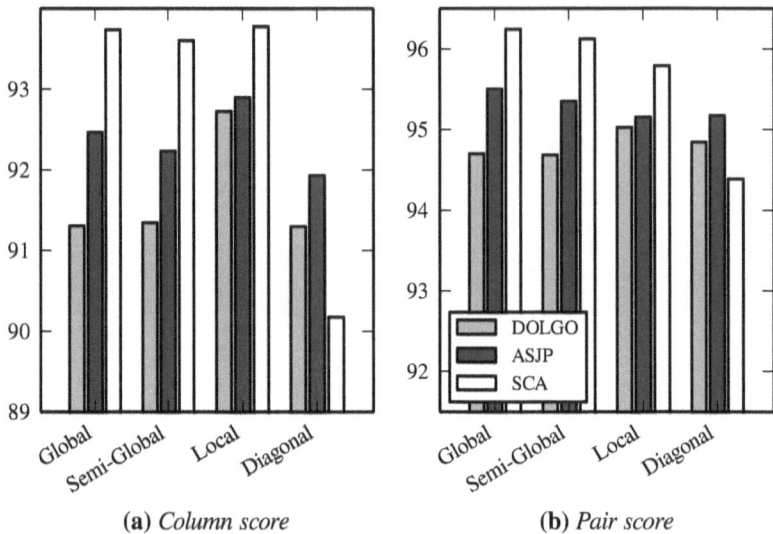

(a) *Column score*   (b) *Pair score*

Figure 4.15: *Results of the PSA analysis for different alignment modes*

The results given in Table 4.15 and Figure 4.15 might come as a surprise, since – in contrast to the previous analyses, which all showed a more or less general tendency throughout all sound-class models – the different alignment modes seem to perform quite differently in dependence of the respective sound-class model being used. Thus, for the SCA model, a more or less clear hierarchy ranging from global via semi-global and local to diagonal mode can be determined.[11] The ASJP model seems to have a similar tendency, yet the differences between the diagonal mode and the other modes are much smaller. For the DOLGO model, the column and pair scores of the Diagonal mode are equal or even better than for the Global and Semi-Global mode, and the best results in terms of pair and column scores are achieved with the Local mode. Hence, while it seems to be the best choice to align in global mode when using the SCA model, it is much more difficult to find the right mode for the ASJP

---

[11] The high column scores in the local modes for all sound-class models are probably due to the fact that only the core blocks of the gold standard alignments were used for the evaluation of alignments produced by the local mode. The general tendency is therefore much more reliably reflected in the row and pair scores.

4.2 Phonetic Alignment

Model	Measure	Mode			
		Basic	Library	Iteration	Lib-Iter
DOLGO	PAS	70.13	73.07	74.13	75.60
	RS	81.35	81.46	83.69	83.77
	CS	85.80	87.36	87.75	88.49
	PS	97.19	97.82	97.85	98.12
ASJP	PAS	74.00	76.53	78.93	79.33
	RS	82.98	84.46	86.04	87.05
	CS	88.05	89.52	90.53	90.87
	PS	97.69	98.58	98.46	98.87
SCA	PAS	76.40	77.87	79.60	81.33
	RS	85.27	85.59	88.58	89.02
	CS	89.02	90.26	91.18	91.96
	PS	97.98	98.64	98.63	98.96

Table 4.16: *Results of the MSA analysis*

and the DOLGO model. Therefore, no final conclusion regarding the reliability of the four alignment modes can be made. When carrying out phonetic alignment analyses, it is important to find the right balance between models and modes.

Multiple Sequence Alignment As for the analysis of the pairwise benchmark, the multiple benchmark was analyzed using the three different sound-class models provided by LingPy. Again, analyses in four different modes were carried out for each model: (1) a progressive alignment analysis (Basic), (2) a progressive alignment analysis with iterative refinement (Iterate), (3) a consistency-based alignment analysis (Library), and (4) a consistency-based alignment analysis in combination with iterative refinement (Lib-Iterate). The iterative refinement analysis was based on the three heuristics described in Section 4.2.3. The library was created from pairwise global, local, and diagonal alignment analyses of all sequence pairs, and the scoring matrix was created from the library as described in Section 4.2.3. Having confirmed that both prosodic context and secondary alignment may significantly improve alignment analyses, the leading question of this analysis was now to clarify

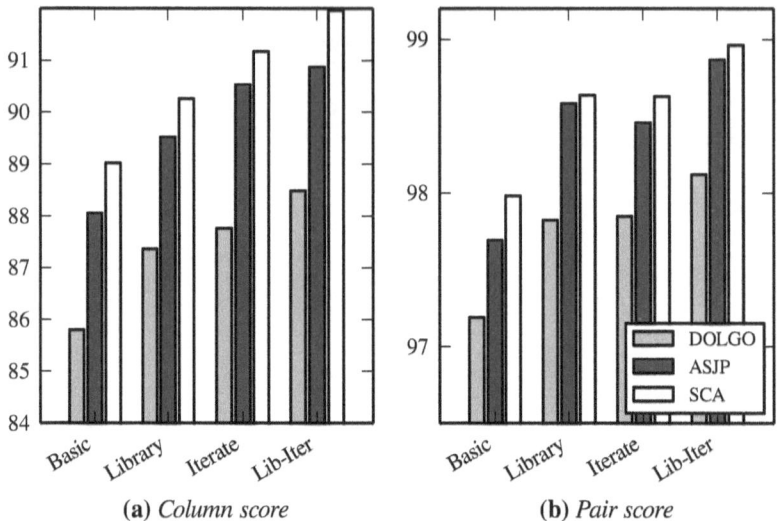

Figure 4.16: *Results of the MSA analysis*

to which degree the modifications to traditional progressive alignment influence the results of multiple alignment analyses.

Looking at the results given in Table 4.16 and Figure 4.16, it becomes obvious that pre- and postprocessing using consistency-based scoring functions and iterative refinement significantly improves the results of multiple alignment analyses ($p < 0.01$ for CS and PS using the Wilcoxon test). The best results are achieved when combining both modes. Similar to the pairwise alignment analyses, the SCA model performs best, followed by ASJP and DOLGO, the difference between all models being significant ($p < 0.01$ for CS and PS).

In order to get some clearer insights into the strengths and weaknesses of the different sound-class models, the performance of the Lib-Iterate analyses on the four subsets of the multiple alignment benchmark was calculated. As can be seen from the results given in Table 4.17 and Figure 4.17, the SCA model again achieves the highest scores in all analyses, followed by ASJP and DOLGO. As one may expect, all models loose accuracy the more divergent the sequences become. The differences between ASJP and SCA, on the one hand, and DOLGO on the other hand, however, are not very great in the PID_70 and

4.2 Phonetic Alignment

Model	Measure	Mode			
		PID_100	PID_70	PID_50	PID_30
DOLGO	PAS	93.33	85.99	71.47	69.93
	RS	93.33	90.35	82.43	77.23
	CS	98.25	95.00	87.03	82.30
	PS	99.92	99.44	98.30	95.71
ASJP	PAS	93.33	88.89	76.27	72.55
	RS	93.33	92.71	85.48	82.63
	CS	98.25	96.16	89.53	86.29
	PS	99.92	99.63	98.81	97.87
SCA	PAS	93.33	90.34	78.40	75.16
	RS	93.33	94.56	87.72	84.26
	CS	98.25	96.78	90.66	88.03
	PS	99.92	99.74	98.88	98.01

Table 4.17: *Results on different gold standard partitions*

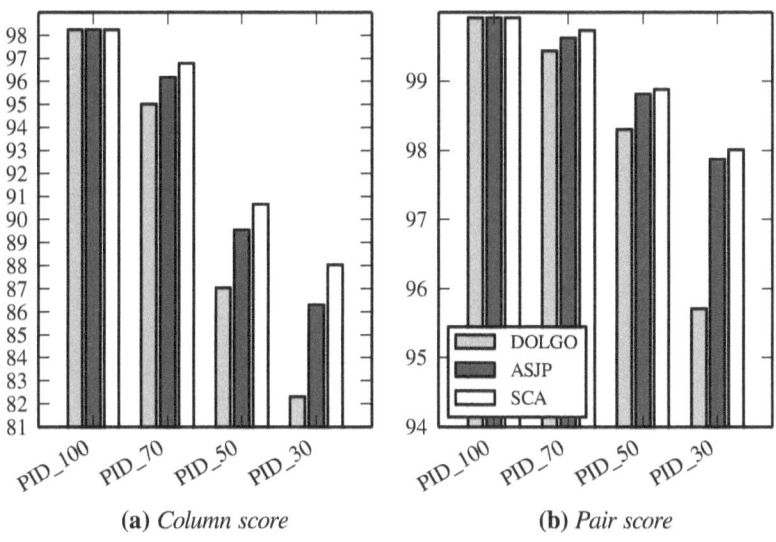

(a) *Column score*   (b) *Pair score*

Figure 4.17: *Results on different gold standard partitions*

the PID_50 subset, while they increase drastically in the PID_30 partition. In List (2012c), a similar increase in the differences could be found between ASJP and SCA. For the most recent version of the SCA approach, this difference can no longer be confirmed. Both model show a comparable accuracy in very divergent sequences.[12]

Swap Detection Of the 750 MSAs in the benchmark, 69 are marked as containing swapped sites. In order to test, how well the method for swap detection described in Section 4.2.3 works, all files were analyzed using the three standard sound-class models of LingPy along with consistency-based scoring functions and iterative refinement (the Lib-Iterate mode). In order to evaluate the accuracy of swap detection, the common distinction between *true positives*, *false positives*, and *false negatives* can be used. *True positives*, however, can be further divided into those which match the respective columns correctly (*true site*) and those which do not (*wrong site*). The results for the analysis are given in Table 4.18. Judging from these results, it is difficult to decide which model really performs best: the DOLGO model with its high recall, or the ASJP model with its high precision. The detection of swapped sites crucially depends on the swap penalty, which was set to −2 for all models. Lowering this penalty will increase the recall, yet it will also decrease the precision, and more testing is needed to find the right balance between false positives and false negatives.

Category		DOLGO	ASJP	SCA
True Positive	True Site	58	51	51
	Wrong Site	2	2	1
False Positive		7	2	2
False Negative		9	16	17

Table 4.18: *Results of the swap-identification task*

---

[12] This may be due to the fact that in the new analyses the weights for prosodic context were further refined, resulting in a generally enhanced performance of phonetic alignment analyses using the ASJP model.

4.2.5 Examples

Pairwise Phonetic Alignment In Figure 4.18 two different alignment analyses of dialect variants of Dutch *berg* [bɛrx] 'mountain' are given. The first one is the typical output of a traditional alignment analysis with an extended scoring scheme (SCA-Basic). The second one is based on the same scoring scheme extended by prosodic weights (SCA-Scale). While the Basic analysis wrongly matches the phonetically similar sounds [ɣ] and [x], the Scale analysis correctly matches [ɣ] with the less similar [ʀ]. The reason can be found in the modified gap penalties and substitution scores of the Scale analysis. While the Basic analysis treats all positions identically, the Scale analysis assigns a lower gap penalty to the insertion of gaps in the end of a word, i.e. [x] in [bɛːʀex] can be more easily gapped than [ʀ]. Furthermore, the Scale analysis gives increased substitution scores for segments appearing in the same sonority context, such as [ɣ] and [ʀ] which both appear in a position of ascending sonority. This also forces the algorithm to prefer the matching of [ɣ] with [ʀ] over the matching of [ɣ] with [x]. This is but one example, how position-specific weights can enhance traditional pairwise alignment analyses.

In the tests on the tone language partition of the benchmark for pairwise alignment analyses, it became especially evident how drastically secondary alignment analyses may increase the accuracy of global alignment analyses. A prototypical example for the difference between primary and secondary alignment analyses is given in Figure 4.19 where two cognates of Chinese

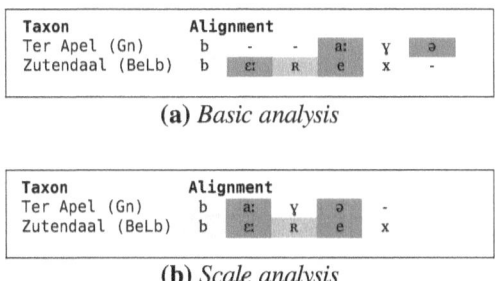

Figure 4.18: *The alignment of dialect variants of Dutch* berg *'mountain' in the Basic (a) and the Scale analysis (b). The data is taken from MAND.*

rìtóu 日頭 [ʐ̩⁵¹tʰou³⁵] 'sun' are aligned. The primary analysis wrongly matches the final [t] of Hǎikǒu *rì* 日 [zit³] 'sun', a reflex of Middle Chinese *ɲit⁴ 日 'sun', with the initial of Yínchuān *tóu* 頭 [tʰəu] 'head', a reflex of Middle Chinese *duw¹ 頭 'head', thereby aligning elements from one syllable in one word with elements from two syllables in the other. Since such a behaviour is prohibited in secondary alignment, the secondary mode correctly matches the corresponding elements of both words with each other.

Analyses using the diagonal alignment mode improved when the DOLGO sound-class model was used, but became worse when using the other models. One reason for this behaviour can be found in the very nature of diagonal alignment. In contrast to global and local alignment, diagonal alignment is based on a very specific scoring function which seeks to maximize the overall alignment score by finding the longest and highest-scoring diagonals (ungapped subalignments). As a result, the method is very conservative regarding diverse sequences and matches only those sounds whose similarity (as assigned by the scoring matrix) is greater than 0. As a result, many divergent matches that global or local algorithms tolerate for the sake of a maximized global score are not accepted in diagonal alignments. In the SCA model and the ASJP model, this leads to a decrease in alignment accuracy, since the models are considerably fine-graded. The DOLGO model, on the other hand, is very broad, in so far as many phonetically quite different sounds are lumped together. As a result, the conservative behaviour of diagonal alignment is weakened by the sound-class model. Although the conservatism seems to be a disadvantage

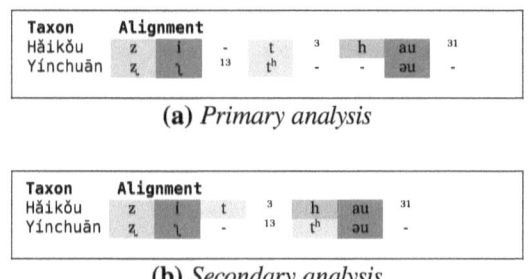

Figure 4.19: *The alignment of dialect variants of Chinese* rìtóu *'sun' in the Primary* (a) *and the Secondary analysis* (b). *The data is taken from YINKU.*

4.2 Phonetic Alignment

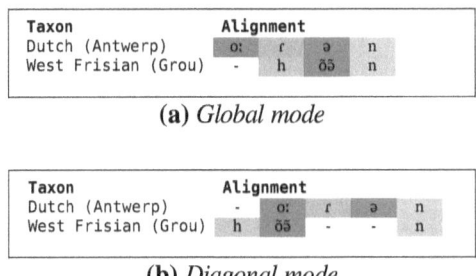

(a) *Global mode*

(b) *Diagonal mode*

Figure 4.20: *The alignment of reflexes of Proto-Germanic* *xurnan *'horn' in Dutch and West Frisian dialects in the Global (a) and the Diagonal mode (b). The data is taken from LOE.*

in general, it may turn out to be an advantage in very specific cases. As an example, consider the alignment of Dutch and West Frisian reflexes of Proto-Germanic **hurna-* 'horn' (KROONEN: 259, based on the SCA model. While the global analysis "accepts" the incorrect matching of [r] and [h], even despite the fact that both occur in different prosodic environments, the diagonal analysis rejects it, correctly aligning only the phonetically most similar segments. The conservative character of diagonal alignments is especially helpful in multiple consistency-based alignments, where diagonal alignments can be used to fill the primary library as a corrective for the less conservative global and local alignment analyses.

Multiple Sequence Alignment The first alignment in Figure 4.21 (MSA 125 in the multiple alignment benchmark) is the typical output of a traditional matrix-based progressive alignment algorithm on a rather tough test alignment, taken from the Bai partition of the phonetic alignment benchmark. Apparently, the phonetic sequences are very diverse, and it is difficult to detect strong similarities when dealing with such an alignment. This is a typical output of traditional matrix-based progressive alignment algorithms. If global similarities cannot be detected, the resulting alignments are mere collections of sound segments in a matrix that are seemingly unreasonably lumped together.

The second alignment in Figure 4.21, on the other hand, is the output of the new consistency-based algorithm that was further improved by iterative

168   4 Sequence Comparison in Historical Linguistics

Taxon	Alignment								
Dàshí	tʂ	-	ɯ	-	21	p	e	21	
Ěryuán	p	-	i	-	31	s	e	42	
Gòngxīng	dʐ	-	i	-	12	b	i	21	
Hèqìng	p	-	i	-	31	sʰ	e	44	
Jiànchuān	p	-	i	-	31	-	-	-	
Jīnxīng	ts	-	ɯ	-	31	p	e	21	
Luòběnzhuō	dʑ	-	ỹ	-	42	-	-	-	
Lánpíng	p	-	ĩ	-	42	s	e	44	
Mǎzhělóng	ɕ	-	e	n	55	p	e	21	
Qīlǐqiáo	p	-	i	-	31	s	e	44	
Tuōluó	d	j	ɯ	-	21	b	i	35	
Yúnlóng	b	j	ɯ	-	21	s	ɛ	55	
Zhōuchéng	ts	-	ɯ	-	0	p	e	21	

(a) *Matrix-based analysis*

Taxon	Alignment											
Dàshí	tʂ	-	ɯ	-	21	p	-	e	21	-	-	-
Ěryuán	-	-	-	-	-	p	-	i	31	s	e	42
Gòngxīng	dʐ	-	i	-	12	b	-	i	21	-	-	-
Hèqìng	-	-	-	-	-	p	-	i	31	sʰ	e	44
Jiànchuān	-	-	-	-	-	p	-	i	31	-	-	-
Jīnxīng	ts	-	ɯ	-	31	p	-	e	21	-	-	-
Lánpíng	-	-	-	-	-	p	-	ĩ	42	s	e	44
Luòběnzhuō	dʑ	-	ỹ	-	42	-	-	-	-	-	-	-
Mǎzhělóng	ɕ	-	e	n	55	p	-	e	21	-	-	-
Qīlǐqiáo	-	-	-	-	-	p	-	i	31	s	e	44
Tuōluó	d	j	ɯ	-	21	b	-	i	35	-	-	-
Yúnlóng	-	-	-	-	-	b	j	ɯ	21	s	ɛ	55
Zhōuchéng	ts	-	ɯ	-	0	p	-	e	21	-	-	-

(b) *Consistency-based analysis*

Figure 4.21: *Alignment of Bai dialect words for 'bark' and 'rain cape' in matrix-* (a) *and consistency-based alignment analyses* (b).

refinement. The method correctly detects the specific local similarities between the words: All words (with the exception of Luòběnzhuō [dʑỹ⁴²] 'rain cape', which might not even be cognate with the other words) have a reflex of Proto-Bai *be¹ 'skin' (Wang 2006a), probably cognate with Chinese pí 皮 [pʰi²¹⁴] 'skin' (< Middle Chinese *bje¹ 皮 < Old Chinese *m-paj 皮, OCBS). Apart from this common morpheme, the dialects can be divided into two classes which actually correspond to two different compounds which are only partially cognate. The first class shows a compound of reflexes of Proto-Bai *dɽɯ³ 'tree' with reflexes of the aforementioned Proto-Bai *be¹ 'skin', as in Jīnxīng [tsɯ³¹pe²¹], with the meaning 'bark' < 'tree' + 'skin' (Wang 2006a). The second class shows a compound of reflexes of Proto-Bai *be¹

'skin' with reflexes of Proto-Bai *$s^h\varepsilon^4$ 'cloth' (ibid.), as in Ěryuán [$pi^{31}se^{42}$],
with the meaning 'rain cape' < 'cape made from (palm) bark (< skin)', (BDS).

Both classes are correctly detected by the algorithm, and the different reflexes are separately aligned. As can be seen from the example, consistency-based methods do not only enhance multiple sequence alignment in biology, but also in linguistics. The specific strength of consistency-based algorithms to be sensitive to both global and local similarities between sequences becomes very apparent in the alignments yielded by the new enhancements of the SCA method.

Swap Detection In order to correctly detect swapped sites in an alignment, it is of great importance that the previous alignment analysis allows the swap to be detected. In Figure 4.22 this is illustrated by contrasting two different alignments (MSA 673 in the multiple alignment benchmark) for reflexes of Proto-Slavic *žьltъ 'yellow' in Bulgarian, Czech, Polish, and Russian (DERKSEN: 565f). The first alignment is based on the ASJP model, using the traditional progressive alignment (Basic mode), the second one is based on the same model but it uses consistency-based progressive alignment with iterative refinement (Lib-Iter). In the output of the Basic mode, the [w] in Polish is misaligned. As a result, no complementary structures can be detected in the alignment, and the method for swap detection fails. In the Lib-Iter mode, the [w] in Polish is correctly aligned with the laterals in the other languages, and the method for swap detection easily identifies the columns 2, 3, and 4 as a swapped site. In the output, this is marked by the white font color of the sounds which appear in swapped columns.

4.3 Automatic Cognate Detection

So far this study focused on alignment analyses as a specific way to compare sequences. In Section 4.1, new approaches to sequence modelling were introduced, and these new sequence models were then used to derive the new method for phonetic alignment presented in Section 4.2. While automatic alignment analyses may surely be useful as a stand-alone tool in historical linguistic and dialectological endeavors, they do not constitute an end in itself. Instead, they are one of the basic tools that can help us approaching one of the "holy grails" of quantitative historical linguistic: the task of *automatic cognate detection* (ACD). Given the basic practice of historical linguistics to base lan-

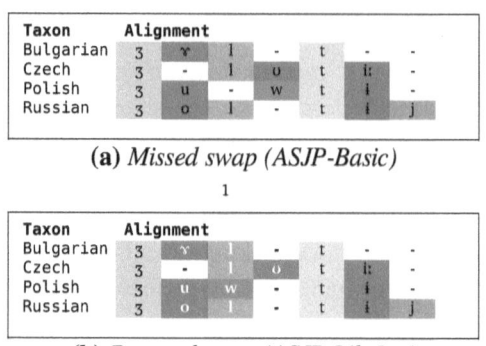

(a) *Missed swap (ASJP-Basic)*

(b) *Detected swap (ASJP-Lib-Iter)*

Figure 4.22: *Missed* (a) *and detected swaps* (b) *in the alignment of descendant words of Proto-Slavic* *žьltъ *'yellow'.*

guage comparison on lexical comparison we can state the *cognate detection problem* as follows:

Cognate Detection Problem: Given a multilingual word list covering a set of arbitrarily selected languages, find all words that are cognate.

In historical linguistics, this problem is usually approached within the framework of the comparative method, as it was outlined in Section 2.6. The most important aspects of the traditional method for cognate detection are the language-specific notion of word similarity, derived from previously identified regular sound correspondences, and the iterative character of the method, by which proposed list of cognates and sound correspondences are constantly refined and updated. Note that the general cognate detection problem was stated as being indifferent regarding a couple of parameters. It is not specified, how many languages are being compared, or whether the genetical relatedness between these languages should be already proven. It is also left open whether the cognate sets to be identified should be restricted to semantically similar words or whether words that greatly diverged semantically should also be included. Furthermore, the size of the word lists is not specified. For the comparative method, only the last point matters. The method is indifferent regarding the number of languages being compared, it has its own procedure to determine genetical relatedness between languages, and semantically different but formally similar words have seldom posed a problem for historical linguists. The size of the word lists, however, is of crucial importance for the method, although nobody has so far been able to determine how many items a word lists should at least contain in order to be applicable. That the popular Swadesh-200 word lists (see Section 2.1.5) are surely not enough when questions of remote relationship have to be solved can be easily demonstrated when considering the amount of cognate words in these word lists for some genetically related languages such as as Armenian, English, French, and German: Given that there are maximally 20 cognates between Armenian and the other three languages, it is hardly possible that these cognates are enough to set up a satisfying set of sound correspondences between these languages.

There is a further aspect of the general cognate detection problem that cannot be solved by the comparative method in its strict form: the distinction between common descent due to borrowing and common descent due to inheritance. As it has been discussed earlier in Sections 2.4.1 and 2.5.2, regular sound correspondences do not necessarily point to common descent but may also result from lexical borrowing. The comparative method thus actually doesn't solve the general cognate detection problem, but rather (merely) solves the *homologue detection problem*:

> **Homologue Detection Problem:** Given a multilingual word list covering a set of arbitrarily selected languages, find all words that are etymologically related.

So far, both the problem of cognate detection and the problem of homologue detection have been stated in general terms. No further preprocessing of the

	Albanian	English	French	German
Albanian		0.07	0.10	0.10
English	14		0.23	0.56
French	20	46		0.23
German	20	111	46	

Table 4.19: *Number and proportion of cognates within Swadesh-200 word lists of four Indo-European languages. The lower triangle of the table indicates the concrete number of shared cognates. The upper triangle gives the percentage of shared cognates. The cognate counts are based on the data given in Kessler (2001).*

data is required by algorithms or methods that solve such a problem, and no restrictions regarding the character of cognates or etymologically related words are being made. Most algorithms for automatic cognate detection which have been proposed so far do not directly deal with this general homologue detection problem, but rather state the problem more specifically. Among the most common specifications of the problem, is to require that etymologically related words should have the same meaning. This problem can be called the *specific cognate detection problem*:

> **Specific Homologue Detection Problem:** Given a multilingual word list, covering a set of arbitrarily selected languages, find all words that are etymologically related (homologous) and have the same meaning.

While semantic identity has never been a requirement for the determination of cognacy in historical linguistics, and it is often explicitly stated, that cognacy can often be determined for semantically quite different words (Szemerényi 1970: 15f), it reflects the heuristic practice of many historical linguists to start the search for cognates by comparing semantically similar words, and to proceed to the comparison of semantically more distant words in later stages.[13] It therefore seems useful to start with the specific homologue detection problem when developing automatic approaches.

4.3.1 Previous Work

Although up to today quite a few methods for automatic cognate detection have been proposed, there are only four recent approaches known to me which explicitly deal with the specific homologue detection problem, as it was defined above. The other methods either restrict cognate detection to pairwise word lists (Mackay and Kondrak 2005), or they require specific parameters, such as a guide tree of the languages, to be known in advance (Hall and Klein 2010). Bergsma and Kondrak (2007) first calculate the longest common subsequence ratio between all word pairs in the input data and then use an integer linear programming approach to cluster the words into cognate sets. Unfortunately, their method is only tested on a dataset containing alphabetic transcriptions; hence, no direct comparison with methods that require phonetic transcriptions as input data is possible. Turchin et al. (2010) determine cognacy in multilingual

---

[13] This practice is already reported in Gabelentz (1891: 177-179), who presents his own "basic vocabulary lists", which he calls "Collectaneen zum Sprachvergleiche", as a heuristic tool for the initial stages of language comparison.

4.3 Automatic Cognate Detection

word lists with help of a simple matching criterion: whenever the first two consonants of two words are identical regarding their Dolgopolsky sound-class, the words are judged to be cognate. Hauer and Kondrak (2011) combine specific language-pair features with common metrics for word similarity (longest common subsequence, etc.) to cluster semantically aligned words into cognate sets. Their method doesn"t employ phonetic similarities, since the authors want to keep it applicable to word lists in orthographical encoding. Steiner et al. (2011) propose an iterative approach which starts by clustering words into tentative cognate sets based on their alignment scores. These preliminary results are then refined by filtering words according to similar meanings, computing multiple alignments, and determining recurrent sound correspondences. The authors test their method on two large datasets. Since no gold standard for their test set is available, they only report intermediate results, and their method cannot be directly compared with other methods.

4.3.2 LexStat − Multilingual Cognate Detection

The LexStat method for automatic cognate detection in multilingual word lists was first proposed in List (2012a). In the following, the most recent version of the method will be introduced in detail. LexStat combines the most important aspects of the comparative method with recent approaches to sequence comparison in historical linguistics and evolutionary biology. The method employs automatically extracted language-specific scoring schemes and computes distance scores from pairwise alignments of the input data. These language-specific scoring schemes come close to the notion of regular sound correspondences in traditional historical linguistics. Similar to the SCA method for phonetic alignment presented in Section 4.2, LexStat is also implemented as a part of the LingPy library. It can either be used in Python scripts or directly be called from the Python prompt.

The basic working procedure of LexStat consists of five stages: (1) sequence conversion, (2) preprocessing, (3) scoring-scheme creation, (4) distance calculation, and (5) sequence clustering. In stage (1), the input sequences are converted into tuples consisting of sound classes and prosodic strings. In stage (2), a simple language-independent ACD method is used to derive preliminary cognate sets. In stage (3), a Monte-Carlo permutation test is used to create language-specific log-odds scoring schemes for all language pairs. In stage (4) the pairwise distances between all word pairs, based on the language-specific scoring schemes, are computed. In stage (5), the sequences are clustered into

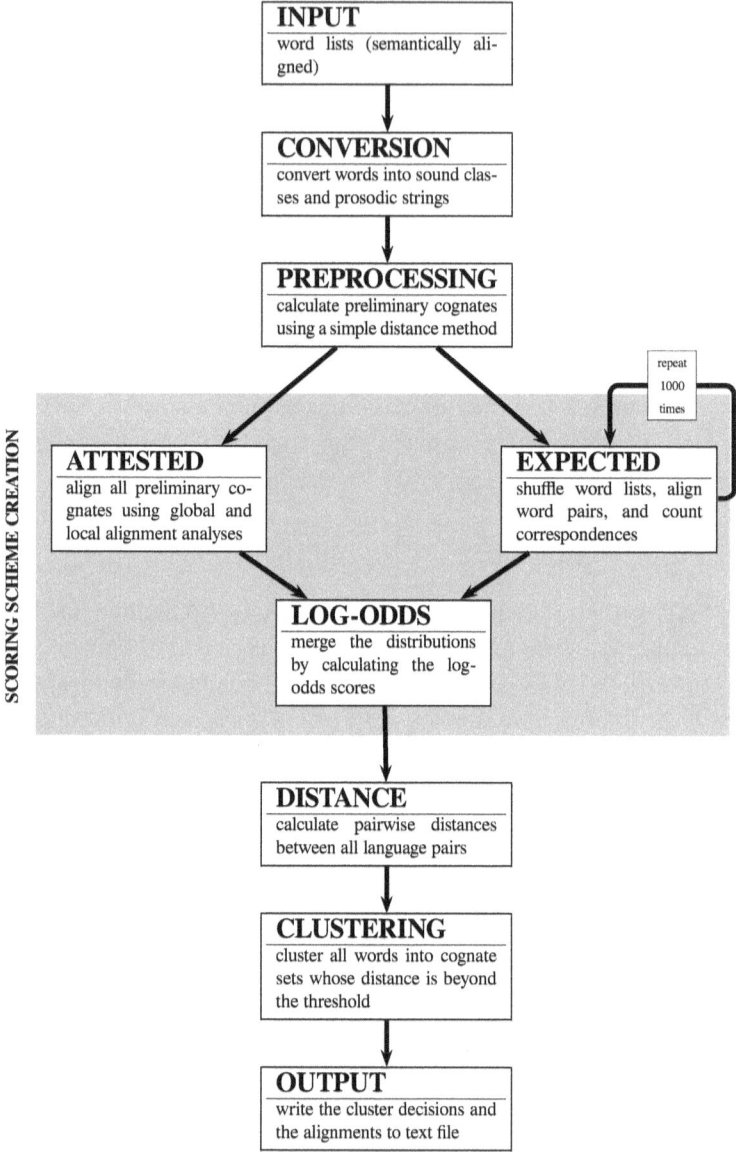

Figure 4.23: *Working procedure of the LexStat method for automatic cognate detection. See the text for a detailed description.*

4.3 Automatic Cognate Detection

cognate sets whose average distance is beyond a certain threshold. Additionally to these five stages, all cognate sets detected by the method are aligned, using the SCA method for multiple phonetic alignment described in Section 4.2. The aligned output is not directly related to the ACD problem, but merely serves as a tool to display the decisions made by the algorithm in a visually appealing way. The different stages of the working procedure of LexStat are illustrated in Figure 4.23.

4.3.3 Specific Features

Input and Output

The basic input format of LexStat is a tab-delimited text file in which the first line indicates the values of the columns and all words are listed in a separate line. The format is pretty flexible. No specific order of columns or rows is required. Whatever additional data the user wants to include can be included, as long as it is in a separate column. Each word has to be characterized by at least four values given in separate columns: (1) ID, an integer that is used to uniquely identify the word during the calculation, (2) Taxa, the name of the language in which the word occurs, (3) GlossID, an identifier which indicates the meaning of the word and which is used to align the words semantically, and (4) IPA, the phonetic transcription of the word given in IPA. The output format is essentially the same as the input format with one additional cognate ID column (CogID) that indicates the clustering decision of the method: All words that are given the same CogID in the output have been identified as cognates by the method (see Table 4.20).[14]

In addition to the simple output, LexStat offers also the possibility to output the data in aligned form. These multiple alignment analyses that are carried out in the last stage of the LexStat method are no direct requirement for an ACD algorithm, since the main task, the identification of cognate sets, is already accomplished after the clustering stage. However, the specific MSA output format provided by LexStat is very convenient for manual checking and editing of automatically detected cognate sets. If the method is used to aid comparative linguists working on less well-studied language families, it may come in handy to have an aligned representation of all cognate sets proposed by the algorithm. Furthermore, since the language-dependent log-odds

---

[14] I am very thankful to Steven Moran for pointing me to the advantages of such a flexible input structure.

scores are also used for the calculation of the alignments, weak positions in the cognate sets will be left unaligned by the algorithm, which may turn out to be a big help when refining ACD analyses manually. Table 4.21 illustrates the basic idea of the aligned output, taking the translations of the basic concept 'woman' in six Germanic languages as an example.

Sequence Conversion

In the stage of sequence conversion, all input sequences are converted to tuples consisting of sound classes and prosodic strings. Thus, German *Sand* [zant] 'sand' has the sound-class representation "SANT" and the prosodic string "#VC$>", and is internally represented as [('S', '#'), ('A', 'V'), ('N', 'C'), ('T', '$')], and German *heiß* [haɪs] 'hot' is internally represented as [('H', '#'), ('A', 'V'), ('S',

ID	Taxa	Word	Gloss	GlossID	IPA	...
...	...	...	...	...	...	...
21	German	Frau	woman	20	frau	...
22	Dutch	vrouw	woman	20	vrɑu	...
23	English	woman	woman	20	wʊmən	...
24	Danish	kvinde	woman	20	kvenə	...
25	Swedish	kvinna	woman	20	kviːna	...
26	Norwegian	kvine	woman	20	kvinə	...
...	...	...	...	...	...	...

(a) *Input*

ID	Taxa	Word	Gloss	GlossID	IPA	CogID
...	...	...	...	...	...	...
21	German	Frau	woman	20	frau	1
22	Dutch	vrouw	woman	20	vrɑu	1
23	English	woman	woman	20	wʊmən	2
24	Danish	kvinde	woman	20	kvenə	3
25	Swedish	kvinna	woman	20	kviːna	3
26	Norwegian	kvine	woman	20	kvinə	3
...	...	...	...	...	...	...

(b) *Output*

Table 4.20: *Input (a) and output format (b) of LexStat. Four columns are required in the input: ID, Taxa, GlossID, and IPA. An additional column is added in the output. Each word is assigned a specific cognate ID (CogID). All words that have the same CogID have been identified as cognates by the algorithm.*

4.3 Automatic Cognate Detection

ID	Language	Word	Gloss	Alignments				
1	German	*Frau*	'woman'	f	r	au		
1	Dutch	*vrouw*	'woman'	v	r	ɑu		
2	English	*woman*	'woman'	wʊmən				
3	Danish	*kvinde*	'woman'	k	v	e	n	ə
3	Swedish	*kvinna*	'woman'	k	v	iː	n	a
3	Norwegian	*kvine*	'woman'	k	ʊ	i	n	ə

Table 4.21: *Aligned output of three cognate sets identified by the LexStat method.*

'$')].[15] Identical segments in one language which differ regarding their position in the word are now treated as different segments. As a result, the initial of *Sand* and the final of *heiß*, which are represented by identical sound classes, are still kept separate, because their tuple representations differ (('S', '#') vs. ('S', '$')). This representation constitutes a novel approach to model phonetic context. It has the advantage of being more "abstract" than *bi-* or *n*-gram approaches which are usually used to incorporate context sensitivity in alignment analyses (Heeringa et al. 2006).

Scoring-Scheme Creation

The idea to compute language-specific similarities by trying to detect regular sound correspondences automatically is definitely not new, and there are many different methods described in the literature (Guy 1994, Kondrak 2003, Oakes 2000, Starostin 2008a). Unfortunately, the applicability and availability of most of these approaches is rather limited. Some are only described in the literature (Guy 1994, Starostin 2008a), some cover only a limited range of sounds (Oakes 2000), and some require specific codings instead of the general IPA standard (Kondrak 2003). The general strategy that all approaches usually follow is to create an *attested distribution* by calculating the (possible) links (segment correspondences, *residue pairs* in biology) between all word pairs in a bilingual word list, and to compare this distribution with an *expected distribution*, i.e. with a distribution of residue pairs one would get if the lan-

---

[15] In this description of the LexStat method, I generally use the SCA model for the examples.

guages were not related. This idea is similar to the way the BLOSUM substitution matrices are calculated in evolutionary biology (see Section 3.3.3). The main difference in the approaches lies in the way these two distributions are calculated. Here, the LexStat method follows Kondrak (2003) in deriving the attested distribution from pairwise alignments. The pairwise alignments are calculated for all possible language pairs in a multilingual word list. In contrast to Kondrak (ibid.), however, LexStat adopts the idea of consistency-based sequence alignment (see Section 3.4.2) in creating a *library* of pairwise alignments. Instead of computing only global or only local pairwise alignments to derive the attested distribution, both global *and* local alignments are computed, and the resulting distribution is averaged. The advantage of this approach is that more information can be taken into account, especially when words exhibit rather "local" similarities, i.e., if they, for example, contain prefixes or suffixes.

The problem all approaches have to deal with is how to handle the noise in the data. Regular sound correspondences can only be determined for cognate words, but not all words in the data are cognate. When linguists determine regular sound correspondences manually, they only count the number of correspondences in those words which they assume to be cognate. Other words are discarded from the count. It is useful to model this behaviour by preprocessing the data for probably fruitful matches. In the first version of LexStat (List 2012a), I employed a very simple strategy to account for this: instead of taking *all* aligned word pairs of each language pair to calculate an attested distribution of correspondence frequencies in pairwise alignments, only those alignments whose SCA distance was beyond a certain threshold were taken into account. The SCA distance (SCAD) was calculated by applying the aforementioned formula of Downey et al. (2008) to the similarity scores produced by the SCA method (see Equation 4.2 on page 142):

$$(4.11) \qquad SCAD = 1 - \frac{2 \cdot S_{AB}}{S_A + S_B},$$

where S_{AB} is the similarity score of an alignment of two words A and B produced by the SCA method, and S_A and S_B are the similarity scores produced by the alignment of A and B with themselves. That SCA distances are not a bad heuristic for the preprocessing of word lists, is illustrated in Table 4.22, where the capability of the three variants of SCA distances to discriminate between cognate words is contrasted with the discriminative force of the normalized edit distance (NED), which is calculated by dividing the edit distance

4.3 Automatic Cognate Detection

by the length of the smaller sequence. The discriminative force of the different distance scores was measured by calculating the *n*-point average precision (cf. the description in Kondrak 2002: 118f) on a small dataset of Swadesh-200 word lists containing manually edited cognate judgments from the literature for Albanian, English, French, and German (Kessler 2001). As can be see from the table, all SCA distances largely outperform the normalized edit distance.

In the most recent version of the LexStat method, a new strategy for the preprocessing of word lists is employed. The main idea is to take *multilingual* instead of *bilingual information* into account. Given that LexStat is but one of four different ACD methods implemented in LingPy, the preprocessing can also be based on one of the three other methods, i.e. the algorithm can first use a simplified language-independent method to search for cognates in a multilingual word list, and than use these preliminary cognate judgments to calculate an attested distribution of correspondence frequencies. The apparent advantage of this approach is that a multilingual ACD method will usually find more cognates than a bilingual one, since false negatives resulting from high distance scores in one language pair may be levelled by the average distances over multiple languages. It is, for example, difficult – if not impossible – to prove the cognacy of German *Zahn* [tsaːn] 'tooth' and English *tooth* [tʊːθ]

Taxa	Cogn. Prop.	NED	SCA distance		
			DOLGO	ASJP	SCA
German / Albanian	0.12	30.62	32.60	38.78	44.58
German / French	0.26	45.97	55.83	54.87	59.84
German / English	0.59	89.16	94.65	93.92	94.45
Albanian / French	0.17	62.74	50.32	61.73	64.12
Albanian / English	0.10	15.74	32.29	31.10	39.86
French / English	0.28	61.92	67.34	70.85	64.65
Average	0.25	51.03	55.50	58.54	61.25

Table 4.22: n-*Point Average Precision of NED and the three variants of SCA distances on Swadesh-200 word lists of four genetically related languages (data taken from Kessler 2001).*

on the basis of Swadesh-200 word lists alone, since there are two gaps in the alignment: | ts a: n - | . Although at least the gap in the English word is regular (see the examples in Section 4.1.1) and might be detected as such in a Swadesh-200 word list of English and German, the missing dental in the German word has no further counterpart in the list, and aggravates the task of finding a correct scenario for an alignment algorithm. This changes when adding Dutch *tand* [tɑnt] 'tooth' to the comparison. This word serves as a missing link. It aligning well with both German: | ts a: n - |), and English: (| t u: - θ | . In the current version of LexStat, the SCA method, by which sequences are clustered into cognate sets whose average SCA distance is beyond a certain threshold, is used for this purpose, since it performed better than the other two methods compared in List (2012a). For this preliminary stage of cognate detection, it is not important that the algorithm finds only true cognates. What is important, is that the recall is considerably high, i.e. that the algorithm finds many of the cognate pairs in the word lists. Therefore, the threshold for this preprocessing stage is set to 0.6 by default.

In contrast to the creation of the attested distribution of matching residue pairs, the creation of the expected distribution is more complicated. In biology, the expected frequencies of matching residue pairs are usually inferred mathematically, under the assumption that all aligned residue pairs are statistically independent of each other. Unfortunately, this is not possible in the LexStat approach, since the attested frequencies are derived from an alignment algorithm which automatically favors and disfavors certain matches. Thus, no matter whether or not two languages are related, there will always be a large amount of vowel-vowel matches in the attested distribution, vowels will never match with consonants, and certain consonant matchings will always be favored while others are disfavored. In order to derive an unbiased expected distribution, I follow the approach by Kessler (2001: 48-50) in using a *Monte Carlo permutation test* (see also Baxter and Manaster Ramer 2000). Thus, in order to create the expected distribution of matching residue pairs, the words in the word lists for a given language pair are repeatedly resampled by shuffling one of the entry columns. In each resampling step, pairwise alignments of the new word pairs are carried out, using the same methods that are used for the creation of the attested distribution. The average of the frequencies of the residue pairs in all samples is then taken to reflect the expected frequencies. In the default settings, the number of repetitions is set to 1000, yet many tests

4.3 Automatic Cognate Detection

showed that even the number of 100 repetitions is sufficient to yield satisfying results that do not vary greatly.

In contrast to most other approaches proposed so far, LexStat does not try to extract the true correspondences in a given dataset, but instead uses the attested and the expected distribution directly to compute log-odds scores which serve as a language-specific scoring matrix for an alignment algorithm. In order to calculate the similarity score $s_{x,y}$ for each residue pair x and y in the dataset, LexStat uses the the formula:

$$(4.12) \quad s_{x,y} = \frac{1}{r_1 + r_2} \left(r_1 \log_2 \left(\frac{a_{x,y}^2}{e_{x,y}^2} \right) + r_2 d_{x,y} \right),$$

where $a_{x,y}$ is the attested frequency of the segment pair, $e_{x,y}$ is the expected frequency, r_1 and r_2 are scaling factors, and $d_{x,y}$ is the similarity score of the original scoring function which was used to retrieve the attested and the expected distributions. This formula combines different approaches from the literature on sequence comparison in historical linguistics and biology. The idea of squaring the frequencies of attested and expected frequencies was adopted from Kessler (2001: 150), reflecting "the general intuition among linguists that the evidence of phoneme recurrence grows faster than linearly". As mentioned above, the calculation of log-odds scores follows the practice in biology to retrieve similarity scores which are apt for the computation of alignment analyses (Henikoff and Henikoff 1992). The incorporation of the alignment score $d_{x,y}$ of the original language-independent scoring-scheme copes with possible problems resulting from small word lists: If the dataset is too small to allow the identification of recurrent sound correspondences, the language-independent alignment scores prevent the method from treating generally probable and generally improbable matchings alike. The ratio of language-specific to language-independent alignment scores is determined by the scaling factors r_1 and r_2. In the default settings of LexStat, it is set to 3:2.

As an example of the computation of language-specific scoring schemes, Table 4.23 shows attested and expected frequencies along with the resulting similarity scores for the matching of word-initial and word-final sound classes in the aforementioned test set of Kessler (2001). The word-initial and word-final classes T = [t, d], C = [ts], S = [ʃ, s, z] in German are contrasted with the word-initial and word-final sound classes T = [t, d] and D = [θ, ð] in English. As can be seen from the table, the scoring scheme correctly reflects the basic sound correspondences between English and German resulting from

English		German		Att.	Exp.	Score
IPA	Cl.	IPA	Cl.			
t, d	T	t, d	T	3.00	1.24	5.50
		ts	C	3.00	0.38	5.10
		ʃ, s, z	S	1.00	1.87	-2.20
θ, ð	D	t, d	T	7.00	0.69	5.83
		ts	C	0.00	0.21	-2.20
		s, z	S	1.00	1.64	-0.60

(a) *Word-initial*

English		German		Att.	Exp.	Score
IPA	Cl.	IPA	Cl.			
t, d	T	t, d	T	22.00	9.03	4.78
		ts	C	3.00	1.69	-0.60
		ʃ, s, z	S	7.50	4.93	1.11
θ, ð	D	t, d	T	4.00	1.17	4.02
		ts	C	0.00	0.23	-2.20
		s, z	S	0.00	0.79	-0.60

(b) *Word-final*

Table 4.23: *Attested versus expected frequencies of residue pairs and the resulting log-odds scores in* (a) *word-initial and* (b) *word-final position for German and English in the dataset of Kessler (2001). The attested distribution reflects the average of one global and one local alignment analysis. For the expected distribution, a Monte-Carlo permutation test of 1000 runs was carried out.*

the High German Consonant Shift (Trask 2000: 300-302), which is reflected in such cognate pairs as English *town* [taʊn] vs. German *Zaun* [tsaun] 'fence', English *thorn* [θɔːn] vs. German *Dorn* [dɔrn] 'thorn', English *dale* [deɪl] vs. German *Tal* [taːl] 'valley', and German *hot* [hɔt] vs. German *heiß* [haɪs] 'hot'. The specific benefit of representing the phonetic segments as tuples consisting of their respective sound class along with their prosodic context also becomes evident: The correspondence of English [t] with German [s] is only attested in word-final position, correctly reflecting the complex change of former [t] to [s]

4.3 Automatic Cognate Detection

in non-initial position in German. If it were not for the specific representation of the phonetic segments by both their sound class and their prosodic context, the evidence would be blurred.[16]

Distance Calculation

Once the language-specific scoring scheme is computed, the distances between all word pairs are calculated. Here, LexStat uses the semi-global alignment algorithm. This modification is useful when words contain prefixes or suffixes which might distort the calculation. The alignment analysis requires no further parameters such as gap penalties, since they have already been calculated in the previous stage. The similarity scores for pairwise alignments are converted to distance scores using the same formula which is used to calculate the language-independent SCA distances (see Equation 4.11 on page 178). This formula does not only require the similarity score between two different sequences as input, but also the similarity score of the sequences compared with themselves. The similarity of one sequence compared with itself is calculated by applying the same Monte Carlo permutation test to all languages compared with themselves and calculating the respective log-odds scores.

The benefits of language-specific in comparison to language-independent sequence distances are illustrated in Figure 4.24. The figure shows the cross-product of 100 cognates which were randomly chosen from a larger sample of 658 cognate pairs between English and German, extracted from KLUGE. In the figures, four different distance scores are compared: percentage identity (PID, see Equation 3.1 on page 74), converted to a distance score, normalized edit distance (NED), the SCA distance (SCA model), and the LexStat distances, which were computed for the two language pairs. In each plot, the real cognates are given in the diagonal cells from bottom left to top right. All other cells of the matrices reflect unrelated word pairs. A certain "cognate signal" can be detected in all plots. However, the signal is quite weak in the PID and the NED plots. In the SCA plot, the signal is stronger, but blurred by generally low distances between non-cognate word pairs. In the LexStat plot, the signal is the strongest: Most of the cognates receive a distance score around or beyond 0.3, while most non-cognates receive a considerably higher distance

---

[16] The alignments along with the distance scores for all word pairs between German and English are given in Appendix C.2.

score. This clearly illustrates the superiority of language-specific distances for the task of distinguishing cognates from non-cognates.[17]

Sequence Clustering

Distance scores do not directly reflect cognate judgments, since they only indicate the similarity between sequence pairs, but not between whole groups of sequences. Applying a threshold beyond which cognacy is assumed for a

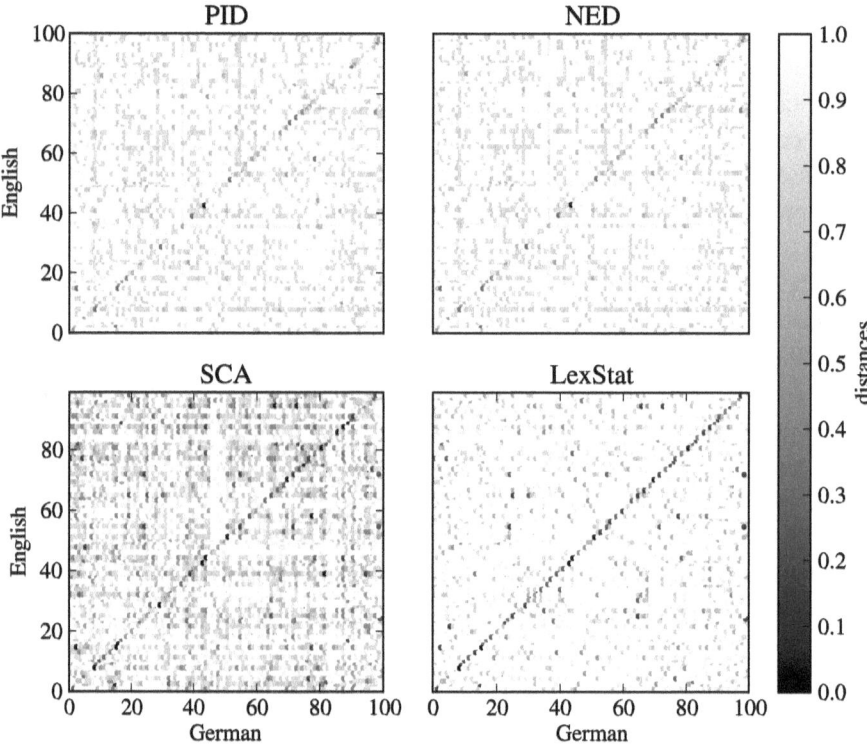

Figure 4.24: *Percentage identities (PID), normalized edit distances (NED), SCA distances, and* LexStat *distances for the cross product of a sample of 100 cognates between English and German.*

---

[17] All distance scores for the 100 cognate pairs are given in Appendix D.1.

given word pair does not solve the problem, since the resulting cognate decision may create intransitive relations (Hauer and Kondrak 2011: 868f). In order to retrieve transitive cognate judgments, a cluster method has to be applied. LexStat uses a flat cluster variant of the UPGMA algorithm (Sokal and Michener 1958) to cluster all words occurring in the same semantic slot into cognate sets. This flat cluster algorithm was written by the author. In contrast to traditional UPGMA clustering, it terminates when a user-defined threshold of average pairwise distances is reached. The threshold itself reflects the maximally allowed average distance between all word pairs in a given cluster.

Figure 4.25 shows how pairwise distances of German, English, Danish, Swedish, Dutch!Standard Dutch, and Norwegian translations of the basic concept 'woman', taken from the GER dataset (see Table 4.25), are merged into cognate sets by the flat cluster algorithm.

4.3.4 Evaluation

Gold Standard

What was said about benchmark datasets for phonetic alignment in Section 4.2.4 also holds for automatic cognate detection: The number of available gold standards is very limited. Kessler (2001) compiled a dataset in which the 200 basic vocabulary items of Swadesh (1952) are translated into eight languages. Apparently, this dataset has only rarely been used as a gold standard for cognate detection before, and the only approach known to me is only based on the comparison of language pairs (Mackay and Kondrak 2005). The advantage of this dataset is the quality of the material: All words are given in orthography and IPA transcription, the cognate judgments are all substantiated by numerous references taken from the literature, and borrowings are especially marked by the author. The drawback of this dataset is its limited size and the languages chosen by the author. The dataset contains Latin and French, which – taken together – are of little use for the evaluation of ACD methods, since the former is the ancestor of the latter. Because the author also deliberately selected genetically unrelated languages, the number of actual cognate sets in the dataset is considerably low. Thus, although the dataset by Kessler (2001) should surely be considered when testing ACD methods, it is not enough to base the evaluation on this dataset alone.

There are a couple of publicly available lexicostatistical databases which offer manually edited cognate judgments that are supposed to reflect the *com-*

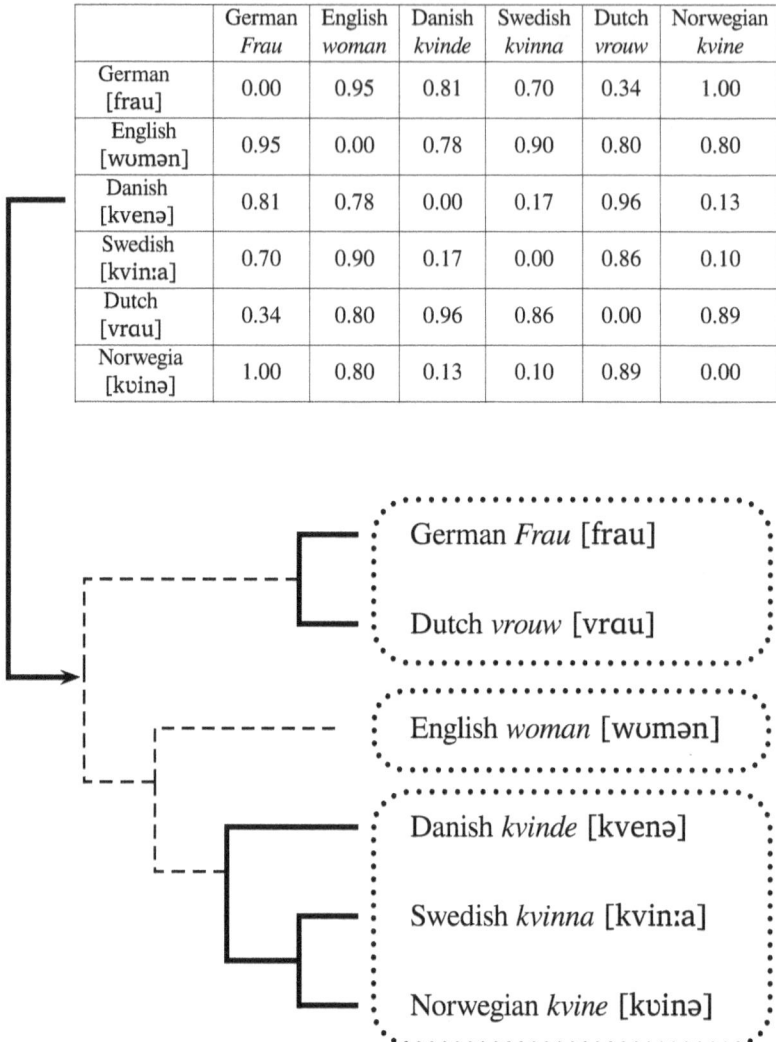

Figure 4.25: *The flat clustering variant of the UPGMA algorithm applied to the basic vocabulary item 'woman' in a couple of Germanic languages. The algorithm successively merges words into larger clusters until a user-defined threshold indicating the maximum of the average distances between all word pairs in a cluster is reached.*

4.3 Automatic Cognate Detection

munis opinio for a given language family. Among these are the *Dyen-Kruskal-Black database* (DKBD, Dyen et al. 1992) which covers almost 100 Indo-European languages, the *Indo-European Lexical Cognacy Database* (IELex), an improved version of the DKBD, the *Tower of Babel database* (ToB) and its successor, the *Global Lexicostatistical Database* (GLD), which cover many different language families, and the *Austronesian Basic Vocabulary Database* (ABVD, Greenhill et al. 2008). Of all these databases, the DKBD has been most frequently used as a benchmark for various applications (Bergsma and Kondrak 2007, Delmestri and Cristianini 2010, Hall and Klein 2010, Hauer and Kondrak 2011, Mackay and Kondrak 2005). Unfortunately, of all these databases, only parts of the IELex can be directly used as a gold standard for the kind of ACD evaluation that is proposed in this study, since none of the other databases offers true phonetic transcriptions. They are either based on orthography, or employ inconsistent idiosyncratic transcription systems which cannot be directly converted into IPA format. While these databases can be used for methods which do not directly depend on IPA transcriptions as in-

Dataset	Languages	I	W	CS	D	T	Source
BAI	Bai dialects	110	1028	205	0.10	9	Wang 2006a
IEL	Indo-European Languages	207	4393	1778	0.38	20	IELex
JAP	Japanese dialects	200	1985	458	0.14	10	Shirō 1973
OUG	Uralic languages	110	2055	239	0.07	21	GLD
PAN	Austronesian languages	210	4358	2730	0.61	20	ABVD
SIN	Chinese dialects	140	2789	1025	0.33	15	YINKU

Table 4.24: *The general partition of the gold standard for the evaluation of methods for automatic cognate detection. Columns* I, W, CS, *and* T *show the numbers of items, words, cognate-sets, and taxa. The diversity index* D *is calculated by dividing the difference between the number of cognate sets and items by the difference between the number of words and items. The lower the value the less diverse are all languages in the respective subset on average.*

put format (Bergsma and Kondrak 2007, Hauer and Kondrak 2011), they are surely not apt for the method proposed in this study.

For the evaluation of an earlier version of the algorithm presented in this study (List 2012a) a specific benchmark dataset was compiled by taking publicly available datasets with authoritative cognate judgments and converting the orthographical entries into IPA. For this study the former benchmark was extended and updated. The new benchmark database for cognate detection can be downloaded from the supporting online material accompanying this study (see Supplementary Material III). In contrast to the benchmark used in List (ibid.), three new subsets were included: The first one (IDS) consists of 550 items translated into four languages (German, English, Dutch, and French) which were taken from the *Intercontinental Dictionary Series* (IDS). The orthographical entries were converted into IPA transcriptions by the author, and cognate judgments were applied manually. The sources which were considered for transcriptions and cognate judgments are given in Appendix A.1. The second one (PAN) is a small part of the ABVD which was kindly provided by Simon Greenhill. It consists of 20 languages given in a very consistent transcription system that could be easily converted to IPA by the author. The third one (IEL) is a small part of the IELex, kindly provided by Micheal Dunn, consisting of 20 languages for which full phonetic transcriptions were available.

The new benchmark divided into two partitions: one "basic" partition and one "specific" partition. The basic partition consists of the six largest subsets, each reflecting a different language family (see Table 4.24). The specific partition consists of various subsets of different sizes which can be used to test specific characteristics of ACD methods (see Table 4.25). It is useful to get a rough impression regarding the diversity of a given dataset. I propose to calculate it with help of the formula:

$$(4.13) \qquad D = \frac{C - I}{W - I},$$

where C is the number of cognate sets, I is the number of basic vocabulary items, and W is the number of language entries (words). This index contrasts the number of cognate sets in a dataset with the number of possible cognate sets. A score of 0 indicates full cognacy, i.e. all words in all semantic slots would be cognate for such a dataset, a high score points to a large amount of unrelated words. As can be seen from the indices for the two partitions of the gold standard, the diversity of the subsets shows a great variation, ranging from dataset with a very high density, such as the OUG data, up to very diverse

4.3 Automatic Cognate Detection

Dataset	Languages	I	W	CS	D	T	Source
GER	Germanic languages and dialects	110	814	182	0.10	7	ToB
IDS	Romance and Germanic languages	550	2429	1490	0.50	4	IDS
KSL	Various languages (partially unrelated)	200	1400	1179	0.82	7	Kessler 2001
PIE	Indo-European languages	110	2172	615	0.24	19	ToB
ROM	Romance language	110	589	177	0.14	5	ToB
SLV	Slavic languages	110	454	165	0.16	4	ToB

Table 4.25: *The* specific partition *of the gold standard for the evaluation of methods for automatic cognate detection. Regarding the* diversity index D*, see the description in Table 4.24.*

ones, such as the PAN data. This is exactly what is needed for a representative gold standard.

Evaluation Measures

The ACD task is essentially a clustering task. The evaluation of clustering tasks is much more complicated than the evaluation of simple pairwise classification tasks (Hauer and Kondrak 2011). Most clustering evaluation measures can be assigned to two different perspectives: the *set perspective*, or the *pair perspective*. The set perspective treats clusters as indivisible wholes. The pair perspective treats a set of clustered items as a set of pairwise decisions between all items in the set.

Bergsma and Kondrak (2007) test the performance of their ACD method by calculating the *set precision* (SP), and the *set recall* (SR). The set precision is defined as the "proportion of sets proposed by [the] system which are also sets in the gold standard" (Bergsma and Kondrak 2007: 659), and can be calculated with the formula:

$$SP = 100 \cdot \frac{|C_r \cap C_t|}{|C_t|},\tag{4.14}$$

where C_r is the set of cognate sets in the reference and C_t is the number of cognate sets in test set. Accordingly, the set recall is defined as the "proportion of gold standard sets that [the] system correctly proposes" (ibid.), and can be calculated with the formula:

$$SR = 100 \cdot \frac{|C_r \cap C_t|}{|C_r|}.\tag{4.15}$$

Both set precision and set recall can be combined by calculating their *harmonic mean*, the *set F-score* (SF):

$$SF = 2 \cdot \frac{SP \cdot SR}{SP + SR}.\tag{4.16}$$

Words	"BAUCH"	"BELLY"	"BUK"	"MAGE"
Reference	1	2	1	3
Test	1	1	1	2

(a) *Cluster decision*

Pairs		Ref.	Test
"BAUCH"	"BELLY"	0	1
"BAUCH"	"BUK"	1	1
"BAUCH"	"MAGE"	0	0
"BELLY"	"BUK"	0	1
"BELLY"	"MAGE"	0	0
"BUK"	"MAGE"	0	0

(b) *Pairwise perspective*

Table 4.26: *The pair perspective in clustering evaluation. Clusters (a) are represented by assigning an integer ID to a given cluster. If two words have the same ID, they are assigned to the same cluster. When comparing cluster decisions within the pair perspective (b), all possible pairs of clustered items are considered, and cluster decisions are displayed by 1 (in the same cluster) and 0 (in different clusters).*

4.3 Automatic Cognate Detection

The set scores are a very conservative evaluation measure, since only identical clusters in reference and test set count positively while identical tendencies are ignored. As a result, the performance of an algorithm may be blurred, especially when the test data is considerably diverse. As an alternative one can turn to the pair perspective which, instead of checking for identical clusters, checks for the identity of pairwise decisions implied by a cluster, as illustrated in Table 4.26. In List (2012a) I used the pair perspective to calculate the proportion of *identical decisions* (ID score). Following the contingency table in Table 4.27, this score can be calculated by dividing the number of true positives and true negatives by the total number of decisions:

$$(4.17) \qquad ID = \frac{a+d}{a+b+c+d}.$$

However, this measure suffers from the shortcoming that it is extremely dependent on the size of the clusters in the dataset. For example, if a dataset contains only a small amount of cognate sets, a poorly performing algorithm which fails to identify most of the cognates may still receive a considerably high ID score as long as it only correctly identifies the non-cognates. In order to avoid these problems, it seems more useful to calculate the *pair precision* (PP) and the *pair recall*, which are formally identical with pair precision and pair recall as evaluation measures for alignment analyses introduced in Section 4.2.4. Thus, given all pairwise decisions in reference and test set, the pair precision can be defined as:

$$(4.18) \qquad PP = 100 \cdot \frac{|P_t \cap P_r|}{|P_t|},$$

	Cognate Reference	Non-Cognate Reference
Cognate Test	true positives a	false positives b
Non-Cognate Test	false negatives c	true negatives d

Table 4.27: *Pairwise decisions in reference and test set*

where P_t is the set of all cognate pairs in the test set and P_r is the set of all cognate pairs in the reference set. Note that this is equivalent to calculating:

(4.19) $$PP = 100 \cdot \frac{a}{a+b},$$

when applying the contingency table in Table 4.27. The pair precision gives an account on the number of false positives produced by an algorithm: The higher the pair precision, the lower the number of false positive decisions made by an algorithm. Accordingly, the pair recall can be calculated with the formula:

(4.20) $$PR = 100 \cdot \frac{|P_t \cap P_r|}{|P_r|},$$

which is again identical to:

(4.21) $$PR = 100 \cdot \frac{a}{a+c}.$$

The pair recall gives an account on the number of false negatives produced by an algorithm: The higher the pair recall, the lower the number of false negative cognate decisions made by an algorithm. Accordingly, the *pair F-score* (PFS) can be calculated by the formula:

(4.22) $$PFS = 2 \cdot \frac{PP \cdot PR}{PP + PR}.$$

Although the pair scores, as they were defined above, show a clear improvement over both the set scores and the ID score, they are still intimately dependent on the cluster size (Amigó et al. 2009). In order to avoid this problem, Hauer and Kondrak (2011) test their ACD method by calculating B-Cubed scores. B-Cubed scores were originally introduced as part of an algorithm by Bagga and Baldwin (1998), but Amigó et al. (2009) could show that they are especially apt as a clustering evaluation measure. In B-Cubed metrics, precision and recall are computed for each word in the dataset taken as a separate item. The *B-Cubed precision* (BP) for one word w in the dataset can be defined as:

(4.23) $$BP_w = 100 \cdot \frac{|R_w \cap T_w|}{|T_w|},$$

4.3 Automatic Cognate Detection

where R_w is the cognate set to which w is assigned by the reference set, and T_w is the cognate set to which w is assigned in the test set. Accordingly, the *B-Cubed recall* (BR) for one word w in the dataset can be defined as:

$$BR_w = 100 \cdot \frac{|R_w \cap T_w|}{|R_w|}, \tag{4.24}$$

and the *B-Cubed F-score* (BF) can be calculated with help of the formula:

$$BF_w = 2 \cdot \frac{BF_w \cdot BR_w}{BF_w + BR_w}. \tag{4.25}$$

The B-Cubed scores for the whole dataset are calculated by taking the average of the separate scores for each word.

The LingPy library, which I wrote for this study, offers a module which calculates all above-mentioned scores for a given reference and test set (see the documentation for details). From the literature it is not clear, how singletons (words that are not cognate with any other word) should be treated. While in the pair scores they are excluded *per definitionem*, it seems that they are usually calculated for the set and the B-Cubed scores. However, while it seems understandable to include singletons in the set calculations, since a correctly assigned singleton should certainly score somehow in the evaluation, this is less true for the B-Cubed scores, because they always yield 1, and no further discrimination between true singletons and false singletons is made. Nevertheless, since the literature remains silent regarding this point, singletons are generally included in the calculations produced by LingPy.

Results

All results which will be reported in the following were achieved by using the most recent version of LexStat along with the same parameters for the different parts of the analysis. For the creation of the language-specific scoring function, attested and expected distributions were calculated by carrying out global and local alignment analyses of the sequences in all language pairs, using the SCA model, and the default SCA scoring function. The GOP was set to –2 for global and to –1 for local alignment analyses. For the creation of the attested distribution, the threshold for the preprocessing was set to 0.6. The ratio between language-specific and language-independent similarity scores was set to 3:2.

Along with the language-specific LexStat method, three language-independent methods, which are all implemented as part of the LingPy library, were tested: The method by Turchin et al. (2010) (Turchin), a simple ACD method based on the normalized edit distance (NED), and the aforementioned ACD method based on SCA distances (SCA), which was also used for the preprocessing. Since the cognate judgments produced by the Turchin method are either positive or negative, no further clustering of words into cognate sets is required. For the NED and SCA methods, the cognate judgments are produced by applying the same clustering method which is also used for the LexStat procedure to the distance scores produced by the methods. Using a "good" threshold is crucial for the performance of all methods. In order to guarantee comparability regarding specific strengths and weaknesses of the different methods, I decided to "anchor" all thresholds to the average B-Cubed precision received by the Turchin method for the general partition of the gold standard, since it doesn't require a threshold. As a result, the thresholds for NED, SCA, and LexStat were set to 0.65, 0.2, and 0.55, respectively. All results of the analyses which are discussed in the following are available as part of the supporting online material accompanying this study (see Supplementary Material IV).

General Results Table 4.28 and Figure 4.26 summarize the results of the ACD methods for the basic partition of the gold standard. As can be seen from the table and the figure, the language-specific LexStat method largely outperforms all language-independent methods, in all "unanchored" evaluation measures apart from the Pair precision, where LexStat performs slightly worse than the SCA method. Furthermore, the language-independent SCA method outperforms the two remaining methods. The Turchin method shows the worst performance. Nevertheless, the NED method is only slightly better. The intention of the authors of this method was to derive a method which is considerably conservative and avoids false positives, and this is certainly guaranteed by the method, although it, unfortunately, misses many cognates.

Being conservative rather then liberal when it comes to cognate judgments is an important requirement for ACD methods. Historical linguists usually have the feeling that false positives are worse than false negatives. Given that the for the three threshold-based methods, the precision was anchored to a value which is allows only a small amount of false positives, the remaining question is, how well the methods identify true cognates. Judging from the results on the

4.3 Automatic Cognate Detection

Measure	Score	Method			
		Turchin	NED	SCA	LexStat
Pair-Scores	ID-Score	75.26	77.31	82.13	84.46
	Precision	81.39	84.09	85.96	85.91
	Recall	47.71	51.51	60.85	66.61
	F-Score	59.48	62.32	70.50	72.19
B-Cubed Scores	Precision	89.83	90.01	90.36	90.30
	Recall	67.23	68.63	75.92	80.58
	F-Score	76.81	77.11	82.45	84.83
Set-Scores	Precision	33.35	34.08	42.78	49.64
	Recall	46.83	46.75	52.99	57.73
	F-Score	38.60	38.72	47.16	53.07

Table 4.28: *Average scores for the subsets of the gold standard*

general partition of the gold standard, it seems to make a difference, whether one compares simple phonetic sequences, as done by the NED method, or complex ones, as done by SCA. Given that Turchin is also based on sound classes, it further seems to make a differences whether one uses alignment analyses, or a simplified matching scheme. Last not least, the language-specific component of LexStat helps to identify a lot more cognates than could be done by the language-independent methods.

As a result of the adjustments of the thresholds to the high B-Cubed precision predefined by the Turchin method, all methods show a higher precision than recall in the pair and the B-Cubed measures. For the set scores the precision is lower than the recall. This is, however, not surprising, since in contrast to the pair and B-Cubed measures, a low set precision doesn't directly point to a high amount of false positives. It may instead also result from a large amount of singletons proposed by an algorithm, since – within the set perspective – a singleton also counts as a set. Therefore, a low set precision – i.e. a low proportion of cognate sets proposed by an algorithm which are also reflected in the gold standard – may also refer to a rather large amount of undetected cognate relations, and – judging from the pair and B-Cubed measures – this seems to be exactly the case.

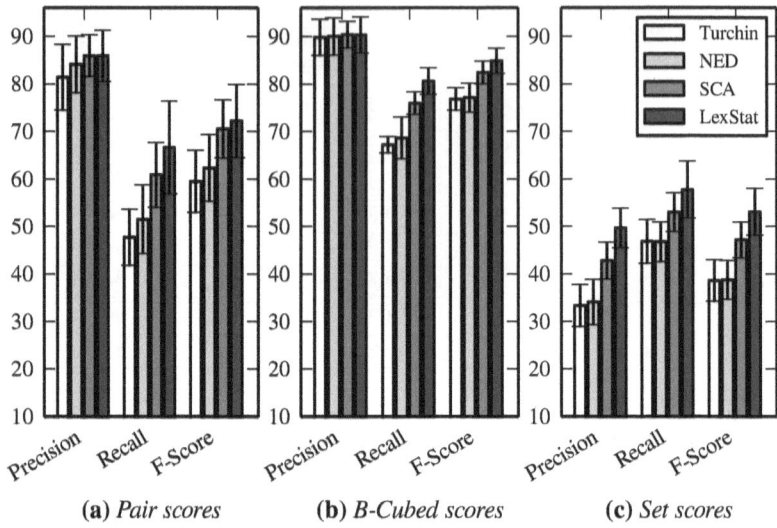

Figure 4.26: *Average scores for the subsets of the gold standard*

Specific Results The general results suggest the superiority of the language-specific LexStat approach compared to the language-independent approaches. An important question is, however, whether these results are also consistent throughout all individual subsets of the gold standard, or whether the superiority applies only to a small part of them. The F-scores for the specific results on the subsets of the general partition of the gold standard are given in Table 4.29. As one can see, the LexStat method again performs best in almost all subsets, the only exceptions being the pair F-scores for the IEL subset and the set F-score for the SIN subset, where the SCA method outperforms LexStat, and the pair F-scores for the PAN subset, where LexStat is outperformed by NED and SCA.

The B-Cubed F-scores which are already given in Table 4.29 are also plotted in Figure 4.27, clearly illustrating that LexStat performs best throughout all subsets. What can also be seen from the figure are large differences in the scores received by the methods in dependence of the subset. This becomes less surprising, when taking into account that the subsets differ greatly regarding the diversity of the languages and the time depth separating them. Thus,

4.3 Automatic Cognate Detection

Subset	Score	Method			
		Turchin	NED	SCA	LexStat
BAI	Pair-F-Score	73.10	68.57	84.05	86.91
	B-Cubed F-Score	80.04	75.43	87.16	88.72
	Set-F-Score	31.10	24.48	44.18	45.02
IEL	Pair-F-Score	46.53	36.52	53.23	49.40
	B-Cubed F-Score	75.31	72.81	79.10	80.62
	Set-F-Score	42.74	45.12	51.64	58.60
JAP	Pair-F-Score	74.34	83.09	83.48	91.48
	B-Cubed F-Score	81.26	86.78	87.20	92.50
	Set-F-Score	38.51	43.33	44.84	58.55
OUG	Pair-F-Score	77.31	82.06	86.85	90.01
	B-Cubed F-Score	81.80	85.58	88.80	91.59
	Set-F-Score	38.46	45.11	53.02	63.34
PAN	Pair-F-Score	35.96	55.64	50.68	45.38
	B-Cubed F-Score	77.52	77.12	80.09	80.74
	Set-F-Score	57.63	49.09	59.45	63.31
SIN	Pair-F-Score	49.67	48.04	64.68	69.98
	B-Cubed F-Score	64.90	64.94	72.32	74.78
	Set-F-Score	23.19	25.21	29.83	29.57

Table 4.29: *Specific results (F-scores) for the six subsets of the general partition of the gold standard.*

the BAI, the JAP, and the OUG subset all consist of languages and dialects which separated not too long ago, while IEL an PAN represent large language families with a considerably long history of divergence. This difference is also reflected in the *diversity index* of the languages given in Table 4.24 above: The indices of BAI (0.10), JAP (0.14), and OUG (0.07) are all very low compared to those for IEL (0.38), and PAN (0.61). One would expect, however, that the algorithms perform better on the SIN dataset, since the Sinitic languages did not diverge too long ago. Nevertheless, the Sinitic data is highly diverse, as reflected by the high diversity index (0.33), and the fact that the glosses in the word lists of the SIN dataset do not entirely belong to the realm of basic vocabulary but also reflect "cultural" words which are much more prone to change. Furthermore, the data is especially challenging, since in the Chinese

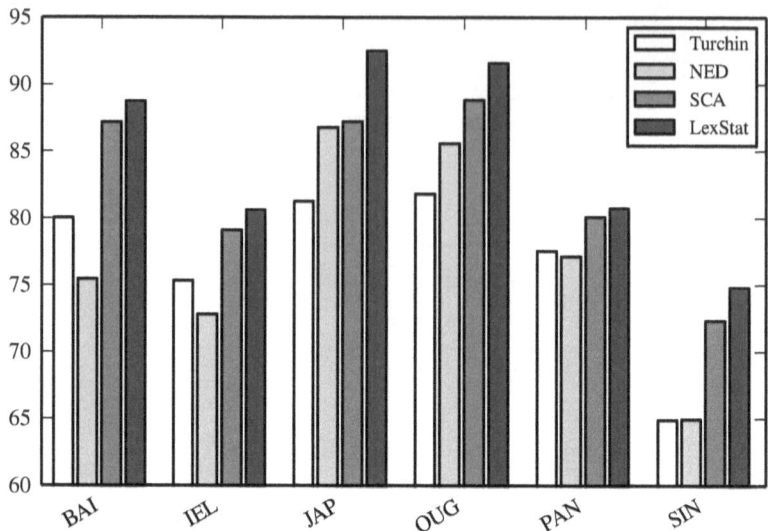

Figure 4.27: *B-Cubed F-scores for the subsets of the general partition of the gold standard.*

dialects there are many compound words which are only partially cognate, i.e. they have morphemes that are cognate, but the compound as a whole is not. Such cases were coded as non-cognate in the data and can easily betray the algorithms.

Time Depth and Diversity   The results on the subsets of the general partition suggest that the accuracy of all methods somehow depends on the diversity of the languages being investigated. Following up this question, a further analysis was carried out. This time, the PIE dataset from the *specific partition* of the gold standard, and its three subsets, GER, ROM, and SLV, were analyzed, using the four methods and the same settings (including the thresholds) as in the previous analyses. The three subsets are directly extracted from the PIE dataset. Thus, their gold standard cognate assignments differ only regarding the number of languages from the PIE data. However, since the subsets reflect the rather "young" Germanic, Romance, and Slavic language families, the time depth that separates the languages in the subsets is much more shallow than

4.3 Automatic Cognate Detection

that of the whole Indo-European language family reflected in the PIE dataset. This is also confirmed by the low diversity indices of the subsets (0.10, 0.14, and 0.16 for GER, ROM and SLV) compared to the index of the combined and extended dataset (0.24, see Equation 4.13 on page 188). The goal of this analysis was to test to which degree time depth and diversity may influence the accuracy of the methods.

The results for the analyses (B-Cubed scores) are given in Table 4.30. As can be seen from the F-scores in the table, diversity and time depth have a crucial impact on the results of the analyses. This is surely no great surprise, since it is well-known that it is easier to compare genetically closely related languages than to compare distantly related ones. However, what might be interesting is that there is only a slight increase in precision, while recall increases greatly. Thus, the majority of problems one faces when entering more shallow time depths in language comparison is not provoked by false positives, but by undetected remote cognate relations.

One further point which is interesting in this context is that in shallow time depths the greatest increase in recall can be recorded for both LexStat (plus 19.9 points on average), followed by NED (15.2), SCA (14.9) and Turchin

Partition	Score	Method			
		Turchin	NED	SCA	LexStat
PIE	B-Cubed Precision	72.59	80.67	79.00	93.48
	B-Cubed Recall	58.69	54.34	66.68	74.21
	B-Cubed F-Score	64.90	64.94	72.32	82.74
GER	B-Cubed Precision	97.02	98.18	97.24	94.09
	B-Cubed Recall	68.11	61.24	78.97	93.42
	B-Cubed F-Score	80.04	75.43	87.16	93.75
ROM	B-Cubed Precision	88.14	95.02	91.14	96.09
	B-Cubed Recall	65.75	59.02	69.87	91.66
	B-Cubed F-Score	80.04	75.43	87.16	93.75
SLV	B-Cubed Precision	98.28	95.34	95.56	98.30
	B-Cubed Recall	69.26	79.63	80.19	97.28
	B-Cubed F-Score	80.04	75.43	87.16	93.75

Table 4.30: *Comparing the B-Cubed scores achieved by the methods on the PIE dataset with those achieved on the three less diverse subsets of PIE (GER, ROM, and SLV).*

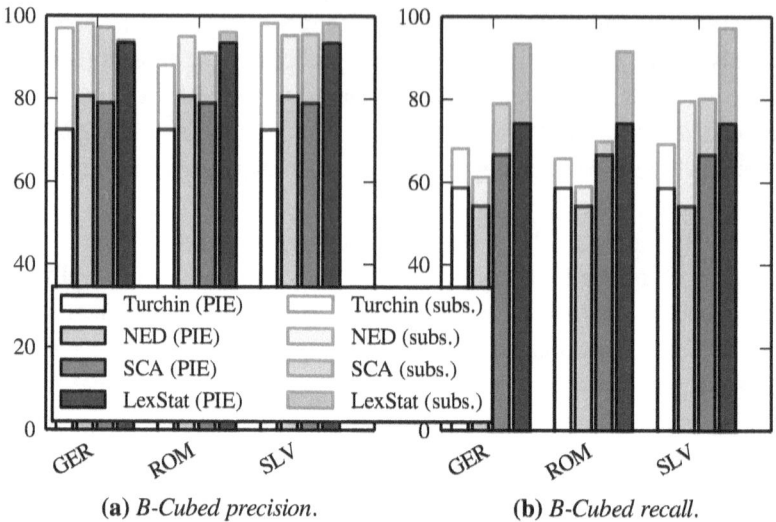

(a) *B-Cubed precision.*   (b) *B-Cubed recall.*

Figure 4.28: *Comparing the B-Cubed precision and recall achieved by the methods on the PIE dataset with the B-Cubed precision and recall achieved on the three less diverse subsets of PIE (GER, ROM, and SLV).*

(9.2). The reason for this increase seems to lie in the fact that genetically closely related languages share a higher amount of cognates than genetically distantly related languages. Thus, there is more signal available which is relevant for methods that rely on language-specific, correspondence-based similarities, such as LexStat. Since genetically closely related languages are also phenotypically more similar, there is also more signal available which is relevant for methods that rely on surface similarities, such as NED.

Sample Size It has been stated above that the sample size is of crucial importance for the comparative method. One can generalize this statement and claim that sample size is of crucial importance for all language-specific methods. In order to test this claim, an analysis of different, randomly created partitions of the IDS dataset was carried out. With its 550 glosses translated into four languages, the IDS is the largest dataset in the gold standard with respect to sample size. The data for this test was created as follows: Starting

4.3 Automatic Cognate Detection

from the basic IDS dataset containing all 550 items, 110 new subsets of the data were created by reducing the data stepwise. In each iteration step, 5 items were randomly deleted from the previous dataset. This process was repeated five times, yielding 550 datasets, covering the whole range of possible sample sizes between 5 and 550 in steps of 5. These datasets were then analysed, using the same settings for the algorithms, as in the analyses reported before.

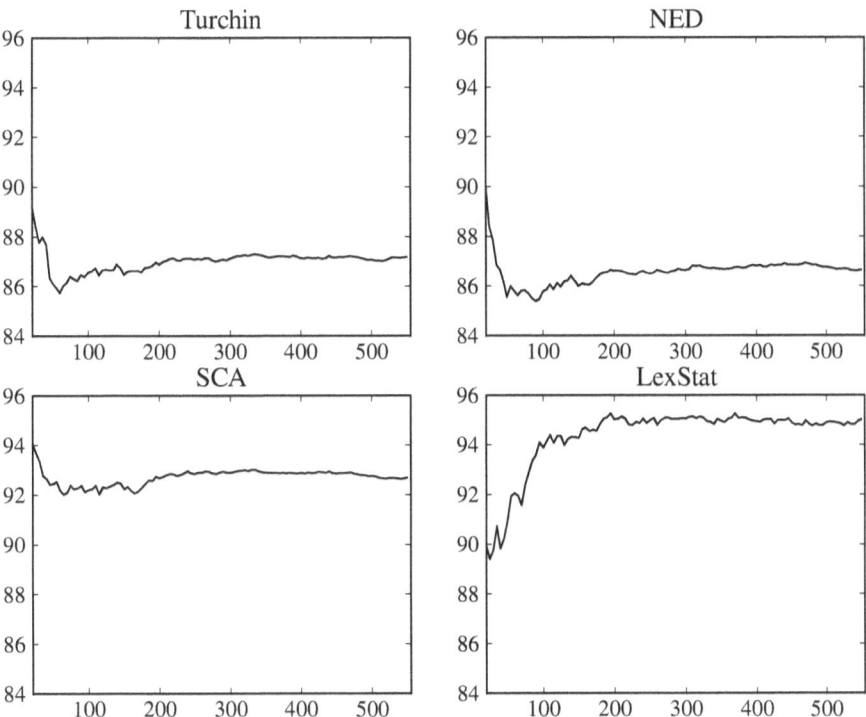

Figure 4.29: *Performance of the ACD methods in dependence of the sample size (number of "basic" vocabulary items per word list). The figures show the B-Cubed recall for the four methods.*

For each specific sample size, the average B-Cubed recall for all five subsets was calculated.[18]

The results of this analysis are plotted in Figure 4.29. As can be seen from the figure, the results of the three language-independent methods are quite similar regarding their tendency. Only the degrees of the scores differ. The scores themselves show only marginal variations and remain constant regardless of the sample size. The results for the language-specific LexStat analysis, on the other hand, clearly depend on the sample size, growing logistically, until converging around a sample size of 200 items. This nicely reflects the language-specific character of the LexStat method: If the word-lists fed to the algorithm are too small, no language-specific similarities can be inferred, and no cognates can be detected, as reflected by the low recall for small word lists. This changes dramatically once the sample size is increased. Comparing the scores for a sample size of 50 items (90.88) with those of 100 items (93.89), an increase of about 3 points can be attested, and between 100 and 200 items (95.02), there is still an increase of more than 1 point (see Table 4.31).

One might wonder whether the fact that the scores converge at a sample size of 200 allows to conclude that 200 words are enough for the preliminary stages

Items	B-Cubed Recall			
	Turchin	NED	SCA	LexStat
50	86.10	85.55	92.44	90.88
100	86.55	85.77	92.20	93.89
200	86.88	86.61	92.68	95.02
300	87.13	86.64	92.90	95.05
400	87.14	86.81	92.89	94.94
500	87.07	86.77	92.75	94.90

Table 4.31: *B-Cubed recall (BR) of the four different ACD methods in randomly created subsamples of varying sample size extracted from the IDS dataset.*

---

[18] In order to guarantee comparability, the thresholds were again "tuned" on the results of the Turchin method, using the whole IDS dataset for the fine-grading, in order to achieve a similar precision between all models. This lead to thresholds of 0.58 for LexStat, 0.18 for SCA, and 0.65 for NED.

4.3 Automatic Cognate Detection 203

of language comparison. Since, to my knowledge, the IDS dataset is the only available gold standard covering more than 500 items, it may be questioned whether the data is representative enough to draw general conclusions regarding the necessary size of word lists for ACD methods. Nevertheless, what the results of the analysis show is that word list size indeed has an impact on the results. Thus, when using language-specific methods, there is no use in taking word lists with less than 100 items, and – as the next paragraph will show – when seeking for very remote genetic relationships, 200 words are surely *not* enough.

Proof of Language Relationship So far, I have presented and discussed the results of the new method for automatic cognate detection. Given that the method works quite well, apparently avoiding false positives while at the same time finding more true cognates than alternative methods, one question that surely comes to mind is whether this method is also capable to prove that two languages are genetically related. In order to test the capability of the method to distinguish related from unrelated languages, the KSL dataset (Kessler 2001) is especially apt, since the compiler of the dataset deliberately chose to include genetically unrelated languages. Thus, apart from the four related Indo-European languages Albanian, English, French, and German, the author also included the three mutually unrelated languages Hawaiian, Navajo, and Turkish.

In Table 4.32 the shared cognates between all language pairs as postulated by the four methods (lower triangle) are contrasted with the cognates postulated by the gold standard (upper triangle).[19] Note that borrowings, which are indicated by Kessler, have been included in this comparison, thus "cognates" in this context are understood as etymologically related words. From a first glance, one can see that all four methods "fail" in so far as they all postulate far more cognates or homologues between unrelated languages than there are in the gold standard. However, the methods fail differently. The Turchin method, which – as could be seen in the previous analyzes – is a very conservative method with a high precision, finds a maximum of 9 cognates in the set of unrelated languages (between Albanian and Hawaiian), while all related languages receive considerably higher scores. One may therefore argue that these false positives do not necessarily invalidate the method, since they can easily be crossed out once genetic relationship is only assumed for languages

---

[19] The results for this test are given in detail in Appendix D.2.

	Albanian	English	French	German	Hawaiian	Navajo	Turkish
Albanian		20	33	25	0	0	1
English	16		56	118	1	0	0
French	23	16		51	0	0	0
German	18	82	19		0	0	0
Hawaian	9	3	4	2		0	0
Navajo	4	4	3	1	0		0
Turkish	7	3	3	1	2	5	

(a) *Turchin*

	Albanian	English	French	German	Hawaiian	Navajo	Turkish
Albanian		20	33	25	0	0	1
English	5		56	118	1	0	0
French	19	16		51	0	0	0
German	9	64	12		0	0	0
Hawaian	2	2	5	3		0	0
Navajo	1	1	2	2	1		0
Turkish	10	5	5	2	1	3	

(b) *NED*

	Albanian	English	French	German	Hawaiian	Navajo	Turkish
Albanian		20	33	25	0	0	1
English	9		56	118	1	0	0
French	19	26		51	0	0	0
German	10	103	18		0	0	0
Hawaian	5	3	10	3		0	0
Navajo	5	8	4	4	4		0
Turkish	7	8	6	4	3	7	

(c) *SCA*

	Albanian	English	French	German	Hawaiian	Navajo	Turkish
Albanian		20	33	25	0	0	1
English	3		56	118	1	0	0
French	11	18		51	0	0	0
German	6	99	11		0	0	0
Hawaian	1	0	0	0		0	0
Navajo	0	1	2	1	0		0
Turkish	2	0	1	0	0	1	

(d) *LexStat*

Table 4.32: *Results of the four methods on the KSL test set. The upper triangle gives the number of shared homologues (cognates and borrowings) in the gold standard, the lower triangle gives the number of shared homologues as determined by the methods.*

4.3 Automatic Cognate Detection

sharing more than a certain amount of "sound-class-cognates". The NED method, on the other hand, finds more cognates between Albanian and Turkish, than between Albanian and English. Given the generally rather high number of matches between Turkish and the Indo-European languages produced by NED, the method suggests that Turkish is an Indo-European language. A similar scenario is drawn by the SCA method which postulates quite a few cognates for the unrelated languages. LexStat postulates the lowest number of cognates for the unrelated languages. However, the high precision of the method comes with a cost, since the status of Albanian as an Indo-European language is now no longer evident. However, that it is difficult – if not impossible – to prove that Albanian is an Indo-European language when relying on small word lists of 200 items only, is not a specific problem of automatic methods, but applies also to the comparative method.

4.3.5 Examples

For reasons of convenience, all examples which are given in the following are drawn from the analysis of the KSL dataset (Kessler 2001). Since the data for the results of all methods on this test set is also given in Appendix D.2, I won't dive too deep into the details here, but only point to some general tendencies which can be easily spotted when comparing the concrete cluster decisions of the algorithms. All examples given in the following follow the same structure. Cognate decisions are displayed with help of integers assigned to each language entry for an item of a multilingual Swadesh list. If the integers are the same for two or more entries, the respective method assigns the entries to the same cluster and therefore judges the words to be etymologically related or cognate. Cluster decisions where the methods differ from the gold standard decisions are especially marked by shading the cells which differ in gray.

Note that the KSL dataset gives the phonetic sequences in different formats. The user can choose between three levels of representation: *word*, *stem*, and *root*. Since the representation on the word level in the KSL data is not optimal for automatic comparison (employing the third person singular for verbs), and the root representation reflects deep historical knowledge of the languages, the stem representation was used for this analysis. Since the data was not further modified, I will use the same orthographic and phonetic representations which can be found in the original data. Since the different representation levels are only applied to the phonetic transcriptions, the orthographic entries in the data represent verbs by using their third person singular form.

"dig" (30)			GLD	TUR	NED	SCA	LxS
Albanian	gërmon	gərmo	1	1	1	1	1
English	*digs*	dıg	2	2	2	2	2
French	*creuse*	krøze	3	1	3	3	3
German	gräbt	graːb	4	1	1	3	4
Hawaiian	'eli	ʔeli	5	5	5	5	5
Navajo	hahashgééd	hahageːd	6	6	6	6	6
Turkish	kazıyor	kaz	7	7	3	7	7

Table 4.33: *Cognate judgments of the four methods for the item 'dig' in the KSL test set. Entries whose orthography is in bold font have been borrowed. Cells shaded in gray mark deviations of the respective method from the gold standard cluster decision.*

False Positives Table 4.33 shows a more or less typical example for false positive cognate judgments which may often occur when using language-independent ACD methods. The false decisions result from the specific weaknesses of the three language-independent methods. According to the Turchin method, Albanian *gërmon* [gərmo] is related with French *creuse* [krøze] and German *gräbt* [graːb], since, according to the DOLGO model, all words have the same first two consonant classes "K" and "R". NED identifies two false cognate sets consisting of two entries each, namely Albanian *gërmon* [gərmo] and German *gräbt* [graːb], and French *creuse* [krøze] and Turkish *kazıyor* [kaz]. Both word pairs exhibit a strong phenotypic similarity. As it has been mentioned before, the NED score is derived from the edit distance by dividing the edit distance by the length of the longer word. As can be seen from, $\left|\begin{smallmatrix} g & ə & r & m & o \\ g & - & r & aː & b \end{smallmatrix}\right|$, the alignment of the Albanian and the German word, there are two matches, one empty match, and two substitutions, summing up to an edit distance of 3, which, divided by the length of the longer word, yields the score $\frac{3}{5} = 0.6$. In $\left|\begin{smallmatrix} k & r & ø & z & e \\ k & a & - & z & - \end{smallmatrix}\right|$, the alignment of the French and the Turkish word, there are again two matches, only one mismatch, but two empty matches, which again yields an edit distance of 3, and an NED score of $\frac{3}{5} = 0.6$. Since the threshold for the NED method was set to 0.65, the distances for both word pairs are beyond the threshold, and the words are therefore judged to be cognate. The SCA method wrongly matches French *creuse* [krøze] with German *gräbt* [graːb]. The low distance score of 0.17 results from the high scores for the matching sound classes "K" and "R" in

4.3 Automatic Cognate Detection

"mouth" (104)			GLD	TUR	NED	SCA	LxS
Albanian	*gojë*	goj	1	1	1	1	1
English	*mouth*	mauθ	2	2	2	2	2
French	*bouche*	buʃ	3	3	3	3	3
German	*Mund*	mund	2	4	4	4	2
Hawaiian	*waha*	waha	5	5	5	5	5
Navajo	*'azéé'*	zeː?	6	6	6	6	6
Turkish	*ağız*	aɣz	7	7	7	7	7

Table 4.34: *Cognate judgments of the four methods for the item 'mouth' in the KSL test set.*

identical prosodic contexts. Since the threshold for the SCA method was set to 0.2, this results again in a false positive decision.

False Negatives In Table 4.34, a more or less typical example for false cognate judgments is given. According to the gold standard, English *mouth* and German *Mund* are cognate, yet, except from the LexStat method, all other methods fail to detect the cognate relation between the two words. The reason for the failure of the Turchin method is obvious: since the method is not based on alignment analyses, it cannot correctly match the relevant sounds. Other, but similarly obvious reasons lead to the failure of the NED method. There is only one identical sounds, since all calculations were applied to tokenized items whereby diphtongs were tokenized into single tokens, the resulting edit distance between both words is 3, and the NED score of 0.75 exceeds the threshold. The SCA method correctly aligns both words, but since the GOP is set to −2, the resulting SCA distance of 0.21 slightly exceeds the threshold. The LexStat distance between the two words is 0.38, and therefore far beyond the threshold of 0.55. An important reason for this low score lies in the low gap penalty of −1 for the gapping of German [n] in a position of descending sonority. Since the correspondence German [n] ≈ English [-] is also reflected in other words of the dataset, such as German *anderer* [andər] 'other' ≈ English *other* [əðər], and German *Zahn* [tsaːn] 'tooth' ≈ English *tooth* [tuθ], the gap penalty is lowered to a considerable degree.

As can be seen from the full record of results given in Appendix D.2, not all cases are as clearcut as the two examples discussed above. The LexStat methods also commits some false positive cognate judgments which a trained historical linguist would never have made, and misses cognates which seem to be obvious. Nevertheless, the apparent weaknesses of language-independent ACD methods are nicely reflected, as is the great improvement resulting from the use of language-specific scoring schemes.

5
Conclusion

> [T]o say that all sound-laws are regular is rather like saying that all Russians are communists.
>
> Allen (1953: 62)

In the begin of the 1950s, Morris Swadesh (1909 – 1967) presented a method that was supposed to measure the genetic closeness between languages on the basis of the statistical analysis of shared cognates in bilingual word lists (Swadesh 1950, Swadesh 1952, Swadesh 1955). At first, the method seemed to breathe fresh wind into historical linguistics. The discipline had past its prime since the structuralist turn in linguistics in the begin of the 1920s (Alter 2001: 1929), and apart from the decipherment of Hittite going along with the proof that it was an Indo-European language (Hrozný 1915), no radical improvements, neither regarding the methods, nor regarding the reconstruction of Proto-Indo-European had been made since the begin of the 20th century. Soon, however, the method was heavily critized (Bergsland and Vogt 1962, Hoijer 1956) and eventually went out of vogue.

When, in the begin of the second millenium, Gray and Atkinson (2003) used similar data but different statistical methods to date the age of the Indo-European language family, they caused a similar stir as Swadesh had done almost half a century ago. But while Swadesh's method was filed away soon after it had been proposed, the method of Gray and Atkinson was part of a general quantitative turn in historical linguistics, which started at the begin of the second millenium. This quantitative turn is reflected in a large bunch of literature on such different topics as phonetic alignment (Kondrak 2002, Prokić et al. 2009), automatic cognate detection (Hall and Klein 2010, Steiner et al. 2011), and phylogenetic reconstruction (Atkinson and Gray 2006, Brown et al. 2008, Nelson-Sathi et al. 2011).

The quantitative turn is not unique to historical linguistics. Not many disciplines could resist the storm of numbers, bits, and bytes that swept over the spires of the ivory tower during the second half of the 20th century. Today, biologists do not need to dissect strange creatures brought home from trips around the world in order to study biological evolution, and linguists do not need to breath the dust of centuries-old books in order to investigate the history of languages. Eventually, even detectives do not need to play the violine while holding out for the spark of inspiration that saves innocent lives and brings real murderers to justice. Statistics, computers, and new procedures which were developed with help of statistics and computers save biologists, linguists, and detectives a lot of time and make their lives a lot easier. If the *Murder on the Orient Express* happened today, CSI Miami would probably solve the case in less than one hour.

Despite the unfortunate fact that quantitative approaches deprive detective fiction of its wit, I feel myself comitted to the quantitative paradigm. Given the increasing amount of data and the well-known problems inherent in our traditional comparative method, we cannot go on comparing words in dictionaries that are so large that they fill a whole shelf without the aid of computers and database tools. However, we should never commit the fallacy to assume that these new methods provide us with new indisputable truths. Algorithms are only as good as their input, and as long as we lack the data to test the new methods rigorously, all results should be treated with care.

So far, no method has been designed that could compete with a trained linguist's intuitions, and, maybe, there is even no need for such a method. There is, however, a definite need for methods that help linguists to *develop* their intuitions. The purpose of this study was to develop and present such methods which can ease the life of historical linguistics. The strategy I followed was to employ the most recent developments in evolutionary biology and computer science while at the same time trying to model the traditional methods as closely as possible.

Following this strategy, the theoretical and practical foundations of traditional historical linguistics were briefly outlined in Chapter 2. After defining languages and words as the basic entities of historical linguistics (Section 2.1), I pointed to the basic types of change these entities are subject to (Section 2.2) and derived basic relations between these entities from them (Section 2.3). The reconstruction of the specific historical relations between words and languages is based on the identification of specific kinds of resemblances (Section

2.4) which are explained with help of historical-fact abduction (Section 2.5). All these questions are addressed more or less explicitly within the traditional framework of the comparative method (Section 2.6).

Given that the main aspect of the comparative method is the comparison of sound sequences, it was important to check whether approaches to sequence comparison in other scientific disciplines might prove useful for historical linguistics. Therefore, the most important aspects of sequence comparison in evolutionary biology and computer science were introduced in Chapter 3. Based on the discussion of formal characteristics of sequences (Section 3.1) and differences between sequences (Section 3.2), an introduction to the basic algorithms for pairwise (Section 3.3) and multiple alignment analyses (Section 3.4) was given.

The new methods for sequence comparison in historical linguistics were introduced in Chapter 4. Since there are some crucial differences between sound sequences and sequences in evolutionary biology and computer science, it was important to develop a new framework for sequence modelling in historical linguistics that – one the one hand – reflects phonetic sequences quite closely, while – on the other hand – being easy to compute (Section 4.1). The solutions proposed in this study consist of a multi-layered representation of phonetic sequences as *sound classes* for which specific *scoring functions* are defined, and *prosodic strings*. It is further accompanied by a specific algorithm that conducts *secondary* as opposed to *primary* alignment analyses.

Sound classes serve as a meta-alphabet that reduces phonetic and phonological detail in order to guarantee the comparability of phonetic tokens between the languages of the world. For this study, three sound-class models were employed. Two were taken from the literature, and one was compiled by myself. In contrast to previous approaches that made use of sound classes in their pure form, specific scoring functions were developed for each of the three sound-class models. These scoring functions define specific transition probabilities between sound classes and account for the fact that not all types of sound change have the same probability to occur during language history.

Prosodic strings allow the linear representation of abstract contextual information when dealing with phonetic sequences. They are an alternative to *n*-gram approaches that are traditionally used to account for context in automatic sequence comparison. Since they are more abstract than *n*-gram approaches, prosodic strings have the advantage of being less dependent on the data size. Furthermore, they make it possible to weight the introduction of gaps and the matching of segments in alignment analyses in dependence of such factors as prosodic strength.

In addition to specific syntagmatic characteristics due to prosodic factors, secondary sequence structures are a second major difference of phonetic sequences compared to sequences in biology and computer science. Apart from sound-class models and prosodic strings, the algorithm for secondary alignment that was developed in Section 3.3.3 was therefore also incorporated in the new method for pairwise and multiple phonetic alignment outlined in Section 4.2. In order to evaluate the performance of this new method, a large benchmark database was created that contains sequence sets that cover many different language families and many different degrees of divergence. As the evaluation of the new method on this benchmark shows, all new approaches to sequence modelling significantly increase the accuracy of phonetic alignment analyses.

Phonetic alignment is a very useful tool in dialectology where due to the relative closeness of the varieties the problem of cognate detection can be solved in a rather straightforward way by relying solely on phonetic and semantic similarity. The more divergent languages become, however, the more difficult it is to distinguish between words that are phonetically similar as a result of non-historical or historical factors. Moreover, historically related words may even have diverged to such a degree that phonetic similarity is almost completely lost. The algorithm for automatic cognate detection introduced in Section 4.3 tries to cope with this problem by deriving language-specific scoring schemes from previously conducted alignment analyses. These scoring schemes come close to the notion of genotypic similarity which is sometimes used to address the specific kind of similarity that surfaces in form of regular sound correspondences. As for the evaluation of the new method for phonetic alignment, a large benchmark database was compiled in order to test the new method for automatic cognate detection. As the results have shown, the new method largely outperforms all language-specific methods. Nevertheless, the new method is not error-free and can only approximate the results which have been achieved by the traditional methods. One reason for this lies surely in the rather small samples of data to which the method was applied. Further reasons are the method's ignorance for morphological information, the restriction to semantically aligned words, and the general problem of cognate assignment in datasets where mostly oblique cognacy can be determined. Despite all these limitations, the method can surely ease the initial stages of linguistic reconstruction, and its results can be taken as a starting point for an in-depth manual evaluation by trained historical linguists.

All methods that I presented in this study are implemented as part of LingPy (see Supplementary Material and http://lingpy.org), a Python library for quantitative endeavours in historical linguistics. The library is freely available and will hopefully be constantly developed further, since there are still many possibilities for improvement. Apart from the theoretical work that has been done to develop the methods, and the practical work that has been done to implement the algorithms, a great deal of time has been devoted to the compilation of new benchmark datasets for phonetic alignment and automatic cognate detection that were used to test the methods presented here. I hope that these datsets will also be of use for other scholars who propose alternative methods in the future. The goal of this study was not to replace the traditional methods, but to provide a tool that can be of real help for historical linguists working on language families that are still less well understood than Indo-European.

My work on LingPy is understood as work in progress. This study reflects its most recent state, yet there are still many things to be done in order to make it a really useful tool for historical linguistic research. Among the most important issues that could not be addressed in the current version of LingPy is the problem of oblique cognacy. Oblique cognacy occurs in all cases where only parts of the words of two genetically related languages share a common history. This is usually the case when specific morphological changes (derivation, compounding) occured only in parts of a language family. In the introduction to Section 4.2 I illustrated this issue by taking various reflexes of Proto-Indo-European *séh₂u̯el- 'sun' in different branches of Indo-European as an example. The current version of LingPy is generally unaware of these specific relations and will necessarily yield alignments and cognate judgments that are simply wrong compared to what we know about the history of the Indo-European languages. One way to solve this problem in the future might be to conduct morphological analyses of the data before comparing the sequences. The secondary alignment algorithm presented in Section 3.3.3 may prove useful in this context, since morphological structures can easily be modelled within the general paradigm of secondary sequence structures. At the moment, however, it is not clear, whether the datasets used in historical linguistics are sufficient to enable full automatic morphological analyses.

A second big issue that could not be addressed in this study is that of semantic change and and semantic similarity. The current version of LingPy requires that the lexical entries are identical regarding their meaning, semantically similar but not identical entries are generally kept distinct. As a result, only those words are judged to be cognate by the LexStat method that have an identical meaning, and cognate words having different meanings, such as, e.g., German *Hund* [hʊnt] 'dog' ≈ English *hound* [haʊnd] cannot be detected. In the literature there are promising proposals to handle semantic similarity when searching for cognates (Steiner et al. 2011). The drawback of these methods is that they require large datasets that are rigorously tagged for meaning. Furthermore, large benchmark databases and training sets are required to test and tune the methods. Since these were not available for this study, it remains for future research to evaluate to which degree such methods can increase the accuracy of algorithms for automatic cognate detection.

Despite the difficulties that are inherent in historical linguistic research in particular and linguistic research in general, I am nevertheless optimistic that the field of historical linguistics will profit from the quantitative turn and sooner or later provide us with new and insteresting insights into language history and the history of languages.

Bibliography

Allen, W. S. (1953). "Relationship in comparative linguistics". *T. Philol. Soc.* 52–108.
Allwood, J. (2003). "Meaning potentials and context: Some consequences for the analysis of variation in meaning". In: *Cognitive approaches to lexical semantics*. Ed. by H. Cuyckens, R. Dirven, and J. R. Taylor. Berlin and New York: Mouton de Gruyter, 29–65.
Alonso, L., I. Castellon, J. Escribano, M. Xavier, and L. Padro (2004). "Multiple sequence alignment for characterizing the linear structure of revision". In: *Proceedings of the 4th International Conference on Language Resources and Evaluation*. "LREC 2004" (Lisbon, 05/26–05/28/2004), 403–406.
Alpher, B. and D. Nash (1999). "Lexical replacement and cognate equilibrium in Australia". *Australian Journal of Linguistics* 19.1, 5–56.
Alter, S. G. (2001). "The linguistic legacy of William Dwight Whitney". In: *History of the language sciences. An international handbook on the evolution of the study of language from the beginnings to the present*. Ed. by S. Auroux, E. F. K. Koerner, H.-J. Niederehe, and K. Versteegh. Vol. 2. Berlin and New York: de Gruyter, 1923–1931.
Amigó, E., J. Gonzalo, J. Artiles, and F. Verdejo (2009). "A comparison of extrinsic clustering evaluation metrics based on formal constraints". *Information Retrieval* 12.4, 461–486.
Anttila, R. (1972). *An introduction to historical and comparative linguistics*. New York: Macmillan.
Arapov, M. V. and M. M. Xerc (1974). *Matematičeskie metody v istoričeskoj lingvistike* [Mathematical methods in historical linguistics]. Moscow: Nauka; German translation: Arapov, M. V. and M. M. Cherc (1983). *Mathematische Methoden in der historischen Linguistik*. Trans. by R. Köhler and P. Schmidt. Bochum: Brockmeyer.
Arens, H. (1955). *Sprachwissenschaft. Der Gang ihrer Entwicklung von der Antike bis zur Gegenwart*. Freiburg: Alber.
Arlotto, A. (1972). *Introduction to historical linguistics*. Boston: Mifflin.
Atkinson, Q. D. and R. D. Gray (2006). "How old is the Indo-European language family? Illumination or more moths to the flame?" In: *Phylogenetic methods and the prehistory of languages*. Ed. by P. Forster and C. Renfrew. Cambridge, Oxford, and Oakville: McDonald Institute for Archaeological Research, 91–109.
Bagga, A. and B. Baldwin (1998). "Entity-based cross-document coreferencing using the vector space model". In: *Proceedings of the 36th Annual Meeting of the Asso-*

ciation for Computational Linguistics and 17th International Conference on Computational Linguistics. "COLING-ACL '98" (Montréal, Quebec, Canada, 08/10–08/14/1998), 79–85.

Barbour, S. and P. Stevenson (1998). *Variation im Deutschen. Soziolinguistische Perspektiven*. Berlin: de Gruyter.

Barton, G. J. and M. J. E. Sternberg (1987). "A strategy for the rapid multiple alignment of protein sequences. Confidence levels from tertiary structure comparisons". *J. Mol. Biol.* 198.2, 327–337.

Baxter, W. H. (1992). *A handbook of Old Chinese phonology*. Berlin: de Gruyter.

Baxter, W. H. and A. Manaster Ramer (2000). "Beyond lumping and splitting: Probabilistic issues in historical linguistics". In: *Time depth in historical linguistics*. Ed. by C. Renfrew, A. McMahon, and L. Trask. Cambridge: McDonald Institute for Archaeological Research, 167–188.

Bennet, P. R. (1976). "Some problems of Bantu lexicostatistics". *Cahiers de l'Institut de Linguistique de Louvain* 3.5-6, 147–173.

Bergsland, K. and H. Vogt (1962). "On the validity of glottochronology". *Curr. Anthropol.* 3.2, 115–153.

Bergsma, S. and G. Kondrak (2007). "Multilingual cognate identification using integer linear programming". In: *Proceedings of the RANLP Workshop on Acquisition and Management of Multilingual Lexicons*. (Borovets, Bulgaria, 09/03/2007).

Bilu, Y., P. K. Agarwal, and R. Kolodny (2006). "Faster algorithms for optimal multiple sequence alignment based on pairwise comparisons". *IEEE/ACM Transactions on Computational Biology and Bioinformatics* 3.4, 408–422.

Branner, D. P. (2006). "Some composite phonological systems in Chinese". In: *The Chinese rime tables. Linguistic philosophy and historical-comparative phonology*. Ed. by D. P. Branner. Amsterdam: Benjamins, 209–232.

Brown, C. H., E. W. Holman, S. Wichmann, V. Velupillai, and M. Cysouw (2008). "Automated classification of the world's languages. A description of the method and preliminary results". *Sprachtypologie und Universalienforschung* 61.4, 285–308.

Brown, C. H., E. W. Holman, and S. Wichmann (2013). "Sound correspondences in the world's languages". *Language* 89.1, 4–29.

Bussmann, H., ed. (1996). *Routledge dictionary of language and linguistics*. Trans. from the German by G. Trauth and K. Kazzazi. London and New York: Routledge.

Böckenbauer, H.-J. and D. Bongartz (2003). *Algorithmische Grundlagen der Bioinformatik*. Stuttgart, Leipzig, and Wiesbaden: Teubner.

Campbell, L. (1999). *Historical linguistics. An introduction*. 2nd ed. Edinburgh: Edinburgh Univ. Press.

Campbell, L. and M. Mixco (2007). *A glossary of historical linguistics*. Edinburgh: Edinburgh University Press.

Chao, K.-M. and L. Zhang (2009). *Sequence comparison. Theory and methods*. London: Springer.

Chao, Y. (1968). *A grammar of spoken Chinese*. Berkeley, Los Angeles, and London: University of California Press.
- (1930 [2006]). "A system of 'tone letters'". In: *Linguistic Essays by Yuenren Chao*. Ed. by Z.-j. Wu and X.-n. Zhao. Běijīng: Shāngwù, 98–102.
Chén Bǎoyà 陳保亞 (1996). *Lùn yǔyán jiēchù yǔ yǔyán liánméng* 論語言接觸與語言聯盟 [Language contact and language unions]. Běijīng 北京: Yǔwén 語文.
Chen, M. (1972). "The time dimension. Contribution toward a theory of sound change". *Foundations of Language* 8.4, 457–498.
Chomsky, N. (1959). "On certain formal properties of grammars". *Information and Control* 2, 137–167.
Chomsky, N. and M. Halle (1968). *The sound pattern of English*. New York, Evanston, and London: Harper and Row.
Coseriu, E. (1973). *Probleme der strukturellen Semantik. Vorlesung gehalten im Wintersemester 1965/66 an der Universität Tübingen*. Tübingen: Narr.
Covington, M. A. (1996). "An algorithm to align words for historical comparison". *Computational Linguistics* 22.4, 481–496.
- (1998). "Alignment of multiple languages for historical comparison". In: *Proceedings of the 36th Annual Meeting of the Association for Computational Linguistics and 17th International Conference on Computational Linguistics*. "COLING-ACL 1998" (Montreal, 08/10–08/14/1998), 275–279.
Croft, W. (2008). "Evolutionary linguistics". *Annu. Rev. Anthropol.* 37, 219–234.
Cronbach, L. J. and P. E. Meehl (1955). "Construct validity in psychological tests". *Psychol. Bull.* 52, 281–302.
Damerau, F. J. (1964). "A technique for computer detection and correction of spelling errors". *Communications of the Association for Computing Machinery* 7.3, 171–176.
Delmestri, A. and N. Cristianini (2010). "Robustness and statistical significance of PAM-like matrices for cognate identification". *J Commun. Comput.* 7.73, 21–31.
DIALIGN. DIALIGN. Multiple sequence alignment. URL: http://bibiserv.techfak.uni-bielefeld.de/dialign/. (Visited on 10/06/2011).
Do, C. B., M. S. P. Mahabhashyam, M. Brudno, and S. Batzoglou (2005). "Prob-Cons. Probabilistic consistency-based multiple sequence alignment". *Genome Res.* 15, 330–340.
Dolgopolsky, A. B. (1964). "Gipoteza drevnejšego rodstva jazykovych semej Severnoj Evrazii s verojatnostej točky zrenija [A probabilistic hypothesis concering the oldest relationships among the language families of Northern Eurasia]". *Voprosy Jazykoznanija* 2, 53–63; English translation: – (1986). "A probabilistic hypothesis concerning the oldest relationships among the language families of northern Eurasia". In: *Typology, relationship and time. A collection of papers on language change and relationship by Soviet linguists*. Ed. by V. V. Shevoroshkin. Trans. from the Russian by V. V. Shevoroshkin. Ann Arbor: Karoma Publisher, 27–50.
Downey, S. S., B. Hallmark, M. P. Cox, P. Norquest, and S. Lansing (2008). "Computational feature-sensitive reconstruction of language relationships: developing the

ALINE distance for comparative historical linguistic reconstruction". *J. Quant. Linguist.* 15.4, 340–369.

Durbin, R., S. R. Eddy, A. Krogh, and G. Mitchinson (1998 [2002]). *Biological sequence analysis. Probabilistic models of proteins and nucleic acids.* 7th ed. Cambridge: Cambridge University Press.

Durie, M., ed. (1996). *The comparative method reviewed. Regularity and irregularity in language change.* With an intro. by M. D. Ross and M. Durie. New York: Oxford University Press.

Dybo, A. and G. Starostin (2008). "In defense of the comparative method, or the end of the Vovin controversy". In: *Aspekty komparativistiki* [Aspects of comparative linguistics]. Vol. 3. Ed. by I. S. Smirnov. Moscow: RGGU, 119–258.

Dyen, I., J. B. Kruskal, and P. Black (1992). "An Indoeuropean classification. A lexicostatistical experiment". *T. Am. Philos. Soc.* 82.5, iii–132.

Eco, U. and T. A. Sebeok, eds. (1983). *The sign of three. Dupin, Holmes, Peirce.* Bloomington: Indiana University Press.

Eddy, S. R. (2004). "Where did the BLOSUM62 alignment score matrix come from?" *Nat. Biotechnol.* 22.8, 1035–1036.

Edgar, R. C. (2004). "MUSCLE. Multiple sequence alignment with high accuracy and high throughput". *Nucleic Acids Res.* 32.5, 1792–1797.

Engstrand, O. (1999). "Swedish". In: *Handbook of the International Phonetic Association. A guide to the use of the international phonetic alphabet.* Cambridge: Cambridge University Press, 140–142.

Feng, D. F. and R. F. Doolittle (1987). "Progressive sequence alignment as a prerequisite to correct phylogenetic trees". *J. Mol. Evol.* 25.4, 351–360.

Fitch, W. M. (2000). "Homology. A personal view on some of the problems". *TRENDS Genet.* 16.5, 227–231.

Fox, A. (1995). *Linguistic reconstruction. An introduction to theory and method.* Oxford: Oxford University Press.

Frege, G. (1892). "Über Sinn und Bedeutung". *Zeitschrift für Philosophie und philosophische Kritik* 100, 25–50.

Gabelentz, H. G. C. (1891). *Die Sprachwissenschaft. Ihre Aufgaben, Methoden und bisherigen Ergebnisse.* Leipzig: T. O. Weigel.

Geisler, H. (1992). *Akzent und Lautwandel in der Romania.* Tübingen: Narr.

Geisler, H. and J.-M. List (2013). "Do languages grow on trees? The tree metaphor in the history of linguistics". In: *Classification and evolution in biology, linguistics and the history of science. Concepts – methods – visualization.* Ed. by H. Fangerau, H. Geisler, T. Halling, and W. Martin. Stuttgart: Franz Steiner Verlag, 111–124.

– (forthcoming). "Beautiful trees on unstable ground. Notes on the data problem in lexicostatistics". In: *Die Ausbreitung des Indogermanischen. Thesen aus Sprachwissenschaft, Archäologie und Genetik.* Ed. by H. Hettrich. Wiesbaden: Reichert.

Geoffrey, N., G. N. O'Grady, and T. Klokeid (1969). "Australian linguistic classification: A plea for coordination of effort". *Oceania* 39.4, 298–311.

Goossens, J. (1973). "Sprache". In: *Niederdeutsch. Sprache und Literatur. Eine Einführung*. Vol. 1. Ed. by J. Goossens. Neumünster: Karl Wachholtz.

Gotoh, O. (1982). "An improved algorithm for matching biological sequences". *J. Mol. Biol.* 162.3, 705–708.

– (1996). "Significant improvement in accuracy of multiple protein sequence alignments by iterative refinement as assessed by reference to structural alignments". *J. Mol. Biol. Direct* 264, 823–838.

Gray, G. S. and W. M. Fitch (1983). "Evolution of antibiotic resistance genes. The DNA sequence of a kanamycin resistance gene from Staphylococcus aureus". *Mol. Biol. Evol.* 1.1, 57–66.

Gray, R. D. and Q. D. Atkinson (2003). "Language-tree divergence times support the Anatolian theory of Indo-European origin". *Nature* 426.6965, 435–439.

Greenhill, S. J., R. Blust, and R. D. Gray (2008). "The Austronesian Basic Vocabulary Database: From bioinformatics to lexomics". *Evol. Bioinformatics* 4, 271–283.

Grimm, J. (1822). *Deutsche Grammatik*. 2nd ed. Vol. 1. Göttingen: Dieterichsche Buchhandlung.

Grønnum, N. (1998). "Danish". *J. Int. Phonet. Assoc.* 28: *Illustrations of the IPA*, 99–105.

Gusfield, D. (1997). *Algorithms on strings, trees and sequences*. Cambridge: Cambridge University Press.

Guy, J. B. M. (1994). "An algorithm for identifying cognates in bilingual wordlists and its applicability to machine translation". *J. Quant. Linguist.* 1.1, 35–42.

Haas, M. R. (1969). *The prehistory of languages*. The Hague and Paris: Mouton.

Hall, D. and D. Klein (2010). "Finding cognate groups using phylogenies". In: *Proceedings of the 48th Annual Meeting of the Association for Computational Linguistics*. "ACL 2010" (Uppsala, 07/11–07/16/2010). Stroudsburg, 1030–1039.

Hall, T. A. (2000). *Phonologie. Eine Einführung*. Berlin and New York: de Gruyter.

Hamming, R. W. (1950). "Error detection and error detection codes". *AT&T TECH J* 29.2, 147–160.

Hauer, B. and G. Kondrak (2011). "Clustering semantically equivalent words into cognate sets in multilingual lists". In: *Proceedings of the 5th International Joint Conference on Natural Language Processing*. (Chiang Mai, Thailand, 11/08–11/13/2011), 865–873.

Heeringa, W. J., P. Kleiweg, C. Gooskens, and J. Nerbonne (2006). "Evaluation of string distance algorithms for dialectology". In: *Proceedings of the Linguistic Distances Workshop at the joint conference of International Committee on Computational Linguistics and the Association for Computational Linguistics*. "Linguistic Distances" (Sydney, 07/23/2006), 51–62.

Henikoff, S. and J. G. Henikoff (1991). "Automated assembly of protein blocks for database searching". *Nucleic Acids Res.* 19.23, 6565–6572.

– (1992). "Amino acid substitution matrices from protein blocks". *Proc. Natl. Acad. Sci. U.S.A.* 89.22, 10915–10919.

Higgins, D. G. and P. M. Sharp (1988). "CLUSTAL. A package for performing multiple sequence alignment on a microcomputer". *Gene* 73, 237–244.

Hirosawa, M., Y. Totoki, M. Hoshida, and M. Ishikawa (1995). "Comprehensive study on iterative algorithms of multiple sequence alignment". *Comput. Appl. Biosci.* 11, 13–18.

Hock, H. H. (1991). *Principles of historical linguistics*. 2nd ed. Berlin: Mouton de Gruyter.

Hock, H. H. and B. D. Joseph (1995 [2009]). *Language history, language change and language relationship. An introduction to historical and comparative linguistics.* 2nd ed. Berlin and New York: Mouton de Gruyter.

Hoenigswald, H. M. (1959). "Some uses of nothing". *Language* 35.3, 409–420.

– (1960). "Phonetic similarity in internal reconstruction". *Language* 36.2, 191–192.

Hogeweg, P. and B. Hesper (1984). "The alignment of sets of sequences and the construction of phyletic trees. An integrated method". *J. Mol. Evol.* 20.2, 175–186.

Hoijer, H. (1956). "Lexicostatistics. A critique". *Language* 32.1, 49–60.

Holm, H. J. (2000). "Genealogy of the main Indo-European branches applying the separation base method". *J. Quant. Linguist.* 7.2, 73–95.

Holman, E. W., S. Wichmann, C. H. Brown, V. Velupillai, A. Müller, and D. Bakker (2008). "Explorations in automated lexicostatistics". *Folia Linguistica* 20.3, 116–121.

Holman, E. W. et al. (2011). "Automated dating of the world's language families based on lexical similarity". *Curr. Anthropol.* 52.6, 841–875.

Holzer, G. (1996). *Das Erschließen unbelegter Sprachen. Zu den theoretischen Grundlagen der genetischen Linguistik*. Frankfurt am Main: Lang.

Hrozný, B. (1915). "Die Lösung des hethitischen Problems". *Mitteilungen der Deutschen Orient-Gesellschaft* 56, 17–50.

Hübschmann, H. (1877). "Ueber die stellung des armenischen im kreise der indogermanischen sprachen". *Zeitschrift für vergleichende Sprachforschung der indogermanischen Sprachen* 23, 5–49.

IPA Handbook (1999). *Handbook of the International Phonetic Association. A guide to the use of the international phonetic alphabet*. Cambridge: Cambridge University Press.

Jakobson, R. (1976 [1978]). *Six lectures on sound and meaning*. Trans. from the French by J. Mepham. With an intro. by C. Lévi-Strauss. Cambridge and London: MIT Press.

Jones, W. (1798). "The third anniversary discourse, delivered 2 February, 1786, by the president. On the Hindus". *Asiatick Researches* 1, 415–431.

Karlgren, B. (1950). *The book of odes. Chinese text, transcription and translation*. Stockholm: Museum of Far Eastern Antiquities.

Katičić, R. (1966). "Modellbegriffe in der vergleichenden Sprachwissenschaft". *Kratylos* 11, 49–67.

Keller, R. (1990). *Sprachwandel. Von der unsichtbaren Hand in der Sprache*. Tübingen: Francke.

Kessler, B. (1995). "Computational dialectology in Irish Gaelic". In: *Proceedings of the seventh conference on European chapter of the Association for Computational Linguistics*. "EACL 1995" (Dublin), 60–66.

– (2001). *The significance of word lists. Statistical tests for investigating historical connections between languages*. Stanford: CSLI Publications.

Kiparsky, P. (1988). "Phonological change". In: *Linguistics. The Cambridge survey*. Vol. 1: *Linguistic theory. Foundations*. Ed. by F. J. Newmeyer. Cambridge et al.: Cambridge University Press, 363–415.

Klein, W. P. (1999). "Die ursprüngliche Einheit der Sprachen in der philologisch-grammatischen Sicht der frühen Neuzeit". In: *The Language of Adam*. Proceedings of a conference held at the Herzog August Bibliothek (Wolfenbüttel, 05/30–05/31/1995). Ed. by A. P. Coudert. Wolfenbütteler Forschungen 84. Wiesbaden: Harrassowitz, 25–56.

– (2004). "Was wurde aus den Wörtern der hebräischen Ursprache? Zur Entstehung der komparativen Linguistik aus dem Geist etymologischer Spekulation". In: *Gottes Sprache in der philologischen Werkstatt. Hebraistik vom 15. bis zum 19. Jahrhundert*. Proceedings of the Symposium "Die Geburt der Philologie aus dem Geist der Hebraistik" (Wittenberg, 10/06–10/06/2002). Ed. by G. Veltri and G. Necker. Studies in European Judaism 11. Leiden: Brill, 3–23.

Kommission "Selbstkontrolle" (2011). *Bericht an die Hochschulleitung der Universität Bayreuth aus Anlass der Untersuchung des Verdachts wissenschaftlichen Fehlverhaltens von Herrn Karl-Theodor Freiherr zu Guttenberg*. Universität Bayreuth. PDF: http://www.uni-bayreuth.de/presse/Aktuelle-Infos/2011/Bericht_der_Kommission_m__Anlagen_10_5_2011_.pdf.

Kondrak, G. (2000). "A new algorithm for the alignment of phonetic sequences". In: *Proceedings of the 1st North American chapter of the Association for Computational Linguistics conference*. (Seattle, 04/29–05/03/2000), 288–295.

– (2002). "Algorithms for language reconstruction". Dissertation. Toronto: University of Toronto. URL: http://webdocs.cs.ualberta.ca/~kondrak/papers/thesis.pdf.

– (2003). "Identifying complex sound correspondences in bilingual wordlists". In: *Computational linguistics and intelligent text processing*. Ed. by A. Gelbukh. Berlin: Springer, 432–443.

Koonin, E. V. (2005). "Orthologs, paralogs, and evolutionary genomics". *Annu. Rev. Genet*. 39, 309–338.

Kormišin, I. V. (1988). "Prajazyk. Bližnjaja i dal'njaja rekonstrukcija [The protolanguage. Narrow and distant reconstruction]". In: *Sravnitel'no-istoričeskoe izučenie jazykov raznych semej* [Comparative-historical investigations of languages of different language families]. Vol. 3: *Teorija lingvističeskoj rekonstrukcii* [Theory of linguistic reconstruction]. Ed. by N. Z. Gadžieva. Moscow: Nauka, 90–105.

Kruskal, J. B. (1983). "An overview of sequence comparison. Time warps, string edits, and macromolecules". *SIAM Review* 25.2, 201–237.

Kruskal, J. B. and M. Liberman (1983 [1999]). "The symmetric time-warping problem. From continuous to discrete". In: *Time warps, string edits, and macromolecules. The theory and practice of sequence comparison.* Ed. by D. Sankoff and J. B. Kruskal. Repr. Stanford: CSLI Publications, 125–161. [Original edition: Reading, Mass.: Addison-Wesley Publishing Company, 1983].

Labov, W. (1994). *Principles of linguistic change.* Vol. 1: *Internal factors.* Malden, Oxford, and West Sussex: Wiley-Blackwell.

Lass, R. (1997). *Historical linguistics and language change.* Cambridge: Cambridge University Press.

Lassmann, T. and E. L. Sonnhammer (2002). "Quality assessment of multiple alignment programs". *FEBS Lett.* 529.1, 126–130.

Lee, W.-S. and E. Zee (2003). "Standard Chinese (Beijing)". *J. Int. Phonet. Assoc.* 33.1: *Illustrations of the IPA*, 109–112.

– (2009). "Hakka Chinese". *J. Int. Phonet. Assoc.* 39.1: *Illustrations of the IPA*, 107–111.

Lees, R. B. (1953). "The basis of glottochronology". *Language* 29.2, 113–127.

Lehmann, W. P. (1962 [1992]). *Historical linguistics. An Introduction.* 3rd ed. London: Routledge.

Leskien, A. (1871 [2002]). *Handbuch der altbulgarischen (altkirchenslavischen) Sprache. Grammatik, Texte, Glossar.* Rev. by O. A. Rottmann. Repr. Heidelberg: Winter. [Original edition: Weimar: Böhlau, 1871].

Levenshtein, V. I. (1965). "Dvoičnye kody s ispravleniem vypadenij, vstavok i zameščenij simvolov [Binary codes with correction of deletions, insertions and replacements]". *Doklady Akademij Nauk SSSR* 163.4, 845–848; English translation:

– (1966). "Binary codes capable of correcting deletions, insertions, and reversals". *Soviet Physics Doklady* 10.8, 707–710.

Lewis, M. P. and C. D. Fennig, eds. (2013). *Ethnologue. Languages of the world.* URL: http://www.ethnologue.com.

List, J.-M. (2010). "Phonetic alignment based on sound classes. A new method for sequence comparison in historical linguistics". In: *Proceedings of the 15th Student Session of the European Summer School for Logic, Language and Information.* (Copenhagen, 08/09–08/20/2010). Ed. by M. Slavkovik, 192–202. PDF: http://lingulist.de/documents/list_sound_classes.pdf.

– (2012a). "LexStat. Automatic detection of cognates in multilingual wordlists". In: *Proceedings of the EACL 2012 Joint Workshop of Visualization of Linguistic Patterns and Uncovering Language History from Multilingual Resources.* "LINGVIS & UNCLH 2012" (Avignon, 04/23–04/24/2012), 117–125.

– (2012b). "Multiple sequence alignment in historical linguistics. A sound class based approach". In: *Proceedings of ConSOLE XIX.* "The 19th Conference of the Student Organization of Linguistics in Europe" (Groningen, 01/05–01/08/2011). Ed. by E.

Boone, K. Linke, and M. Schulpen, 241–260. PDF: http://media.leidenuniv.nl/legacy/console19-proceedings-list.pdf.
- (2012c). "SCA. Phonetic alignment based on sound classes". In: *New directions in logic, language, and computation*. Ed. by M. Slavkovik and D. Lassiter. Berlin and Heidelberg: Springer, 32–51.

List, J.-M., A. Terhalle, and M. Urban (2013). "Using network approaches to enhance the analysis of cross-linguistic polysemies". In: *Proceedings of the 10th International Conference on Computational Semantics – Short Papers.* "IWCS 2013" (Potsdam, 03/19–03/22/2013), 347–353. URL: http://aclweb.org/anthology-new/W/W13/W13-0208.pdf.

Lowrance, R. and R. A. Wagner (1975). "An extension of the string-to-string correction problem". *J. Assoc. Comput. Mach.* 22.2, 177–183.

Löbner, S. (2003). *Semantik. Eine Einführung.* Berlin: de Gruyter.

Mackay, W. and G. Kondrak (2005). "Computing word similarity and identifying cognates with pair hidden markov models". In: *Proceedings of the Ninth Conference on Computational Natural Language Learning.* "CoNLL 2005" (Ann Arbor, 06/29–06/30/2005), 40–47.

Maddieson, I. (2011). "Consonant inventories". In: *The world atlas of language structures online.* Ed. by M. Dryer and M. Haspelmath. Munich: Max Planck Digital Library. URL: http://wals.info/chapter/1.

Makaev, E. A. (1977). *Obščaja teorija sravnitel'nogo jazykoznanija* [Common theory of comparative linguistics]. Moscow: Nauka.

Marchal, J. H. (1975). "On the concept of a system". *Philosophy of Science* 42.4, 448–468.

McGuffin, L. J. (2009). "Insertion and deletion events, their molecular mechanisms, and their impact on sequence alignment". In: *Sequence alignment. Methods, models, concepts, and strategies.* Ed. by M. S. Rosenberg. Berkeley, Los Angeles, and London: University of California Press, 23–38.

McMahon, A. and R. McMahon (2005). *Language classification by numbers.* Oxford: Oxford University Press.

Meier-Brügger, M. (2002). *Indogermanische Sprachwissenschaft.* In collab. with M. Fritz and M. Mayrhofer. 8th ed. Berlin and New York: de Gruyter.

Mel'čuk, I. (2006). *Aspects of the theory of morphology.* Ed. by D. Beck. Berlin and New York: Mouton de Gruyter.

Merrell, F. (2001). "Charles Sanders Peirce's concept of the sign". In: *The Routledge companion to semiotics and linguistics.* Ed. by P. Cobley. London and New York: Routledge, 28–39.

Morgenstern, B., A. Dress, and W. T. David (1996). "Multiple DNA and protein sequence alignment based on segment-to-segment comparison". *Proceedings of the National Acadamy of Science* 93, 12098–12103.

Morgenstern, B., W. R. Atchley, K. Hahn, and A. Dress (1998). "Segment-based scores for pairwise and multiple sequence alignments". In: *Proceedings of the Sixth*

International Conference on Intelligent Systems for Molecular Biology. (Montréal, 06/28–07/01/1998). Ed. by J. Glasgow, T. Littlejohn, F. M. R. Lathrop, D. Sankoff, and C. Sensen. AAAI Press, 115 –121.

Morrison, D. A. (2010). "Review of *Sequence Alignment: Methods, Models, Concepts, and Strategies* ed. by M. S. Rosenberg (2009)". *Syst. Biol.* 359.3, 363–365.

Needleman, S. B. and C. D. Wunsch (1970). "A gene method applicable to the search for similarities in the amino acid sequence of two proteins". *J. Mol. Biol.* 48, 443–453.

Nelson-Sathi, S., J.-M. List, H. Geisler, H. Fangerau, R. D. Gray, W. Martin, and T. Dagan (2011). "Networks uncover hidden lexical borrowing in Indo-European language evolution". *Proc. R. Soc. London, Ser. B* 278.1713, 1794–1803.

Nerbonne, J. and W. Heeringa (2010). "Measuring dialect differences". In: *Language and space. An international handbook of linguistic variation. Vol. 1. Theories and method*. Ed. by P. Auer and J. E. Schmidt. Berlin: De Gruyter Mouton, 550–567.

Nichols, J. (1996). "The comparative method as heuristic". In: *The comparative method reviewed. Regularity and irregularity in language change*. Ed. by M. Durie. With an intro. by M. D. Ross and M. Durie. New York: Oxford University Press, 39–71.

Nietzsche, F. (1869 [1920]). *Homer und die classische Philologie. Antrittsrede an der Universität Basel gehalten am 28. Mai 1869*. In: *Gesammelte Werke*. Vol. 2: *Kleinere Schriften. 1869 - 1874*. München: Musarion, 1–32.

Notredame, C. (2007). "Recent evolutions of multiple sequence alignment algorithms". *PLoS Comput. Biol.* 3.8, 1405–1408.

– (2009). "Computing multiple sequence alignment with template-based methods". In: *Sequence alignment. Methods, models, concepts, and strategies*. Ed. by M. S. Rosenberg. Berkeley, Los Angeles, and London: University of California Press, 55–69.

Notredame, C., L. Holm, and D. G. Higgins (1998). "COFFEE. An objective function for multiple sequence alignment". *Bioinformatics* 14.5, 407–422.

Notredame, C., D. G. Higgins, and J. Heringa (2000). "T-Coffee. A novel method for fast and accurate multiple sequence alignment". *J. Mol. Biol.* 302, 205–217.

Oakes, M. P. (2000). "Computer estimation of vocabulary in a protolanguage from word lists in four daughter languages". *J. Quant. Linguist.* 7.3, 233–243.

Oesterreicher, W. (2001). "Historizität, Sprachvariation, Sprachverschiedenheit, Sprachwandel". In: *Language typology and language universals. An international handbook*. Ed. by M. Haspelmath. Berlin and New York: Walter de Gruyter, 1554–1595.

Ogden, C. K. and I. A. Richards (1923 [1989]). *The meaning of meaning. A study of the influence of language upon thought and of the science of symbolism*. With an intro. by U. Eco. 8th ed. New York: Harcourt, Brace & World Inc.

Oommen, B. J. and R. K. S. Loke (1997). "Pattern recognition of strings with substitutions, insertions, deletions and generalized transpositions". *Pattern Recogn.* 30.5, 789–800.

Osthoff, H. and K. Brugmann (1878). *Morphologische Untersuchungen auf dem Gebiete der indogermanischen Sprachen.* Vol. 1. Leipzig: Hirzel.

Pagel, M. (2009). "Human language as a culturally transmitted replicator". *Nature Reviews. Genetics* 10, 405–415.

Peer, Y. Van de (2009). "Phylogenetic inference based on distance methods. Theory". In: *The phylogenetic handbook. A practical approach to phylogenetic analysis and hypothesis testing.* Ed. by P. Lemey, M. Salemi, and A.-M. Vandamme. 2nd ed. Cambridge: Cambridge University Press, 142–160.

Peirce, C. S. (1931/1958). *Collected papers of Charles Sanders Peirce.* Ed. by C. Hartshorne and P. Weiss. Cont. by A. W. Burke. 8 vols. Cambridge, Mass.: Harvard University Press.

Popper, K. R. (1978). "Three worlds". *The Tanner Lectures on Human Values*, 143–167. URL: http://www.tannerlectures.utah.edu/lectures/documents/popper80.pdf.

Prokić, J., M. Wieling, and J. Nerbonne (2009). "Multiple sequence alignments in linguistics". In: *Proceedings of the EACL 2009 Workshop on Language Technology and Resources for Cultural Heritage, Social Sciences, Humanities, and Education.* "LaTeCH-SHELT&R 2009" (Athens, 03/30/2009), 18–25.

Raghava, G. P. S. and G. J. Barton (2006). "Quantification of the variation in percentage identity for protein sequence alignments". *BMC Bioinformatics* 7.415.

Rask, R. K. (1818). *Undersögelse om det gamle Nordiske eller Islandske sprogs oprindelse* [Investigation of the origin of the Old Norse or Icelandic language]. Copenhagen: Gyldendalske Boghandlings Forlag; English translation: – (1993). *Investigation of the origin of the Old Norse or Icelandic language.* Trans. by N. Ege. Travaux du Cercle Linguistique de Copenhague 26. Copenhagen: The Linguistic Circle of Copenhagen.

Renfrew, C., A. McMahon, and L. Trask, eds. (2000). Cambridge: McDonald Institute for Archaeological Research.

Ringe, D., T. Warnow, and A. Taylor (2002). "Indo-European and computational cladistics". *T. Philol. Soc.* 100.1, 59–129.

Rosenberg, M. S., ed. (2009a). *Sequence alignment. Methods, models, concepts, and strategies.* Berkeley, Los Angeles, and London: University of California Press.

– (2009b). "Sequence alignment. Concepts and history". In: *Sequence alignment. Methods, models, concepts, and strategies.* Ed. by M. S. Rosenberg. Berkeley, Los Angeles, and London: University of California Press, 1–22.

Rosenberg, M. S. and T. H. Ogden (2009). "Simulation approaches to evaluating alignment error and methods for comparing alternate alignments". In: *Sequence alignment. Methods, models, concepts, and strategies.* Ed. by M. S. Rosenberg. Berkeley, Los Angeles, and London: University of California Press, 179–207.

Ross, A. S. C. (1950). "Philological probability problems". *J. R. Stat. Soc. Series B (Methodological)* 12.1, 19–59.
Saitou, N. and M. Nei (1987). "The neighbor-joining method: A new method for reconstructing phylogenetic trees". *Mol. Biol. Evol.* 4.4, 406–425.
Sankoff, D. (1969). "Historical linguistics as stochastic process". Dissertation. Montreal: McGill University.
Saussure, F. de (1916). *Cours de linguistique générale.* Ed. by C. Bally. Lausanne: Payot; German translation: – (1967). *Grundfragen der allgemeinen Sprachwissenschaft.* Trans. from the French by H. Lommel. 2nd ed. Berlin: Walter de Gruyter & Co.
Schleicher, A. (1848). *Zur vergleichenden Sprachengeschichte.* Bonn: König.
– (1861). *Compendium der vergleichenden Grammatik der indogermanischen Sprache.* Vol. 1: *Kurzer Abriss einer Lautlehre der indogermanischen Ursprache.* Weimar: Böhlau.
– (1863). *Die Darwinsche Theorie und die Sprachwissenschaft. Offenes Sendschreiben an Herrn Dr. Ernst Haeckel.* Weimar: Hermann Böhlau.
– (1861 [1866]). *Compendium der vergleichenden Grammatik der indogermanischen Sprache.* Vol. 1: *Kurzer Abriss einer Lautlehre der indogermanischen Ursprache.* 2nd ed. Weimar: Böhlau.
Schmidt, J. (1872). *Die Verwantschaftsverhältnisse der indogermanischen Sprachen.* Weimar: Hermann Böhlau.
Schmitter, P. (1982). *Untersuchungen zur Historiographie der Linguistik. Struktur – Methodik – theoretische Fundierung.* Tübinger Beiträge zur Linguistik 181. Tübingen: Gunter Narr.
Schurz, G. (2008). "Patterns of abduction". *Synthese* 164, 201–234.
Schwarz, M. (1996). *Einführung in die kognitive Linguistik.* Basel and Tübingen: Francke.
Schwink, F. (1994). *Linguistic typology, universality and the realism of reconstruction.* Washington: Institute for the Study of Man.
Searls, D. B. (2002). "The language of genes". *Nature* 420, 211–217.
Sechehaye, A. (1908). *Programme et méthodes de la linguistique théorique. Psychologie du langage.* Paris: Honoré Champion.
Shirō, H. (1973). "Japanese dialects". In: *Diachronic, areal and typological linguistics.* Ed. by H. M. Hoenigswald and R. H. Langacre. Current Trends in Linguistics 11. The Hague and Paris: Mouton, 368–400.
Smith, T. F. and M. S. Waterman (1981). "Identification of common molecular subsequences". *J. Mol. Biol.* 1, 195–197.
Sokal, R. R. and C. D. Michener (1958). "A statistical method for evaluating systematic relationships". *University of Kansas Scientific Bulletin* 28, 1409–1438.
Somers, H. L. (1999). "Aligning phonetic segments for children's articulation assessment". *Computational Linguistics* 25.2, 267–275.

Starostin, G. (2008a). *Making a comparative linguist out of your computer. Problems and achievements*. Talk, given at the Santa Fe Institute (Santa Fe, 08/12/2008).
– (2010). "Preliminary lexicostatistics as a basis for language classification: A new approach". *J. Lang. Relationship* 3, 79–116.
Starostin, S. A. (1989). "Sravnitel'no-istoričeskoe jazykoznanie i leksikostatistika [Comparative-historical linguistics and lexicostatistics]". In: *Lingvističeskaja rekonstrukcija i drevnejšaja istorija Vostoka* [Linguistic reconstruction and the oldest history of the East]. Vol. 1: *Materialy k diskussijam na konferencii* [Materials for the discussion on the conference]. Ed. by S. V. Kullanda, J. D. Longinov, A. J. Militarev, E. J. Nosenko, and V. A. Shnirel'man. Moscow: Institut Vostokovedenija, 3–39; English translation: – (2000). "Comparative-historical linguistics and lexicostatistics". In: *Time depth in historical linguistics*. Ed. by C. Renfrew, A. McMahon, and L. Trask. Trans. from the Russian by I. Peiros. Vol. 1. Papers in the prehistory of languages. Cambridge: McDonald Institute for Archaeological Research, 223–265.
Statt, D. A., comp. (1981 [1998]). *Consise dictionary of psychology*. 3rd ed. London and New York: Routledge.
Steiner, L., P. F. Stadler, and M. Cysouw (2011). "A pipeline for computational historical linguistics". *Lang. Dyn. Change* 1.1, 89–127.
Sturtevant, E. H. (1920). *The pronunciation of Greek and Latin*. Chicago: University of Chicago Press.
Sun, C. (2006). *Chinese: A linguistic introduction*. Cambridge: Cambridge University Press.
Swadesh, M. (1950). "Salish internal relationships". *Int. J. Am. Linguist.* 16.4, 157–167.
– (1952). "Lexico-statistic dating of prehistoric ethnic contacts. With special reference to North American Indians and Eskimos". *Proc. Am. Philol. Soc.* 96.4, 452–463.
– (1955). "Towards greater accuracy in lexicostatistic dating". *Int. J. Am. Linguist.* 21.2, 121–137.
Szemerényi, O. (1970). *Einführung in die vergleichende Sprachwissenschaft*. Darmstadt: Wissenschaftliche Buchgesellschaft.
Taylor, W. R. (1987). "Multiple sequence alignment by a pairwise algorithm". *Comput. Appl. Biosci.* 3.2, 81–87.
Ternes, E. (1987). *Einführung in die Phonologie*. Darmstadt: Wissenschaftliche Buchgesellschaft.
Thompson, J. D. (2009). "Constructing alignment benchmarks". In: *Sequence alignment. Methods, models, concepts, and strategies*. Ed. by M. S. Rosenberg. Berkeley, Los Angeles, and London: University of California Press, 151–177.
Thompson, J. D., D. G. Higgins, and T. J. Gibson (1994). "CLUSTAL W. Improving the sensitivity of progressive multiple sequence alignment through sequence

weighting, position-specific gap penalties and weight matrix choice". *Nucleic Acids Res.* 22.22, 4673–4680.

Thompson, J. D., F. Plewniak, and O. Poch (1999). "A comprehensive comparison of multiple sequence alignment programs". *Nucleic Acids Res.* 27.13, 2682–2690.

Torres, A., A. Cabada, and J. J. Nieto (2003). "An exact formula for the number of alignments between two DNA sequences". *DNA Sequence* 14.6, 427–430.

Trask, R. L. (1996). *Historical linguistics*. London et al.: Arnold.

– comp. (2000). *The dictionary of historical and comparative linguistics*. Edinburgh: Edinburgh University Press.

Turchin, P., I. Peiros, and M. Gell-Mann (2010). "Analyzing genetic connections between languages by matching consonant classes". *J. Lang. Relationship* 3, 117–126.

Wagner, R. A. (1975). "On the complexity of the extended string-to-string correction problem". In: *Proceedings of the seventh annual ACM symposium on theory of computing*. "STOC 1975" (Albuquerque), 218–223.

Wagner, R. A. and M. J. Fischer (1974). "The string-to-string correction problem". *J. Assoc. Comput. Mach.* 21.1, 168–173.

Wallace, I. M., O. O'Sullivan, and D. G. Higgins (2005). "Evaluation of iterative alignment algorithms for multiple alignment". *Bioinformatics* 21.8, 1408–1414.

Wang, F. (2006a). *Comparison of languages in contact. The distillation method and the case of Bai*. Taipei: Institute of Linguistics Academia Sinica.

Wang, L. and T. Jiang (1994). "On the complexity of multiple sequence alignment". *J. Comput. Biol.* 1.4, 337–348.

Wang, W. S.-Y. (1969). "Competing changes as a cause of residue". *Language* 45.1, 9–25.

– (2006b). *Yǔyán, yǔyīn yǔ jìshù* 語言, 語音與技術 [Language, phonology and technology]. Shànghǎi 上海: Xiānggǎng Chéngshì Dàxué.

Weinreich, U. (1954). "Is a structural dialectology possible?" *Word* 10.2/3, 388–400.

Wichmann, S., E. W. Holman, A. Müller, V. Velupillai, J.-M. List, O. Belyaev, M. Urban, and D. Bakker (2010). "Glottochronology as a heuristic for genealogical language relationships". *J. Quant. Linguist.* 17.4, 303–316.

Wilkins, D. P. (1996). "Natural tendencies of semantic change and the search for cognates". In: *The comparative method reviewed. Regularity and irregularity in language change*. Ed. by M. Durie. With an intro. by M. D. Ross and M. Durie. New York: Oxford University Press, 264–304.

Witten, I. H. and E. Frank (2005). *Data mining. Practical machine learning tools and techniques*. 2nd ed. Amsterdam et al.: Elsevier.

Sources

Krátylos	*Krátylos* (after 399 BC). By Plátōn (424–348 BC); English translation: *Cratylus* (1921). In: *Plato in twelve volumes*. Vol. 4: *Cratylus. Parmenides. Greater Hippias. Lesser Hippias*. Trans. from the Greek by H. N. Fowler. London: William Heinemann Ltd.; German translation: *Kratylos* (2001). In: *Platon. Werke in acht Bänden. Griechisch und Deutsch*. Vol. 3: *Phaidon. Das Gastmahl. Kratylos*. Ed. by G. Eigler. Red. by D. Kurz. Greek text by L. Robin and L. Méridier. Trans. from the Greek by F. Schleiermacher. Darmstadt: Wissenschaftliche Buchgesellschaft.
Máoshī Gǔyīnkǎo	*Máoshī Gǔyīnkǎo* 毛詩古音攷 [Investigation of the old sounds in Mao's compilation of the Book of Odes] (1606). By Chén Dì 陳第 (1541–1617); Critical edition: Chén Dì 陳第 (1606). *Máoshī Gǔyīnkǎo* 毛詩古音攷 [Investigation of the old sounds in Mao's compilation of the Book of Odes]. Sìkù Quánshū 四庫全書 [Complete Library of the Four Treasuries]; Jīngbù 經部; Xiǎoxuélèi 小學類; Míng 明.
Shījīng	*Shījīng* 詩經 [The book of odes] (ca. 1050 BC); Critical edition: *Máoshī* (1922). *Máoshī* 毛詩 [Mao's compilation of the Book of Odes]. Comm. by Máo Hēng 毛亨 (Hàn Dynasty: 207 BC–9 AD). Sìbù Cóngkān 四部叢刊 [The collected publications from the Four Categories]. Shanghai: Shāngwù 商務; English translation: B. Karlgren (1950). *The book of odes. Chinese text, transcription and translation*. Stockholm: Museum of Far Eastern Antiquities.

Dictionaries and Databases

ABVD   S. J. Greenhill, R. Blust, and R. D. Gray, eds. (2008/). *The Austronesian Basic Vocabulary Database*. URL: http://language.psy.auckland.ac.nz/austronesian/.

BDS   B. Allen (2007). *Bai Dialect Survey*. SIL International. PDF: http://www.sil.org/silesr/2007/silesr2007-012.pdf.

Buldialect   V. Zhobov, G. Kolev, and P. Shishkov, eds. (2009). *Buldialect. Measuring linguistic unity and diversity in Europe*. Eberhard-Karls Universität Tübingen, Rijksuniversiteit Groningen, and Bulgarian Academy of Science. URL: http://www.sfs.uni-tuebingen.de/dialectometry/project.shtml. (Visited on 06/12/2012).

CELEX   R. H. Baayen, R. Piepenbrock, and L. Gulikers, comp. (1995). *The CELEX Lexical Database*. Version 2. Linguistic Data Consortium.

DDO   L. Trap-Jensen, cont. *Den Danske Ordbog* The Danish dictionary. Det Danske Sprog- og Litteraturselskab. URL: http://ordnet.dk/ddo/. (Visited on 10/25/2011).

DERKSEN   R. Derksen, comp. (2008). *Etymological dictionary of the Slavic inherited lexicon*. Leiden Indo-European Etymological Dictionary Series 4. Leiden and Boston: Brill.

DKBD   I. Dyen, J. B. Kruskal, and P. Black, eds. (1997). *Comparative Indo-European database: File IE-data1*. URL: http://www.wordgumbo.com/ie/cmp/iedata.txt. (Visited on 02/26/2009).

FREEDICT   FREEDICT. *The Free Dictionary. Dictionary, Encyclopedia and Thesaurus*. Farlex, Inc. URL: http://www.thefreedictionary.com/. (Visited on 10/25/2011).

GLD   G. Starostin and P. Krylov, eds. (2011). *The Global Lexicostatistical Database. Compiling, clarifying, connecting basic vocabulary around the world: From free-form to tree-form*. URL: http://starling.rinet.ru/new100/main.htm.

HACHETTE   V. Grundy, M.-H. Corréard, J.-B. Ormal-Grenon, and J. Rubery, eds. (2009). *Concise Oxford Hachette French dictionary. French-English, English-French*. 4th ed. Oxford: Oxford University Press. URL: http://www.wordreference.com/fren/.

IDS	M. R. Key and B. Comrie, eds. (2007). *IDS – The Intercontinental Dictionary Series*. URL: http://lingweb.eva.mpg.de/ids/. (Visited on 04/09/2012).
IELex	M. Dunn, ed. (2012). *Indo-European lexical cognacy database (IELex)*. URL: http://ielex.mpi.nl/.
KLUGE	F. Kluge, found. (2002). *Etymologisches Wörterbuch der deutschen Sprache*. Cont. by E. Seebold. 24th ed. Berlin: de Gruyter.
KROONEN	G. Kroonen, comp. (2013). *Etymological dictionary of Proto-Germanic*. Leiden Indo-European Etymological Dictionary Series 11. Leiden and Boston: Brill.
LIV	H. Rix, ed. (2001). *LIV. Lexikon der Indogermanischen Verben. Die Wurzeln und ihre Primärstammbildungen*. In collab. with M. Kümmel, T. Zehnder, R. Lipp, and B. Schirmer. Wiesbaden: Reichert.
LOE	C. Renfrew and P. Heggarty (2009). *Languages and Origins in Europe*. URL: http://www.languagesandpeoples.com/. (Visited on 06/12/2012).
MAND	G. de Schutter, B. van den Berg, T. Goeman, and T. de Jong, eds. (2007). *MAND. Morfologische Atlas van de Nederlandse Dialecten*. Meertens Instituut. URL: http://www.meertens.knaw.nl/mand/database/. (Visited on 06/12/2012).
NIL	D. Wodtko, B. Irslinger, and C. Schneider, eds. (2008). *Nomina im Indogermanischen Lexikon*. Heidelberg: Winter.
NORDAVINDEN	NORDAVINDEN. *Nordavinden og sola. En norsk dialektprøvedatabase på nettet* [The North Wind and the Sun. A Norwegian dialect database on the web]. Recordings and transcriptons by J. Almberg. Technical implementation by K. Skarbø. URL: http://www.ling.hf.ntnu.no/nos/. (Visited on 10/14/2011).
OCBS	W. H. Baxter and L. Sagart (2011). *Baxter-Sagart Old Chinese reconstructions*. Version 20th February 2011. PDF: http://crlao.ehess.fr/document.php?id=1217.
OED	D. Harper, ed. (2011). *Online Etymology Dictionary*. Page design and coding by D. McCormack. URL: http://www.etymonline.com/.
OREL	V. Orel, comp. (2003). *A handbook of Germanic etymology*. Leiden: Brill.
PARAVIA	J. Rubery and F. Cicoira, eds. (2009). *Concise Oxford Paravia Italian dictionary. English-Italian, Italian-English*. URL: http://wordreference.com/iten/.
PFEIFER	W. Pfeifer, comp. (1993). *Etymologisches Wörterbuch des Deutschen*. 2nd ed. 2 vols. Berlin: Akademie. URL: http://www.dwds.de/.

PONS	PONS. *PONS.eu Online-Wörterbuch*. Pons GmbH. URL: http://de.pons.eu/. (Visited on 10/24/2011).
REW	W. Meyer-Lübke, comp. (1911). *Romanisches etymologisches Wörterbuch*. Sammlung romanischer Elementar- und Handbücher 3.3. Heidelberg: Winter.
SAL	P. Heggarty (2006). *Sounds of the Andean languages*. URL: http://www.quechua.org.uk/. (Visited on 06/12/2012).
SCHUESSLER	A. Schuessler, comp. (2006). *ABC Etymological dictionary of Old Chinese*. Honolulu: University of Hawai'i Press.
TPPSR	L. Gauchat, J. Jeanjaquet, and E. Tappolet, eds. (1925). *Tableaux phonétiques des patois suisses romands. Relevés comparatifs d'environ 500 mots dans 62 patois-types. Publiés avec introduction, notes, carte et répertoires*. Neuchâtel: Attinger.
ToB	G. Starostin, ed. (2008b). *Tower of Babel. An etymological database project*. URL: http://starling.rinet.ru.
VAAN	M. Vaan, comp. (2008). *Etymological dictionary of Latin and the other Italic languages*. Leiden Indo-European Etymological Dictionary Series 7. Leiden and Boston: Brill.
VASMER	M. Vasmer, comp. (1986–1987). *Ėtimologičeskij slovar' russkogo jazyka. Ėtimologičeskij slovar' russkogo jazyka*. 4 vols. Moscow: Progress. URL: http://starling.rinet.ru.
WIKTIONARY	WIKTIONARY (2012). *Wiktionary. The free dictionary*. URL: http://en.wiktionary.org/.
YINKU	Hóu Jīngyī 侯精一, ed. (2004). *Xiàndài Hànyǔ fāngyán yīnkù* 現代漢語方言音庫 [Phonological database of Chinese dialects].
ZIHUI	Běijīng Dàxué 北京大學, ed. (1962 [1989]). *Hànyǔ fāngyīn zìhuì* 漢語方音字彙 [Chinese dialect character pronunciation list]. 2nd ed. Běijīng 北京: Wénzì Gǎigé 文字改革; Electronic Edition: W. S.-Y. Wang and C.-C. Cheng, eds. (1969). *DOC. Dictionary On Computer*. URL: http://starling.rinet.ru/.

Supplementary Material

The supplementary material accompanying this study contains the following resources:

 I Phonetic alignment benchmark

 II Results for automatic phonetic alignment analyses

 III Cognate detection benchmark

 IV Results for automatic cognate detection

The supplementary material can be downloaded from:

- https://SequenceComparison.github.io

The website also offers the original source code of the LingPy library (Version 1.0). This is the code which was used for all analyses reported in this study. The LingPy library is constantly being updated. For the most recent official release of LingPy, please visit the project website at:

- http://lingpy.org

For recent updates, please visit the source code repository at:

- http://github.com/lingpy/lingpy/

List of Abbreviations

ABVD Austronesian Basic Vocababulary Database

ACD automatic cognate detection

ASJP Automatic Similarity Judgment Program

BF B-Cubed F-score

BLOSUM blocks substitution matrix

BP B-Cubed precision

BR B-Cubed recall

CDE column dependant evaluation

CP column precision

CR column recall

CS column score

DKBD Dyen-Kruskal-Black Database

DPA dynamic programming algorithm

GEP gap extension penalty

GLD Global Lexicostatistical Database

GOP gap opening penalty

ID identical decisions score

IDS Intercontinental Dictionary Series

IPA International Phonetic Alphabet

MPA multiple phonetic alignment

MRI modified rand index

MSA multiple sequence alignment

NED normalized edit distance

NW Needleman-Wunsch algorithm

PAS perfect alignments score

PFS pair F-score

PID percentage identity

PP pair precision

PPA pairwise phonetic alignment

PR pair recall

PS pair score

PSA pairwise sequence alignment

RS row score

SCA Sound-Class-Based Phonetic Alignment

SCAD SCA distance

SF set F-score

SP set precision

SP sum-of-pairs

SPS sum-of-pairs score

SR set recall

SW Smith-Waterman algorithm

ToB Tower of Babel (database)

Indices

Index of Topics

abduction, *see* inference
ACD evaluation, 185–208
    B-Cubed F-score, 193
    B-Cubed precision, 192
    B-Cubed recall, 193
    evaluation measures, 189–193
    gold standard, 185–189
    pair F-score, 192
    pair perspective, 189
    pair precision, 191
    pair recall, 191
    proportion of identical decisions, 191
    set F-score, 190
    set perspective, 189
    set precision, 189
    set recall, 189
alignment, 6, 67, 69–76, 134–137
    gap, 70
    multiple, *see* multiple alignment
    pairwise, *see* pairwise alignment
    phonetic alignment, *see* phonetic alignment
alignment analysis, *see* alignment
alignment evaluation, 147–169
    BulDial Benchmark, 147, 149
    column dependent evaluation, 153
    column perspective, 151
    column precision, 151
    column recall, 151
    column score, 152
    Covington Benchmark, 147, 149, 155, 156
    evaluation measures, 150–154
    gold standard, 147–150
    modified rand index, 153
    pair precision, 153
    pair recall, 153
    pair score, 153
    perfect alignments score, 150
    precision, 151
    recall, 151
    row perspective, 151
    row score, 151
    sum-of-pairs score, 153
assimilation, *see* sound change types

basic vocabulary, 23
basic vocabulary list, 23, 24
biological evolution, 119
Book of Odes, 24
borrowing, 40, 171

Chinese writing system, 25
cluster algorithm
    flat cluster algorithm, 185
    Neighbor-Joining algorithm, 100–105, 142, 154
    UPGMA algorithm, 100–105, 185

cognate detection, 5, 6
  automatic cognate detection, 7, 119, 120, 169–208
  comparative method, *see* comparative method
  language-specific methods, 200
  LexStat method, 173, 175, 177–181, 183, 193–196, 199, 202
  NED method, 194
  permutation test, 180
  SCA method, 180, 194
  Turchin method, 194
cognate relation, *see* sign relations
cognate set, 38
cognation, *see* sign relations
common descent, 41, 171
  direct, 40
  due to lateral transfer, 40
  indirect, 40
comparative method, 6, 10, 54, 57–59, 119, 170, 171, 173, 200, 211
  cognate list, 58
  correspondence list, 58
compression and expansion, *see* edit operations
continuation, *see* sound change types
correspondences
  of segments, *see* segment correspondences
  of sounds, *see* form resemblances

databases
  Austronesian Basic Vocabulary Database, 187
  Dyen-Kruskal-Black database, 187
  EvoBench, *see* ACD evaluation, *see* alignment evaluation
  Global Lexicostatistical Database, 187
  Indo-European Lexical Cognacy Database, 187
  Intercontinental Dictionary Series, 188
  Tower of Babel database, 187
deduction, *see* inference
deletion, *see* edit operations, *see* sound change types
DIALIGN algorithm, *see* pairwise alignment
diasystem, 13
  Dachsprache, 13
  dialect, 13
  linguistic variety, 13
  sociolect, 13
  standard language, 13
  variety space, 13
dynamic programming, 78, 137

edit distance
  normalized, 194
edit operations, 67–69, 76, 145
  compression and expansion, 68
  deletion, 67
  indel, 67
  insertion, 67
  substitution, 67
  transposition, 68
elision, *see* sound change types
epenthesis, *see* sound change types
Ethnologue, 5
etymology, 15
evaluation
  of ACD algorithms, *see* ACD evaluation
  of alignment algorithms, *see* alignment evaluation
evaluation measures, *see* ACD evaluation, *see* alignment evaluation
evolution

Index of Topics

biological, *see* biological evolution
linguistic, *see* language history

form resemblances, 48–50
    genotypic similarity, 49, 121, 122
    language-independent, 50
    language-specific, 50, 59, 170
    phenotypic similarity, 49, 122
    regular sound correspondences, 19, 49, 59, 134, 170, 171, 173, 177
    structural similarity, 48
    substantial similarity, 48
    surface resemblances, 59
    systematic correspondences, 49
    systematic form resemblances, 55
fusion, *see* sound change types

gap, *see* segment correspondences
gap penalty, 96, 99
    affine gap penalty, 96
    gap function, 91, 96
    GEP, 96
    GOP, 96, 132, 207
    linear gap penalty, 96
    position-specific, 140
    position-specific gap penalty, 98
gene relations
    homology, 39–41
    orthology, 40
    paralogy, 40
    xenology, 40, 43
genotypic similarity, *see* form resemblances

High German Consonant Shift, 182
homology, *see* gene relations

indel, *see* edit operations
induction, *see* inference
inference
    abduction, 51–57

construct, 51
deduction, 52
factual abduction, 53
historical-fact abduction, 53
induction, 52
insertion, *see* edit operations, *see* sound change types
International Phonetic Alphabet, *see* IPA
IPA, 20, 123, 139, 140, 142, 150, 175, 185

language
    langue, 14
    parole, 14
language change, 25–38
    catastrophic view on, 26
    Hebrew paradigm, 26
    lexical change, *see* lexical change
    semantic change, *see* semantic change
    sound change, *see* sound change
language history, 15, 119
language relations, 44–47
    ancestor-descendant relation, 44
    contact relation, 45
    genetic relation, 45
    genetic relationship, 39, 134
    historical relation, 47
language system, 14
    lexicon, 15
    phonological system, 15
lateral transfer, 40
lenition, *see* sound change types
lexical change, 37–38
    lexical replacement, 37, 38
    word gain, 37, 44
    word loss, 37, 44
lexical diffusion, *see* sound change mechanisms
lexicostatistics, 15, 38

LingPy, 6, 121, 125, 128, 131–134, 139, 154–156, 161, 164, 173, 179, 193, 194, 213
linguistic reconstruction, *see* reconstruction, 5, 15, 19
linguistic sign, 15–18, 20, 21, 48
  arbitrariness, 16
  form, *see* sign form
  language of a, 16
  meaning, *see* meaning
  signified, *see* meaning
  signifier, *see* sign form
loss, *see* sound change types

match, *see* segment correspondences
  complex, *see* segment correspondences
  crossed, *see* segment correspondences
  direct, *see* segment correspondences
  divergent, *see* segment correspondences
  emtpy, *see* segment correspondences
  uniform, *see* segment correspondences
matching types, *see* segment correspondences
meaning, 21, 22
  reference, 21
  reference potential, 21, 34, 35
meaning resemblances, 50–51
  semantic identity, 51
mismatch, *see* segment correspondences
multiple alignment, 6, 74, 99–115, 135, 143
  enhancements, 108
  Feng-Doolittle algorithm, 105
  flat-cluster partitioning, 143
  guide tree, 100–105
  iterative refinement, 113, 141
  multi-type partitioning, 114
  orphan partitioning, 143
  postprocessing, 108, 113–115
  preprocessing, 108–113
  profile
    profile, 106
  progressive alignment, 100, 108, 140
  random partitioning, 114
  sequence alignment, 105–108
  similar-gap-sites partitioning, 143
  single-type partitioning, 114
  sum-of-pairs, 106
  T-Coffee algorithm, 112, 143
  tree-dependent partitioning, 114
multiple alignment analysis, *see* multiple alignment

Needle man-Wunsch algorithm, 155, 156
Needleman-Wunsch algorithm, 77–82, 100
  matrix construction, 79
  matrix initialization, 79
  structural extensions, 82–91
  substantial extensions, 91
  traceback, 79
Neighbor-Joining algorithm, *see* cluster algorithm
Neogrammarian Hypothesis, *see* sound change mechanisms

orthology, *see* gene relations

pairwise alignment, 6, 74, 76–99
  algorithm, *see* Needleman-Wunsch algorithm
  alignment score, 76
  diagonal, 87
  diagonal alignment, 86–88
  DIALIGN algorithm, 87
  global alignment, 82

local alignment, 83–85
optimal, 77
primary alignment, 89
scoring scheme, *see* scoring scheme
secondary alignment, 88–91, 140
secondary alignment algorithm, 89, 90
semi-global alignment, 83
Smith-Waterman algorithm, 84
pairwise alignment analysis, *see* pairwise alignment
paralogy, *see* gene relations
percentage identity, 149
phonetic alignment, 120, 132, 134–169, 209
ALINE algorithm, 138, 155
ALPHAMALIG algorithm, 138
consistency-based scoring scheme, 143–144
iterative refinement, 142–143
JAKARTA, 138
multiple phonetic alignment, 137, 140–142
pairwise phonetic alignment, 137, 140
SCA method, 132, 139–147
secondary alignment, 140, 157, 165
swap detection, 144–147
phylogenetic reconstruction, *see* reconstruction
problem
sequence alignment problem, 120
problems
cognate detection problem, 170
homologue detection problem, 171
secondary alignment problem, 89
specific cognate detection problem, 172

specific homologue detection problem, 172
profile, 106, 109, 114
proof, 51–57
cumulative evidence, 53
evidence, 54–57
individual-identifying evidence, 53
laws, 54–55
of language relations, 51–57
of sign relations, 51–57
reconstruction
phylogenetic reconstruction, 209
regular sound correspondences, *see* form resemblances
relations, 39–47
gene relations, *see* gene relations
language relations, *see* language relations
sign relations, *see* sign relations
resemblances, 47–51
between forms, *see* form resemblances
between meanings, *see* meaning resemblances
rhotacism, *see* sound change types

scoring function, 78, 80, 82, 87, 90–96
attested distribution, 180
attested frequency, 95
BLOSUM, 95, 178
expected distribution, 180
expected frequency, 95
log-odds score, 94
log-odds scores, 181
scoring matrix, 94
scoring scheme, xiii, 76–78, 84, 86, 87, 90–93, 96, 97
con sis ten cy-based, 141
consistency-based, 108
extended library, 112
gap penalty, *see* gap penalty

general, 110
library, 109
matrix-based, 108
position-specific, 110, 130, 140
primary library, 112
scoring function, *see* scoring function
segment correspondences, 67–69, 73, 76, 77, 137
complex match, 68
crossed match, 68, 144
divergent match, 67, 76, 138
empty match, 67, 70, 76
gap, 76
indel, 77
matching types, 69
mismatch, 67
proper match, 67
uniform match, 67, 76
semantic change, 34, 37
accumulation, 34
reduction, 34
sequence, 62–66
alphabet, 64
characters, 64
definitions, 64–66
modelling of, *see* sequence modelling
paradigmatic aspects, 120
prefix, 66
primary structure, 88
secondary structure, 88, 133
sequences vs. sets, 64
subsequence, 65
substring, 66
suffix, 66
syntagmatic aspects, 120
sequence comparison, 5, 6, 61, 66–145
alignment, *see* alignment
correspondence perspective, 67, 68

Damerau-Le ven shtein distance, 146
Damerau-Levenshtein distance, 145
edit distance, 78, 178, 207
edit operations, *see* edit operations
edit perspective, 67, 68
Hamming distance, 67, 128, 129
listing, 69–72, 99
models of, 69–72
normalized edit distance, 178, 183
percentage identity, 74, 148, 183
SCA distance, 178, 180, 183
SCA distances, 194
segment correspondences, *see* segment correspondences
trace, 69–72, 99
sequence modelling, 119–134
ascending sonority, 131
ASJP model, 125, 128, 155, 157, 158, 160, 164, 166
ASJP scoring function, 128
Chomsky-Halle model, 128
descending sonority, 131
DOLGO model, 123–125, 128, 129, 155, 157, 158, 160, 164, 166
DOLGO scoring function, 128
maximum sonority, 131
paradigmatic aspects, 121–129
prosodic context, 130–133, 140, 157, 161
prosodic string, 131, 140, 176
SCA model, 123, 129, 142, 162, 166, 193
SCA scoring function, 128, 193
scoring function, 129
secondary structure, 133–134
sequence representation, 131
sonority profile, 131

Index of Topics

sound classes, 121–125, 176
   syntagmatic aspects, 130–134
sign form, 18–20
   algebraic perspective, 19
   phonemic perspective, 18
   phonetic perspective, 18
   structure, 18
   substance, 18
   substantial perspective, 19
sign relations, 41–43
   ancestor-descendant relation, 41, 42, 44
   cognacy, 39–42, 134, 172, 184, 188
   cognate relation, 41, 45
   direct cognate relation, 42
   donor-recipient relation, 42, 46
   etymological relation, 41, 42
   oblique cognacy, 40
   oblique cognate relation, 42
   oblique etymological relation, 43
singletons, 193
Smith-Waterman algorithm, *see* pairwise alignment
sonority, *see* sequence modelling
sound change, 26–34, 121
   alternation, 34
   directionality of, 126
   High German Consonant Shift, 20
   mechanisms, *see* sound change mechanisms
   paradigmatic, *see* sound change types
   patterns, *see* sound change patterns
   procedural aspects, 27
   regularity of, 28
   substantial aspects, 27
   syntagmatic, *see* sound change patterns
   systematic aspects, 27
   type, 31
   types, *see* sound change types
sound change mechanisms, 27–31
   lexical diffusion, 29, 31, 54
   lexical diffusion, 31
   Neogrammarian Hypothesis, 28–31, 54
   Neogrammarian sound change, 31
   sporadic sound change, 31
sound change patterns, 27
   loss, 27
   merger, 27
   split, 27
sound change types, 27, 31–34, 126, 138
   assimilation, 32, 128
   continuation, 32
   deletion, 32–34
   elision, 33
   epenthesis, 33
   fusion, 34
   insertion, 32, 34
   lenition, 20, 31, 126, 128
   loss, 33
   metathesis, 32, 33, 49
   palatalization, 126–128
   rhotacism, 31
   split, 34
   substitution, 32
sound classes, *see* sequence modelling
split, *see* sound change types
substitution, *see* edit operations, *see* sound change types
Swadesh list, *see* word list

The Northwind and the Sun, 11
transposition, *see* edit operations

UPGMA algorithm, *see* cluster algorithm

word, *see* linguistic sign
word list, 22–24, 38, 171

bilingual, 23
entry of a, 22
item of a, 22
lexicostatistical, 38, 119
monolingual, 23
multilingual, 23, 170–173, 178, 179, 205

Index of Persons

Brugmann, Karl, 28

Christie, Agatha, 1
Chén Dì 陳第, 25

Damerau, F. J., 68, 145
Dolgopolsky, A. B., 122

Fischer, M. J., 78

Gabelentz, Georg, 54
Galliéron, Jules, 29
Grimm, Jacob, 28

Hamming, R. W., 67
Holmes, Sherlock, 2

Jakobson, Roman, 15

Levenshtein, V. I., 68, 76, 145

Needleman, S. B., 78

Osthoff, Hermann, 28

Peirce, Charles Sanders, 52
Plato, 26
Poirot, Hercule, 1, 2

Rask, Rasmus, 28

Saussure, Ferdinand, 14, 15
Schleicher, August, 9, 28
Schmidt, Johannes, 51
Smith, T. F., 84
Swadesh, Morris, 23, 24, 209

Wagner, R. A., 78
Waterman, M. S., 84
Weinreich, Uriel, 13
Wunsch, C. D., 78

Index of Languages

Albanian, 179, 203, 205–207
Armenian, 56, 171

Bai
    Jīnxīng, 168
    Luòběnzhuō, 168
    Ěryuán, 169
Bulgarian, 33, 131, 133, 138, 142, 145, 146, 169

Chinese
    Běijīng, 11
    Hakka, 11
    Hǎikǒu, 166
    Middle Chinese, 29, 30, 166, 168
    Old Chinese, 24, 168
    Shuāngfēng, 29, 30
    Shànghǎi, 11, 63
    Standard Chinese, 37, 55, 166, 168
    Yínchuān, 166
Choctaw, 135
Cree, 135
Czech, 33, 142, 146, 169

Danish, 11, 12, 175, 176, 185
Dutch
    Antwerp, 167
    Standard Dutch, 23, 35, 38, 50, 165, 167, 175, 176, 180, 185, 188
    Ter Apel, 165
    Zudendaal, 165

English, 5, 16, 17, 20, 22, 23, 34, 35, 38, 40–42, 47, 50, 55, 59, 76, 89, 121, 122, 128, 140, 171, 175, 176, 179, 180, 182, 183, 185, 188, 203, 205, 207, 214

French, 5, 43, 48, 49, 55, 136, 171, 179, 185, 188, 203, 206, 207

German
    Old High German, 32, 33, 41
    Standard German, 5, 16, 17, 20, 22–24, 32–35, 38, 40–43, 47, 48, 50, 55, 59, 76, 121, 122, 136, 140, 171, 175, 176, 179, 180, 182, 183, 185, 188, 203, 206, 207, 214
Greek
    Modern Greek, 50, 55
    Mycenaean Greek, 50
    Old Greek, 2, 9, 20, 53

Hawaiian, 203, 207
Hebrew, 26
Hittite, 209

Italian, 5, 26, 27, 48–50, 136

Koasati, 135

Latin
    Classical Latin, 2, 9, 20, 26, 27, 40, 43, 50, 53, 136, 185
    Old Latin, 50
    Vulgar Latin, 136
Latvian, 43

Navajo, 203, 207
Norwegian, 11, 12, 175, 176, 185

Polish, 42, 136, 142, 146, 169
Proto-Bai, 168, 169
Proto-Germanic, 5, 20, 34, 42, 43, 50, 136, 167

Index of Languages

Proto-Indo-European, 5, 40, 51, 136, 209, 213
Proto-Romance, 5
Proto-Slavic, 33, 42, 136, 169
Proto-World, 44

Russian, 23, 33, 34, 38, 42, 50, 136, 142, 145, 146, 169

Sanskrit, 2, 9, 20
Spanish, 50, 55
Swedish, 11, 12, 136, 175, 176, 185

Turkish, 203, 205–207

West Frisian
    Grou, 167

Index of Word Forms

Albanian
    gojë, 207
    gërmon, 207
    gērmon, 206

Bai
    Jīnxīng
        tsɯ^{31}pe^{21}, 168
    Luòběnzhuō
        ʥỹ^{42}, 168
    Ěryuán
        pi^{31}ṣe^{42}, 169

Bulgarian
    глава, 33
    жълт, 146, 169
    ябълка, 131, 133, 142, 145

Chinese
    Hǎikǒu
        rìtóu 日頭, 166
        rì 日, 166
    Shuāngfēng
        bù 步, 30
        bǔ 捕, 30
        dào 盜, 30
        dǎo 導, 30
        páo 刨, 30
        páo 跑, 30
    Shànghǎi
        tàiyáng 太陽, 63
    Standard Chinese
        māma 妈妈, 55
        pǐ 皮, 168
        rìtóu 日頭, 166
        shǒu 首, 37
    Yínchuān
        rìtóu 日頭, 166
        tóu 頭, 166

Choctaw
    fani, 135

Cree
    il̥, 135

Czech
    jablko, 142
    žlutý, 33, 146
    žlytý, 169

Danish
    kvinde, 175, 176, 185

Dutch
    Antwerp
        oːrən, 167
    Standard Dutch
        hand, 23, 38
        hoofd, 23, 38
        tand, 23, 38
        vrouw, 175, 176, 185
        berg, 165
        hoofd, 38
        kop, 35, 50
        tand, 180
    Ter Apel
        baːɣə, 165
    Zudendaal
        bɛʀex, 165

English
    cup, 16, 17, 35, 41, 42, 50
    dale, 182
    daughter, 122, 140
    digs, 207
    fact, 50
    form, 50
    function, 50

Index of Word Forms

hand, 23, 38
head, 23, 38
heart, 76
hot, 182
hound, 214
mountain, 55
mount, 121
mouth, 121, 207
other, 121, 207
ship, 20
short, 40
thorn, 182
token, 59
tongue, 59
tooth, 5, 23, 38, 55, 179, 207
town, 182
weak, 59
woman, 175, 176, 185
cup, 34
melon, 34
skull, 35

French
   bouche, 207
   clé, 49
   coupe, 43
   creuse, 206, 207
   dent, 5
   fleur, 49
   langue, 49
   larme, 49
   lune, 49
   montagne, 55
   plume, 49
   soleil, 136

German
   Old High German
     angust, 33
     hant, 32
     ioman, 33
     snēo, 32
     swīn, 41

Standard German
   Fakt, 50
   Form, 50
   Frau, 175, 176, 185
   Funktion, 50
   Hand, 23, 38
   Kopf, 16, 23, 38
   Mama, 55
   Mund, 207
   Zahn, 23, 38, 55
   gräbt, 207
   Angst, 33
   Birne, 34
   Dach, 34
   Ding, 22
   Dorn, 182
   Flaschen, 48
   Hand, 32
   Haupt, 38
   Herz, 76
   Hund, 214
   Kerker, 48
   Kopf, 17, 34, 35, 38, 42, 43, 50
   Maus, 121
   Mund, 121, 207
   Obst, 48
   Post, 48
   Rübe, 34
   Sand, 176
   Schiff, 20
   Schnee, 32
   Schwein, 41
   Schädel, 34
   Sonne, 136
   Stein, 22
   Tal, 182
   Tanten, 48
   Tochter, 122, 140
   Zahn, 5, 179, 207
   Zaun, 182
   Zeichen, 59
   Zunge, 59

anderer, 207
anders, 121
gräbt, 206
heiß, 176, 182
jemand, 33
kurz, 40
schlafen, 48
weich, 59

Greek
   Modern Greek
      θεός, 50, 55
   Mycenaean Greek
      tʰehós, 50
   Old Greek
      ζυγόν, 2
      πατήρ, 2
      φέρω, 2
      φράτηρ, 2
      ἀγρός, 2

Hawaiian
   'eli, 207
   waha, 207

Italian
   chiave, 26, 49
   dente, 5
   fiore, 26, 49
   lacrima, 27, 49
   lingua, 27, 49
   luna, 27, 49
   piuma, 26, 49
   sole, 136

Koasati
   ip̥lu, 135

Latin
   Classical Latin
      ager, 2
      fero, 2
      frater, 2

iugum, 2
pater, 2
clāvis, 26
curtus, 40
cūpa, 43
cŭrtus, 40
flōs, 26
lacrima, 27
lingua, 26
lūna, 27
plūma, 26
sōlis, 136
   Old Latin
      deivos, 50

Latvian
   gubt, 43

Navajo
   'azé', 207
   hahashgééd, 207

Norwegian
   kvine, 175, 176, 185

Polish
   jabłko, 142
   ptak, 42
   słońce, 136
   żółty, 146, 169

Russian
   голова, 23, 34, 38
   жёлтый, 33, 146, 169
   зуб, 23, 38
   птица, 42
   рука, 23, 38
   солнце, 136
   факт, 50
   форма, 50
   функция, 50
   яблоко, 142, 145

Sanskrit
- अग्र, 2
- पितृ, 2
- भरमि, 2
- भ्रातृ, 2
- युग, 2

Spanish
- *dios*, 50, 55

Swedish
- *kvinna*, 175, 176, 185
- *sol*, 136

Turkish
- *ağız*, 207
- *kazıyor*, 206, 207

West Frisian
- Grou
  - hõə̃n, 167

Index of Reconstructed Forms

Chinese
    Middle Chinese
        *bje¹ 皮, 168
        *bo³ 捕, 30
        *bo³ 步, 30
        *bæw¹ 刨, 30
        *bæw¹ 跑, 30
        *daw³ 導, 30
        *daw³ 盜, 30
        *duw¹ 頭, 166
        *ɳit⁴ 日, 166
    Old Chinese
        *m-paj 皮, 168

Latin
    Vulgar Latin
        *sōlĭculus, 136

Proto-Bai
    *be¹, 168, 169
    *drɯ³, 168
    *sʰɛ⁴, 169

Proto-Germanic
    *hurna-, 167
    *kuppa-, 34, 42, 43, 50
    *skipa-, 20
    *sunnōn-, 136
    *sōel-, 136
    *tanθ, 5

Proto-Indo-European
    *(s)sker-, 40
    *dent, 5
    *séh₂u̯el-, 136, 213

Proto-Romance
    *dente, 5

Proto-Slavic
    *golvà, 33
    *pъt-, 42
    *pъtìca, 42
    *pъtákъ, 42
    *sъ̀lnьce, 136
    *žьltъ, 33, 169

A
Language-Specific Resources

A.1 Phonetic Transcriptions

The following table summarizes the sources of the phonetic transcriptions which were used in this study.[1] In most cases I follow the transcriptions directly. Only in rare cases, when the transcription was not available, or when values were obviously miscoded, I corrected the respective transcriptions using my best knowledge of the respective languages.

Language	Author / Editor	Title	Year	Abbr.
Bai	Wang	Comparison of languages in contact. The distillation method and the case of Bai	2006	Wang 2006a
	Allen	Bai Dialect Survey	2007	BDS
Bulgarian		Wiktionary	2012	WIKTIONARY
Chinese	Hóu	Xiàndài Hànyǔ fāngyán yīnkù	2004	YINKU
	Běijīng Dàxué	Hànyǔ Fāngyīn Zìhuì	1989	ZIHUI
Czech		PONS.eu Online-Wörterbuch		PONS
Danish	Trap-Jensen	DDO		DDO
Dutch	Baayen et al.	CELEX	1995	CELEX
English	Baayen et al.	CELEX	1995	CELEX
French	Grundy et al.	Concise Oxford Hachette French dictionary	2009	HACHETTE
German	Baayen et al.	CELEX	1995	CELEX
Greek		PONS.eu Online-Wörterbuch		PONS
Italian	Rubery and Cicoira	Concise Oxford Paravia Italian dictionary	2009	PARAVIA

---

[1] All references whose abbreviation is shaded gray in the table are available in digital form (as an online resource or as CD-ROM).

Latin		Wiktionary	2012	WIKTIONARY
Norwegian		PONS.eu Online-Wörterbuch		PONS
Polish		PONS.eu Online-Wörterbuch		PONS
Russian		The Free Dictionary		FREEDICT
Spanish		PONS.eu Online-Wörterbuch		PONS
Swedish		PONS.eu Online-Wörterbuch		PONS

A.2 Etymological Sources

The following table summarizes the etymological sources for language families and individual languages which were used in this study.[2]

Language	Author / Editor	Title	Year	Abbr.
Bai	Wang	Comparison of languages in contact. The distillation method and the case of Bai	2006	
Chinese	Baxter and Sagart	Baxter-Sagart Old Chinese reconstructions	2011	OCBS
	Schuessler	ABC Etymological dictionary of Old Chinese	2006	SCHUESSLER
English	Harper	Online Etymology Dictionary	2011	OED
German	Kluge	Etymologisches Wörterbuch der deutschen Sprache	2002	KLUGE
	Pfeifer	Etymologisches Wörterbuch des Deutschen	1993	PFEIFER
Germanic	Orel	A handbook of Germanic etymology	2003	OREL
	Kroonen	Etymological dictionary of Latin	2013	KROONEN
Indo-Eur.	Wodtko et al.	Nomina im Indogermanischen Lexikon	2008	NIL
	Rix	LIV. Lexikon der Indogermanischen Verben	2001	LIV
Latin	Vaan	Etymological dictionary of Latin	2008	VAAN
Romance	Meyer-Lübke	Romanisches etymologisches Wörterbuch	1911	REW
Russian	Vasmer	Ėtimologičeskij slovar' russkogo jazyka	1986	VASMER
Slavic	Derksen	Etymological dictionary of the Slavic inherited lexicon	2008	DERKSEN

---

[2] Middle Chinese readings from OCBS are rendered in IPA with superscript numbers instead of the capital symbols used in the original.

B
Sequence Modelling

The following three tables illustrate the current state of the scoring functions for the three default sound-class models of the LingPy library. For reasons of space, the tone characters were excluded in the tables.

B.1 The DOLGO Scoring function

	H	J	K	M	N	P	R	S	T	V	W
H	10	0	0	0	0	0	0	0	0	−10	0
J	0	10	0	0	0	0	0	0	0	−10	0
K	0	0	10	0	0	0	0	0	0	−10	0
M	0	0	0	10	0	0	0	0	0	−10	0
N	0	0	0	0	10	0	0	0	0	−10	0
P	0	0	0	0	0	10	0	0	0	−10	0
R	0	0	0	0	0	0	10	0	0	−10	0
S	0	0	0	0	0	0	0	10	0	−10	0
T	0	0	0	0	0	0	0	0	10	−10	0
V	−10	−10	−10	−10	−10	−10	−10	−10	−10	5	−10
W	0	0	0	0	0	0	0	0	0	−10	10

B.2 The SCA Scoring function

	A	B	C	D	E	G	H	I	J	K	L	M	N	O	P	R	S	T	U	W	Y
A	5	-10	-10	-10	4	-10	-10	4	-6	-10	-10	-10	-10	4	-10	-10	-10	-10	4	-6	4
B	-10	10	0	0	-10	0	0	-10	0	0	0	0	0	-10	6	0	0	0	-10	6	-9
C	-10	0	10	2	-10	2	2	-10	0	6	0	0	0	-10	0	0	6	6	-10	0	-10
D	-10	0	2	10	-10	0	2	-10	0	0	0	0	0	-10	0	0	6	6	-10	0	-10
E	4	-10	-10	-10	5	-10	-10	4	-6	-10	-10	-10	-10	4	-10	-10	-10	-10	4	-6	4
G	-10	0	2	0	-10	10	2	-10	0	6	0	0	0	-10	0	0	6	0	-10	0	-10
H	-10	0	2	2	-10	2	10	-10	0	0	0	0	0	-10	0	0	6	0	-10	0	-10
I	4	-10	-10	-10	4	-10	-10	5	-5	-10	-10	-10	-10	4	-10	-10	-10	-10	4	-6	4
J	-6	0	0	0	-6	0	0	-5	10	0	0	0	0	-6	0	0	0	0	-6	0	-6
K	-10	0	6	0	-10	6	0	-10	0	10	0	0	0	-10	0	0	2	0	-10	0	-10
L	-10	0	0	0	-10	0	0	-10	0	0	10	0	0	-10	0	4	0	0	-10	0	-10
M	-10	0	0	0	-10	0	0	-10	0	0	0	10	1	-10	0	0	0	0	-10	0	-10
N	-10	0	0	0	-10	0	0	-10	0	0	0	1	10	-10	0	0	0	0	-10	0	-10
O	4	-10	-10	-10	4	-10	-10	4	-6	-10	-10	-10	-10	5	-10	-10	-10	-10	4	-6	4
P	-10	6	0	0	-10	0	0	-10	0	0	0	0	0	-10	10	0	0	0	-10	2	-10
R	-10	0	0	0	-10	0	0	-10	0	0	4	0	0	-10	0	10	0	0	-10	0	-10
S	-10	0	6	6	-10	6	6	-10	0	2	0	0	0	-10	0	0	10	2	-10	0	-10
T	-10	0	6	6	-10	0	0	-10	0	0	0	0	0	-10	0	0	2	10	-10	0	-10
U	4	-10	-10	-10	4	-10	-10	4	-6	-10	-10	-10	-10	4	-10	-10	-10	-10	5	-6	4
W	-6	6	0	0	-6	0	0	-6	0	0	0	0	0	-6	2	0	0	0	-6	10	-5
Y	4	-9	-10	-10	4	-10	-10	4	-6	-10	-10	-10	-10	4	-10	-10	-10	-10	4	-5	5

B.3 The ASJP Scoring function

C
Phonetic Alignment

C.1 Covington's Testset

The following three tables give the bad alignments yielded by the different sound class models in comparison with the respective gold standard alignments on the Covington test set (Covington 1996). Since true gold standard alignments for the Covington test set were never published, the reference alignments were carried out by myself, and compared with the correct alignments yielded by the ALINE algorithm (Kondrak 2000) which are discussed in Kondrak (2002).

Language	Word	Gold Standard	Test Alignment
Spanish	*ver*	b - e r	- b e r
French	*voir*	v w a r	v w a r
Spanish	*decir*	d e θ i r	d e θ i r
French	*dire*	d - - i r	- - d i r
English	*full*	f u l - - - -	f - u l - -
Latin	*plenus*	p - l eː n u s	p l eː n u s
Fox	*kiinwaawa*	k iː n w aː w a	k iː n w aː w a -
Menomini	*kenuaq*	k e n u a ʔ -	k e n - u - a ʔ
Old Grk.	δίδωμι	d i d oː m i	d i d oː m i
Latin	*do*	- - d oː - -	d oː - - - -
Latin	*ager*	a g e r - -	a g - e r
Sanskrit	*ajras*	a ʤ - r a s	a ʤ r a s

(a) DOLGO-Model

Language	Word	Gold Standard							Test Alignment							
English	tooth	t	u	-	θ	-	-		-	-	-	-	t	u	θ	
Latin	dentis	d	e	n	t	i	s		d	e	n	t	i	s		
Fox	kiinwaawa	k	iː	n	w	aː	w	a	k	iː	n	w	aː	w	a	-
Menomini	kenuaq	k	e	n	u	a	ʔ	-	k	e	n	-	u	-	a	ʔ

(b) SCA-Model

Language	Word	Gold Standard						Test Alignment					
English	this	ð	i	s	-	-		ð	i	-	-	s	
German	dieses	d	iː	z	e	s		d	iː	z	e	s	
English	tooth	t	u	-	θ	-	-	-	-	-	-	t	u	θ
Latin	dentis	d	e	n	t	i	s	d	e	n	t	i	s	

(c) ASJP-Model

C.2 Language-Specific Pairwise Alignments

The following table gives the distances scores and the alignments along with the similarity scores between all segments for German-English word pairs taken from Kessler (2001) as they are produced by the LexStat when calculating global alignments.[1] Columns that are shaded in gray are beyond the default threshold of 0.55, and are therefore judged to be cognate by the algorithm. Items which are double-underlined indicate that the respective words are etymologically related, following the cognate assignments of the Kessler (2001). Words whose orthographical representation is given in bold font are borrowings.

No.	Item	Score	Alignment					
1	"all"	0.07	Eng. *all* Ger. *alle*	ɔ a 1.0	l l 7.0			
2	"and"	0.57	Eng. *and* Ger. *und*	a u 0.0	n n 1.0	d t 5.0		
3	"animal"	1.28	Eng. *animal* Ger. *Tier*	a - -1.0	n - -3.0	ə - -1.0	m t -3.0	ə iː -1.0	l r -1.0

---

[1] Normally, LexStat calculates semi-global alignments, but since in semi-global alignment analyses long parts of very diverse sequences are left unaligned, I used the global mode instead. Otherwise, many of the specific segment similarities would not be visible.

C.2 Language-Specific Pairwise Alignments

#	Gloss	Score	Lang	Word							
4	"ashes"	0.40	Eng.	ashes	a	ʃ	-				
			Ger.	Asche	a	ʃ	ə				
					1.0	7.0	-0.0				
5	"at"	1.16	Eng.	at	a	t	-				
			Ger.	an	a	-	n				
					1.0	-2.0	-1.0				
6	"back"	1.16	Eng.	back	b	a	k	-	-		
			Ger.	Rücken	r	y	k	ə	n		
					-3.0	0.0	1.0	-1.0	-1.0		
7	"bad"	0.85	Eng.	bad	-	b	a	-	d		
			Ger.	schlecht	ʃ	l	e	x	t		
					-3.0	-3.0	1.0	1.0	5.0		
8	"bark"	1.12	Eng.	bark	b	ɑ	r	-	-	k	-
			Ger.	Rinde	-	-	r	i	n	d	ə
					-3.0	-1.0	1.0	1.0	-1.0	-3.0	-0.0
9	"because"	1.22	Eng.	because	b	ə	k	ɔ	z		
			Ger.	weil	v	ai	-	l			
					-1.0	0.0	-3.0	-3.0			
10	"belly"	0.83	Eng.	belly	b	ɛ	l	i			
			Ger.	Bauch	b	au	x	-			
					7.0	0.0	-3.0	-3.0			
11	"big"	1.15	Eng.	big	b	ɪ	g	-	-	-	
			Ger.	groß	-	-	g	r	o:	s	
					-3.0	-0.0	1.0	-2.0	-3.0		
12	"bird"	1.11	Eng.	bird	b	ə	-	-	r	d	
			Ger.	Vogel	f	o:	g	ə	l	-	
					-1.0	0.0	-3.0	-1.0	-1.0	-2.0	
13	"bite"	0.35	Eng.	bites	b	ai	t				
			Ger.	beißt	b	ai	s				
					7.0	1.0	1.0				
14	"black"	1.21	Eng.	black	b	l	-	a	-	k	
			Ger.	schwarz	-	ʃ	v	a	r	ts	
					-3.0	-3.0	0.0	1.0	-3.0	-1.0	
15	"blood"	0.02	Eng.	blood	b	l	ə	d			
			Ger.	Blut	b	l	u:	t			
					7.0	7.0	1.0	5.0			
16	"blow"	0.19	Eng.	blows	b	l	o	-			
			Ger.	bläst	b	l	a:	z			
					7.0	7.0	1.0	-0.0			
17	"bone"	0.93	Eng.	bone	-	b	o	-	-	n	
			Ger.	Knochen	k	n	o	x	ə	n	
					-3.0	-3.0	1.0	-3.0	-1.0	6.0	
18	"breast"	0.28	Eng.	breast	b	r	ɛ	s	t		
			Ger.	Brust	b	r	u	s	t		
					7.0	8.0	1.0	1.0	5.0		
19	"breathe"	1.27	Eng.	breathes	b	r	i	ð	-		
			Ger.	atmet	-	-	a:	t	m		
					-3.0	-3.0	-0.0	-1.0	-3.0		
20	"burn"	0.35	Eng.	burns	b	ə	r	-	n		
			Ger.	brennt	b	-	r	e	n		
					7.0	-1.0	1.0	0.0	6.0		
21	"child"	0.87	Eng.	child	tʃ	-	-	ai	l	d	
			Ger.	Kind	k	i	n	-	-	d	
					-1.0	1.0	-1.0	-1.0	-3.0	5.0	
22	"claw"	0.11	Eng.	claw	k	l	ɔ	-			
			Ger.	Klaue	k	l	au	ə			
					7.0	7.0	1.0	-0.0			
23	"cloud"	0.96	Eng.	cloud	-	-	k	l	-	au	d
			Ger.	Wolke	v	o	-	l	k	ə	-
					-3.0	-3.0	-3.0	6.0	1.0	-2.0	
24	"cold"	0.01	Eng.	cold	k	o	l	d			
			Ger.	kalt	k	a	l	t			
					7.0	1.0	8.0	5.0			
25	"come"	0.07	Eng.	comes	k	ə	m				
			Ger.	kommt	k	o	m				
					7.0	0.0	8.0				
26	"count"	1.20	Eng.	counts	k	au	n	t			
			Ger.	zählt	ts	e:	l	-			
					-1.0	1.0	-3.0	-2.0			
27	"cut"	0.90	Eng.	cuts	-	k	ə	t			
			Ger.	schneidet	ʃ	n	ai	d			
					-3.0	-3.0	0.0	5.0			
28	"day"	0.46	Eng.	day	d	e	-				
			Ger.	Tag	t	a:	g				
					5.0	1.0	0.0				

#	Word	Score	Lang.	Word						
29	"die"	1.22	Eng. Ger.	dies stirbt	- ʃ -3.0	d t 1.0	ai e -1.0	- r -3.0	- b -3.0	
30	"dig"	1.20	Eng. Ger.	digs gräbt	d - -3.0	ɪ g -0.0	g r 1.0	- a: -2.0	- - -3.0	- - -3.0
31	"dirty"	1.26	Eng. Ger.	dirty schmutzig	- ʃ -3.0	d m -3.0	ə - 1.0	r - -3.0	t ts -1.0	i i 1.0	- x -3.0
32	"dog"	1.20	Eng. Ger.	dog Hund	- h -3.0	- u -3.0	- n -1.0	d d 1.0	ɑ - -1.0	g - -3.0
33	"drink"	0.09	Eng. Ger.	drinks trinkt	d t 5.0	r r 8.0	ɪ i 1.0	ŋ ŋ 7.0	k k 4.0	
34	"dry"	0.46	Eng. Ger.	dry trocken	d t 5.0	r r 8.0	ai o -1.0	- k 1.0	- ə -1.0	- n -1.0
35	"dull"	1.18	Eng. Ger.	dull stumpf	- ʃ -3.0	d t 1.0	ə u 1.0	l m -3.0	- p͡f -3.0	
36	"dust"	1.14	Eng. Ger.	dust Staub	d - -3.0	ə - -1.0	s ʃ 1.0	t t 1.0	- au -3.0	- b -3.0
37	"ear"	0.10	Eng. Ger.	ear Ohr	ɪ ɔ: 0.0	r r 7.0				
38	"earth"	0.55	Eng. Ger.	earth Erde	ə e: 1.0	r r 8.0	θ d -1.0	- ə -0.0		
39	"eat"	0.82	Eng. Ger.	eats ißt	i - -0.0	- e 0.0	t s 1.0			
40	"egg"	1.40	Eng. Ger.	egg Ei	ɛ ai 0.0	g - -3.0				
41	"eye"	0.77	Eng. Ger.	eye Auge	ai au 1.0	- g 1.0	- ə -0.0			
42	"fall"	0.00	Eng. Ger.	falls fällt	f f 6.0	ɔ a 1.0	l l 7.0			
43	"far"	0.40	Eng. Ger.	far fern	f f 6.0	ɑ e 1.0	r r 5.0	- n -1.0		
44	"father"	0.01	Eng. Ger.	father Vater	f f 6.0	ɑ a: 1.0	ð t 7.0	ə ə 2.0	r r 7.0	
45	"feather"	0.03	Eng. Ger.	feather Feder	f f 6.0	ɛ e: 1.0	ð d 7.0	ə ə 2.0	r r 7.0	
46	"few"	0.86	Eng. Ger.	few wenige	f v 6.0	- e: 0.0	j n -3.0	u i -1.0	- g 0.0	
47	"fight"	1.21	Eng. Ger.	fights kämpft	- k -3.0	- a -3.0	- m -3.0	f p͡f 1.0	ai - -1.0	t - -2.0
48	"fire"	0.32	Eng. Ger.	fire Feuer	f f 6.0	ai oi -1.0	ə - -1.0	r r 7.0		
49	"fish"	0.03	Eng. Ger.	fish Fisch	f f 6.0	ɪ i 1.0	ʃ ʃ 6.0			
50	"five"	0.61	Eng. Ger.	five fünf	f f 6.0	ai y 0.0	- n -1.0	v f 1.0		
51	"flow"	0.17	Eng. Ger.	flows fließt	f f 6.0	l l 7.0	o i: 1.0	- s -0.0		
52	"flower"	0.91	Eng. Ger.	flower Blume	f b -1.0	l l 7.0	au u: 0.0	ə - -3.0	r m -3.0	
53	"fly"	0.17	Eng. Ger.	flies fliegt	f f 6.0	l l 7.0	ai i: 2.0	- g 0.0		

C.2 Language-Specific Pairwise Alignments

54	"fog"	1.24	Eng. *fog*	-	-	f	ɑ	g		
			Ger. *Nebel*	n	e:	b	ə	l		
				-3.0	0.0	-1.0	-1.0	-3.0		
55	"foot"	0.34	Eng. *foot*	f	ʊ	t				
			Ger. *Fuß*	f	u:	s				
				6.0	2.0	1.0				
56	"four"	0.11	Eng. *four*	f	ɔ	r				
			Ger. *vier*	f	i:	r				
				6.0	-1.0	7.0				
57	"freeze"	0.39	Eng. *freezes*	f	r	i	z	-	-	
			Ger. *friert*	f	r	-	-	i:	r	
				6.0	8.0	-0.0	-3.0	1.0	-3.0	
58	"fruit"	0.11	Eng. *fruit*	f	r	u	-	t		
			Ger. *Frucht*	f	r	u	x	t		
				6.0	8.0	2.0	1.0	5.0		
59	"full"	0.03	Eng. *full*	f	ʊ	l				
			Ger. *voll*	f	o	l				
				6.0	1.0	7.0				
60	"give"	0.61	Eng. *gives*	g	-	ɪ	v			
			Ger. *gibt*	g	e:	-	b			
				7.0	0.0	-0.0	-1.0			
61	"go"	0.06	Eng. *goes*	g	o					
			Ger. *geht*	g	e:					
				7.0	2.0					
62	"good"	0.06	Eng. *good*	g	ʊ	d				
			Ger. *gut*	g	u:	t				
				7.0	2.0	5.0				
63	"grass"	0.00	Eng. *grass*	g	r	a	s			
			Ger. *Gras*	g	r	a:	z			
				7.0	8.0	1.0	6.0			
64	"grease"	1.31	Eng. *grease*	g	r	i	s	-	-	
			Ger. *Fett*	-	-	-	f	e	t	
				-3.0	-3.0	-0.0	-3.0	0.0	-3.0	
65	"green"	0.00	Eng. *green*	g	r	i	n			
			Ger. *grün*	g	r	y:	n			
				7.0	8.0	1.0	6.0			
66	"guts"	1.28	Eng. *guts*	g	ə	t	-	-	-	
			Ger. *Därme*	-	-	d	a	r	m	
				-3.0	-1.0	1.0	-3.0	-3.0	-3.0	
67	"hair"	0.00	Eng. *hair*	h	ɛ	r				
			Ger. *Haare*	h	a:	r				
				7.0	0.0	7.0				
68	"hand"	0.03	Eng. *hand*	h	a	n	d			
			Ger. *Hand*	h	a	n	d			
				7.0	1.0	7.0	5.0			
69	"he"	1.43	Eng. *he*	h	i	-				
			Ger. *er*	-	e:	r				
				-3.0	-1.0	-3.0				
70	"head"	1.39	Eng. *head*	h	ɛ	d				
			Ger. *Kopf*	k	o	p͡f				
				-3.0	0.0	-3.0				
71	"hear"	0.01	Eng. *hears*	h	ɪ	r				
			Ger. *hört*	h	ø:	r				
				7.0	0.0	7.0				
72	"heart"	0.37	Eng. *heart*	h	ɑ	r	t	-	-	
			Ger. *Herz*	h	e	r	ts	ə	n	
				7.0	1.0	7.0	4.0	-1.0	-1.0	
73	"heavy"	1.14	Eng. *heavy*	h	ɛ	v	i	-		
			Ger. *schwer*	ʃ	-	v	e:	r		
				-1.0	-1.0	1.0	-1.0	-3.0		
74	"here"	0.00	Eng. *here*	h	ɪ	r				
			Ger. *hier*	h	i:	r				
				7.0	1.0	7.0				
75	"hit"	1.18	Eng. *hits*	h	-	ɪ	t			
			Ger. *schlägt*	ʃ	l	a:	g			
				-1.0	-3.0	-0.0	0.0			
76	"hold"	0.00	Eng. *holds*	h	o	l	d			
			Ger. *hält*	h	a	l	t			
				7.0	1.0	8.0	5.0			
77	"horn"	0.00	Eng. *horn*	h	ɔ	r	n			
			Ger. *Horn*	h	o	r	n			
				7.0	1.0	7.0	6.0			
78	"hot"	0.33	Eng. *hot*	h	ɑ	t				
			Ger. *heiß*	h	ai	s				
				7.0	1.0	1.0				

#	Word	Score	Lang.		Alignment								
79	"human"	0.79	Eng.	*human*	h	j	u	m	-	-	-	ə	n
			Ger.	*Mensch*	-	-	-	m	e	n	ʃ	ə	n
					-3.0	-3.0	2.0	1.0	0.0	-1.0	-3.0	2.0	6.0
80	"hunt"	1.27	Eng.	*hunts*	h	ə	n	t					
			Ger.	*jagt*	j	aː	-	g					
					-3.0	0.0	-3.0	0.0					
81	"husband"	1.27	Eng.	*husband*	h	ə	z	b	ə	n	d	-	
			Ger.	*Gatte*	-	-	g	-	a	-	t	ə	
					-3.0	-1.0	-2.0	-3.0	-1.0	-3.0	1.0	-0.0	
82	"I"	1.09	Eng.	*I*	ai	-	-						
			Ger.	*ich*	-	i	x						
					-1.0	1.0	-3.0						
83	"ice"	0.13	Eng.	*ice*	ai	s							
			Ger.	*Eis*	ai	s							
					1.0	6.0							
84	"if"	0.93	Eng.	*if*	ɪ	f	-	-					
			Ger.	*wenn*	-	v	e	n					
					-0.0	1.0	0.0	-1.0					
85	"in"	0.05	Eng.	*in*	ɪ	n							
			Ger.	*in*	i	n							
					1.0	6.0							
86	"kill"	1.37	Eng.	*kills*	k	ɪ	l						
			Ger.	*tötet*	t	øː	t						
					-3.0	0.0	-3.0						
87	"knee"	1.06	Eng.	*knee*	-	n	i						
			Ger.	*Knie*	k	n	iː						
					-3.0	1.0	-1.0						
88	"knife"	1.30	Eng.	*knife*	n	ai	f	-	-				
			Ger.	*Messer*	m	e	s	ə	r				
					-3.0	1.0	-3.0	-1.0	-3.0				
89	"know"	1.18	Eng.	*knows*	n	o	-						
			Ger.	*weiß*	v	i	s						
					-3.0	1.0	-0.0						
90	"lake"	1.41	Eng.	*lake*	l	e	k	-	-				
			Ger.	*See*	-	-	z	eː					
					-3.0	-1.0	-3.0	-3.0	-0.0				
91	"laugh"	0.61	Eng.	*laughs*	l	a	f						
			Ger.	*lacht*	l	a	x						
					9.0	1.0	-3.0						
92	"leaf"	1.19	Eng.	*leaf*	-	l	i	f					
			Ger.	*Blatt*	b	l	a	t					
					-3.0	1.0	-0.0	-3.0					
93	"left"	0.67	Eng.	*left*	l	ɛ	f	-	-	t			
			Ger.	*link*	l	-	-	i	ŋ	k			
					9.0	-1.0	-3.0	1.0	-1.0	0.0			
94	"lie"	0.24	Eng.	*lies*	l	ai	-						
			Ger.	*liegt*	l	iː	g						
					9.0	2.0	0.0						
95	"liver"	0.33	Eng.	*liver*	l	ɪ	-	v	ə	r			
			Ger.	*Leber*	l	-	eː	b	ə	r			
					9.0	-0.0	0.0	-1.0	2.0	7.0			
96	"long"	0.00	Eng.	*long*	l	ɔ	ŋ						
			Ger.	*lang*	l	a	ŋ						
					9.0	1.0	6.0						
97	"louse"	0.00	Eng.	*louse*	l	au	s						
			Ger.	*Laus*	l	au	z						
					9.0	1.0	6.0						
98	"man"	0.00	Eng.	*man*	m	a	n						
			Ger.	*Mann*	m	a	n						
					8.0	1.0	6.0						
99	"many"	1.35	Eng.	*many*	m	ɛ	n	-	-	i			
			Ger.	*viele*	-	-	f	iː	l	-			
					-3.0	-1.0	-3.0	1.0	-3.0	-			
100	"meat"	1.15	Eng.	*meat*	-	m	i	t					
			Ger.	*Fleisch*	f	l	ai	ʃ					
					-3.0	-3.0	-0.0	1.0					
101	"moon"	0.56	Eng.	*moon*	m	u	n	-					
			Ger.	*Mond*	m	oː	n	d					
					8.0	1.0	1.0	-3.0					
102	"mother"	0.02	Eng.	*mother*	m	ə	ð	ə	r				
			Ger.	*Mutter*	m	u	t	ə	r				
					8.0	1.0	7.0	2.0	7.0				
103	"mountain"	1.28	Eng.	*mountain*	m	au	-	t	ə	n	-		
			Ger.	*Berg*	-	-	b	e	r	g			
					-3.0	-1.0	-3.0	-3.0	-1.0	-3.0	0.0		

266   C Phonetic Alignment

C.2 Language-Specific Pairwise Alignments

#	Word	Score	Lang	Form							
104	"mouth"	0.36	Eng. Ger.	mouth Mund	m m 8.0	au u 0.0	- n -1.0	θ d 4.0			
105	"name"	0.65	Eng. Ger.	name Name	n n 8.0	e aː 0.0	m m 1.0	- ə -1.0	- - -1.0		
106	"narrow"	1.16	Eng. Ger.	narrow eng	- e 0.0	n ŋ 1.0	a - -1.0	r - -3.0	o - -3.0		
107	"near"	0.61	Eng. Ger.	near nah	n n 8.0	ɪ aː -1.0	r - -3.0				
108	"neck"	1.28	Eng. Ger.	neck Hals	n h -3.0	ɛ a 0.0	k l -3.0	- z -0.0			
109	"new"	0.36	Eng. Ger.	new neu	n n 8.0	u oi -1.0					
110	"night"	0.20	Eng. Ger.	night Nacht	n n 8.0	ai a 1.0	- x 1.0	t t 5.0			
111	"nose"	0.19	Eng. Ger.	nose Nase	n n 8.0	o aː 1.0	z z 7.0	- ə -0.0			
112	"not"	0.27	Eng. Ger.	not nicht	n n 8.0	ɑ - -1.0	- ɪ 1.0	- x 1.0	t t 5.0		
113	"now"	0.47	Eng. Ger.	now nun	n n 8.0	au uː -1.0	- n -1.0				
114	"old"	0.01	Eng. Ger.	old alt	o a 1.0	l l 7.0	d t 5.0				
115	"one"	0.49	Eng. Ger.	one eins	w - -3.0	ə ai 0.0	n n 6.0				
116	"other"	0.40	Eng. Ger.	other anderer	ə a 0.0	- n -3.0	ð d 7.0	ə ə 1.0	r r 7.0		
117	"path"	0.69	Eng. Ger.	path Pfad	p pf -1.0	a aː 1.0	θ d 4.0				
118	"play"	1.04	Eng. Ger.	plays spielt	- ʃ -3.0	p p 1.0	- iː 1.0	l l 1.0	e - -3.0		
119	"pull"	1.37	Eng. Ger.	pulls zieht	p ts -3.0	ʊ - 2.0	l - -3.0	- iː -3.0			
120	"push"	0.77	Eng. Ger.	pushes stößt	- ʃ -3.0	p t -3.0	ʊ oː 1.0	ʃ s 6.0			
121	"rain"	0.58	Eng. Ger.	rain Regen	r r 1.0	e eː 1.0	- g -1.0	- ə -1.0	n n 6.0		
122	"red"	0.58	Eng. Ger.	red rot	r r 1.0	ɛ oː 0.0	d t 5.0				
123	"right"	0.60	Eng. Ger.	right recht	r r 1.0	ai e 1.0	- x 1.0	t t 5.0			
124	"river"	1.23	Eng. Ger.	river Fluss	r - -3.0	ɪ - -0.0	v f 1.0	- l -3.0	ə u -1.0	r - -3.0	- s -0.0
125	"root"	0.97	Eng. Ger.	root Wurzel	- v -3.0	- u -3.0	r r 1.0	u - 2.0	t ts 4.0	- ə -1.0	- l -3.0
126	"rotten"	1.38	Eng. Ger.	rotten faul	r - -3.0	ɑ - -1.0	t f -3.0	ə au -1.0	n l -3.0		
127	"round"	0.39	Eng. Ger.	**round** **rund**	r r 1.0	au u 0.0	n n 7.0	d d 5.0			
128	"rub"	0.87	Eng. Ger.	rubs reibt	r r 1.0	ə ai 0.0	b b 1.0				

#	Word	Score	Lang.							
129	"salt"	0.32	Eng. Ger.	salt Salz	s z 5.0	ɔ a 1.0	l l 8.0	t ts -1.0		
130	"sand"	0.07	Eng. Ger.	sand Sand	s z 5.0	a a 1.0	n n 7.0	d d 5.0		
131	"say"	0.41	Eng. Ger.	says sagt	s z 5.0	e aː 1.0	- g 0.0			
132	"scratch"	0.63	Eng. Ger.	scratches kratzt	s k 0.0	k - 0.0	r r 8.0	a a 1.0	tʃ ts 1.0	
133	"sea"	0.41	Eng. Ger.	sea See	s z 5.0	i eː -1.0				
134	"see"	0.41	Eng. Ger.	sees sieht	s z 5.0	i eː -1.0				
135	"seed"	0.91	Eng. Ger.	seed Same	s z 5.0	i aː -0.0	d m -3.0	- ə -1.0	- n -1.0	
136	"sew"	1.16	Eng. Ger.	sews näht	s n -3.0	o eː 2.0				
137	"sharp"	0.43	Eng. Ger.	sharp scharf	ʃ ʃ 5.0	a a 1.0	r r 7.0	p f -1.0		
138	"short"	0.72	Eng. Ger.	short kurz	ʃ k 0.0	ɔ u -1.0	r r 7.0	t ts -1.0		
139	"sing"	0.03	Eng. Ger.	sings singt	s z 5.0	ɪ i 1.0	ŋ ŋ 6.0			
140	"sit"	0.56	Eng. Ger.	sits sitzt	s z 5.0	ɪ i 1.0	t ts -1.0			
141	"skin"	1.03	Eng. Ger.	skin Haut	s h 3.0	k - 0.0	ɪ au -0.0	n t -3.0		
142	"sky"	1.01	Eng. Ger.	sky Himmel	s h 3.0	k - 0.0	- i 1.0	- m -3.0	ai ə -1.0	- l -3.0
143	"sleep"	0.44	Eng. Ger.	sleeps schläft	s ʃ 5.0	l l 7.0	i aː -0.0	p f -1.0		
144	"small"	0.91	Eng. Ger.	small klein	s k 0.0	m l 3.0	ɔ ai 1.0	l - -3.0	- n -1.0	
145	"smell"	1.24	Eng. Ger.	smells riecht	- r -3.0	- iː 1.0	s x -1.0	m - -3.0	e - -1.0	l - -3.0
146	"smoke"	1.14	Eng. Ger.	smoke Rauch	s - -3.0	m r -3.0	o au 1.0	k x -1.0		
147	"smooth"	0.66	Eng. Ger.	smooth glatt	s g 0.0	m l 3.0	u a 0.0	ð t 4.0		
148	"snake"	0.95	Eng. Ger.	snake Schlange	s ʃ 5.0	- l -3.0	- a -3.0	n ŋ 1.0	e - -1.0	k ə -3.0 - -0.0
149	"snow"	0.49	Eng. Ger.	snow Schnee	s ʃ 5.0	n n 1.0	o eː 2.0			
150	"some"	1.12	Eng. Ger.	some einige	s - -3.0	ə ai 0.0	m n -3.0	- i 1.0	- g 0.0	
151	"spit"	0.29	Eng. Ger.	spits spuckt	s ʃ 5.0	p p 9.0	ɪ u 1.0	t k 0.0		
152	"split"	0.20	Eng. Ger.	splits spaltet	s ʃ 5.0	p p 9.0	- a -3.0	l l 6.0	ɪ - -0.0	t t 5.0
153	"squeeze"	1.23	Eng. Ger.	squeezes drückt	- d -3.0	s r -3.0	k - 0.0	w - -3.0	i y 1.0	- k 0.0 z - -3.0

C.2 Language-Specific Pairwise Alignments

#	Word	Score	Lang.	Form							
154	"stab"	0.58	Eng. Ger.	stabs sticht	s ʃ 5.0	t t 6.0	a e 1.0	b x -3.0			
155	"stand"	0.53	Eng. Ger.	stands steht	s ʃ 5.0	t t 6.0	a e: 1.0	n - -3.0	d - -2.0		
156	"star"	0.34	Eng. Ger.	star Stern	s ʃ 5.0	t t 6.0	ɑ e 1.0	r r 5.0	- n -1.0		
157	"stick"	0.20	Eng. Ger.	stick Stock	s ʃ 5.0	t t 6.0	ɪ o 0.0	k k 4.0			
158	"stone"	0.05	Eng. Ger.	stone Stein	s ʃ 5.0	t t 6.0	o ai 1.0	n n 6.0			
159	"straight"	0.77	Eng. Ger.	straight gerade	s g 0.0	t - -3.0	- ə 0.0	r r 8.0	e a: -1.0	t d 1.0	- ə -0.0
160	"suck"	0.25	Eng. Ger.	sucks saugt	s z 5.0	ə au 0.0	k g 4.0				
161	"sun"	0.59	Eng. Ger.	sun Sonne	s z 5.0	ə o 0.0	n n 1.0	- ə -0.0			
162	"swell"	0.45	Eng. Ger.	swells schwillt	s ʃ 5.0	w v -1.0	ɛ e 1.0	l l 7.0			
163	"swim"	0.40	Eng. Ger.	swims schwimnt	s ʃ 5.0	w v -1.0	ɪ i 1.0	m m 8.0			
164	"tail"	1.21	Eng. Ger.	tail Schwanz	- ʃ -3.0	- v 0.0	- a -3.0	- n -1.0	t ts -1.0	e - -1.0	l - -3.0
165	"that"	0.45	Eng. Ger.	that das	ð d 6.0	a a 1.0	t s 1.0				
166	"there"	0.75	Eng. Ger.	there da	ð d 6.0	ɛ a: -1.0	r - -3.0				
167	"they"	1.13	Eng. Ger.	they sie	ð z -1.0	e i: -1.0					
168	"thick"	0.25	Eng. Ger.	thick dick	θ d 6.0	ɪ ɪ 1.0	k k 4.0				
169	"thin"	0.14	Eng. Ger.	thin dünn	θ d 6.0	ɪ y 1.0	n n 6.0				
170	"think"	0.22	Eng. Ger.	thinks denkt	θ d 6.0	ɪ - -0.0	- e 0.0	ŋ ŋ 7.0	k k 4.0		
171	"this"	0.14	Eng. Ger.	this dieses	ð d 6.0	ɪ i: 1.0	s z 6.0				
172	"thou"	1.31	Eng. Ger.	you du	j d -3.0	u u: -1.0					
173	"three"	0.22	Eng. Ger.	three drei	θ d 6.0	r r 8.0	i ai -1.0				
174	"throw"	1.33	Eng. Ger.	throws wirft	θ v -3.0	- e 0.0	r r 1.0	o - -3.0	- f -3.0		
175	"tie"	1.15	Eng. Ger.	ties bindet	- b -3.0	- i 1.0	- n -1.0	t d 1.0	ai - -3.0		
176	"tongue"	0.63	Eng. Ger.	tongue Zunge	t ts 5.0	ə u 1.0	ŋ ŋ 2.0	- ə -0.0			
177	"tooth"	0.82	Eng. Ger.	tooth Zahn	t ts 5.0	u - 2.0	θ - -3.0	- a: -3.0	- n -1.0		
178	"tree"	1.39	Eng. Ger.	tree Baum	t - -3.0	r b -3.0	i au -1.0	- m -3.0			

179	"true"	1.40	Eng. Ger.	*true* *wahr*	- v -3.0	- aː -3.0	t - -3.0	r r 1.0	u - -3.0	
180	"two"	0.68	Eng. Ger.	*two* *zwei*	t ts 5.0	- v 0.0	u ai -1.0			
181	"vomit"	1.11	Eng. Ger.	**vomits** *erbricht*	- e 0.0	- r -2.0	v b -1.0	ɑ - -1.0	m r 2.0	ə e -1.0	t x -3.0
182	"wash"	0.22	Eng. Ger.	*washes* *wäscht*	w v 4.0	ɑ a 1.0	ʃ ʃ 6.0			
183	"water"	0.50	Eng. Ger.	*water* *Wasser*	w v 4.0	ɑ a 1.0	t s -2.0	ə ə 2.0	r r 7.0	
184	"we"	0.86	Eng. Ger.	*we* *wir*	w v 4.0	- iː 1.0	- r -3.0	i - -3.0		
185	"wet"	1.12	Eng. Ger.	*wet* *nass*	w n -3.0	ɛ a 0.0	t s 1.0			
186	"what"	0.74	Eng. Ger.	*what* *was*	w v 4.0	ɑ - -1.0	t - -2.0			
187	"white"	0.55	Eng. Ger.	*white* *weiß*	w v 4.0	ai ai 1.0	t s 1.0			
188	"who"	1.43	Eng. Ger.	*who* *wer*	h v -3.0	u eː -1.0				
189	"wide"	0.25	Eng. Ger.	*wide* *weit*	w v 4.0	ai ai 1.0	d t 5.0			
190	"wife"	1.36	Eng. Ger.	*wife* *Gattin*	w g -3.0	ai a 1.0	f t -3.0	- i -3.0	- n -1.0	
191	"wind"	0.16	Eng. Ger.	*wind* *Wind*	w v 4.0	ɪ i 1.0	n n 7.0	d d 5.0		
192	"wing"	1.01	Eng. Ger.	**wing** *Flügel*	w f 4.0	- l -3.0	ɪ yː 1.0	- g 1.0	- ə -1.0	ŋ l -3.0
193	"wipe"	0.80	Eng. Ger.	*wipes* *wischt*	w v 4.0	ai - -1.0	p - -3.0	- i 1.0	- ʃ -0.0	
194	"with"	0.86	Eng. Ger.	*with* *mit*	w m -3.0	ɪ i 1.0	θ t 4.0			
195	"woman"	0.77	Eng. Ger.	*woman* *Frau*	w f 4.0	ʊ - 2.0	m r 2.0	ə au -1.0	n - -3.0	
196	"woods"	0.60	Eng. Ger.	*woods* *Wald*	w v 4.0	- a -3.0	- l -3.0	ʊ - 2.0	d d 5.0	
197	"worm"	0.14	Eng. Ger.	*worm* *Wurm*	w v 4.0	ə u 1.0	r r 7.0	m m 8.0		
198	"year"	0.53	Eng. Ger.	*year* *Jahr*	j j 1.0	ɪ aː -0.0	r r 7.0			
199	"yellow"	1.08	Eng. Ger.	*yellow* *gelb*	j g -3.0	ɛ e 1.0	l l 6.0	o - -3.0	- b -3.0	
200	"you"	1.22	Eng. Ger.	*you* *ihr*	j - -3.0	u - -3.0	- iː 1.0	- r -3.0		

D
Cognate Detection

D.1 Comparison of Phonetic Distances

The following word lists illustrate the differences in the distance scores resulting from the different methods discussed in Section 4.3.3 for cognates between German and English. Cells which are shaded in gray indicate, where these methods fail to detect cognacy when applying the standard thresholds which have been used in the studies for automatic cognate detection. The list was created by randomly selecting 100 cognate pairs from a larger dataset of 658 English-German cognate pairs taken from Kluge (KLUGE). The IPA transcriptions were added by the author of this study.

No.	German		English		Distance Scores			
	Orth.	IPA	Orth.	IPA	PID	NED	SCA	LxS
1	saufen	zaufən	sup	sʌp	1.00	1.00	0.61	0.25
2	Miete	miːtə	meed	miːd	0.50	0.50	0.18	0.17
3	gebaeren	gəbɛːrən	bear	bɛər	0.71	0.71	0.81	0.80
4	Zunge	tsʊŋə	tongue	tʌŋ	0.75	0.75	0.37	0.34
5	Seife	zaifə	soap	səʊp	1.00	1.00	0.36	0.23
6	Volk	fɔlk	folk	fəʊk	0.50	0.50	0.32	0.49
7	Bube	buːbə	boy	bɔɪ	0.75	0.75	0.75	1.30
8	leben	leːbən	live	laɪv	0.80	0.80	0.61	0.28
9	Schulter	ʃʊltər	shoulder	ʃəʊldər	0.33	0.33	0.00	0.13
10	Nacht	naxt	night	naɪt	0.50	0.50	0.29	0.23
11	Hilfe	hɪlfə	help	hɛlp	0.60	0.60	0.25	0.23
12	Storch	ʃtɔrx	stork	stɔːk	0.80	0.80	0.30	0.26
13	Knabe	knaːbə	nave	neɪv	0.80	0.80	0.64	0.50
14	gehen	geːən	go	gəʊ	0.67	0.67	0.41	0.24
15	Tod	toːt	death	dɛθ	1.00	1.00	0.14	0.33
16	Bier	biːr	beer	bɪər	0.33	0.33	0.00	0.06
17	Heu	hɔy	hay	heɪ	0.50	0.50	0.00	0.42

18	bluehen	blyːən	blow	bləʊ	0.50	0.50	0.28	0.29
19	lispeln	lɪspəln	lisp	lɪsp	0.43	0.43	0.46	0.29
20	Sorge	zɔrgə	sorrow	sɔrəʊ	0.60	0.60	0.31	0.36
21	Knopf	knɔpf	knob	nɔb	0.60	0.60	0.53	0.57
22	Distel	dɪstəl	thistle	θɪsl̩	0.67	0.67	0.49	0.58
23	Wagen	vaːgən	wain	weɪn	0.80	0.80	0.66	0.68
24	leisten	laɪstən	last	lɑːst	0.50	0.50	0.33	0.16
25	Lerche	lɛrxə	lark	lɑːk	0.80	0.80	0.63	0.33
26	Segel	zeːgəl	sail	seɪl	0.80	0.80	0.50	0.20
27	Krueppel	krʏpəl	cripple	krɪpl̩	0.50	0.50	0.14	0.13
28	Gewicht	gəvɪxt	weight	weɪt	0.83	0.83	0.83	0.76
29	Wasser	vasər	water	wɔːtər	0.60	0.60	0.27	0.42
30	Griff	grɪf	grip	grɪp	0.25	0.25	0.05	0.18
31	schlagen	ʃlaːgən	slay	sleɪ	0.83	0.83	0.70	0.53
32	Galle	galə	gall	gɔːl	0.50	0.50	0.22	0.22
33	sehen	zeːən	see	siː	1.00	1.00	0.46	0.46
34	Grund	grʊnt	ground	graʊnd	0.40	0.40	0.00	0.14
35	speien	ʃpaɪən	spew	spjuː	0.80	0.75	0.60	0.33
36	waten	vaːtən	wade	weɪd	1.00	1.00	0.62	0.35
37	hundert	hʊndərt	hundred	hʌndrəd	0.50	0.57	0.26	0.26
38	Schwarte	ʃvartə	sward	swɔːd	1.00	1.00	0.47	0.33
39	Leid	laɪt	loath	ləʊθ	0.67	0.67	0.14	0.26
40	Kinn	kɪn	chin	tʃɪn	0.33	0.33	0.10	0.32
41	Span	ʃpaːn	spoon	spuːn	0.50	0.50	0.00	0.21
42	schleissen	ʃlaɪsən	slit	slɪt	0.83	0.83	0.55	0.30
43	Zipfel	tsɪpfəl	tip	tɪp	0.67	0.67	0.76	0.58
44	Fisch	fɪʃ	fish	fɪʃ	0.00	0.00	0.00	0.11
45	Hut	huːt	hood	hʊd	0.67	0.67	0.00	0.11
46	meinen	maɪnən	mean	miːn	0.60	0.60	0.49	0.25
47	Tau	tau	dew	djuː	1.00	1.00	0.62	0.53
48	Knie	kniː	knee	niː	0.33	0.33	0.48	0.50
49	Bug	buːk	bough	baʊ	0.67	0.67	0.46	0.54
50	Nessel	nɛsəl	nettle	nɛtl̩	0.60	0.60	0.40	0.29
51	Zwist	tsvɪst	twist	twɪst	0.40	0.40	0.12	0.19
52	Lamm	lam	lamb	læm	0.33	0.33	0.00	0.07

D.1 Comparison of Phonetic Distances

53	sacken	zakən	sag	sæg	1.00	1.00	0.49	0.23
54	Regen	reːgən	rain	reɪn	0.60	0.60	0.50	0.24
55	Winter	vɪntər	winter	wɪntər	0.17	0.17	0.01	0.15
56	Lauch	laux	leek	liːk	0.67	0.67	0.14	0.25
57	hacken	hakən	hack	hæk	0.60	0.60	0.49	0.21
58	reiten	raitən	ride	raɪd	0.80	0.80	0.46	0.22
59	Foehre	fœːrə	fir	fɜːr	0.50	0.50	0.22	0.27
60	Zimmer	tsɪmər	timber	tɪmbər	0.33	0.33	0.32	0.59
61	kommen	kɔmən	come	kʌm	0.60	0.60	0.49	0.23
62	Weizen	vaitsən	wheat	wiːt	1.00	1.00	0.75	0.45
63	Borste	bɔrstə	bristle	brɪsl̩	0.57	0.67	0.74	0.82
64	Adel	aːdəl	addle	ædl̩	0.75	0.75	0.33	0.26
65	Weib	vaip	wife	waɪf	1.00	1.00	0.27	0.29
66	Seele	zeːlə	soul	səʊl	0.75	0.75	0.18	0.17
67	singen	zɪŋən	sing	sɪŋ	0.60	0.60	0.46	0.22
68	stillen	ʃtɪlən	still	stɪl	0.50	0.50	0.33	0.17
69	Schwein	ʃvain	swine	swaɪn	0.75	0.75	0.05	0.20
70	bruehen	bryːən	broth	brɔθ	0.50	0.50	0.26	0.51
71	Meer	meːr	mere	mɪər	0.33	0.33	0.00	0.12
72	duenken	dyŋkən	think	θɪŋk	0.67	0.67	0.46	0.26
73	Loch	lɔx	lock	lɔk	0.33	0.33	0.10	0.21
74	Suende	zyndə	sin	sɪn	0.80	0.80	0.51	0.78
75	Besen	beːzən	besom	biːzəm	0.40	0.40	0.19	0.45
76	Otter	ɔtər	adder	ædər	0.50	0.50	0.00	0.18
77	Harm	harm	harm	hɑːm	0.50	0.50	0.29	0.18
78	Schaf	ʃaːf	sheep	ʃiːp	0.67	0.67	0.14	0.29
79	vier	fiːr	four	fɔːr	0.33	0.33	0.00	0.26
80	Heide	haidə	heath	hiːθ	0.75	0.75	0.36	0.36
81	sondern	zɔndərn	sunder	sʌndər	0.43	0.43	0.13	0.22
82	Tor	toːr	door	dɔːr	0.67	0.67	0.00	0.11
83	zehn	tseːn	ten	tɛn	0.67	0.67	0.10	0.27
84	winken	vɪŋkən	wink	wɪŋk	0.50	0.50	0.43	0.23
85	Jugend	juːgənt	youth	juːθ	0.67	0.67	0.76	0.45
86	Ohr	oːr	ear	ɪər	0.50	0.50	0.00	0.29
87	Welt	vɛlt	world	wɜːld	0.75	0.75	0.05	0.18

88	wirken	vɪrkən	work	wɜːk	0.83	0.83	0.82	0.44
89	Saat	zaːt	seed	siːd	1.00	1.00	0.00	0.16
90	Floh	floː	flea	fliː	0.33	0.33	0.00	0.33
91	fasten	fastən	fast	fɑːst	0.50	0.50	0.33	0.19
92	Bad	baːt	bath	bɑːθ	0.67	0.67	0.10	0.27
93	binden	bɪndən	bind	baɪnd	0.50	0.50	0.36	0.22
94	Rabe	raːbə	raven	rævn̩	0.80	0.75	0.57	0.42
95	Spaten	ʃpaːtən	spade	speɪd	0.83	0.83	0.36	0.21
96	schauen	ʃauən	show	ʃəu	0.67	0.67	0.46	0.30
97	neun	nɔyn	nine	naɪn	0.33	0.33	0.00	0.21
98	Busen	buːzən	bosom	buzəm	0.40	0.40	0.17	0.42
99	Halle	halə	hall	hɔːl	0.50	0.50	0.22	0.21
100	Lauge	laugə	lie	laɪ	0.75	0.75	0.71	0.44

D.2 Cognate Detection

The following tables give a detailed comparison of the cognate decisions made by the four methods on the KSL testset (Kessler 2001). Of the 200 items in the original list, only those have been included where at least one of the four methods differs. Cluster decisions are indicated by integers assigned to each entry. If the integers are identical in two entries, the entries are judged to be cognate by the respective method. Cells shaded in gray indicate that the cluster decision made by the respective method differs from the gold standard. Orthographical forms in bold font indicate that the respective entry was borrowed.

"all" (1)			GLD	TUR	NED	SCA	LxS
Albanian	gjithë	ɟiθ	1	1	1	1	1
English	all	ɔl	2	2	2	2	2
French	tous	tut	3	3	3	1	3
German	alle	al	2	2	2	2	2
Hawaiian	apau	apau	5	5	5	5	5
Navajo	tʼáá ʼáłtso	ʔayɬtso	6	6	6	6	6
Turkish	bütün	bytyn	7	7	7	7	7

D.2 Cognate Detection

	"and" (2)		GLD	TUR	NED	SCA	LxS
Albanian	*e*	e	1	1	1	1	1
English	*and*	and	2	2	2	2	2
French	*et*	e	1	1	1	1	3
German	*und*	unt	2	2	4	2	4
Hawaiian	*ā*	aː	5	1	5	1	5
Navajo	*dóó*	doː	6	6	6	6	6
Turkish	*ve*	ve	7	7	1	7	7

	"animal" (3)		GLD	TUR	NED	SCA	LxS
Albanian	*kafshë*	kafʃ	1	1	1	1	1
English	*animal*	anəməl	2	2	2	2	2
French	*animal*	animal	2	2	2	2	3
German	*Tier*	tiːr	4	4	4	4	4
Hawaiian	*holoholona*	holoholona	5	5	5	5	5
Navajo	*naaldeehii*	naːldeːhiː	6	6	6	6	6
Turkish	*hayvan*	hajvan	7	7	7	7	7

	"at" (5)		GLD	TUR	NED	SCA	LxS
Albanian	*në*	nə	1	1	1	1	1
English	*at*	at	2	2	2	2	2
French	*à*	a	2	3	2	3	3
German	*an*	an	4	1	2	4	1
Hawaiian	*ma*	ma	5	5	5	5	5
Navajo	*-di*	di	6	2	6	6	6
Turkish	*-de*	de	7	2	6	6	6

	"back" (6)		GLD	TUR	NED	SCA	LxS
Albanian	*shpinë*	ʃpin	1	1	1	1	1
English	*back*	bak	2	2	2	2	2
French	*dos*	do	3	3	3	3	3
German	*Rücken*	rykən	4	4	4	4	4
Hawaiian	*kua*	kua	5	5	5	5	5
Navajo	*'anághah*	nayɣah	6	6	6	6	6
Turkish	*arka*	arka	7	4	7	7	7

	"bad" (7)		GLD	TUR	NED	SCA	LxS
Albanian	*keq*	kec	1	1	1	1	1
English	*bad*	bad	2	2	2	2	2
French	*mauvais*	mɔvɛz	3	3	3	3	3
German	*schlecht*	ʃlext	4	4	4	4	4
Hawaiian	*'ino*	ʔino	5	5	5	5	5
Navajo	*doo yá'áshóǫ da*	jayʔayʃõõ	6	6	6	6	6
Turkish	*kötü*	køty	7	7	7	1	7

	"because" (9)		GLD	TUR	NED	SCA	LxS
Albanian	sepse	sepse	1	1	1	1	1
English	**because**	bəkɔz	2	2	2	2	2
French	parce que	pars	1	3	3	3	3
German	weil	vail	4	4	4	4	4
Hawaiian	ā mea	aːmea	5	5	5	5	5
Navajo	háálá	haːlay	6	6	6	6	6
Turkish	çünkü	tʃynky	7	7	7	7	7

	"belly" (10)		GLD	TUR	NED	SCA	LxS
Albanian	bark	bark	1	1	1	1	1
English	belly	bɛli	2	1	2	2	2
French	ventre	vãtr	3	3	3	3	3
German	Bauch	baux	4	4	4	1	4
Hawaiian	'ōpū	ʔoːpuː	5	5	5	5	5
Navajo	'abid	bid	6	6	6	6	4
Turkish	karın	karn	7	7	1	7	7

	"big" (11)		GLD	TUR	NED	SCA	LxS
Albanian	madh	mað	1	1	1	1	1
English	big	bıg	2	2	2	2	2
French	grand	grãd	3	3	3	3	3
German	groß	groːs	4	3	3	3	3
Hawaiian	nui	nui	5	5	5	5	5
Navajo	'áníłtso	ʔayniłtso	6	6	6	6	6
Turkish	büyük	byjyk	7	7	7	2	7

	"bite" (13)		GLD	TUR	NED	SCA	LxS
Albanian	kafshon	kafʃo	1	1	1	1	1
English	bites	bait	2	2	2	2	2
French	mord	mɔr	3	3	3	3	3
German	beißt	bais	2	4	2	2	2
Hawaiian	nahu	nahu	5	5	5	5	5
Navajo	'aháshháásh	ʔahayłhaːʃ	6	6	6	6	6
Turkish	ısırıyor	ɯsɯr	7	7	7	7	7

	"black" (14)		GLD	TUR	NED	SCA	LxS
Albanian	zi	zez	1	1	1	1	1
English	black	blak	2	2	2	2	2
French	noir	nwar	3	3	3	3	3
German	schwarz	ʃvarts	4	4	3	4	4
Hawaiian	'ele'ele	ʔeleʔele	5	5	5	5	5
Navajo	łizhin	łiʒin	6	6	6	6	6
Turkish	kara	kara	7	7	7	7	7

D.2 Cognate Detection

"blood" (15)			GLD	TUR	NED	SCA	LxS
Albanian	gjak	ɟakr	1	1	1	1	1
English	blood	bləd	2	2	2	2	2
French	sang	sã	3	3	3	3	3
German	Blut	bluːt	2	2	2	2	2
Hawaiian	koko	koko	5	1	5	5	5
Navajo	dił	dił	6	6	6	6	6
Turkish	kan	kan	7	7	7	7	7

"blow" (16)			GLD	TUR	NED	SCA	LxS
Albanian	fryn	fry	1	1	1	1	1
English	blows	blo	2	1	2	2	2
French	vente	vãte	3	3	3	3	3
German	bläst	blaːz	2	1	2	2	2
Hawaiian	puhi	puhi	5	5	5	5	5
Navajo	ních'i	nitʃʔi	6	6	6	6	6
Turkish	esiyor	es	7	7	7	7	7

"bone" (17)			GLD	TUR	NED	SCA	LxS
Albanian	kockë	kotsk	1	1	1	1	1
English	bone	bon	2	2	2	2	2
French	os	ɔs	3	3	3	3	3
German	Knochen	knoxən	4	4	4	4	4
Hawaiian	iwi	iwi	5	5	5	5	5
Navajo	ts'in	tsʔin	6	4	6	6	6
Turkish	kemik	kemik	7	7	1	7	7

"breathe" (19)			GLD	TUR	NED	SCA	LxS
Albanian	marr frymë	frym	1	1	1	1	1
English	breathes	brið	2	1	2	2	2
French	**respire**	rɛspire	3	3	3	3	3
German	atmet	aːtm	4	4	4	4	4
Hawaiian	hanu	hanu	5	5	5	5	5
Navajo	ńdísdzih	ńdidʑih	6	6	6	6	6
Turkish	**nefes alıyor**	nefes	7	7	7	7	7

"burn" (20)			GLD	TUR	NED	SCA	LxS
Albanian	digjet	diɟ	1	1	1	1	1
English	burns	bərn	2	2	2	2	2
French	**brûle**	bryle	2	2	3	3	3
German	brennt	bren	2	2	2	2	2
Hawaiian	'ā	ʔaː	5	5	5	5	5
Navajo	diltłi'	diltʰiʔ	6	6	6	6	6
Turkish	yanıyor	jan	7	7	7	7	7

"child" (21)			GLD	TUR	NED	SCA	LxS
Albanian	*fëmiljë*	fəmiʎ	1	1	1	1	1
English	child	tʃaild	2	2	2	2	2
French	enfant	ɑ̃fɑ̃t	3	3	3	3	3
German	Kind	kind	4	4	4	4	4
Hawaiian	keiki	keiki	5	5	4	5	5
Navajo	'ashkii	ʔʃkiː	6	6	6	6	6
Turkish	çocuk	tʃodʒuk	7	5	7	7	7

"claw" (22)			GLD	TUR	NED	SCA	LxS
Albanian	thua	θon	1	1	1	1	1
English	claw	klɔ	2	2	2	2	2
French	*griffe*	grif	3	2	3	3	3
German	Klaue	klauə	2	2	2	2	2
Hawaiian	miki'ao	mikiʔao	5	5	5	5	5
Navajo	'akéshgaan	keʃgaː	6	6	6	6	6
Turkish	tırnak	tɯrnak	7	7	7	7	7

"cold" (24)			GLD	TUR	NED	SCA	LxS
Albanian	ftohët	ftohət	1	1	1	1	1
English	cold	kold	2	2	2	2	2
French	froid	frwad	3	3	3	3	3
German	kalt	kalt	2	2	2	2	2
Hawaiian	anu	anu	5	5	5	5	5
Navajo	sik'az	sikʔaz	6	6	6	6	6
Turkish	soğuk	soɣuk	7	6	7	6	7

"come" (25)			GLD	TUR	NED	SCA	LxS
Albanian	*vjen*	vjen	1	1	1	1	1
English	comes	kəm	1	2	2	2	2
French	vient	vjẽ	1	1	1	1	3
German	kommt	kom	1	2	2	2	2
Hawaiian	hele mai	hele	5	5	5	5	5
Navajo	yíghááh	jiɣaːh	6	6	6	6	6
Turkish	geliyor	gel	7	7	5	7	7

"count" (26)			GLD	TUR	NED	SCA	LxS
Albanian	*numëron*	numəruar	1	1	1	1	1
English	*counts*	kaunt	2	2	2	2	2
French	compte	kɔ̃te	2	3	3	2	2
German	zählt	tseːl	4	4	4	4	4
Hawaiian	helu	helu	5	5	5	5	5
Navajo	'íínishta'	iːniɬtaʔ	6	6	6	6	6
Turkish	sayıyor	saj	7	7	7	7	7

D.2 Cognate Detection

	"cut" (27)		GLD	TUR	NED	SCA	LxS
Albanian	*pres*	pres	1	1	1	1	1
English	***cuts***	kət	2	2	2	2	2
French	***coupe***	kupe	3	3	3	3	3
German	*schneidet*	ʃnaid	4	4	4	4	4
Hawaiian	*'oki*	ʔoki	5	5	5	5	5
Navajo	*'aháshgéésh*	ʔahayge:ʃ	6	6	6	6	6
Turkish	*kesiyor*	kes	7	7	1	2	7

	"day" (28)		GLD	TUR	NED	SCA	LxS
Albanian	*ditë*	dit	1	1	1	1	1
English	*day*	de	2	2	2	2	2
French	*jour*	ʒur	3	3	3	3	3
German	*Tag*	ta:g	2	4	4	4	2
Hawaiian	*lā*	la:	5	5	5	5	5
Navajo	*jį́*	ʤį́	6	6	6	2	6
Turkish	*gün*	gyn	7	7	7	7	7

	"dig" (30)		GLD	TUR	NED	SCA	LxS
Albanian	*gërmon*	gərmo	1	1	1	1	1
English	***digs***	dɪg	2	2	2	2	2
French	***creuse***	krøze	3	1	3	3	3
German	*gräbt*	gra:b	4	1	1	3	4
Hawaiian	*'eli*	ʔeli	5	5	5	5	5
Navajo	*hahashgééd*	hahage:d	6	6	6	6	6
Turkish	*kazıyor*	kaz	7	7	3	7	7

	"dog" (32)		GLD	TUR	NED	SCA	LxS
Albanian	***qen***	cen	1	1	1	1	1
English	*dog*	dɑg	2	2	2	2	2
French	*chien*	ʃjɛn	1	3	3	1	1
German	*Hund*	hund	1	4	4	4	4
Hawaiian	*'īlio*	ʔi:lio	5	5	5	5	5
Navajo	*łééchąą'í*	łe:tʃãːʔi	6	6	6	6	6
Turkish	*köpek*	køpek	7	7	7	7	7

	"drink" (33)		GLD	TUR	NED	SCA	LxS
Albanian	*pi*	pi	1	1	1	1	1
English	*drinks*	drɪŋk	2	2	2	2	2
French	*bois*	bwa	1	3	3	3	3
German	*trinkt*	trɪŋk	2	2	2	2	2
Hawaiian	*inu*	inu	5	5	5	5	5
Navajo	*'adlą́*	ʔadˡą́	6	6	6	6	6
Turkish	*içiyor*	itʃ	7	7	7	7	7

"dry" (34)

			GLD	TUR	NED	SCA	LxS
Albanian	*thatë*	θat	1	1	1	1	1
English	*dry*	drai	2	2	2	2	2
French	*sec*	sɛʃ	3	3	3	3	3
German	*trocken*	trokən	2	2	4	2	2
Hawaiian	*maloʻo*	maloʔo	5	5	5	5	5
Navajo	*yíłtseii*	jiɬtseiː	6	6	6	6	6
Turkish	*kuru*	kuru	7	7	7	7	7

"dust" (36)

			GLD	TUR	NED	SCA	LxS
Albanian	*pluhur*	pluhur	1	1	1	1	1
English	*dust*	dəst	2	2	2	2	2
French	*poussière*	pusjɛr	3	3	3	3	3
German	*Staub*	ʃtaub	4	4	4	4	4
Hawaiian	*ʻehu*	ʔehu	5	5	5	5	5
Navajo	*łeezh*	ɬeːʒ	6	6	6	6	6
Turkish	*toz*	toz	7	2	7	2	7

"ear" (37)

			GLD	TUR	NED	SCA	LxS
Albanian	*vesh*	veʃ	1	1	1	1	1
English	*ear*	ɪr	1	2	2	2	2
French	*oreille*	ɔrɛj	1	3	3	3	3
German	*Ohr*	oːr	1	2	2	2	2
Hawaiian	*pepeiao*	pepeiao	5	5	5	5	5
Navajo	*ʼajaaʼ*	ʥaːʔ	6	6	6	6	6
Turkish	*kulak*	kulak	7	7	7	7	7

"earth" (38)

			GLD	TUR	NED	SCA	LxS
Albanian	*dhe*	ðer	1	1	1	1	1
English	*earth*	ərθ	2	2	2	2	2
French	*terre*	tɛr	3	1	3	1	3
German	*Erde*	eːrdə	2	2	4	2	2
Hawaiian	*lepo*	lepo	5	5	5	5	5
Navajo	*łeezh*	ɬeːʒ	6	6	6	6	6
Turkish	*toprak*	toprak	7	7	7	7	7

"eat" (39)

			GLD	TUR	NED	SCA	LxS
Albanian	*ha*	ha	1	1	1	1	1
English	*eats*	it	2	2	2	2	2
French	*mange*	mãʒe	3	3	3	3	3
German	*ißt*	es	2	4	4	4	4
Hawaiian	*ʻai*	ʔai	5	1	5	1	5
Navajo	*ʼayą́*	ʔajã́	6	6	5	1	6
Turkish	*yiyor*	je	7	7	7	7	7

D.2 Cognate Detection

	"egg" (40)		GLD	TUR	NED	SCA	LxS
Albanian	vezë	vez	1	1	1	1	1
English	**egg**	ɛg	1	2	2	2	2
French	œuf	œf	1	3	3	3	3
German	Ei	ai	1	4	4	4	4
Hawaiian	hua	hua	5	5	5	5	5
Navajo	'ayęęzhii	jẽːʒiː	6	6	6	6	6
Turkish	yumurta	jumurta	7	7	7	7	7

	"eye" (41)		GLD	TUR	NED	SCA	LxS
Albanian	sy	syr	1	1	1	1	1
English	eye	ai	2	2	2	2	2
French	œil	œj	2	3	3	3	3
German	Auge	augə	2	4	4	4	4
Hawaiian	maka	maka	5	5	5	4	5
Navajo	'anáá'	naːʔ	6	6	6	6	6
Turkish	göz	gøz	7	7	7	7	7

	"fall" (42)		GLD	TUR	NED	SCA	LxS
Albanian	bie	bie	1	1	1	1	1
English	falls	fɔl	2	2	2	2	2
French	**tombe**	tɔ̃be	3	3	3	3	3
German	fällt	fal	2	2	2	2	2
Hawaiian	hina	hina	5	5	5	5	5
Navajo	naashtłííshh	naːtˡiːʃ	6	6	6	6	6
Turkish	düşüyor	dyʃ	7	7	7	6	3

	"far" (43)		GLD	TUR	NED	SCA	LxS
Albanian	**larg**	larg	1	1	1	1	1
English	far	fɑr	2	2	2	2	2
French	loin	lwẽ	3	3	3	3	3
German	fern	fern	2	2	2	2	2
Hawaiian	mamao	mamao	5	5	5	5	5
Navajo	nízahgóó	nizah	6	6	6	6	6
Turkish	uzak	uzak	7	7	6	7	7

	"father" (44)		GLD	TUR	NED	SCA	LxS
Albanian	**babë**	babə	1	1	1	1	1
English	father	fɑðər	2	2	2	2	2
French	père	pɛr	2	3	3	3	2
German	Vater	faːtər	2	2	2	2	2
Hawaiian	makua kāne	makuakaːne	5	5	5	5	5
Navajo	'ataa'	taːʔ	6	6	6	6	6
Turkish	baba	baba	1	1	1	1	1

"few" (46)			GLD	TUR	NED	SCA	LxS
Albanian	**pak**	pak	1	1	1	1	1
English	few	fju	1	2	2	2	2
French	peu de	pø	1	3	3	1	1
German	wenige	veːnig	4	4	4	4	4
Hawaiian	kakaʻikahi	kakaʔikahi	5	5	5	5	5
Navajo	tʼáá díkwíí	dikwiː	6	6	6	6	6
Turkish	az	az	7	7	7	7	7

"fight" (47)			GLD	TUR	NED	SCA	LxS
Albanian	**lufton**	lufto	1	1	1	1	1
English	fights	fait	2	2	2	2	2
French	bat	bat	3	2	3	2	2
German	**kämpft**	kampf	4	4	4	4	4
Hawaiian	hakakā	hakakaː	5	5	5	5	5
Navajo	ʼahishgą́	ʔahigã́	6	6	6	5	6
Turkish	dövüşüyor	døvyʃ	7	7	7	7	7

"fish" (49)			GLD	TUR	NED	SCA	LxS
Albanian	**peshk**	peʃk	1	1	1	1	1
English	fish	fɪʃ	1	1	2	2	2
French	poisson	pwasɔ̃	1	3	3	3	1
German	Fisch	fiʃ	1	1	2	2	2
Hawaiian	iʻa	iʔa	5	5	5	5	5
Navajo	łóóʼ	łoːʔ	6	6	6	6	6
Turkish	balık	baluɯk	7	7	7	7	7

"five" (50)			GLD	TUR	NED	SCA	LxS
Albanian	**pesë**	pesə	1	1	1	1	1
English	five	faiv	1	2	2	2	2
French	cinq	sɛ̃k	1	3	3	3	3
German	fünf	fynf	1	4	4	2	4
Hawaiian	lima	lima	5	5	5	5	5
Navajo	ʼashdlaʼ	ʔaʃdˡaʔ	6	6	6	6	6
Turkish	beş	beʃ	7	1	7	1	7

"flow" (51)			GLD	TUR	NED	SCA	LxS
Albanian	rrjedh	rːeð	1	1	1	1	1
English	flows	flo	2	2	2	2	2
French	coule	kule	3	3	3	3	3
German	fließt	fliːs	2	2	2	2	2
Hawaiian	kahe	kahe	5	5	3	3	5
Navajo	yígeeh	jigeːh	6	6	6	6	6
Turkish	akıyor	ak	7	7	7	7	7

D.2 Cognate Detection

"flower" (52)			GLD	TUR	NED	SCA	LxS
Albanian	*lule*	lul	1	1	1	1	1
English	*flower*	flauər	2	2	2	2	2
French	*fleur*	flœr	2	2	2	2	2
German	*Blume*	bluːm	2	2	4	4	4
Hawaiian	pua	pua	5	5	5	5	5
Navajo	ch'ilátah hózhóón	tʃʼilaytah	6	6	6	6	6
Turkish	çiçek	tʃitʃek	7	7	7	7	7

"fly" (53)			GLD	TUR	NED	SCA	LxS
Albanian	fluturon	fluturo	1	1	1	1	1
English	flies	flai	2	1	2	2	2
French	vole	vɔle	3	3	3	2	2
German	fliegt	fliːg	2	1	2	2	2
Hawaiian	lele	lele	5	5	3	5	5
Navajo	yit'ah	jitʔah	6	6	6	6	6
Turkish	uçuyor	utʃ	7	7	7	7	7

"fog" (54)			GLD	TUR	NED	SCA	LxS
Albanian	mjegull	mjeguł	1	1	1	1	1
English	*fog*	fɑg	2	2	2	2	2
French	*brouillard*	brujar	3	3	3	3	3
German	Nebel	neːbəl	4	4	4	4	4
Hawaiian	'ohu	ʔohu	5	5	5	5	5
Navajo	'áhí	ayhi	6	6	6	5	6
Turkish	sis	sis	7	7	7	7	7

"foot" (55)			GLD	TUR	NED	SCA	LxS
Albanian	*këmbë*	kəmb	1	1	1	1	1
English	foot	fʊt	2	2	2	2	2
French	pied	pje	2	3	3	3	3
German	Fuß	fuːs	2	4	4	2	2
Hawaiian	wāwae	waːwae	5	5	5	5	5
Navajo	'akee'	keːʔ	6	6	6	6	6
Turkish	ayak	ajak	7	7	7	7	7

"four" (56)			GLD	TUR	NED	SCA	LxS
Albanian	katër	katər	1	1	1	1	1
English	four	fɔr	1	2	2	2	2
French	quatre	katr	1	1	1	1	1
German	vier	fiːr	1	2	2	2	2
Hawaiian	hā	haː	5	5	5	5	5
Navajo	dį́į́'	dĩːʔ	6	6	6	6	6
Turkish	dört	dørt	7	7	7	7	7

	"fruit" (58)		GLD	TUR	NED	SCA	LxS
Albanian	*pemë*	pem	1	1	1	1	1
English	*fruit*	frut	2	2	2	2	2
French	*fruit*	frui	2	2	2	3	3
German	*Frucht*	fruxt	2	2	2	2	2
Hawaiian	hua	hua	5	5	5	5	5
Navajo	bineest'ą'	bineːst⁷ãʔ	6	6	6	6	6
Turkish	*meyva*	mejva	7	7	7	7	7

	"full" (59)		GLD	TUR	NED	SCA	LxS
Albanian	plotë	plot	1	1	1	1	1
English	full	fʊl	1	1	2	2	2
French	plein	plɛn	1	1	1	1	1
German	voll	fol	1	1	2	2	2
Hawaiian	piha	piha	5	5	5	5	5
Navajo	hadeezbin	hadibin	6	6	6	6	6
Turkish	dolu	dolu	7	7	2	7	7

	"give" (60)		GLD	TUR	NED	SCA	LxS
Albanian	jep	jep	1	1	1	1	1
English	*gives*	gɪv	2	2	2	2	2
French	donne	dɔne	3	3	3	3	3
German	gibt	geːb	2	4	4	2	4
Hawaiian	hāʻawi	haːʔawi	5	5	5	5	5
Navajo	nish'aah	niʔaːh	6	6	6	6	6
Turkish	veriyor	ver	7	7	7	7	7

	"go" (61)		GLD	TUR	NED	SCA	LxS
Albanian	shkon	ʃko	1	1	1	1	1
English	goes	go	2	2	2	1	2
French	va	v	3	3	3	3	3
German	geht	geː	2	2	2	1	2
Hawaiian	hele	hele	5	5	5	5	5
Navajo	yíghááh	jiɣaːh	6	6	6	6	6
Turkish	yürüyor	jyry	7	7	7	7	7

	"good" (62)		GLD	TUR	NED	SCA	LxS
Albanian	mirë	mir	1	1	1	1	1
English	good	gʊd	2	2	2	2	2
French	bon	bɔn	3	3	3	3	3
German	gut	guːt	2	2	4	2	2
Hawaiian	maikaʻi	maikaʔi	5	5	5	5	5
Navajo	yá'át'ééh	jayʔayt⁷eːh	6	6	6	6	6
Turkish	iyi	iji	7	7	7	7	7

D.2 Cognate Detection

	"grease" (64)		GLD	TUR	NED	SCA	LxS
Albanian	**dhjamë**	ðjam	1	1	1	1	1
English	**grease**	gris	2	2	2	2	2
French	graisse	grɛs	2	2	2	2	2
German	**Fett**	fet	4	4	4	4	4
Hawaiian	**ʻaila**	ʔaila	5	5	5	5	5
Navajo	ʼakʻah	kʔah	6	6	6	6	6
Turkish	yağ	jaɣ	7	7	1	7	7

	"green" (65)		GLD	TUR	NED	SCA	LxS
Albanian	gjelbër	ɟelbər	1	1	1	1	1
English	green	grin	2	1	2	2	2
French	vert	vɛrt	3	3	3	3	3
German	grün	gryːn	2	1	2	2	2
Hawaiian	ʻōmaʻomaʻo	ʔoːmaʔomaʔo	5	5	5	5	5
Navajo	dootłʼizh	doːtɬʔiʒ	6	6	6	6	6
Turkish	yeşil	jeʃil	7	7	7	7	7

	"he" (69)		GLD	TUR	NED	SCA	LxS
Albanian	ai	ai	1	1	1	1	1
English	he	hi	2	2	1	2	2
French	il	il	3	3	3	3	3
German	er	eːr	4	3	4	4	4
Hawaiian	ia	ia	5	1	3	1	5
Navajo	bí	bi	6	6	1	6	6
Turkish	o	on	7	7	7	7	7

	"head" (70)		GLD	TUR	NED	SCA	LxS
Albanian	kokë	kok	1	1	1	1	1
English	head	hɛd	2	2	2	2	2
French	tête	tɛt	3	3	3	3	3
German	**Kopf**	kopf	4	4	1	4	4
Hawaiian	poʻo	poʔo	5	5	5	5	5
Navajo	ʼatsiiʼ	tsiːʔ	6	6	6	6	6
Turkish	baş	baʃ	7	7	7	5	7

	"hear" (71)		GLD	TUR	NED	SCA	LxS
Albanian	dëgjon	dəɟo	1	1	1	1	1
English	hears	hır	2	2	2	2	2
French	entend	ãtãd	3	3	3	3	3
German	hört	høːr	2	2	2	2	2
Hawaiian	lohe	lohe	5	5	5	5	5
Navajo	diitsʼaʼ	diːtsʔaʔ	6	1	6	1	6
Turkish	işitiyor	iʃit	7	7	7	3	7

	"heart" (72)		GLD	TUR	NED	SCA	LxS
Albanian	zemër	zemər	1	1	1	1	1
English	heart	hɑrt	2	2	2	2	2
French	cœur	kœr	2	3	3	3	3
German	Herz	hertsən	2	2	4	2	2
Hawaiian	puʻuwai	puʔuwai	5	5	5	5	5
Navajo	ʼajéídíshjool	ʥeidiʃʤoːl	6	6	6	6	6
Turkish	yürek	jyrek	7	7	7	7	7

	"here" (74)		GLD	TUR	NED	SCA	LxS
Albanian	këtu	kətu	1	1	1	1	1
English	here	hɪr	2	2	2	2	2
French	ici	isi	3	3	3	3	3
German	hier	hiːr	2	2	2	2	2
Hawaiian	nei	nei	5	5	5	5	5
Navajo	kweʼé	kweʔe	6	6	6	1	6
Turkish	burada	bura	7	7	7	7	7

	"hit" (75)		GLD	TUR	NED	SCA	LxS
Albanian	qëllon	cəɫo	1	1	1	1	1
English	**hits**	hɪt	2	2	2	2	2
French	*frappe*	frape	3	3	3	3	3
German	schlägt	ʃlaːg	4	4	4	4	1
Hawaiian	kuʻi	kuʔi	5	5	5	5	5
Navajo	ńdiistsʼin	ńdiːɬtsʔin	6	6	6	6	6
Turkish	vuruyor	vur	7	7	7	7	7

	"horn" (77)		GLD	TUR	NED	SCA	LxS
Albanian	bri	brir	1	1	1	1	1
English	horn	hɔrn	2	2	2	2	2
French	corne	kɔrn	2	3	2	2	2
German	Horn	horn	2	2	2	2	2
Hawaiian	kiwi	kiwi	5	5	5	5	5
Navajo	ʼadeeʼ	deːʔ	6	6	6	6	6
Turkish	boynuz	bojnuz	7	7	7	7	7

	"hot" (78)		GLD	TUR	NED	SCA	LxS
Albanian	nxehtë	nʤeht	1	1	1	1	1
English	hot	hɑt	2	2	2	2	2
French	chaud	ʃod	3	3	3	2	2
German	heiß	hais	2	4	4	4	2
Hawaiian	wela	wela	5	5	5	5	5
Navajo	sido	sido	6	3	6	2	6
Turkish	sıcak	sɯjak	7	7	7	7	7

D.2 Cognate Detection

	"human" (79)		GLD	TUR	NED	SCA	LxS
Albanian	njerí	ɲeri	1	1	1	1	1
English	**human**	hjumən	2	2	2	2	2
French	**humain**	ymɛn	2	3	3	2	2
German	Mensch	menʃən	4	3	4	4	4
Hawaiian	kanaka	kanaka	5	5	5	5	5
Navajo	diné	dine	6	6	6	6	6
Turkish	**adam**	adam	7	7	7	7	7

	"hunt" (80)		GLD	TUR	NED	SCA	LxS
Albanian	gjuan	ɟua	1	1	1	1	1
English	hunts	hənt	2	2	2	2	2
French	chasse	ʃase	3	3	3	3	1
German	jagt	jaːg	4	4	4	4	4
Hawaiian	hahai	hahai	5	5	5	3	5
Navajo	haalzheeh	haːlʒeːh	6	6	6	6	6
Turkish	avlıyor	avla	7	7	7	7	7

	"husband" (81)		GLD	TUR	NED	SCA	LxS
Albanian	burrë	burː	1	1	1	1	1
English	**husband**	həzbənd	2	2	2	2	2
French	mari	mari	3	3	3	3	3
German	Gatte	gatə	4	4	4	4	4
Hawaiian	kāne	kaːne	5	5	5	4	5
Navajo	hastiin	hastiːn	6	2	6	2	6
Turkish	**koca**	koʤa	7	7	7	4	7

	"I" (82)		GLD	TUR	NED	SCA	LxS
Albanian	unë	unə	1	1	1	1	1
English	I	ai	2	2	2	2	2
French	je	ʒə	2	3	3	3	3
German	ich	ix	2	4	4	4	4
Hawaiian	au	au	5	2	5	2	5
Navajo	shí	ʃi	6	3	6	3	3
Turkish	ben	ben	7	7	7	7	7

	"ice" (83)		GLD	TUR	NED	SCA	LxS
Albanian	akull	akuɫ	1	1	1	1	1
English	ice	ais	2	2	2	2	2
French	glace	glas	3	1	3	3	3
German	Eis	ais	2	2	2	2	2
Hawaiian	hau	hau	5	5	5	5	5
Navajo	tin	tin	6	6	6	6	6
Turkish	buz	buz	7	7	7	2	7

"in" (85)			GLD	TUR	NED	SCA	LxS
Albanian	në	nə	1	1	1	1	1
English	in	ɪn	1	1	2	2	2
French	dans	dɑ̃	1	3	3	3	3
German	in	in	1	1	2	2	2
Hawaiian	i loko	loko	5	5	5	5	5
Navajo	bii'	iːʔ	6	6	6	6	6
Turkish	içinde	itʃin	7	7	2	2	7

"knee" (87)			GLD	TUR	NED	SCA	LxS
Albanian	gju	ɟur	1	1	1	1	1
English	knee	ni	2	2	2	2	2
French	genou	ʒənu	2	3	3	3	3
German	Knie	kniː	2	4	4	2	4
Hawaiian	kuli	kuli	5	1	5	5	5
Navajo	'agod	god	6	6	6	6	6
Turkish	diz	diz	7	7	7	7	7

"knife" (88)			GLD	TUR	NED	SCA	LxS
Albanian	thikë	θik	1	1	1	1	1
English	knife	naif	2	2	2	2	2
French	couteau	kuto	3	3	3	3	3
German	Messer	mesər	4	4	4	4	4
Hawaiian	pahi	pahi	5	5	5	5	5
Navajo	béésh	beːʃ	6	6	6	5	6
Turkish	bıçak	bɯtʃak	7	7	7	7	7

"lake" (90)			GLD	TUR	NED	SCA	LxS
Albanian	**liqen**	licen	1	1	1	1	1
English	**lake**	lek	2	1	2	2	2
French	**lac**	lak	2	1	2	2	3
German	See	zeː	4	4	4	4	4
Hawaiian	loko	loko	5	1	2	2	5
Navajo	tooh siyínígíí	toːh	6	6	6	6	6
Turkish	göl	gøl	7	7	7	7	7

"laugh" (91)			GLD	TUR	NED	SCA	LxS
Albanian	qesh	ceʃ	1	1	1	1	1
English	laughs	laf	2	2	2	2	2
French	rit	ri	3	3	3	3	3
German	lacht	lax	2	4	2	4	4
Hawaiian	'aka	ʔaka	5	5	5	5	5
Navajo	yidloh	jidˡoh	6	6	6	6	6
Turkish	gülüyor	gyl	7	7	7	7	7

D.2 Cognate Detection

	"leaf" (92)		GLD	TUR	NED	SCA	LxS
Albanian	gjethe	ɟeθ	1	1	1	1	1
English	leaf	lif	2	2	2	2	2
French	feuille	fœj	3	3	3	3	3
German	Blatt	blat	4	4	4	4	4
Hawaiian	lau	lau	5	5	4	5	5
Navajo	'at'ąą'	tʔã:ʔ	6	6	6	6	6
Turkish	yaprak	japrak	7	7	7	7	7

	"lie" (94)		GLD	TUR	NED	SCA	LxS
Albanian	(rri) shtrirë	ʃtrir	1	1	1	1	1
English	lies	lai	2	2	2	2	2
French	(est) allongé	alɔ̃ʒe	3	3	3	3	3
German	liegt	li:g	2	4	4	2	2
Hawaiian	moe	moe	5	5	5	5	5
Navajo	sitį́	sitį̃	6	1	6	6	6
Turkish	yatıyor	jat	7	7	7	7	7

	"liver" (95)		GLD	TUR	NED	SCA	LxS
Albanian	mëlçi	məltʃi	1	1	1	1	1
English	liver	lɪvər	2	2	2	2	2
French	foie	fwa	3	3	3	3	3
German	Leber	le:bər	2	4	2	2	2
Hawaiian	ake	ake	5	5	5	5	5
Navajo	'azid	zid	6	6	6	6	6
Turkish	ciğer	ʤiyer	7	7	7	7	7

	"long" (96)		GLD	TUR	NED	SCA	LxS
Albanian	gjatë	ɟat	1	1	1	1	1
English	long	lɔŋ	1	2	2	2	2
French	long	lɔ̃g	1	3	3	3	3
German	lang	laŋ	1	2	2	2	2
Hawaiian	loa	loa	5	5	5	3	5
Navajo	nineez	nine:z	6	6	6	6	6
Turkish	uzun	uzun	7	7	7	7	7

	"louse" (97)		GLD	TUR	NED	SCA	LxS
Albanian	morr	mor:	1	1	1	1	1
English	louse	laus	2	2	2	2	2
French	pou	pu	3	3	3	3	3
German	Laus	lauz	2	2	2	2	2
Hawaiian	'uku	ʔuku	5	5	5	5	5
Navajo	yaa'	ja:ʔ	6	6	6	6	6
Turkish	bit	bit	7	7	7	3	7

	"many" (99)		GLD	TUR	NED	SCA	LxS
Albanian	*shumë*	ʃum	1	1	1	1	1
English	*many*	mɛni	2	2	2	2	2
French	*beaucoup de*	boku	3	3	3	3	3
German	*viele*	fiːl	4	4	4	4	4
Hawaiian	*nui*	nui	5	5	5	5	5
Navajo	*lą'í*	lãʔi	6	6	6	6	6
Turkish	*çok*	tʃok	7	7	3	7	7

	"meat" (100)		GLD	TUR	NED	SCA	LxS
Albanian	*mish*	miʃ	1	1	1	1	1
English	*meat*	mit	2	2	1	2	2
French	*viande*	vjãd	3	3	3	3	3
German	*Fleisch*	flaiʃ	4	4	4	4	4
Hawaiian	*'i'o*	ʔiʔo	5	5	5	5	5
Navajo	*'atsį'*	tsĩʔ	6	6	6	6	6
Turkish	*et*	et	7	7	7	2	7

	"mother" (102)		GLD	TUR	NED	SCA	LxS
Albanian	*nënë*	nən	1	1	1	1	1
English	*mother*	məðər	2	2	2	2	2
French	*mère*	mɛr	2	3	2	2	2
German	*Mutter*	mutər	2	2	2	2	2
Hawaiian	*makuahine*	makuahine	5	5	5	5	5
Navajo	*'amá*	may	6	6	6	6	6
Turkish	*anne*	anne	7	1	7	7	7

	"mountain" (103)		GLD	TUR	NED	SCA	LxS
Albanian	*mal*	mal	1	1	1	1	1
English	***mountain***	mauntən	2	2	2	2	2
French	*montagne*	mõtaɲ	2	3	1	2	2
German	*Berg*	berg	4	4	4	4	4
Hawaiian	*mauna*	mauna	5	2	5	5	5
Navajo	*dził*	dziɬ	6	6	6	6	6
Turkish	*dağ*	daɣ	7	7	7	7	7

	"mouth" (104)		GLD	TUR	NED	SCA	LxS
Albanian	***gojë***	goj	1	1	1	1	1
English	*mouth*	mauθ	2	2	2	2	2
French	*bouche*	buʃ	3	3	3	3	3
German	*Mund*	mund	2	4	4	4	2
Hawaiian	*waha*	waha	5	5	5	5	5
Navajo	*'azéé'*	zeːʔ	6	6	6	6	6
Turkish	*ağız*	aɣɯz	7	7	7	7	7

D.2 Cognate Detection

"name" (105)			GLD	TUR	NED	SCA	LxS
Albanian	emër	emər	1	1	1	1	1
English	name	nem	1	2	2	2	2
French	nom	nõ	1	3	3	3	2
German	Name	naːmən	1	2	1	2	2
Hawaiian	inoa	inoa	5	3	5	5	5
Navajo	'ázhi'	ʒiʔ	6	6	6	6	6
Turkish	ad	ad	7	7	7	7	7

"narrow" (106)			GLD	TUR	NED	SCA	LxS
Albanian	**ngushtë**	nguʃt	1	1	1	1	1
English	narrow	naro	2	2	2	2	2
French	étroit	etrwat	3	3	3	3	3
German	eng	eŋ	1	4	4	4	4
Hawaiian	lā'iki	laːʔiki	5	5	5	5	5
Navajo	'álts'óózí	ʔayɬtsʔoːzi	6	6	6	6	6
Turkish	dar	dar	7	3	2	7	7

"near" (107)			GLD	TUR	NED	SCA	LxS
Albanian	afèr	afər	1	1	1	1	1
English	near	nɪr	2	2	2	2	2
French	près de	prɛ	3	1	3	3	3
German	nah	naː	2	4	4	2	2
Hawaiian	kokoke	kokoke	5	5	5	5	5
Navajo	'áhání	ʔayhayni	6	6	6	6	6
Turkish	yakın	jakɯn	7	7	7	7	7

"neck" (108)			GLD	TUR	NED	SCA	LxS
Albanian	**qafë**	caf	1	1	1	1	1
English	neck	nɛk	2	2	2	2	2
French	cou	ku	3	3	3	3	3
German	Hals	halz	3	4	4	4	4
Hawaiian	'ā'ī	ʔaːʔiː	5	5	5	5	5
Navajo	'ak'os	kʔos	6	6	6	3	6
Turkish	boyun	bojn	7	7	7	7	7

"new" (109)			GLD	TUR	NED	SCA	LxS
Albanian	ri	ri	1	1	1	1	1
English	new	nu	2	2	2	2	2
French	nouveau	nuvɛl	2	3	3	3	3
German	neu	noi	2	2	2	2	2
Hawaiian	hou	hou	5	5	5	5	5
Navajo	'ániid	niːd	6	6	6	2	6
Turkish	yeni	jeni	7	7	7	7	7

	"night" (110)		GLD	TUR	NED	SCA	LxS
Albanian	natë	nat	1	1	1	1	1
English	night	nait	1	1	1	1	2
French	nuit	nɥi	1	3	3	3	3
German	Nacht	naxt	1	4	1	1	2
Hawaiian	pō	poː	5	5	5	5	5
Navajo	tl'éé'	tˡˀeːʔ	6	6	6	6	6
Turkish	gece	gedʒe	7	7	7	7	7

	"nose" (111)		GLD	TUR	NED	SCA	LxS
Albanian	hundë	hund	1	1	1	1	1
English	nose	noz	2	2	2	2	2
French	nez	ne	2	3	3	2	2
German	Nase	naːzə	2	2	2	2	2
Hawaiian	ihu	ihu	5	5	5	5	5
Navajo	áchį́į́h	tʃĩːh	6	6	6	6	6
Turkish	burun	burn	7	7	7	7	7

	"not" (112)		GLD	TUR	NED	SCA	LxS
Albanian	nuk	nuk	1	1	1	1	1
English	not	nɑt	2	2	2	2	2
French	ne...pas	pa	3	3	3	3	3
German	nicht	nixt	2	1	2	2	2
Hawaiian	'a'ole	ʔaʔole	5	5	5	5	5
Navajo	doo...da	doː	6	6	6	6	6
Turkish	değil	deɣil	7	7	7	7	7

	"now" (113)		GLD	TUR	NED	SCA	LxS
Albanian	tani	tani	1	1	1	1	1
English	now	nau	2	2	2	2	2
French	maintenant	mɛ̃tnɑ̃	3	3	3	3	3
German	nun	nuːn	2	4	4	2	2
Hawaiian	'ānō	ʔaːnoː	5	5	5	1	5
Navajo	k'ad	kˀad	6	6	6	6	6
Turkish	şimdi	ʃimdi	7	7	7	7	7

	"old" (114)		GLD	TUR	NED	SCA	LxS
Albanian	**vjetër**	vjetər	1	1	1	1	1
English	old	old	2	2	2	2	2
French	vieil	vjɛj	1	1	3	3	3
German	alt	alt	2	2	4	2	2
Hawaiian	o'o	oʔo	5	5	5	5	5
Navajo	sání	sayni	6	6	6	6	6
Turkish	**ihtiyar**	ihtijar	7	7	7	7	7

D.2 Cognate Detection

	"one" (115)		GLD	TUR	NED	SCA	LxS
Albanian	një	ɲə	1	1	1	1	1
English	one	wən	2	2	2	2	2
French	un	œ̃	2	3	3	3	3
German	eins	ain	2	1	4	2	2
Hawaiian	'ekahi	ʔekahi	5	5	5	5	5
Navajo	łáa'ii	łayʔiː	6	6	6	6	6
Turkish	bir	bir	7	7	7	7	7

	"other" (116)		GLD	TUR	NED	SCA	LxS
Albanian	tjetër	tjetər	1	1	1	1	1
English	other	əðər	2	2	2	2	2
French	autre	otr	3	2	3	2	1
German	anderer	andər	2	4	2	2	2
Hawaiian	'ē a'e	ʔeː	5	5	5	5	5
Navajo	łah	łah	6	6	6	6	6
Turkish	başka	baʃka	7	7	7	7	7

	"path" (117)		GLD	TUR	NED	SCA	LxS
Albanian	shteg	ʃteg	1	1	1	1	1
English	path	paθ	2	2	2	2	2
French	sentier	sɑ̃tje	3	1	3	3	3
German	Pfad	pfaːd	2	2	4	2	4
Hawaiian	ala	ala	5	5	5	5	5
Navajo	'atiin	tiːn	6	6	6	6	6
Turkish	yol	jol	7	7	7	7	7

	"pull" (119)		GLD	TUR	NED	SCA	LxS
Albanian	tërheq	tərhec	1	1	1	1	1
English	pulls	pʊl	2	2	2	2	2
French	tire	tire	3	1	1	3	3
German	zieht	tsiː	4	4	4	4	4
Hawaiian	huki	huki	5	5	5	5	5
Navajo	yisdzı̨́ı̨́s	jidʑı̨́ːs	6	6	6	6	6
Turkish	çekiyor	tʃek	7	7	7	4	7

	"push" (120)		GLD	TUR	NED	SCA	LxS
Albanian	shtyn	ʃty	1	1	1	1	1
English	**pushes**	pʊʃ	2	2	2	2	2
French	pousse	puse	2	2	3	2	2
German	stößt	ʃtoːs	1	1	1	1	4
Hawaiian	pahu	pahu	5	5	5	2	5
Navajo	béshhííł	beyiːł	6	6	6	6	6
Turkish	itiyor	it	7	7	7	7	7

"rain" (121)

			GLD	TUR	NED	SCA	LxS
Albanian	shi	ʃi	1	1	1	1	1
English	rain	rɛn	2	2	2	2	2
French	pluie	plɥi	3	3	3	3	3
German	Regen	reːgən	2	4	2	2	2
Hawaiian	ua	ua	5	5	5	5	5
Navajo	níłtsą́	niɬtsã́	6	6	6	6	6
Turkish	yağmur	jaɣmur	7	7	7	7	7

"red" (122)

			GLD	TUR	NED	SCA	LxS
Albanian	**kuq**	kuc	1	1	1	1	1
English	red	rɛd	2	2	2	2	2
French	rouge	ruʒ	2	3	3	2	2
German	rot	roːt	2	2	4	2	2
Hawaiian	'ula	ʔula	5	5	5	5	5
Navajo	łichíín	ɬitʃiːh	6	6	6	6	6
Turkish	kızıl	kɯzɯl	7	7	7	7	7

"right" (123)

			GLD	TUR	NED	SCA	LxS
Albanian	djathtë	djaθt	1	1	1	1	1
English	right	rait	2	2	2	2	2
French	droit	drwat	2	3	1	3	3
German	recht	rext	2	4	2	2	2
Hawaiian	'ākau	ʔaːkau	5	5	5	5	5
Navajo	nish'ná	niʃnay	6	6	6	6	6
Turkish	sağ	saɣ	7	7	7	7	7

"river" (124)

			GLD	TUR	NED	SCA	LxS
Albanian	lumë	lum	1	1	1	1	1
English	**river**	rɪvər	2	2	2	2	2
French	*fleuve*	fløv	3	3	1	3	3
German	Fluss	flus	4	3	1	3	4
Hawaiian	kahawai	kahawai	5	5	5	5	5
Navajo	tooh	toːh	6	6	6	6	6
Turkish	**nehir**	nehir	7	7	7	7	7

"root" (125)

			GLD	TUR	NED	SCA	LxS
Albanian	rrënjë	rːəɲ	1	1	1	1	1
English	**root**	rut	1	2	2	2	2
French	racine	rasin	1	3	3	1	1
German	Wurzel	vurtsəl	1	4	4	4	4
Hawaiian	a'a	aʔa	5	5	5	5	5
Navajo	'akétl'óól	ketˀoːl	6	6	6	6	6
Turkish	kök	køk	7	7	7	7	7

D.2 Cognate Detection

	"rotten" (126)		GLD	TUR	NED	SCA	LxS
Albanian	kalbur	kalbur	1	1	1	1	1
English	**rotten**	rɑtən	2	2	2	2	2
French	pourri	puri	3	3	3	3	3
German	faul	faul	3	3	4	4	4
Hawaiian	pilau	pilau	5	3	5	3	5
Navajo	diłdzííd	diłdziːd	6	6	6	6	6
Turkish	çürük	tʃyryk	7	1	7	7	7

	"round" (127)		GLD	TUR	NED	SCA	LxS
Albanian	rrumbullák	rːumbuɫak	1	1	1	1	1
English	**round**	raund	2	2	2	2	2
French	rond	rɔ̃d	2	3	2	2	2
German	**rund**	rund	2	2	2	2	2
Hawaiian	poepoe	poepoe	5	5	5	5	5
Navajo	nímaz	nimaz	6	6	6	6	6
Turkish	yuvarlak	juvarlak	7	7	1	7	7

	"rub" (128)		GLD	TUR	NED	SCA	LxS
Albanian	**fërkon**	fərko	1	1	1	1	1
English	rubs	rəb	2	2	2	2	2
French	frotte	frɔte	3	1	3	3	3
German	reibt	raib	4	2	2	2	2
Hawaiian	'ānai	ʔaːnai	5	5	5	5	5
Navajo	bídinishhish	bidiniɣiʃ	6	6	6	6	6
Turkish	sürtüyor	syrt	7	7	7	7	7

	"salt" (129)		GLD	TUR	NED	SCA	LxS
Albanian	kripë	krip	1	1	1	1	1
English	salt	sɔlt	2	2	2	2	2
French	sel	sɛl	2	2	2	2	3
German	Salz	zalts	2	2	4	2	2
Hawaiian	pa'akai	paʔakai	5	5	5	5	5
Navajo	'áshįįh	ʔayʃĩːh	6	6	6	6	6
Turkish	tuz	tuz	7	7	7	7	7

	"sand" (130)		GLD	TUR	NED	SCA	LxS
Albanian	**rërë**	rər	1	1	1	1	1
English	sand	sand	2	2	2	2	2
French	sable	sabl	3	3	2	3	3
German	Sand	zand	2	2	2	2	2
Hawaiian	one	one	5	5	5	5	5
Navajo	séí	sei	6	6	6	6	6
Turkish	kum	kum	7	7	7	7	7

"say" (131)			GLD	TUR	NED	SCA	LxS
Albanian	thotë	θ	1	1	1	1	1
English	says	se	2	2	2	2	2
French	dit	di	3	1	3	3	3
German	sagt	zaːg	2	4	4	2	2
Hawaiian	'ōlelo	ʔoːlelo	5	5	5	5	5
Navajo	ní	ni	6	6	3	6	6
Turkish	diyor	de	7	1	2	3	1

"scratch" (132)			GLD	TUR	NED	SCA	LxS
Albanian	gërvish	gərviʃ	1	1	1	1	1
English	scratches	skratʃ	2	2	2	2	2
French	*gratte*	grat	1	1	2	2	3
German	kratzt	krats	1	1	2	2	3
Hawaiian	walu	walu	5	5	5	5	5
Navajo	'ashch'id	ʔatʃʔid	6	6	6	6	6
Turkish	tırmalıyor	tɯrmala	7	7	7	7	7

"sea" (133)			GLD	TUR	NED	SCA	LxS
Albanian	det	det	1	1	1	1	1
English	sea	si	2	2	2	2	2
French	mer	mɛr	3	3	3	3	3
German	See	zeː	2	2	4	2	2
Hawaiian	kai	kai	5	5	5	5	5
Navajo	tónteel	tonteːl	6	6	6	6	6
Turkish	deniz	deniz	7	6	1	7	7

"see" (134)			GLD	TUR	NED	SCA	LxS
Albanian	sheh	ʃ	1	1	1	1	1
English	sees	si	1	1	2	1	1
French	voit	vwa	3	3	3	3	3
German	sieht	zeː	1	1	4	1	1
Hawaiian	'ike	ʔike	5	5	5	5	5
Navajo	yish'į́	jiʔĩ	6	6	6	6	6
Turkish	görüyor	gør	7	7	7	7	7

"seed" (135)			GLD	TUR	NED	SCA	LxS
Albanian	farë	far	1	1	1	1	1
English	seed	sid	2	2	2	2	2
French	graine	grɛn	3	3	3	3	3
German	Same	zaːmən	2	4	4	4	4
Hawaiian	'ano'ano	ʔanoʔano	5	5	5	5	5
Navajo	k'eelyéí	kʼeːljei	6	3	6	6	6
Turkish	*tohum*	tohum	7	7	7	7	7

D.2 Cognate Detection

	"sew" (136)		GLD	TUR	NED	SCA	LxS
Albanian	qep	cep	1	1	1	1	1
English	sews	so	2	2	2	2	2
French	coud	kuz	2	3	3	3	3
German	näht	neː	4	4	4	4	4
Hawaiian	humu	humu	5	5	5	5	5
Navajo	náiłkad	nayiłkad	6	6	6	6	6
Turkish	dikiyor	dik	7	7	7	7	7

	"short" (138)		GLD	TUR	NED	SCA	LxS
Albanian	**shkurtër**	ʃkurtər	1	1	1	1	1
English	short	ʃɔrt	1	2	1	1	2
French	court	kurt	1	3	1	1	2
German	**kurz**	kurts	1	3	1	1	4
Hawaiian	pōkole	poːkole	5	5	5	5	5
Navajo	yázhí	jayʒi	6	6	6	6	6
Turkish	kısa	kɯsa	7	7	7	7	7

	"sing" (139)		GLD	TUR	NED	SCA	LxS
Albanian	**këndon**	kəndo	1	1	1	1	1
English	sings	sɪŋ	2	2	2	2	2
French	chante	ʃãte	1	3	3	3	3
German	singt	ziŋ	2	2	4	2	2
Hawaiian	mele	mele	5	5	5	5	5
Navajo	hataał	hataːɬ	6	6	6	3	6
Turkish	şarkı söylüyor	ʃarkɯ	7	7	7	7	7

	"sit" (140)		GLD	TUR	NED	SCA	LxS
Albanian	(rri) ndenjur	ndeɲ	1	1	1	1	1
English	sits	sɪt	2	2	2	2	2
French	(est) assis	asiz	2	3	3	3	3
German	sitzt	zits	2	4	4	2	4
Hawaiian	noho	noho	5	5	5	5	5
Navajo	sidá	siday	6	2	6	2	2
Turkish	oturuyor	otur	7	7	7	7	7

	"sky" (142)		GLD	TUR	NED	SCA	LxS
Albanian	**qiell**	cieł	1	1	1	1	1
English	**sky**	skai	2	2	2	2	2
French	ciel	sjɛl	1	3	3	3	3
German	Himmel	himəl	4	4	4	4	4
Hawaiian	lani	lani	5	5	5	5	5
Navajo	yá	yay	6	6	6	6	6
Turkish	gök	gøk	7	7	7	7	7

"sleep" (143)			GLD	TUR	NED	SCA	LxS
Albanian	*fle*	fle	1	1	1	1	1
English	*sleeps*	slip	2	2	2	2	2
French	*dort*	dɔr	3	3	3	3	3
German	*schläft*	ʃlaːf	2	2	4	2	2
Hawaiian	*moe*	moe	5	5	5	5	5
Navajo	*'ałhosh*	ʔaɬhoʃ	6	6	6	6	6
Turkish	*uyuyor*	uju	7	7	7	7	7

"smoke" (146)			GLD	TUR	NED	SCA	LxS
Albanian	**tym**	tym	1	1	1	1	1
English	*smoke*	smok	2	2	2	2	2
French	*fumée*	fyme	1	3	1	3	3
German	*Rauch*	raux	4	4	4	4	4
Hawaiian	*uahi*	uahi	5	5	5	5	5
Navajo	*łid*	ɬid	6	6	6	6	6
Turkish	*duman*	duman	7	1	7	1	7

"snake" (148)			GLD	TUR	NED	SCA	LxS
Albanian	*gjarpër*	ɟarpər	1	1	1	1	1
English	*snake*	snek	2	2	2	2	2
French	*serpent*	sɛrpɑ̃	1	3	3	1	3
German	*Schlange*	ʃlaŋə	4	3	4	4	4
Hawaiian	**naheka**	naheka	2	5	5	5	5
Navajo	*tł'iish*	tˡʔiːʃ	6	6	6	6	6
Turkish	*yılan*	jɯlan	7	7	7	7	7

"snow" (149)			GLD	TUR	NED	SCA	LxS
Albanian	*borë*	bor	1	1	1	1	1
English	*snow*	sno	2	2	2	2	2
French	*neige*	nɛʒ	2	3	3	3	3
German	*Schnee*	ʃneː	2	2	4	2	2
Hawaiian	*hau kea*	hau	5	5	5	5	5
Navajo	*zas*	zas	6	6	6	6	3
Turkish	*kar*	kar	7	7	7	7	7

"some" (150)			GLD	TUR	NED	SCA	LxS
Albanian	*disa*	disa	1	1	1	1	1
English	*some*	səm	2	2	2	2	2
French	*quelques*	kɛlkə	3	3	3	3	3
German	*einige*	ainig	4	4	4	4	4
Hawaiian	*kekahi*	kekahi	5	5	5	3	5
Navajo	*ła'*	ɬaʔ	6	6	6	6	6
Turkish	**bazı**	bazɯ	7	7	7	7	7

D.2 Cognate Detection

	"spit" (151)		GLD	TUR	NED	SCA	LxS
Albanian	pështyn	pəʃty	1	1	1	1	1
English	spits	spɪt	2	2	2	2	2
French	**crache**	kraʃe	3	3	3	3	3
German	**spuckt**	ʃpuk	4	2	4	2	2
Hawaiian	kuha	kuha	5	5	5	3	5
Navajo	dishsheeh	diʒeːh	6	6	6	6	6
Turkish	tükürüyor	tykyr	7	7	7	7	7

	"squeeze" (153)		GLD	TUR	NED	SCA	LxS
Albanian	shtrydh	ʃtryð	1	1	1	1	1
English	squeezes	skwiz	2	2	2	2	2
French	presse	prɛse	3	3	3	3	3
German	drückt	dryk	4	4	1	4	4
Hawaiian	'uwī	ʔuwiː	5	5	5	5	5
Navajo	yiishnih	jiːnih	6	6	6	6	6
Turkish	sıkıyor	sɯk	7	2	7	7	7

	"stab" (154)		GLD	TUR	NED	SCA	LxS
Albanian	ther	θer	1	1	1	1	1
English	stabs	stab	2	2	2	2	2
French	poignarde	pwaɲarde	3	3	3	3	3
German	sticht	ʃtex	4	2	4	2	2
Hawaiian	hou	hou	5	5	5	5	5
Navajo	bighá'níshgééd	biɣayʔniɬgeːd	6	6	6	6	6
Turkish	**hançerliyor**	hantʃerle	7	7	7	7	7

	"stand" (155)		GLD	TUR	NED	SCA	LxS
Albanian	(rri) më këmbë	kəmb	1	1	1	1	1
English	stands	stand	2	2	2	2	2
French	**(est) debout**	dəbu	3	3	3	3	3
German	steht	ʃteː	2	2	4	2	2
Hawaiian	kū	kuː	5	5	5	5	5
Navajo	sizį́	sizį́	6	6	6	6	6
Turkish	duruyor	dur	7	7	7	7	7

	"star" (156)		GLD	TUR	NED	SCA	LxS
Albanian	yll	yɫ	1	1	1	1	1
English	star	stɑr	2	2	2	2	2
French	étoile	etwal	2	3	3	3	3
German	Stern	ʃtern	2	2	2	2	2
Hawaiian	hōkū	hoːkuː	5	5	5	5	5
Navajo	sǫ'	sõʔ	6	6	6	6	6
Turkish	yıldız	jɯldɯz	7	7	7	7	7

"stick" (157)			GLD	TUR	NED	SCA	LxS
Albanian	shkop	ʃkop	1	1	1	1	1
English	stick	stɪk	2	2	2	2	2
French	**bâton**	batɔ̃	3	3	3	3	3
German	Stock	ʃtok	4	2	1	2	2
Hawaiian	lā'au	la:ʔau	5	5	5	5	5
Navajo	tsin	tsin	6	6	6	6	6
Turkish	değnek	deɣnek	7	7	7	7	7

"straight" (159)			GLD	TUR	NED	SCA	LxS
Albanian	**drejtë**	drejt	1	1	1	1	1
English	straight	stret	2	2	2	1	2
French	droit	drwat	1	1	1	1	3
German	gerade	gəra:də	4	4	4	4	4
Hawaiian	pololei	pololei	5	5	5	5	5
Navajo	k'éhózdon	kʔehozdon	6	6	6	6	6
Turkish	doğru	doɣru	7	7	7	7	7

"suck" (160)			GLD	TUR	NED	SCA	LxS
Albanian	thith	θiθ	1	1	1	1	1
English	sucks	sək	2	2	2	2	2
French	suce	syse	2	3	3	3	3
German	saugt	zaug	2	2	4	2	2
Hawaiian	omo	omo	5	5	5	5	5
Navajo	yisht'o'	jiɬtʔoʔ	6	6	6	6	6
Turkish	emiyor	em	7	5	7	5	7

"sun" (161)			GLD	TUR	NED	SCA	LxS
Albanian	diell	dieɫ	1	1	1	1	1
English	sun	sən	2	2	2	2	2
French	soleil	sɔlɛj	2	3	3	3	3
German	Sonne	zonə	2	2	4	2	2
Hawaiian	lā	la:	5	5	5	5	5
Navajo	shá	ʃay	6	6	6	2	6
Turkish	güneş	gyneʃ	7	7	7	7	7

"swell" (162)			GLD	TUR	NED	SCA	LxS
Albanian	ënj	əɲ	1	1	1	1	1
English	swells	swɛl	2	2	2	2	2
French	enfle	ãfle	3	3	3	3	3
German	schwillt	ʃvel	2	2	4	2	2
Hawaiian	ho'opehu	hoʔopehu	5	5	5	5	5
Navajo	niishchaad	ni:tʃa:d	6	6	6	6	6
Turkish	şişiyor	ʃiʃ	7	7	7	7	7

D.2 Cognate Detection

	"swim" (163)		GLD	TUR	NED	SCA	LxS
Albanian	noton	noto	1	1	1	1	1
English	swims	swɪm	2	2	2	2	2
French	nage	naʒe	3	3	3	1	3
German	schwimmt	ʃvim	2	2	4	2	2
Hawaiian	'au	ʔau	5	5	5	5	5
Navajo	'ashkǫ́ǫ́h	ʔałkõːh	6	6	6	6	6
Turkish	yüzüyor	jyz	7	7	7	7	7

	"tail" (164)		GLD	TUR	NED	SCA	LxS
Albanian	bisht	biʃt	1	1	1	1	1
English	tail	tel	2	2	2	2	2
French	queue	kø	3	3	3	3	3
German	Schwanz	ʃvants	4	4	4	4	4
Hawaiian	huelo	huelo	5	5	2	5	5
Navajo	'atsee'	tseːʔ	6	6	6	6	6
Turkish	kuyruk	kujruk	7	7	7	7	7

	"that" (165)		GLD	TUR	NED	SCA	LxS
Albanian	ai	ai	1	1	1	1	1
English	that	ðat	2	2	2	2	2
French	cela	səla	3	3	3	3	3
German	das	das	2	4	4	4	2
Hawaiian	kēlā	keːlaː	5	5	5	3	5
Navajo	'éi	ʔeiː	6	6	6	6	6
Turkish	o	on	7	7	7	7	7

	"there" (166)		GLD	TUR	NED	SCA	LxS
Albanian	aty	aty	1	1	1	1	1
English	there	ðɛr	2	2	2	2	2
French	là	la	3	3	3	3	3
German	da	daː	2	1	4	4	4
Hawaiian	laila	laila	5	5	3	5	5
Navajo	'áadi	ʔaːdi	6	6	6	1	6
Turkish	orada	ora	7	3	7	7	7

	"they" (167)		GLD	TUR	NED	SCA	LxS
Albanian	ata	ata	1	1	1	1	1
English	**they**	ðe	2	1	2	2	2
French	ils	il	3	3	3	3	3
German	sie	ziː	4	4	4	2	4
Hawaiian	lākou	laːkou	5	5	5	5	5
Navajo	daabí	bi	6	6	6	6	6
Turkish	onlar	on	7	7	7	7	7

"thick" (168)			GLD	TUR	NED	SCA	LxS
Albanian	trashë	traʃ	1	1	1	1	1
English	thick	θɪk	2	2	2	2	2
French	épais	epɛs	3	3	3	3	3
German	dick	dik	2	2	4	2	2
Hawaiian	mānoa	maːnoa	5	5	5	5	5
Navajo	ditą́	ditã́	6	6	4	6	6
Turkish	kalın	kalɯn	7	7	7	7	7

"thin" (169)			GLD	TUR	NED	SCA	LxS
Albanian	hollë	hoɫ	1	1	1	1	1
English	thin	θɪn	2	2	2	2	2
French	mince	mɛ̃s	3	3	3	3	3
German	dünn	dyn	2	2	4	2	2
Hawaiian	wīwī	wiːwiː	5	5	5	5	5
Navajo	'áłt'ą́'í	ʔayɬt'ʔã́ʔi	6	1	6	6	6
Turkish	ince	indʒe	7	7	7	7	7

"think" (170)			GLD	TUR	NED	SCA	LxS
Albanian	**mendon**	mendo	1	1	1	1	1
English	thinks	θɪŋk	2	2	2	2	2
French	**pense**	pɑ̃se	3	3	3	3	3
German	denkt	deŋk	2	2	2	2	2
Hawaiian	mana'o	manaʔo	5	1	1	5	5
Navajo	nízin	nizin	6	6	6	6	6
Turkish	düşünüyor	dyʃyn	7	7	7	6	7

"this" (171)			GLD	TUR	NED	SCA	LxS
Albanian	ky	k	1	1	1	1	1
English	this	ðɪs	2	2	2	2	2
French	ceci	səsi	3	3	3	3	3
German	dieses	diːz	2	2	4	2	2
Hawaiian	kēia	keːia	5	1	5	5	5
Navajo	díí	diː	6	6	4	2	6
Turkish	bu	bun	7	7	7	7	7

"thou" (172)			GLD	TUR	NED	SCA	LxS
Albanian	ti	t	1	1	1	1	1
English	you	ju	2	2	2	2	2
French	tu	ty	1	1	1	1	3
German	du	duː	1	1	4	1	1
Hawaiian	'oe	ʔoe	5	5	5	5	5
Navajo	ni	ni	6	6	6	6	6
Turkish	sen	sen	7	7	7	7	7

D.2 Cognate Detection

	"three" (173)		GLD	TUR	NED	SCA	LxS
Albanian	tre	tre	1	1	1	1	1
English	three	θri	1	1	2	1	1
French	trois	trwa	1	1	1	1	3
German	drei	drai	1	1	4	1	1
Hawaiian	kolu	kolu	5	5	5	5	5
Navajo	táá'	ta:ʔ	6	6	6	6	6
Turkish	üç	ytʃ	7	7	7	7	7

	"tongue" (176)		GLD	TUR	NED	SCA	LxS
Albanian	gjuhë	ɟuh	1	1	1	1	1
English	tongue	təŋ	2	2	2	2	2
French	langue	lãg	2	3	3	3	3
German	Zunge	tsuŋə	2	4	4	2	4
Hawaiian	alelo	alelo	5	5	5	5	5
Navajo	'atsoo'	tso:ʔ	6	1	6	1	6
Turkish	dil	dil	7	7	7	7	7

	"tooth" (177)		GLD	TUR	NED	SCA	LxS
Albanian	dhëmb	ðəmb	1	1	1	1	1
English	tooth	tuθ	2	2	2	2	2
French	dent	dã	2	3	3	2	3
German	Zahn	tsa:n	2	4	4	4	4
Hawaiian	niho	niho	5	5	5	5	5
Navajo	'awoo'	ɣo:ʔ	6	6	6	6	6
Turkish	diş	diʃ	7	7	7	2	7

	"tree" (178)		GLD	TUR	NED	SCA	LxS
Albanian	dru	drur	1	1	1	1	1
English	tree	tri	1	1	2	1	1
French	arbre	arbr	3	3	1	3	3
German	Baum	baum	4	4	4	4	4
Hawaiian	lā'au	la:ʔau	5	5	5	5	5
Navajo	tsin	tsin	6	6	6	6	6
Turkish	ağaç	aɣaʤ	7	7	7	7	7

	"true" (179)		GLD	TUR	NED	SCA	LxS
Albanian	vërtetë	vərtet	1	1	1	1	1
English	true	tru	2	2	2	2	2
French	vrai	vrɛ	1	1	3	3	1
German	wahr	va:r	1	1	4	3	4
Hawaiian	'oia'i'o	ʔoiaʔiʔo	5	5	5	5	5
Navajo	'aaníí	ʔa:ni:	6	6	6	6	6
Turkish	doğru	doɣru	7	7	2	2	7

	"two" (180)		GLD	TUR	NED	SCA	LxS
Albanian	*dy*	dy	1	1	1	1	1
English	*two*	tu	1	1	2	1	2
French	*deux*	dø	1	1	1	1	3
German	*zwei*	tsvai	1	4	4	4	4
Hawaiian	*lua*	lua	5	5	5	5	5
Navajo	*naaki*	naːki	6	6	6	6	6
Turkish	*iki*	iki	7	7	6	6	7

	"wash" (182)		GLD	TUR	NED	SCA	LxS
Albanian	*lau*	la	1	1	1	1	1
English	*washes*	wɑʃ	2	2	2	2	2
French	*lave*	lave	1	3	1	1	1
German	*wäscht*	vaʃ	2	2	4	2	2
Hawaiian	*holoi*	holoi	5	5	5	5	5
Navajo	*yiisgis*	jiːgis	6	6	6	6	6
Turkish	*yıkıyor*	jɯka	7	6	7	6	7

	"water" (183)		GLD	TUR	NED	SCA	LxS
Albanian	*ujë*	uj	1	1	1	1	1
English	*water*	wɑtər	1	2	2	2	2
French	*eau*	o	3	3	3	3	3
German	*Wasser*	vasər	1	4	2	2	2
Hawaiian	*wai*	wai	5	5	5	5	5
Navajo	*tó*	to	6	6	3	6	6
Turkish	*su*	suj	7	7	1	1	7

	"we" (184)		GLD	TUR	NED	SCA	LxS
Albanian	*né*	n	1	1	1	1	1
English	*we*	wi	2	2	2	2	2
French	*nous*	nu	1	1	1	1	3
German	*wir*	viːr	2	4	4	4	4
Hawaiian	*mākou*	maːkou	5	5	5	5	5
Navajo	*nihí*	nihi	6	6	6	6	6
Turkish	*biz*	b	7	7	7	7	7

	"what" (186)		GLD	TUR	NED	SCA	LxS
Albanian	*ç'*	tʃ	1	1	1	1	1
English	*what*	wɑt	2	2	2	2	2
French	*quoi*	kwa	2	3	3	3	3
German	*was*	v	2	4	4	4	4
Hawaiian	*aha*	aha	5	5	5	5	5
Navajo	*ha'át'íísh*	haʔaytʔiːʃ	6	6	6	6	6
Turkish	*ne*	ne	7	7	7	7	7

D.2 Cognate Detection

	"white" (187)		GLD	TUR	NED	SCA	LxS
Albanian	bardhë	barð	1	1	1	1	1
English	white	wait	2	2	2	2	2
French	**blanc**	blɑ̃ʃ	3	1	3	3	3
German	weiß	vais	2	4	4	3	2
Hawaiian	keʻokeʻo	keʔokeʔo	5	5	5	5	5
Navajo	łigai	łigai	6	6	6	6	6
Turkish	ak	ak	7	7	7	7	7

	"who" (188)		GLD	TUR	NED	SCA	LxS
Albanian	kush	k	1	1	1	1	1
English	who	hu	1	2	2	2	2
French	qui	ki	1	1	1	1	1
German	wer	veː	1	4	4	4	4
Hawaiian	wai	wai	5	4	5	5	5
Navajo	háí	hayi	6	2	6	2	6
Turkish	kim	kim	7	7	1	1	7

	"wide" (189)		GLD	TUR	NED	SCA	LxS
Albanian	gjerë	ɟer	1	1	1	1	1
English	wide	waid	2	2	2	2	2
French	large	larʒ	3	3	3	3	3
German	weit	vait	2	2	4	2	2
Hawaiian	ākea	aːkea	5	5	5	5	5
Navajo	niteel	niteːl	6	6	6	6	6
Turkish	geniş	geniʃ	7	7	7	7	7

	"wife" (190)		GLD	TUR	NED	SCA	LxS
Albanian	grua	gru	1	1	1	1	1
English	wife	waif	2	2	2	2	2
French	femme	fam	3	3	3	3	3
German	Gattin	gatin	4	4	4	4	4
Hawaiian	wahine	wahine	5	5	4	5	5
Navajo	ʼaʼáád	ʔaːd	6	6	6	6	6
Turkish	karı	karɯ	7	1	7	1	7

	"wind" (191)		GLD	TUR	NED	SCA	LxS
Albanian	**erë**	er	1	1	1	1	1
English	wind	wɪnd	2	2	2	2	2
French	vent	vã	2	3	3	3	3
German	Wind	vind	2	2	2	2	2
Hawaiian	makani	makani	5	5	5	5	5
Navajo	nítchʼi	niɬtʃʼi	6	6	6	6	6
Turkish	**rüzgar**	ryzgaːr	7	7	7	7	7

"wing" (192)			GLD	TUR	NED	SCA	LxS
Albanian	fletë	flet	1	1	1	1	1
English	**wing**	wɪŋ	2	2	2	2	2
French	aile	ɛl	3	3	3	3	3
German	Flügel	flyːgəl	4	1	4	4	4
Hawaiian	'ēheu	ʔeːheu	5	5	5	5	5
Navajo	'at'a'	t'aʔ	6	6	6	6	6
Turkish	kanat	kanad	7	7	7	7	7

"wipe" (193)			GLD	TUR	NED	SCA	LxS
Albanian	fshin	fʃi	1	1	1	1	1
English	wipes	waip	2	2	2	2	2
French	essuie	esɥije	3	3	3	3	3
German	wischt	viʃ	4	4	4	1	4
Hawaiian	**kāwele**	kaːwele	5	5	5	5	5
Navajo	náníshť'od	naynitʔod	6	6	6	6	6
Turkish	siliyor	sil	7	7	7	7	7

"with" (194)			GLD	TUR	NED	SCA	LxS
Albanian	me	me	1	1	1	1	1
English	with	wɪθ	2	2	2	2	2
French	avec	avɛk	3	3	3	3	3
German	mit	mit	1	4	4	1	4
Hawaiian	me	me	5	1	1	1	1
Navajo	bił	ił	6	6	6	6	6
Turkish	ile	ile	7	6	7	6	7

"woman" (195)			GLD	TUR	NED	SCA	LxS
Albanian	grua	gru	1	1	1	1	1
English	woman	wʊmən	2	2	2	2	2
French	femme	fam	3	3	3	3	3
German	Frau	frau	4	4	4	4	1
Hawaiian	wahine	wahine	5	5	5	5	5
Navajo	'asdzání	ʔasdzayni	6	6	6	6	6
Turkish	**kadın**	kadɯn	7	7	7	7	7

"woods" (196)			GLD	TUR	NED	SCA	LxS
Albanian	**pyll**	pył	1	1	1	1	1
English	woods	wʊd	2	2	2	2	2
French	**bois**	bwa	3	3	3	3	3
German	Wald	vald	4	4	4	4	2
Hawaiian	ulu lā'au	ululaːʔau	5	5	5	5	5
Navajo	tsintah	tsintah	6	6	6	6	6
Turkish	orman	orman	7	7	7	7	7

D.2 Cognate Detection

"worm" (197)			GLD	TUR	NED	SCA	LxS
Albanian	*krimb*	krimb	1	1	1	1	1
English	*worm*	wərm	2	2	2	2	2
French	*ver*	vɛr	2	2	2	2	3
German	*Wurm*	vurm	2	2	2	2	2
Hawaiian	*ko'e*	koʔe	5	5	5	5	5
Navajo	*ch'osh*	tʃˀoʃ	6	6	6	6	6
Turkish	***solucan***	soluʤan	7	7	7	7	7

"year" (198)			GLD	TUR	NED	SCA	LxS
Albanian	*vit*	vit	1	1	1	1	1
English	*year*	jɪr	2	2	2	2	2
French	*année*	ane	3	3	3	3	3
German	*Jahr*	jaːr	2	2	2	2	2
Hawaiian	*makahiki*	makahiki	5	5	5	5	5
Navajo	*hai*	hai	6	6	6	6	6
Turkish	***sene***	sene	7	7	3	3	7

"yellow" (199)			GLD	TUR	NED	SCA	LxS
Albanian	***verdhë***	verð	1	1	1	1	1
English	*yellow*	jɛlo	2	2	2	2	2
French	*jaune*	ʒon	2	3	3	3	3
German	*gelb*	gelb	2	4	4	4	4
Hawaiian	*melemele*	melemele	5	5	5	5	5
Navajo	*łitso*	łitso	6	6	6	6	6
Turkish	*sarı*	sarɯ	7	7	7	7	7

"you" (200)			GLD	TUR	NED	SCA	LxS
Albanian	*ju*	ju	1	1	1	1	1
English	*you*	ju	2	1	1	1	2
French	*vous*	vu	1	3	1	3	3
German	*ihr*	iːr	2	4	4	4	4
Hawaiian	*'oukou*	ʔou	5	5	5	5	5
Navajo	*nihí*	nihi	6	6	6	6	6
Turkish	*siz*	s	7	7	7	7	7

www.ingramcontent.com/pod-product-compliance
Lightning Source LLC
Chambersburg PA
CBHW032221010526
44113CB00032B/197